P9-CAL-781

ABBOTT AND

COSTELLO
IN HOLLYWOOD

BOB FURMANEK AND RON PALUMBO

A PERIGEE BOOK

Preceding page: Abbott and Costello with Frances Rafferty and Jean Porter in *Abbott and Costello in Hollywood* (1945).

PHOTO CREDITS

Abbott and Costello Enterprises, pages: 15 (top), 16, 19, 21, 23 (right), 93, 153, 219, 220 (left), 231, 234, 257, 259, 261, 262, 267.

Academy of Motion Picture Arts and Sciences—Margaret Herrick Library (Universal Collection), pages: title page (second from left and seventh from left), 10, 12, 15 (bottom), 17, 31, 81 (right), 149 (left), 154, 156, 167, 170 (left), 179, 183, 194, 197, 201, 202, 204, 207, 215, 227, 237, 238, 243, 247, 254.

The Bettmann Archive/Bettmann Newsphotos, pages: 23 (left), 104.

Billy Rose Theatre Collection of the New York Public Library at Lincoln Center (Universal Collection), pages: 24, 25, 33 (left), 102 (left), 149 (right).

Culver Pictures, Inc., pages: 20, 102 (right).

Princeton University Library—William Seymore Theatre Collection (Warner Bros. Archives), pages: 220 (right).

Turner Entertainment Co., pages: 1, title page (from left: fourth and tenth photos), 80, 81 (left), 115, 116, 131, 129.

Universal City Studios, Inc., pages: cover, title page (from left: first, third, fifth, sixth, eighth, and ninth photos), 33 (right), 36, 39, 41, 46, 51, 53, 58, 61, 65, 67, 71, 72, 75, 85, 86, 90, 92, 97, 101, 105, 109, 111, 120, 121, 123, 125, 137, 138, 143, 144, 147, 170 (right), 214, 224, 252, 267.

Wisconsin Center for Film and Theatre Research (United Artists Collection), pages: 161, 187.

Back cover photos: Poster of *Abbott and Costello in Hollywood* courtesy of Abbott and Costello Enterprises; other photos courtesy of Universal City Studios, Inc.

Perigee Books
are published by
The Putnam Publishing Group
200 Madison Avenue
New York, NY 10016

Copyright © 1991 by Bob Furmanek and Ron Palumbo

Designed by Sheree L. Goodman

All rights reserved. This book, or parts thereof,
may not be reproduced in any form without permission.
Published simultaneously in Canada

Library of Congress Cataloging-in-Publication Data

Furmanek, Bob, date.
    Abbott and Costello in Hollywood / Bob Furmanek and Ron Palumbo.
        p.   cm.
    Includes index.
    ISBN 0-399-51605-0
    1. Abbott, Bud.   2. Costello, Lou.   3. Comedy films—United States—History.
    I. Palumbo, Ron.   II. Title.
PN2287.A217F8   1991   90-22097 CIP
791.43′028′0922—dc20

Printed in the United States of America

1   2   3   4   5   6   7   8   9   10

This book is printed on acid-free paper.
∞

To my wife, Karen, and our daughter, Vienna, who taught me more about love, patience, and support than I taught them about Bud and Lou.

—Ron Palumbo

To my mother, who has shown the patience of a saint in putting up with me through the many years of researching this book, and to the memory of my father, who is not only responsible for my interest in film, but who always encouraged me to pursue my dreams, no matter how far out of reach they may have seemed. Somehow I can't help but think that he's been pulling some strings for me to help make this dream a reality.

—Bob Furmanek

ACKNOWLEDGMENTS

The authors wish to express our deepest appreciation to the families of Bud and Lou for being so generous with their time, efforts, and memories: Bud Abbott, Jr.; Vickie Abbott Wheeler and Don Wheeler for providing unprecedented access to Bud's personal scrapbook; Paddy Costello Humphreys and Fred Humphreys for permitting unlimited access to Lou's scrapbook; and a special thanks to Chris Costello for donating hours of interviews she conducted for her own book, *Lou's On First* (St. Martin's Press).

We are also greatly indebted to the following research organizations and their staffs: American Film Institute/Louis B. Mayer Library (Ruth Spencer); The Academy of Motion Picture Arts and Sciences Margaret Herrick Library (Robert Cushman, Howard H. Prouty, Alison Pinsler, Stacey Endres, Robert Rioux, David Marsh, and the entire staff); Billy Rose Theatre Collection of the New York Public Library at Lincoln Center (Dorothy L. Swerdlove, Louis Paul, and the entire staff); The Book Sail, Orange, California (John McLaughlin); Culver Pictures Inc. (Thomas R. Logan); Paterson Museum (Giacomo DeStefano); Princeton University Library, William Seymour Theatre Collection, Warner Bros. Archives (Mary Ann Jensen, Andros Thomson); Theatre Historical Society of America (Bill Benedict); Turner Entertainment Co. (Cathy Manolis, Irma Kraus, Beverly Laufer, Carole Orgel); UCLA Theatre Arts Library (Raymond Soto, Brigitte J. Kueppers); UPI/Bettman Photo (Darby Harper, Liz Orr); The Universal Collection/USC Cinema-Television Library and Archives of Performing Arts (Ned Comstock, Anne G. Schlosser); Universal Pictures Corporate Records Management (Armando Ponce, Rita Duenas); Universal Pictures Publicity/Photo Department (Corinne DeLuca, Frank Rodriguez, Lucia Bernard, Jim Chaparas); Warner Bros. Archives/USC School of Cinema-Television (Leith Adams); and the Wisconsin Center for Film and Theatre Research/United Artists Collection (Reg Shrader, Tim Hawkins).

We would like to acknowledge the invaluable assistance of the following companies and organizations: The Official Abbott and Costello Fan Club (P.O. Box 2084, Toluca Lake, CA 91610-0084); APCO Photo, New York; Adrian's Camera and Bowling Shop, Passaic, New Jersey; Archives of Music Preservation (Paul Surratt); CBS Photo Library (Marty Silverstein); Clifton Camera Shop (Joseph Siuta, Craig Van Brookhoven); Fabian Theatre, Paterson, New Jersey (Steve Slone, Ken Beyer); MCA Home Video (Louis Feola, Marty Henry, Mike Fitzgerald); *New York Daily News* Photo Library (Eugene Ferrara); Paterson Free Public Library (Linda Brown); Pictorial Parade, Inc. (Robert Thompson); Photofest (Howard & Ron Mandelbaum); Perigee Books (Eugene Brissie, Laura Shepherd); Shubert Archive (Mark Swartz); Wide World Photos, Inc. (Elvis A. Brathwaite); Hy Zazula Associates (Dave Zazula).

We wish to thank the following family, friends, and colleagues of Abbott and Costello who graciously consented to be interviewed for this book: Norman Abbott, Iris Adrian, Patty Andrews, Michael Ansara, Jess Barker, Carol Bruce, Richard Collins, John Conte, Stanley Cortez, the late Pat Costello, Harry Crane, the late Robert Cummings, Jacqueline DeWit, Howard Dimsdale, Robert Easton, Fritz Feld, Arthur Franz, Devery Freeman, Joe Glaston, Jr., Gale Gordon, Anne Gwynne, Abe Haberman, Edmund L. Hartmann, Paul Jarrico, Allan Jones, Hillary Brooke-Klune, Peggy Moran-Koster, Charles Lamont, Robert Lees, Sheldon Leonard, Jerry Lewis, Arthur Lubin, the late Mike Mazurki, Sidney Miller, Patsy O'Connor-Norton, Vic Parks, Nat Perrin, Don Porter, Jean Porter Dmytryk, the late Eddie Quillan, Robert Shayne, Ginny Simms-Eastvold, Leonard Stern, Marie Windsor.

In addition, we drew from the following interviews conducted by Chris Costello: Mrs. Bud (Betty) Abbott, Maxene Andrews, Robert Arthur, Mrs. Bobby (Maxine) Barber, Charles Barton, Joe & Ernie Besser, Milt Bronson, Howard Christie, Richard Deacon, Gene de Paul, Tom Ewell, Joan Fulton Shawlee, Alex Gottlieb, Kathryn Grayson, Margaret Hamilton, Stan Irwin, Joe Kenny, Howard Koch, Sid Kuller, Patricia Medina, Martin Ragaway, Lewis Rachmil, Stanley Roberts, Harold Slater, Leonard Spigelgass, Charles Van Enger, Elena Verdugo, Sam Weisbord.

Last but not least, we wish to express our lasting gratitude to the following friends of this book: Jefry N. Abraham, Al and Judy Alijewicz, John E. Allen, Tom B'Hend, Charlene Lamont Brumleu, Jerry Burling, Robin Callot, Mrs. Marty Costello, Nancy Cushing-Jones, Paul DeMaria, Bill DiCicco, Mrs. June Easton, Ray Faiola, Chet Furmanek, Ron Furmanek, Garry Garnet, John Heese, Gary Kaskel, Preston Kaufman, the late Mrs. Estelle Bradley Lamont, Gregory William Mank, Ron McCarrell, Andy McKaie, Jim McPherson, Jim Mulholland, Bob Norberg, Virginia O'Brien, Elmar Paeva, Marvin Page, Carl Palumbo, John Patierno, Jay Ranellucci, Mark Ricci, Philip J. Riley, Mitch Rose, Sal Santuzi, Paul Scrabo, Joe Stabile, Paul Surratt, Bob Thomas, Jerry Weinstein, Marc Weilage, Wade Williams, and Marc Zubatkin.

CONTENTS

9

Clowning backstage at the
world premiere benefit of
*Abbott and Costello Meet the
Invisible Man* (1951).

FOREWORD

A RECOLLECTION BY JERRY LEWIS

In reading this book about Abbott and Costello, know that you're reading about pioneers . . . ground-breakers for the kind of comedy that gave birth to today's great comics.

Dean and I had the great fortune of working on a variety of shows with Bud and Lou, and I can honestly say we had more than just a lesson or two. They were the guys that made America forget that "two-acts" were ever around before them (when in fact there were many . . . the likes of Olsen & Johnson . . . Wheeler & Woolsey . . . Smith & Dale . . . Burns & Allen, and so on).

Possibly the key to the genius of Abbott and Costello was their fantastic capacity to leave the men in the dressing room and bring the comics onto the stage, and that stage could have been a club date, a theater, a burlesque house, a sound stage, or a television studio and would function like a well-oiled machine and make great comedy.

They were perfectionists and taskmasters of rehearsal and preparation for great timing and pace. I doubt that there are another two men living today that could make "Who's On First?" work any better than Bud and Lou did . . . and that was but *one* routine.

Yet with all that was clear to the viewing public, possibly the secret to their success was that Bud and Lou were wonderful men . . . decent, caring, and concerned beings about all the right things . . . namely laughter for others, and human rights.

There will never be another Abbott and Costello, and that's sad . . . while I'm kinda glad, only because I'd hate to try to make a comparison . . . a completely impossible idea.

The Abbott and Costello families on the set of *Abbott and Costello in the Foreign Legion* (1950). Clockwise from Bud: Betty Abbott, Anne Costello, Paddy Costello, Lou, Bud Abbott, Jr., Vickie Abbott, Chris Costello, and Carole Costello.

INTRODUCTION

BY BUD ABBOTT, JR., VICKIE ABBOTT WHEELER, CHRIS COSTELLO, AND PADDY COSTELLO HUMPHREYS

Being the children of Bud Abbott and Lou Costello was as wonderful as you might imagine. Our dads were devoted family men who preferred to stay home with their kids than be a part of the Hollywood scene. Even when they had to go to work at the studio, they brought us along dozens of times. We each have indelible memories of these visits, and you'll read them in this book. Two things were common to each film—the spirit of fun and camaraderie, and laughter, always laughter. Of course, we also spent countless hours in our home theaters, watching these movies over and over again. We're particularly fond of the early ones, like *Buck Privates, Hold That Ghost,* and *Ride 'Em Cowboy,* but *Abbott and Costello Meet Frankenstein,* as you might expect, holds a very special place all its own.

At home, Bud and Lou were not at all like the characters they portrayed on the screen. Both were generous to a fault. Bud was a sweet, gentle man, and Lou was thoughtful and ambitious. Our dads would have been hurt by all the attention that's been focused on their squabbles. They were literally with each other more than they were with our mothers. You can't be together for that amount of time and not fight, yet you can't be together that long and not be friends. Bud and Lou were, above all, friends. Bud was always "Uncle Bud" to the Costello kids, and, likewise, Lou was "Uncle Lou" to the Abbott children. They always treated their "nieces" and "nephew" just great.

Looking back, our dads had a lot to be proud of. They were the number one box office stars of 1942. They were also an important part of their country's war effort. Not only did their comedies keep morale up, but the team was personally responsible for the sale of a record $85 million in War Bonds. They were also deeply concerned with the welfare of children. The other important project in their lives was the establishment of the Lou Costello Jr. Youth Center in 1947; it still serves the East Los Angeles community today. Bud and Lou were also proud that their classic "Who's On First?" routine was inducted into the National Baseball Hall of Fame in Cooperstown in 1956. They'd be pleased to know that it remains the most popular exhibit at the museum. But not all of their successes were in the 1940s or 1950s. It was a big thrill for us to see our dads perform "Who's On First?" in *Rain Man,* and an even bigger thrill when the film won the Oscar for Best Picture. We can now say that Abbott and Costello have indeed appeared in an Academy Award-winning film!

But most of all, we think our dads would be proud to know that their comedy is still making people laugh. After all, that's what Bud and Lou loved doing best. To reach across generations and still be funny is no small accomplishment.

This book is about the making of each of their 36 feature films. It includes information we never knew, and some behind-the-scenes stories that oven our dads may not have known about. To know that an entire book has been devoted to their films would honor them enormously. You know, our dads were notorious for never reading the scripts of their movies. But we know they'd read this book, and love it. We know you will, too.

BUD AND LOU BEFORE HOLLYWOOD

First known photograph of the new team of Abbott and Costello (May 1936).

In most interviews, Abbott and Costello preferred to date their teaming at 1929, suggesting that until they hit the big time in 1938, their climb had been long and hard. But in fact, the road to stardom was comparatively short once they formally joined forces in 1936. This should have served as a testament to the sanctity of the match, yet the boys (or was it their press agent?) preferred to tell the classic dues-paying story.

Both men certainly had put in their time. Bud had been in burlesque for twenty-five years, and Lou, after spending a painful year as a Hollywood stuntman, bounced around in burlesque for another eight. From an early age, however, both seemed destined for show business. Bud's father, Harry Abbott, was an advance man for the Barnum and Bailey Circus, and his mother, Rae, was a bareback rider with the troupe. She left the circus to keep house in Asbury Park, New Jersey, and raise four children—Harry Jr., Olive, William Alexander (Bud), and Florence (Babe). Ultimately, all of the Abbott offspring landed in show business—all in burlesque.

Following Bud's birth on October 2, 1895, the Abbotts moved to Coney Island, where they lived for eighteen years. Bud left St. Paul's Grade School when he could finally "outrun the truant officers" for the lures of the boardwalk. "I wish I'd gone to high school," he told an interviewer in 1959. "We came from a very poor family, and we all had to get out and hustle for the folks." One of his first jobs was at Dreamland Park. For 10¢ Bud would rescue customers lost inside the first Crystal Maze. He worked as a candy butcher, sign painter, house mover, and even operated the parachute ride.

Harry Sr., tired of traveling with the circus, went to work for the organizers of the first of the burlesque circuits, the Columbia Wheel. It would be the cleanest and classiest of the "wheels." Bud hounded his father for a job, and Harry relented. There was an opening in the box office of a Brooklyn burlesque house, and sixteen-year-old Bud stepped in.

Bud Abbott as a teenager at a Coney Island concession.

As the assistant treasurer of the Casino Theater (located off Temple Square), Bud met and paid off some of the fast-rising stars of the day, including W.C. Fields, Fanny Brice, Bert Lahr, Jack Pearl and Sophie Tucker. One of the most popular comedy teams of the 1930s, Bobby Clark and Paul McCullough, played the Casino in their formative years. (In 1939, Abbott and Costello would work with Clark on Broadway in *Streets of Paris*.) When he should have been minding the store, young Bud was backstage, studying how the comedians held an audience, timed the jokes, and built the laughs. Bud Abbott obviously was a very good student, with a very discerning eye.

Not long after starting his new job, Bud wandered into a nearby beer joint on Brooklyn's Red Hook waterfront. When he came to, he found himself shanghaied on the Norwegian steamer *Christianafjord*. He stoked coal for his passage, then jumped ship in Bergen. When he

Bud and Betty Abbott in a publicity still for their act, in the early 1930s.

returned nearly a year later, it was on the same *Christianafjord,* as a helper in the steerage kitchen.

After a tearful reunion with his family, Bud returned to the box office, where he remained, in one burlesque theater or another, for the next ten or twelve years. Billy Gilbert, an ex-burlesque comedian probably best remembered for his run-ins with Laurel and Hardy, recalled giving Bud his first taste of the stage. In the introduction to Leonard Maltin's *Movie Comedy Teams,* Gilbert wrote that Bud "was a ticket taker in a theater I played in. When my straight man didn't show up one day I remembered a bright kid out front and sent for him to replace my missing straight man. He was so good, I kept him in the show. I was twenty-two years old and he was nineteen." Bud still had a few years to go before permanently moving on stage.

In 1918, while he was the treasurer of the National Theater, a burlesque house in Washington, D.C., Bud met a pretty chorine whose stage name was Betty Smith (she was born Jenny Mae Pratt). A week later, they were married in the courthouse at Alexandria, Virginia. Bud and Betty moved on to Cleveland for a stint at the Empire Theater, where Bud worked as a manager and Betty as a soubrette. Finally, in 1923, Bud borrowed $1500 from an uncle, a treasurer at Tammany Hall, to stage his own tab show, *Broadway Flashes,* on the Gus Sun circuit. "That consisted of about ten girls, a straight man, a comic, a prima donna, and a soubrette," Bud explained in a 1959 interview. "I put the company together, but I wasn't an actor then. I just got hold of some cheap scenery and some cheap wardrobe and put it out on the road. Those were hard, plugging days. I went into the show as a straight man because I wanted to save the straight man's salary. I looked at him and said, 'Why am I paying this guy $50 a week when I can do the same thing myself?' "

When the tour dissolved, Bud and Betty landed in Detroit at the National Theater, where Bud, now a producer, staged a new show every week for three years. Occasionally, Bud would fill in for an indisposed straight man and work with the comics. When he finally was confident enough to make a permanent move from producer to performer, he and Betty developed an act with Bud as the straight man and Betty the comic. A booker for the Hertigan-Seamans circuit was a friend of Bud's father, and he signed the couple to a three-year contract.

Bud's cousin, Al Golden, was one of the top straight men in the business. (In the 1930s, Golden teamed briefly with future Three Stooges member Joe DeRita.) As the show-business critic Joe Laurie, Jr., once observed, "A good straight man can make a fair comic look good, and a great comic look better." Al instructed Bud on technique, and Bud closely followed his cousin's advice. Bud was always proud of the fact that he succeeded on the stage without resorting to the outlandish costumes or heavy make-up so typical of burlesque comedians. He wore an ordinary business suit, and it became his trademark. Bud quickly became one of burlesque's best straight men, and, although he worked primarily with Betty, comics were lining up to work with him.

Louis Francis Cristillo was born on March 6, 1906, in (of course) Paterson, New Jersey. His father, Sebastian, was an Italian immigrant who worked for an insurance company, and his mother, Helene, was half French and half Irish. Lou was preceded by a brother, Anthony (better known as Pat), and followed by a sister, Marie.

"From the very beginning, my father was both an athlete and a ham," Lou's daughter Chris wrote in *Lou's on First,* a biography of her father. He loved baseball and basketball, becoming Paterson's Foul Shot Champion, and even tried boxing under the name Lou King. But his ring career ended the night his father happened to attend one of his bouts.

"Dad always wanted to be in show business," Chris writes. "From the time he was four years old, he play-acted with his friends or alone in front of a mirror. Nobody knows where he got it; there were no actors on either side of the family." Lou also excelled at being the class clown. Legend has it that after one particularly precocious day, his teacher, Bessie Whitehead, had him stay after school to write "I'm a bad boy" 150 times. While the phrase stuck with him (it later became his trademark line), it didn't dissuade him. Lou even managed a pratfall at his high school graduation.

Lou loved movies, and he and Pat would ditch school and spend their lunch money on westerns or Charlie Chaplin shorts. When he was twelve, Lou was entranced by Chaplin's service comedy, *Shoulder Arms* (1918), reportedly seeing the film twenty-five times. "He absolutely idolized Chaplin, and it was Chaplin, indirectly, who influenced my father to change his course in life. Instead of a dramatic actor, he wanted to be a comic," Chris writes. That Halloween, Lou won a Charlie Chaplin look-alike contest at the Paterson Armory.

After graduating from high school, Lou began making the rounds of local vaudeville agents without success. Finally, in 1927, he announced to his parents that he wanted to try his luck in Hollywood. Sebastian flatly refused to permit it, but Pat successfully lobbied in Lou's favor.

By day, Lou found sparse work as a laborer and extra at MGM, and at night he slept in parked cars adjacent to the lot. Some sources place him in *Bardelys the Magnificent* (1926) and *Taxi Dancer* (1927). He occasionally worked as an extra in crowd scenes, and can be spotted ringside in the Laurel and Hardy silent, *The Battle of the Century* (1927). Reportedly he was hired to shoot basketballs for the Marion Davies film, *The Fair Co-Ed* (1927).

Lou Costello as a member of a semi-pro basketball team in Paterson, NJ.

One fateful day a stuntman was needed to jump off a second-story balcony for Dolores Del Rio in *The Trail of '98* (1928). Lou volunteered, did the stunt, and found a new career. He claimed to have worked in more than sixty films, doubling for George K. Arthur and Tim McCoy, among others. He was trampled by the entire USC football team; donned a gorilla suit for a chase scene in *Circus Rookies* (1928); and was part of a barroom brawl in *Rose Marie* (1928). Lou recalled, "When I was a stuntman—and that was an easier racket than most people suspect—I was clawed on the top of the head by an eagle and once bitten on the finger by a vulture. I was once supposed to lead a hundred cossacks in a mob scene. I fell off my horse and all hundred of the cossacks rode over me. There was also the time the script called for the comedian to sleep with his horse. Before I crawled in with the horse, the guy in charge studies the situation and says, 'Don't worry. He won't touch you. When the horse gets up, he'll get up in the other direction, away from you.' Naturally he gets up on my side of the bed, rolling over me."

After he was hurt doubling for Dolores Del Rio, Lou reconsidered his career. "When the talkies came in, I saw a lot of actors were hotfooting it to New York for voice lessons. I said, if you gotta have voice lessons to be an actor, that's for me. So I decided to go to New York." When his bankroll ran out in Topeka, he learned that a burlesque house in St. Joseph, Missouri, needed a comic.

The Empress (on South 7th Street) had advertised for a "Dutch" comic. In burlesque, every nationality and accent had been fodder for comedy at one time or another. In 1929, Dutch accents were in vogue. The comic misunderstood his straight man (or woman), presumably because of the language barrier. Lou was essentially a Dutch comic minus the accent with Bud Abbott in their various mix-up routines.

Although he'd been to Paterson's burlesque theater, the Orpheum, a few times, Lou really didn't know burlesque. Perhaps because of his Hollywood background, or because the Empress was desperate for a comic, Lou was hired even though he had never performed in front of an audience before. But he learned fast. Harold Slater, then a young reporter for the St. Joseph *News-Press*, became friends with the new comedian. "He was in St. Joseph for maybe eight months, making in those days maybe $25 a week as a Dutch comic. Back then, the Empress had a good burlesque show—four girls in the chorus and he was a good act. He was never dirty; no smut was ever involved. In fact, he was a real clean kid." Lou was now using the name "Costello," which he borrowed from actress Helene Costello.

Lou (left) on the set of *Trail of '98* (1928)

There were about 200 basic burlesque sketches that dated from before the turn of the century. After a year on the circuit, a comic knew them all and could ad-lib variations to freshen them up. In his autobiography, burlesque graduate Phil Silvers cited two myths about burlesque. "The first is that burlesque was a great training ground for comedians. That's true.

17

But the other myth, that all burlesque comics were great, wasn't true. That's why they stayed in burlesque. The ones who rose out of it were able to build creatively on the basics they had learned. Witness Abbott and Costello, Bert Lahr, Jackie Gleason, Bobby Clark, Ed Wynn, Red Skelton, Eddie Cantor, and Fanny Brice." And Phil Silvers.

Lou moved on to a burlesque house in St. Louis, then worked his way home. In the summer of 1930, producer Nat Fields (brother of Lew Fields of Weber and Fields) saw him in a local show in Paterson and hired him for the Orpheum Theater in New York. For the next two years, Lou worked locally, playing burlesque at the Orpheum in Paterson, Minsky's Republic on 42nd Street, and Minsky's Apollo in Harlem. He also first worked with Sidney Fields at Paterson's Orpheum Theater during this period. Fields would later play the irascible landlord in the Abbott and Costello television series.

By now, Lou had shed the old-fashioned puttied nose, funny hats, and baggy pants of a burlesque comic. But he hadn't forgotten his goal of becoming a movie star. In the summer of 1932, with a few years' stage experience under his belt, he grabbed at a chance to appear in stock burlesque at the Follies Theater in Los Angeles. His notices were good, but a second shot at movies never came. He headed back east, stopping for stints in St. Louis, Chicago, and Columbus.

Bud and Betty, meanwhile, had signed a long-term contract with the Minsky brothers in New York and rotated between their Republic, Central, and Apollo theaters. Bud was now working with comedian Harry Steppe, who originated the famous "Lemon Bit"—a hilarious shell game routine that Abbott and Costello would do on Broadway and in *In the Navy* (1941). Bud so impressed the Minskys that he was asked to produce shows with his own stock troupe that included Betty, Harry, Lou DeVine, Gene Schuler and Joe Hill. A second Minsky producer with his own unit was a tall, handsome straight man named John Grant.

If Bud and Lou hadn't bumped into each other before, they certainly did in January 1933, when Costello was booked into the Republic at the same time as Bud and Betty. Lou was teamed with Jimmy Francis at this time, but worked with Abbott for one sketch—the "Piano Scene" (also known as "All Right"). The Abbott, in this case was not Bud, but Betty, who was an excellent straight woman in her own right. Over the next two years, Bud and Lou's paths would cross many times.

At the end of 1933, Bud was producing the stock shows at Newark's Empire theater and working with a comedian named Harry Evanson. Betty Abbott and Milt Bronson were also in the company. Lou was back at Minsky's Republic in a show headlined by Ann Corio. A pretty chorus girl named Anne Battler caught his eye, and in January 1934, they were married in Boston. Late one summer night in 1934, Lou and Anne were in an automobile accident driving home from a theater in Connecticut. Anne suffered a broken neck, and it ended her career as a dancer.

Soon after, Lou joined forces with straight man Joe Lyons, and the pair signed with the Independent Wheel, a Minsky competitor. John Grant was now producing shows for the Independent Wheel. By the end of 1934, Lyons and Costello's contract with the Indy and Abbott and Evanson's contract with the Minskys had ended. Both teams landed in stock burlesque at the Eltinge Theater on 42nd Street in January 1935. Over the next three months, Bud and Lou really got to know each other and, although they had other partners, perform together. Betty Abbott appeared in sketches with both teams, as did Milt Bronson. "Bud put on a scene for Lou," Betty recalled in an interview in 1979. "It was the 'Lemon Bit' that Bud had done with Harry Steppe. And they worked wonderfully together. People started to say, 'Why don't you team up?'" After the engagement, Abbott and Costello went their separate ways until the end of the year, when they met up again and decided to formally team. Their first show together was probably early in January 1936.

The new team was immediately signed by the Minskys, and for three months they bounced back and forth between the Republic and Minsky's Brooklyn theater. In April, Bud and Lou briefly toured with *Life Begins at Minsky's,* a show that brought that unique brand of burlesque to cities in the east. Despite their surroundings, Bud and Lou always kept their act clean. "An audience may laugh at you for off-color jokes when they're in the theater," Bud once explained, "but when they get outside and talk it over, their opinion of you is pretty low." When they returned to New York in May, Abbott and Costello were spotted by a young talent booker named Eddie Sherman. Sherman needed a couple of comics to round out a minstrel show at Atlantic City's Steel Pier for the summer season. "In those days," Sherman explained in an interview, "the strippers were the big attraction, and they had to follow the strippers. Which made it a little difficult for a few minutes. But once they got into their routines, they just wrecked the audience." Sherman brought the minstrel show's producer, Frank Elliott, to have a look. On May 19, Abbott and Costello signed with Elliott's show for eleven weeks, commencing June 26, at $145 a week. "Never got in the water," Bud recalled, "because we were busy doing 812 shows a day. But we could see it occasionally." Lou and Anne Costello also had their first child, Patricia, at the end of that summer.

The boys then returned to burlesque with an exclusive thirty-nine-week contract with another burlesque impresario, Max Wilner. The team shuttled between Wilner's two showcases—the Apollo on 42nd Street (a few doors down from Minsky's Republic) and the Shubert in Philadelphia. Bud and Lou developed their consummate sense of timing and honed their classic material—including "Who's On First?"—to perfection during this period. "Bud had done the baseball bit a long time before he worked with Lou," Betty Abbott said. "That was public domain. He did it with some comic, I don't remember who it was. And it was a little different, because he and Lou put an awful lot of stuff in it, a lot of new material. Eddie Sherman had them copyright it." In fact, while Bud and Lou were working at the Steel Pier that summer, Steve Mills and Brownie Sick were doing a version of "Who's On First?" in Los Angeles in *Minsky's Goes Hollywood.*

By the time the team's contract with Wilner expired in April 1937, burlesque itself didn't have much longer to live. Abbott and Costello worked at the Star Theater in Brooklyn for just two days before Mayor LaGuardia ordered all the burlesque theaters closed on April 30. Bud and Lou were forced to go legitimate. Fortunately, the boys had already been booked for a second summer at the Steel Pier . . . with a $5 raise.

"After the Steel Pier," Bud explained, "we signed with Leddy and Smith, producers of a traveling [vaudeville] unit called *Hollywood Bandwagon.*" The troupe toured Springfield, Boston, Cleveland, Montreal, Toronto, Detroit, and Indianapolis. Bud and Lou performed the "Drill Routine" and "Who's On First?," which, according to *Variety,* was the big hit of the show.

"We remained with Leddy and Smith," Bud continued, "until we got stranded in Milwaukee. Then we went to work for Eddie Sherman." Sherman got them humble gigs at first, like the Willow Grove amusement park in Pennsylvania for $20. They paid Sherman his $2 commission. "And you know how much Abbott and I spent that afternoon on the rides at the park? Right—$18!" Lou recalled.

"I talked Eddie into booking us into Paterson for three days at $60 for the pair of us," Lou continued. "We were terrific. Next, Baltimore and Philadelphia for split-week engagements. We were dynamite. So much so that we shuttled back and forth for six weeks."

Finally, a booker for the Loew's circuit caught them in Washington, D.C., and signed them for a stage show at Loew's State in New York for the first week of February 1938. The boys were now earning $600 a week. But the star of the show, which included a dog and pony act, tap dancers and chorus line, was a young and pre-*Wizard of Oz* Judy Garland. *Variety* called Judy "an undeniable smash," while Abbott and Costello, performing the "Drill Routine," evoked only a "not bad" from the trade paper.

"We were playing Loew's State when Ted Collins, Kate Smith's manager, caught us during the Wednesday show and right off invited us to the Thursday broadcast," Lou recalled. Longtime A&C pal Milt Bronson recalled, "Henny Youngman had seen Bud and Lou and urged Ted Collins to go to Loew's State to see the team work. Ted went, but was not impressed. Since *The Kate Smith Hour* was radio, Ted was afraid Bud and Lou were too visual and would die on the airwaves." Sherman turned to Sam Weisbrod of the William Morris Agency to join the lobby to persuade Collins to hire Bud and Lou. "They're going to be big

On the boardwalk between performances at Atlantic City's Steel Pier (probably the summer of 1938).

19

ABOVE RIGHT: Regulars on
the *Kate Smith Hour* in
1938. ABOVE LEFT: With
Bobby Clark in *Streets of
Paris* (1939).

stars, Ted," Weisbrod warned. "Now, you wouldn't want to be known as the man who passed
up Abbott and Costello, would you?"

Collins agreed to a one-shot that night, February 3, 1938, for $350. In their first appearance
the boys did their "Mudder/Fodder" routine, but their voices tended to sound alike over the
air. This detracted from the effectiveness of the bit, since, as Lou put it, "the listeners couldn't
tell who was asking and who was answering." The similarity was never discovered on stage,
Lou said, probably because "I shout and jump around so much." Lou agreed to adapt a piping
falsetto, and their next appearance was a great improvement.

Lou continued, "Although we weren't terrific starting out in radio, Ted had confidence in
me and Bud and kept inviting us back. We couldn't get any of those thirteen-week contracts,
but boy did that turn out good for me and Bud. We had to sign a new contract for every
guest shot and when we started to click the ante was boosted every week. When we finally
did get a contract, that was all right, too. It was a straight thirty-nine week agreement with
no options." The boys would ultimately remain with the program ninety-nine weeks, until
the summer of 1940.

Legend has it that Bud and Lou tried for weeks to do "Who's On First?" on the show,
but Collins didn't think the routine was funny. Lou recalled in an interview in 1956, "We
started to do the routine and we got as far as the outfield before he stopped us and said,
'Well, boys, I don't think you ought to do that on radio.'" Bud interrupted, "He was a little
more severe than that, Lou. He said, 'If you do that, you'll never do another radio show
again.'" Lou finally tricked Collins by claiming it was the only thing left in their repertoire.
Rather than have them skip a week, Collins relented, and on March 24, 1938, a national radio
audience heard "Who's On First?" for the very first time. It was an instant smash. Collins
raised the team's salary to $500 a week and ordered "Who's On First?" repeated once a
month.

But the team really was running low on material. Not many burlesque bits were purely
verbal and right for radio. A week later, an old acquaintance from burlesque named John
Grant was hired on as their writer. Grant had been in Toronto producing burlesque and
vaudeville shows. It was the start of an auspicious association that would last seventeen years.

Abbott and Costello began doing stage shows at the prestigious Roxy Theater in 1938, and
their stature grew with each appearance. By October, they were headliners. In November the
boys branched out with their first nightclub engagement at Billy Rose's Casa Mañana. They
were now attracting a lot of attention within the industry and reportedly received their first
film offer around Thanksgiving. They turned this down (and another in 1940) because of their
commitment to Kate Smith and because the offers were single shots. As Lou explained, "We
don't want to make a picture; we want to keep on making them. We'll wait for the right
story to come along."

Meanwhile, another opportunity knocked. While the team played the Paramount Theater
in February, 1939, producer Harry Kaufman approached them about a Broadway show he

was preparing, *Streets of Paris.* Kaufman's other show, *Hellzapoppin'* with Ole Olsen and Chick Johnson, was a big hit. Kaufman, Olsen, and Johnson would produce the new show, to star veteran comic Bobby Clark. It promised to be a rowdy, naughty show—perfect for two ex-burlesquers.

Streets of Paris, which also introduced Carmen Miranda to American audiences, contained two acts and twenty-eight scenes. Bud and Lou appeared in four scenes, including the burlesque standards "Hole in The Wall," "Lemon Bit," and "Crazy House," which stopped the show every night. When *Streets of Paris* opened on Broadway at the Broadhurst Theater on June 19, 1939, legendary *New York Times* theater critic Brooks Atkinson welcomed "the hilarious team of Lou Costello and Bud Abbott, who carry laughter to the point of helpless groaning. . . . It is a patter act primarily. Abbott is the overbearing master mind whose feverish and impatient guidance of the conversation produces the crises. Costello is the short, fat he-who-gets-slapped. He is a moon-faced zany with wide, credulous eyes, a high voice and puffy hands that struggle in futile gestures. Both men work themselves up into a state of excitement that is wonderful to behold."

Bud's nephew, Norman, who is today an Emmy-winning director, was just a stage kid who ran errands for his uncle in 1939. "You never heard laughter like that," he recalled. "You know a Broadway audience is more sedate; Noel Coward is their idea of a comedian. And here come these two guys from burlesque. They just *rocked* the Broadhurst Theatre."

In one scene, Bud threw Lou across the stage; one night, Costello sailed into the orchestra pit and demolished a bass viola. Bud and Lou also rose to the challenge posed by Bobby Clark, a comic's comic who was never upstaged. Clark loved to add bits of business himself, which frequently threw his co-stars. But one night, when Clark dropped his beret in a scene, Lou and Bud grabbed a hatrack and a cane, and the team proceeded to play hockey with Clark's cap. Clark was nonplussed. On other nights, Lou would step out of character to recap the show for the latecomers. *Streets* became a huge hit—and Abbott and Costello were the reason.

Bud and Lou became the darlings of New York. They made their television debut on July 19, 1939, on a fifteen-minute program called *So This Is New York.* Mayor La Guardia invited the boys to City Hall several times and remained good friends with them. September 6, 1939, was Abbott and Costello Day at the New York World's Fair. Schoolchildren presented them with medals in honor of Lou's "I'm a bad boy" tagline. New York University bestowed degrees of Doctor of Hilarity on them. Perhaps as final affirmation of their popularity, Bud and Lou turned up in advertisements for Horn and Hardart restaurants, Edelbrau beer, Garcia cigars, and Adams Hats.

Earliest known photograph of "Who's On First?" (circa 1937).

To accommodate the team's weekly appearance on the Kate Smith program, the *Streets* curtain was delayed ten minutes every Friday night. In November, Bud and Lou began doing late shows at the Versailles nightclub on East 50th Street. One critic, citing all the concurrent appearances by the team, suggested that Bud and Lou had reached the peak of popularity. They were making $1250 a week on radio, $1500 on Broadway, and $1000 in nightclubs. Christmas was particularly sweet that year. Lou and Anne had their second child, Carole, and Bud and Betty bought their first house, in Stony Brook, Long Island.

Streets closed after 274 performances on February 10, 1940. Then the show went out on a tour that included Washington, D.C. where President Roosevelt enjoyed the boys immensely and invited Abbott and Costello to entertain at a White House dinner party on March 16, 1940 (the first of several command performances for U.S. Presidents). The team left the musical when the tour took them too far from New York to continue appearing on the Smith program.

That summer, Mike Todd mounted a streamlined *Streets of Paris* at the World's Fair starring Minsky alumni Abbott and Costello and Gypsy Rose Lee. NBC signed Bud and Lou as Fred Allen's summer replacement, and Hollywood began making overtures in earnest. Abbott and Costello fully expected to do one picture, *One Night in the Tropics,* then return to New York and continue working on radio and Broadway. Fortunately, that's not what became of Bud Abbott and Lou Costello. Their talents had to be captured on film.

MAKING THE MOVIES

The Abbott and Costello films instantly became the most lucrative series of comedies ever made, and because of that the films were churned out with remarkable dispatch. In the team's first twenty-four months in Hollywood, they made ten films. After that, Bud and Lou averaged between two and three films a year for the next fourteen years. No other Universal feature series was so prolific. Even Deanna Durbin, who saved the studio from bankruptcy in the late 1930s, made only two films per year at her peak. Later, in the 1950s, Universal turned out one profitable Ma and Pa Kettle and Francis the Talking Mule picture per year, while Bud and Lou's contract still called for two at Universal, plus one independent picture, per year.

With such a relentless production schedule, the prime concern for the team's producers was coming up with story ideas. Frequently one film inspired a series of sequels. The blockbuster *Buck Privates,* which was originally inspired by current events (Congress had just passed the first peacetime selective service act), begat the team's other service comedies, *In the Navy* and *Keep 'Em Flying.* Much later, the inspired (and profitable) teaming of Abbott and Costello with the Frankenstein monster led the way to several horror spoofs.

But early in 1941, producer Alex Gottlieb's immediate concern was developing an adequate supply of scripts for future A&C vehicles. "I made a list," Gottlieb recalled in 1979. "I had gone through all the 'team' pictures and made a list of all the backgrounds they had used. RKO had Wheeler and Woolsey, a comedy team that worked almost the same way as Bud and Lou did, only they weren't anywhere as good. And other studios had teams like that. I made a list of all the backgrounds they had used."

Bert Wheeler and Robert Woolsey were vaudeville and Broadway comedians who broke into RKO musicals in 1929. Like Abbott and Costello, they began their own series of features with a service comedy, *Half Shot at Sunrise* (1930). Over the next eight years Wheeler and Woolsey would appear in twenty-one films—a pace matched only by Abbott and Costello ten years later. There are other, more eerie similarities between the teams. Like Lou, Bert was born in Paterson, New Jersey. Bert and his wife, like Bud and Betty Abbott, had been a team on stage. And, like Lou, Bob fell ill at the height of the team's career and was confined to bed for a year. Unlike Lou, however, he never recovered, and he died in 1938. His partner outlived him by nearly 20 years (Bud outlived Lou by 15).

Wheeler and Woolsey's second starring film, *Hook, Line and Sinker* (also 1930) clearly inspired Abbott and Costello's second film, *Hold That Ghost* (1941). In the former, co-star Dorothy Lee inherits a run-down hotel that W&W help turn into a swanky resort. Along the way they get mixed up with gangsters who try to hide stolen loot there. In *Hold That Ghost,* Bud and Lou inherit a run-down roadhouse that they turn into a resort. Along the way they get mixed up with gangsters searching for hidden loot. In *The Nitwits* (1935) Wheeler and Woolsey run a

22

ABOVE: With the third
member of the team,
writer John Grant. ABOVE
LEFT: Arthur Lubin, who
directed the team's first
five hits, on the set of In
the Navy (1941).

cigar store in a midtown skyscraper. When a magazine publisher in the building is murdered, Bert and Bob try to solve the crime themselves. In *Who Done It?* (1942), Bud and Lou are soda jerks at Radio City. When the president of the network is murdered, Bud and Lou try to solve the crime themselves. MGM followed suit in 1942 when it dusted off Wheeler and Woolsey's *Rio Rita* (1929) and retailored it for A&C. A western dude ranch was the locale for Wheeler and Woolsey's *Girl Crazy* (1932) and for Abbott and Costello's *Ride 'Em Cowboy* (1942). *Mummy's Boys* (1936) presages *Abbott and Costello Meet the Mummy* (1955). And in *Cracked Nuts* (1932), Wheeler and Woolsey examined a map with towns named "Which" and "What," thus anticipating "Who's On First?" as well.

This is not to say that Gottlieb, the writers, or Bud and Lou stole from Wheeler and Woolsey. The settings may be similar, but the plots, excecutions, and gags are completely different. "I picked Bud and Lou's pictures out of that list," Gottlieb continued. "I suggested a premise to a writer, and he would write an outline. Then John Grant would put in the routines. As a result, from then on, I'd look at this list to make a picture." Gottlieb's list was so extensive that in an interview in 1942 he boasted that he had ninety-two story properties awaiting Bud and Lou—enough, he said, to take them into the year 1983. The list was also, it seems, well guarded; the writers we spoke with seemed genuinely surprised to learn about it. They recalled Gottlieb doling out story ideas one at a time.

In that interview, Gottlieb explained that there had to be a definite story before any of the funny stuff could be written. There was a stable of young writers who worked on these early Abbott and Costello treatments and scripts: True Boardman, Edmund L. Hartmann, Arthur Horman, Edmund Joseph, Robert Lees and Fred Rinaldo, Nat Perrin, Stanley Roberts, and Harold Shumate. "It was common for us to be writing an Abbott and Costello while there was one in release and another one shooting," explained Robert Lees. Frequently, two writers would be assigned to write treatments for, say, "The Abbott and Costello Cowboy Picture." Once a treatment was selected, it was submitted to the story department, which might or might not assign the same writer to do the screenplay. Usually, a writer had eight weeks to do a screenplay, from treatment to final draft, at his own pace. Arthur Horman, however, wrote *In the Navy* in five weeks.

Second and third drafts of the script were passed on to Abbott and Costello's writer, John Grant. "John looked like a very successful banker—tall, stately; he could have been a British character actor," recalled Edmund Hartmann, who, after writing some of the early A&C vehicles, succeeded Alex Gottlieb as the team's producer. "John was a wonderful guy; a quiet, decent man. He had been in burlesque with Bud and Lou. There are about 15 to 20 basic burlesque comedy routines. John's job was to take a finished script and go through it and see where they could inject these comedy routines. They were the only things that Lou would

23

Lou with producer Edmund L. Hartmann on the set of *The Naughty Nineties* (1945)

willingly do, because they didn't have to rehearse—they knew them all. And if the routines weren't in, Lou would put them in. They were very resistant to using new material—especially Lou." The formula had served Bud, Lou, and Universal's bankbook incredibly well, and there was no need or desire to experiment now.

The other screenwriters hardly collaborated with John Grant. When they finished a treatment or script, it was practically shoved under Grant's door. His revisions generally went uncontested because he was the only writer Bud and Lou listened to. Robert Lees and Fred Rinaldo wrote some of the team's best films, including *Hold That Ghost* and *Abbott and Costello Meet Frankenstein*. "You didn't have conferences with anybody but the producer," Lees recalled. "John Grant would occasionally come in and talk to us, but more or less he was off somewhere else. He had nothing to do with the stories, but he'd write so much dialogue that he'd get a screen credit. Fred and I were screenwriters, not gagwriters. The problem was, we wanted to write stories that held up, had character, and developed. And we would write what we would consider Abbott and Costello routines which were verbal or physical. Sometimes we felt that John Grant would take perfectly good dialogue that was advancing the script and turn it into one of those things they had done a thousand times before. And they'd put it in just because it was Grant. They were more sure of their routines, or more sure of John's stuff. And there would go your continuity. They usually kept him on the set to jazz up scenes that had no reason being jazzed up in the first place." The writers frequently wouldn't know what of their original script survived until they saw the finished film. Tired of trying to develop their own comedy scenes for A&C, many of the other writers surrendered. It is not uncommon to see in some second and third draft screenplays notations like, "John Grant comes up with a great ending," or "An A&C routine here."

Grant did do his homework. He bought books on the subjects of the films and screened related movies for ideas and material to parody. He would also compile a list of props that applied to the setting, such as a hammock or a water fountain, then work out gags based on the props. Sometimes, however, John's facility with material wasn't always inspired by the muses. Alex Gottlieb recalled, "I went to John one day and said, 'The script feels a little empty here; we need an extra routine. Can you dream something up?' He said, 'I'll write it tonight.' And he came in the next day with an absolutely brilliant routine. And I said, 'This is the best thing you've ever written.' Bud and Lou read it and said, 'John, this is great.' And he said, 'I just got inspired.' Now, John was a very nice guy. But it bothered me that a guy who wrote certain types of routines had written this thing; it was damn good. I said to myself, this guy is not that clever a comedy writer. Suddenly I remembered something. I had a book published in 1876, *A Compendium of Humor*. I looked through this book very carefully, and John had taken the whole routine right out of the book. I never told him that I knew, or Bud and Lou."

As the scripts were written, they were fed, section by section, to the Production Code Administration, where Joseph Breen's staff scrutinized them for potentially offensive material. "There were pages and pages of things you couldn't do or say," recalled Edmund Hartmann. "It's a wonder pictures were made at all." The standards were quaint compared to what if anything is labeled "offensive" today. Double entendre was blue penciled, and anything remotely suggestive was ordered changed. Gangsters had to be punished or redeemed. In a bedroom scene, the man had to keep one foot on the floor at all times. A scene could not fade out on a kiss—it had to have a discernible end—and a kiss could only last a prescribed length of time. Sometimes a writer or producer could argue his case if the "questionable" material was integral to the plot, or genuinely innocent in intent. Robert Lees remembered, "We had a line once, 'Here we go again,' and it came down that we couldn't use the line. We said, 'What's wrong with that?' They said, 'It's the punchline to a dirty joke.' We had to cut it out. We knew they were a little nuts, but we never paid too much attention; you can't write anticipating what they're going to delete." Still, lots of things slipped through, including the name of the acrobatic troupe in *Who Done It?*—the Flying Bordellos! In any case, the final script and the completed film would have to be approved by the Breen Office or the picture couldn't be released. Frequently their suggestions made good business sense; why have local censor boards hack up your film? The Breen Office was also invaluable in spotting potential trouble in foreign markets, where customs are different. For example, in the United States the word "bum" means tramp, but in England it's the posterior, and therefore, offensive. In Arabia, scenes of Bud slapping Lou were excised because it is considered an affront to Allah to slap someone.

The working script would also go to Universal's Production Office, where a budget and shooting schedule would be worked out. The A&C films never received "A" budgets at Universal, but did at Metro. Typically, an Abbott and Costello film shot six days a week, a minimum of ten hours a day. Arthur Lubin, who directed the team's first five films, remembered the grueling pace. "In those days, before the Director's Guild, you had to shoot so many pages a day, and if you didn't finish in so many hours, you worked until you dropped dead, at night or on a Saturday or Sunday. The studio didn't ask how good did you do, but how many pages did you shoot." It was rare for an Abbott and Costello film to be in production more than four weeks. One exception was *Buck Privates Come Home* (1947), which was in production an epic fifty days. Post-production, including editing and scoring, usually took another four to six weeks. The Production Office also scrutinized the script for any extravagances. If, for example, a writer put in, say, a rooftop chase, the department might suggest scaling it down to a series of alleyways, thus saving money.

Writers were further hindered from realizing their original vision, because they were discouraged from visiting the set. That wasn't the policy on just the A&C films, but on all of the films at Universal. Robert Lees recalled, "It was like working on a conveyor belt. The producer would take the script from you and get it to the director. Then he'd take the film from the director and get it into the cutting room, get it scored, and so forth. It wasn't collaborative, and I think that hurt the quality at Universal. Because they wanted directors to direct, and writers to write. It would be a terrible waste of time if a writer and a director ever got together. If we wandered onto the set of an Abbott and Costello picture on the way back from lunch, the director would yell, 'What are you fellows doing here?' For two reasons: first of all, we weren't doing what we were supposed to be doing—writing. Secondly, they didn't want us to see what a mess they were making of our story. And God help us if we made a suggestion! We'd be watching them shoot a scene with Bud and Lou being chased all over the place and then we'd say, 'What are they chasing them for?' The director would say, 'Because they've got the jewels!' We'd say, 'But you cut the scene where you see them get the jewels, so you're chasing them for no reason.' And he'd say, 'Don't worry, no one will notice.' That was the attitude at Universal."

Edmund Hartmann explained that this attitude was fostered at the very top. After the Laemmle family, which founded Universal, was deposed in 1936, a committee was brought in to turn the failing studio around. "The studio executives were all theater exhibitors, owners, and operators. They knew nothing about the technique of making movies. But they knew what would bring a crowd in on the marquee. So they would assign contract people to do something that had nothing to do with the picture at all, just to be able to use the name. And they never talked about movies; you could talk about football, you could talk about horse racing. But if you talked about movies they looked at you like you were some kind of nut." Later, in 1947, when Universal merged with International Pictures, erudite producers William Goetz and Leo Spitz showed little interest in the Abbott and Costello series. Director Charles Barton explained, "Mr. Spitz was a nice man, but he wouldn't talk to either Bud or Lou. I think he was scared of them. Mr. Goetz was a very fine independent producer. But you had two people in charge of the studio who didn't know anything about comedy at all."

How much did Bud and Lou contribute to the scripts? "They never had script approval," Alex Gottlieb said. They weren't writers; they trusted that to John Grant. Generally, Bud and Lou had little to say about their scripts simply because they barely read them. But in 1946,

Shooting a scene from *Keep 'Em Flying* (1941) on location.

Lou initiated a campaign to break away from their previous formula. Whether this occurred because of a well-publicized rift with Bud, or because the team's most recent films, *The Naughty Nineties* and *Here Come the Co-Eds* were box office disappointments, is open to debate. In any case, the studio consented and the two films produced during this period, *Little Giant* and *The Time of Their Lives,* effectively split the team as separate characters in the same story. While these films are among the team's most interesting work, they are not among their funniest. The experiment failed, and Lou wisely turned the controls over to his new producer at Universal, Robert Arthur. By the 1950s, Abbott and Costello's enthusiasm and input at Universal had waned considerably. Disenchanted with the studio's apparent apathy toward them, Bud and Lou were more concerned with their own TV series (1952–54) and appearances on *The Colgate Comedy Hour*—projects that clearly meant more to them. Charles Lamont, the team's last director at Universal, remembered how distracted they were. "Things were left entirely to John Grant and myself. In fact, neither one of them even bothered about okaying a script. We'd present them with a finished script and they'd do it. Once in a while they'd suggest a gag or maybe ad-lib something, but not too often. Bud never did, and Lou very seldom. I think this was because their minds really weren't on what they were doing."

Once before the cameras, however, Bud and Lou were always improving on the material, and if they weren't full of ideas reading a script cold, performing brought out their innovations. During his radio days, Lou claimed he couldn't be funny reading words off a piece of paper. While he reviewed his lines beforehand, he invariably elaborated and improvised during a scene. "You get too mechanical if you rehearse," Lou told an interviewer in 1947. "That's what killed vaudeville, guys never changing their timing. After all these years I can tell by the gleam in Abbott's eye when he's going to throw me a line and I have to hit that dumb kisser of mine." Arthur Lubin was the first director to realize that at least in Abbott and Costello's case, rehearsals were detrimental. "I found that if we rehearsed too much with them, their material got stale, and they'd start adding things that didn't mean anything. All I needed a rehearsal for was to place my cameras. There was nothing I could tell them because no one could direct their routines as well as they."

And so a method of working evolved. "We just ad-lib our pictures," said Lou. "Bud and me get the gist of the scene from the director, and then we're off on whatever comes into our minds." Director Charles Lamont remembered, "Lou would come to me and say, 'What do I do here?' He never knew what he was going to do, never knew what the hell the story was about. I'd tell him, then he'd twist the lines around. They were just as good as the lines that were written, so I never made a fuss about it." Frequently, however, Lou wandered off the point—far off. He confessed that "sometimes I don't know where I'm at and it's Bud who gets me back on the track."

Here was Bud Abbott's great talent—knowing just how much rope to give Lou before pulling him back into the scene. Arthur Lubin explained, "I thought Lou Costello would have been lost without Bud, and Bud without Lou. I don't think there was a more wonderful 'feed' man. Lou would start to get away from the script, and he'd go on ad-libbing, and Bud could bring him right back to the script, which was wonderful. They were a great, great pair."

Standard moviemaking practice was to shoot a scene from three different angles: first in a wide shot, then in close-ups for each of the principal characters. The dialogue and action in each set-up had to match closely so the sequence could be cut together and make sense. Early on, Arthur Lubin discovered that with Abbott and Costello, no two takes were ever the same; Lou would add things, physically and verbally, each time, and Bud, naturally, would respond perfectly to him. Having them repeat a scene three times for the various camera angles became a continuity nightmare.

"Because Lou never did a scene the same way twice," Lubin explained, "I shot all their scenes with two or three cameras simultaneously: a close-up for Lou, because he had such a dollface, and a close two-shot. I usually tried to have a camera on a dolly so I could move with them. You couldn't keep them in one position; Lou was all over the place. This actually saved time and money, because they always knew what they were going to do when they walked on a set." The three-camera set-up became standard procedure on all future A&C films.

Directors also learned to keep the cameras running even after they yelled "Cut," since Lou would be off exploring uncharted comedy regions. Sometimes his new stuff was incorporated into the picture as a bonus. Edmund Hartmann explained, "We would simply let the cameras run and start him in the right direction. Whatever he did would go on *forever,* and a great deal of it was not funny. But we *knew* it was going to happen that way and we could occasionally find a gem." An editor could always cut away to Bud or another character, cut out a big section of Lou's improvisations that misfired, then return to Lou for more funny business.

Of course John Grant was always on the set, offering his advice and vast stockpile of gags. "Lou and John Grant would come up with terrible jokes," producer Robert Arthur recalled. "I'd say, 'Oh, for God's sake, I heard that when I was this big.' Lou always had a thing with me. He'd say, 'Let's shoot it, and I'll bet you $100 that you won't cut it out of the picture.' I never won one of those. They were such terrible jokes, as in *The Wistful Widow of Wagon Gap,* Lou says, 'Marriage is a three-ring circus: the engagement ring, the wedding ring, and then suffering.' We did it, and the audience fell down laughing."

Eventually, directors learned to accept the team's method of working. Two that didn't, Erle C. Kenton and William Seiter, did their assignments and moved on. "Actually, it's a simple matter of using child psychology on Lou," said director Jean Yarbrough. "If you try to force him to do it your way, he loses his spontaneity. If he has to stick to the letter of the script, he becomes mechanical. That's why it's necessary to keep a very loose rein on him so that the picture will benefit by the added laughs. Lou contributes on the spur of the moment."

Co-stars did the best they could in scenes with Bud and Lou. Those that couldn't adapt stood and waited for cues that never came. "We understood when a co-star flubbed," said Edmund Hartmann, "and we would pick it up later in an isolated shot. They knew what they were getting into with an Abbott and Costello picture—it was all over town what these two guys were doing." Many actors and actresses feared the worst when they stepped on an A&C set the first day, only to be pleasantly surprised. Bud and Lou treated their co-stars with great respect, and working on one of their films was a unique, enjoyable experience. "I thought everyone should do at least one Abbott and Costello film," explained actress Hillary Brooke. Still, Robert Arthur explained, not everyone took the chance. "We always had a hard time with the girls. I used to be a contract breaker. If the studio had a girl under contract and they wanted to get out of the contract, they'd send her down to me to interview for the lead in an Abbott and Costello picture. Of course, she'd ask, 'Is it a good part?' All I had to do was be honest with her: 'As good as it can be in an Abbott and Costello picture.' If the jokes were going over the only thing we'd cut was the girl and boy story. Then the last question was, 'Do you think it's good or bad for my career?' And I would have to say, 'It's not going to do your career one bit of good.' Then she'd ask to be let out of her contract and the studio was happy and it'd hire someone else."

If keeping Bud and Lou in camera range once they began ad-libbing posed a challenge to directors, just getting them in front of the cameras could require Herculean effort. Once again, it was a deeply ingrained habit from burlesque that had to be overcome. It was a legendary and perpetual card game. In burlesque, the boys relieved the boredom between shows by playing gin rummy or poker. Gypsy Rose Lee recalled in her autobiography that the team kept score on the cardboard stuffed in shirts from the laundry. When they ran out of cardboard, Bud and Lou wrote on the dressing room wall—and the running tally ran out into the hallway. These games—or was it one long, continuous game?—continued in radio, on Broadway, and in Hollywood, with the stakes raised with each jump in salary.

"The minute a scene was done," recalled Alex Gottlieb, "instead of studying the next scene as any actor would, they ran to a little card table they had set up and the two of them played poker. Can you imagine *two* people playing poker? And everybody used to sit around and watch them, the two worst poker players in the world. They would always play draw poker, and Bud would look at Lou's cards and no matter what he drew, he could not outdraw Lou. But he'd draw a card anyway! They were just playing to play. They didn't care about winning or losing. When they would play with one another they really didn't lose any money; one would win one day, and one would win another day."

Edmund Hartmann observed, "They played some pretty high-staked games, and if they were losing they weren't about to quit the game and go and do a shot. Generally you had to wait until they were ready, and it might take an hour. Those are the things you can do when your pictures are making money." A fixture on the soundstage was a gangster named Mike Potson, who Bud and Lou met on a personal appearance tour in 1941. Potson ran a night club in Chicago called Colisimo's, but made such a lucrative living off Bud and Lou that he sold his interest in the club and moved to California. "Mike Potson took them for I don't know how many dollars," Joe Kenny, then an assistant director, recalled. Kenny and Howard Christie were usually able to cajole the boys out of their trailers. "I'd say 'Come on, cut out this nonsense. We're waiting for you. You're not being right to the company. These are the people that are paying you.' They'd say, 'Aw, okay.' I'd say to Potson, 'I'm going to have you barred from the lot! [laughs] Well, I could no more have him barred than the man in the moon!" Christie also maintained his sense of humor. "I used to put Potson on the call sheet in the morning and say, 'Be here at nine o'clock,' knowing that if he was in at nine, the boys would be in at nine—to play poker. And when they were in the middle of a poker game I would get Joe Kenny and we'd just carry Lou into the scene. He got a big kick out of it and that's the way we got him on the set."

Charles Barton just sat and waited. "I never tried to get them away from the game. The head of the studio couldn't do it—how could one of us? So the whole company had to sit and wait. Whenever they ran out of money, the game stopped, because IOUs weren't allowed. One time Bud owed Lou something like $10,000, and Lou demanded the money. Bud said, 'I don't have it right now.' So Lou said, 'Well, you better get it.' So Bud had one of their stooges go to the bank and withdraw $10,000. Meanwhile, the boys wouldn't film while the money was being picked up. They just sat and waited. The funny part about it was, the film was their money, too. The cheaper the films were produced, the more money they could make. This didn't matter." Charles Lamont actually found that the poker games were beneficial to the team's on-camera performance. "Every take they did was terrific, because they wanted to get back to that card game."

On weekends, or nights, the stakes were staggering. Joe Kenny recalled, "When they went over to MGM, Lou started playing poker with people like you wouldn't believe—Joe Schenck, Louis B. Mayer, Eddie Mannix. He came back one Monday and said, 'I won $18,000!' Then the next four Mondays he wouldn't say a word. You'd say, 'Lou, how'd you do?' He'd say, 'Oh, I dropped a few,' or 'I dropped $42,000,' or 'I dropped this or that.' You wouldn't *believe* the money he lost to the MGM crowd. It was just like taking candy from a baby." Robert Arthur added, "And the most insulting thing that ever happened was, one of them called Lou and asked if he would like to join a game. They said, 'We'll give you half your losses back.' They just wanted to fill up the game."

The gambling wasn't confined to cards. Bud and Lou, it seems, would bet on anything— that you'd flub your next line, that a light bulb would blow out—anything. Kenny remembered, "I'd be at Lou's house when he'd call Abbott on the phone and say, 'You got a coin, Abbott? Toss you for $100.' Lou would say, 'Heads.' Abbott would say, 'Right. I owe you $100.' Lou would say, 'Okay, I'll toss. Call it, Bud. Okay, we're even. Now once for $200.' And whoever won, the next day they'd give the other $200. *Really.*"

While Bud avoided playing the horses, Lou was obsessed enough for the both of them. After the team's initial success, he began buying thoroughbreds. Charles Lamont recalled, "He owned a race horse name Bazooka, and when Bazooka was running, he'd have one of his stooges place a bet for him. And he never made a small bet; a typical wager was $3,000 to win, $2,000 to place, and $1,000 to show. But there were many times when he wanted to go to the track and see the race. He would just take off, which made it difficult for me: I'd have a straight man but no comic. But he could get away with those things because he was a star. It just made their pictures more expensive and, frankly, I wonder why I didn't get ulcers. Sometimes I had to get firm with him, though. One day he said, 'Tomorrow my horse is running and I'm going to go see him. I want you to cover for me.' I said to him, in front of all the crew, 'Look, Lou, I'm not going to cover for you. If you're going to go to the track, you're going to pay the day's salary for everyone on this set and we'll *all* take the day off.' I made my stand. I called the front office and said, 'Mr. Costello wants to go to the track to see his horse run. Who the hell's running this studio, Costello or you?' And they backed me up. I felt you have to bring it to a stop. You can only have one boss on the set."

Surely no one who walked on an Abbott and Costello set would mistake it for a production by the Royal Shakespeare Company. Because when Bud and Lou weren't playing cards, betting with bookies, or cutting up in front of the cameras, they were busy playing practical jokes and tossing dozens of pies. This reached high art in the late 1940s when a short, bald bit player named Bobby Barber was designated court jester. "Bobby Barber to me was one of the nicest people that ever walked on the face of this earth," recalled Joe Kenny, assistant director on many of their films. "He was just a delightful man." Bobby found himself on both ends of the pies, seltzer bottles, water pistols, hotfoots and goosings that were *de rigueur* on the team's sets. He and Lou had great affection for each other. Lou would roar when he gave it to Bobby, but he'd roar just as hard when Bobby got him. One day Bud Jr. asked his dad why they abused Bobby. "They'd drop firecrackers in his shorts, everything. My dad said, 'Don't worry, he gets paid for that.' "

Robert Arthur understood the method to the madness: "So many people looked down their noses at some of the nonsense that went on on the set. But you had to keep the momentum going." Hillary Brooke agreed. "All the shenanigans that went on on the set were necessary for Lou. His whole schooling was the stage, where he could build up to the end of the gag. But in films you had to start in the middle of a scene, so all this was necessary to him in order to keep his energy level up, in order to get to the top of the gag. If you fool around, it's like playing to an audience, and when you start the scene you're up. The people working with him understood that it was necessary and all these things kept it up. It was also Lou's way of showing affection for you. You didn't feel 'in' if they didn't play tricks on you."

The A&C set was the most popular on the lot, both for performers and crew. Bud Abbott, Jr., recalled that when he worked at Universal in the 1960s, oldtimers would tell him how much they relished being assigned to an A&C picture. There was always a familial atmosphere on the set. Early on, Bud's nephew Norman served as his uncle's stand-in, and, later, as dialogue director. Pat Costello was Lou's stand-in and stunt double, and brother-in-law Joe Kirk turned up in bit parts. They added cronies from burlesque like Milt Bronson and Charlie Murray. "Something funny was going on every single minute and the crews loved him," Charles Barton recalled. "Everybody adored working with Lou Costello. Abbott, too, but Abbott was quiet and more subdued. Lou was always kidding around and doing funny things to break you up." Expensive gifts were lavished on cast and crew at the end of a production, and Christmas was another thing entirely. "Come Christmas, you never saw such presents as they gave out to *everybody*," recalled Alex Gottlieb. "They never gave out anything cheap." Joe Kenny recalled, "The things he would do for people after people after people. Guys on the set, he'd come up to them and hand them a hundred-dollar bill and say, 'Here, take this home.' He was always giving people money. You'd say, 'Damn you, Lou—this guy's a phoney.' He'd say, 'What the hell. It's only money.' He was magnificent that way. And so was Bud. Bud was really a *good* person."

"Lou was always very nice to the people he worked with," recalled Robert Arthur. "One of the only times I saw him get angry was when someone on the set didn't give him a message that his mother had called. He'd stop whatever he was doing to speak to her."

The Abbott and Costello children frequently visited their dads at work. "We spent so much time at that studio I can hardly believe it," Lou's daughter Paddy recalled. "We would run around the sets. Albert Deano, the costume guy, was so good to us. He was the best babysitter in the world. If it was real boring, the make-up man would put scars on us, or make us up like the current glamour queen. Or we'd sit in the projection room watching every western I think Universal ever made." Lou had a little scooter that he used to tool around the back lot. Edmund Hartmann remembered, "If a small child visited the set, Lou would stop in the middle of a shot and take the child for a ride in his scooter."

"Their wives were wonderful," said Robert Arthur. "They weren't around the set too often, but when they were you were delighted to see them. They never interfered. All they ever were was helpful."

Although it often seemed as though Bud and Lou preferred to be someplace else besides a movie set, they couldn't resist bringing pieces of those sets home with them. Lou more so than Bud became notorious for stealing furniture and props from the soundstages. He once quipped that his home was furnished in "early Universal." Norman Abbott explained that these things were taken as souvenirs of the pictures. "They had all the money in the world; if they wanted something all they had to do was buy it." Charles Barton agreed, "Lou was like a small boy. If he saw something pretty that he liked, he'd take it home with him. He was never malicious, and even if he made it tough to get a prop back, he did it in fun—not to hurt anyone." The problem, however, was that Lou rarely waited until the end of the film to liberate these souvenirs. This was a constant source of headaches to prop men and set dressers who had to match set-ups. Universal came up with a few defenses. "There was a rule," Edmund Hartmann explained, "that when Lou drove his car out, it was to be stopped at the gate, and the guard had a list of 'hot' props—props that we were still going to use. And if he had taken a 'hot' prop, the guard was to take it back and get it back to the set. If it was a prop we were through with, we let him have it. And when I went to his house one night after a showing, you could see the props from all the pictures."

Norman Abbott recalled one time the studio finally decided to fight fire with fire. "One day there was a knock on the door at Lou's house on Longridge Avenue, and Anne was home and there were two uniformed piano movers at the door. They said, 'Mr. Costello wants the piano on the set.' So they moved the piano out. Lou came home that night and said, 'Where's the piano, Anne?' She said, 'What are you talking about—you sent for it.' Lou said, 'I didn't send for it.' Right about then the phone rang and it was Bryan Foy at the studio. He said, 'When you bring back all the props you took off my set, I'll send your piano back.' Lou returned all the props."

Lunch at the studio commissary was always an event. Edmund Hartmann recalled, "When they first came to the studio, they used to go to the commissary for lunch, and they were very quiet and subdued. They'd go to their little corner table, have their lunch, go back to the set. Then they got to be tremendously successful. And now, each time they came to lunch, they made an entrance. A couple of them I still remember. I remember Lou and Bud and two or three of their stooges, with the stooges coming in first and making way, and Bud coming with about thirty cigar boxes that he balanced all the way to the ceiling, doing a performance all the way through the restaurant to the table, balancing the cigar boxes. Then about a week later they came in and their stooges were dressed as clowns in full make-up, and they had a three-piece band playing their entrance. All this just to have lunch! I've never seen anything like it." Even the pie throwing carried over into the commissary. "Not only did they throw pies in the commissary," recalled Robert Arthur, "but they once hit the head table, and then Lou sent for some more. But actually that was just to say to the bosses, 'Don't forget we're around, fellas.' "

Getting the work done, then, was a challenge. Joe Kenny tried to cajole the boys into working. "To try to keep things moving and get in the day's quota, I had said, 'Lou, nothing's funny after four o'clock.' And he looked at me and said, 'You know, you're right.' I said, 'Yeah, because you get tired and lose all your inner stuff. So let's get it all done by four o'clock.' So he pipes up and announces, 'We're not working past four o'clock!' [laughs] And at four o'clock, they'd both go home! Boy, did *that* boomerang on me!''

The team's health could be another problem. Bud Abbott was epileptic, and although seizures were mercifully rare on the set, he was so worried about them that he kept to himself a great deal. After a scene was completed, Bud was more likely than Lou to head for his trailer until needed again. "Bud worried about having an epileptic fit in front of the audience during their personal appearances," said Charles Barton. "He tried to make sure nobody saw him have an attack." A man named Charlie Murray was Bud's driver, and occasional stunt double. But his primary responsibility was to take care of Bud if he had a seizure.

Lou looked strong as an ox, but even before *Buck Privates,* he failed a studio health insurance examination because of a heart murmur. Bud, meanwhile, regularly passed these examinations. The studio could only insure Lou against an accident. The most critical illness of his career was in 1943, when, at the peak of the team's success, he was bedridden with rheumatic fever and missed one year of work. After that, he suffered serious recurring lapses throughout his life that either delayed production of some films or kept the team out of others. Still, Lou worked incredibly hard for a man in his condition, performing many stunts against doctor's orders.

"Lou had us by the throat," Robert Arthur explained. "All he had to do was call in six doctors and they could put him on a ten-to-three day. So whenever we renegotiated his contract, we'd try to get him to work nine to five or nine to six, and we were at his mercy, because he had everything on his side to work five hours a day, or three days a week, or not at all."

Universal executives were hardly used to coddling their stars, and Bud and Lou always felt they were underappreciated. One major bone of contention was the budgets on their films, and the fact that the studio never gave them a color production. In 1949 Lou complained to an interviewer, "Comedians like Danny Kaye and Red Skelton get color and good stories and girls like Esther Williams in their pictures. We're a bigger box office draw than any of them. But we've never done a color picture. We've never gone on location. And instead of Jane Russell, we get Pat Alphin." Still, the team rarely fought with its bosses. "The TV movie *Bud and Lou* was the most disgraceful thing I ever saw," Alex Gottlieb said, "because they portrayed Lou as a tough guy—tough with the studio, tough with the producer. That's not Lou Costello at all. He was a very sweet little guy who never fought with the studio. He'd just tell them very nicely, 'I won't be in for work,' or 'We're going to tear up my contract.' He would say it to needle them, to drive them crazy. And Eddie Sherman would plead with him, 'Let me

BOTTOM LEFT: Director Charles Lamont and dialogue director Milt Bronson on the set of *Foreign Legion* (1950) BOTTOM: Director Charles Barton and John Grant work out a scene with Lou and Lenore Aubert in *Abbott and Costello Meet the Killer, Boris Karloff* (1949).

do it, let me talk to them.' And Lou would say, 'Go ahead and talk. If you have any trouble, call me.' He never fought or had an argument with any of them. And we were the best of friends. I never had one argument with Lou, Bud, or John Grant. Bud never raised his voice about *anything*. And anything I wanted Lou to do—at least during the first four pictures— he would do. Later it became a little tougher to get him to do more than one or two takes. But it didn't make any difference because he was always funny."

"There were so many people buzzing at them, saying, 'The studio is getting rich and you fellows aren't getting as much as you should,'" said Robert Arthur. "It also generated a lot of excitement for them. Some things were just pure teasing. Lou delighted in having Joe Kenny call me and say, 'There's a crisis on the set, would you come down?' I walked in one day and Joe said, 'Lou wants to see you.' And Lou said, 'That tobacco you smoke—it smells very good. Have you got any?' And then he died laughing, you see. And we had dozens of instances of small crises. But I never felt that I was in any serious crisis with them."

"They had the first trailers that were ever put in at Universal," Joe Kenny remembered. "They said they wanted portable dressing rooms. See, the studio had built a dressing room for Deanna Durbin that was on wheels. Bud and Lou said they wanted trailers. And in those days they were big trailers. So the studio said, 'Give them to them. Keep them happy.' So Bud got one and Lou got one."

Charles Barton reasoned, "They were making more money for Universal than anybody. But at the same time, they were being compensated to what they and Eddie Sherman had agreed to. They would look at their contract and see what Universal was making and get mad at Eddie. 'Look what you've done to us!' And they'd tear up their contracts. You have to look at it two ways. Who made Bud and Lou? Certainly not Kate Smith. She brought them to national attention, but she could never have made A&C what they became. Never. It was the studio in back of them that said we'll gamble on them. They were unknowns—who the hell were they? A couple of very funny radio guys."

Bud and Lou's personal relationship was, for the most part, quite good, but there were times when it could be quite stormy and could affect production in many ways. There were battles over the split of their earnings and even over the billing. They were very competitive with each other, and when one bought something, the other tried to top it. They amassed swimming pools, yachts, nightclubs, and ranches, forever arguing over whose was the better, the bigger, or the more expensive. Bud took a more passive role in the team's business decisions. These were generally left up to Lou, and in time Lou grew to resent the burden. In an interview in 1958, Costello explained, "Bud Abbott and me have worked together since, I think, late in 1934. Bud was a dandy, a real sharp dresser. Easy-going kind of guy. Me, I'm a worrier. I worried about Bud for twenty-two years. Would he be there for rehearsal? Would he make the airport on time? Did he know the new material?"

Robert Arthur saw the team's relationship like a marriage. "They would not get along, and then they would get along. It was kind of like husband and wife. Now, I didn't know for the longest time that Bud was an epileptic. And Lou was the one who would hit Bud in the stomach, and Bud would come out of it. But when Bud was having those moments, nobody could have cared more for him than Lou. Next day, he and Bud may be back in an argument about a card game or something."

Joe Kenny said, "When both of them came in and were happy, it was the most beautiful set in the world. You never could tell what would trigger it. They were brothers and [laughs] haters. It was like two stray cats facing one another. Then the two stray cats would dissolve and suddenly they're two brothers—arms around each other, loving each other."

Charles Barton recalled, "When I started working with them [in 1946], I could sense an animosity between them. They wouldn't even speak to one another in one film. In another, they'd have a riff one day and the next day it would be completely forgotten. But nobody could ever say anything bad about Bud to Lou, and don't say anything to Bud about Lou— even when they weren't speaking."

ABOVE: Bud and Lou's second favorite pastime, playing cards on the set during *Hit the Ice* (1942).
ABOVE LEFT: Producer Robert Arthur, who was responsible for the team's comeback in the late 1940s, visits Lou on the set of *Abbott and Costello Meet Frankenstein* (1948).

"Did I ever see them in an argument?" Charles Lamont said. "I'll say no, because the only time I'd ever see them in an argument was over a poker game. I think these stories about misunderstandings between the two of them were just a publicity thing. They said the boys had no rapport, which was not true at all. Have you ever heard of a successful team that hasn't been accused of fighting?"

Hillary Brooke agreed that it was more like a marriage. "It's being so close for so long and so dependent on each other in a working sense. Lou couldn't work with anyone else, and Bud couldn't work with anyone else. They'd been together so long. And that's a very intimate relationship between a comic and a straight man." But professionally, on the sets of their films, and on their radio show and personal appearances, they never let their differences interfere with their performance.

Bud and Lou rarely looked at the dailies. It apparently never occurred to them that their scenes could be reshot if they weren't happy with them. They were still operating as though they were on stage, where once their performance was done it was gone forever. "As far as they were concerned," Edmund Hartmann explained, "what they had on film was the picture. I don't think it ever occurred to them that you could change that." The only reason to reshoot was if there was a technical problem. Similarly, they never questioned the producer's or editor's choice of scenes or cut. But because the boys ad-libbed so much, and continuity was broken off in mid-picture, dialogue was frequently post-dubbed to bridge the plot, cover goofs, or fix inaudible lines. Costello would frequently have to cover scenes where he unintentionally called Bud "Abbott." (They missed at least two—in *In Society* and in *Meet Frankenstein*.) Bud would add lines to scenes of Lou's pantomimes so you wouldn't forget he was there, too.

An Abbott and Costello film was previewed two or three times for fine-tuning before release. "When word got out that there was going to be a preview of an Abbott and Costello picture," recalled Edmund Hartmann, "by six o'clock at night there'd be a line around the block. By eight o'clock, when the picture would start, the place would be jammed. And they'd be laughing before the picture even started." Often entire scenes were drowned in laughter. "You actually recut the picture after the first preview," Lubin recalled, "to try to put a breath in so they can hear the dialogue and what's going to happen. We would bring it back after a preview and say, 'My God, they couldn't hear this whole next scene!' " Many of the loudest laughs anyone had ever heard were at A&C screenings. Hartmann is still awed by *In Society*, and Robert Lees will never forget *Hold That Ghost* and *A&C Meet Frankenstein*: "One of the biggest damn laughs was when the boys stack everything up against the bedroom door, and the door opens the wrong way and they're face-to-face with the monster. That was the biggest scream at the previews."

There seems to be a misconception that Bud and Lou were not embraced by the critics of their day. The fact is, Bud and Lou were rarely attacked by the critics—the studio and the films were. In 1944 a *New York Times* critic wrote, "Probably no other comedy team in pictures has been so sincerely and enthusiastically supported by screen observers and critics generally. Whatever criticisms have been leveled, they have been pointed, not at the comedians, but at their vehicles. This almost universal loyalty from the press springs from the personal warmth of the comedians themselves plus a deep faith, on the parts of most critics, in the real comedy potentialities of the two men. Thus we find a team generally accredited with having all the qualifications of a long-enduring comedy and money-earning combination being bled white, so to speak, in pieces below their abilities."

It was a losing battle. "These pictures were doing so well that the studio wasn't about to tamper with success," explained Edmund Hartmann. Charles Barton offered, "The films sold, no matter how bad the content, on their names alone." The public wanted and expected Abbott and Costello in the team's films and, as *Little Giant* and *The Time of Their Lives* had shown, wouldn't accept anything else. The studio counted too heavily on the team's films to keep the gates open to experiment again. Bud and Lou simply were typecast. Producer Robert Arthur explained, "They wanted to do *Don Quixote*. Lou had spent a lot of thought on it and it all made sense to him. But it didn't make sense for us as a studio, and I had the difficult task of explaining to him that, with a totally bankable formula, why would we depart into an area we didn't know? He never quite understood. Perhaps if they had made the break first on the stage, they might have been able to get away from slapstick. But I'd often talk to Lou about the problem that ZaSu Pitts had. She was put in a dramatic role in *All Quiet on the Western Front* (1930) and the preview audiences laughed at her. They were accustomed to the ZaSu Pitts that they knew, the comedienne, and they wouldn't accept her as anything else."

"If Universal had put the kind of money into the Abbott and Costellos, or given them the kind of directors that, say, Danny Kaye had, they would have been bigger than anyone," offered screenwriter Robert Lees. "But Abbott and Costello were keeping the studio alive so they just wanted to turn out as many as they possibly could. I'm just sorry that they really didn't turn Lou into a Chaplin, because they turned the pictures out like sausages."

Director Charles Barton explained, "Universal was making so much money that they flooded the market with them. The same time that a new film came out, a rerelease would also be on the market. I believe what really happened to them was, they were overexposed. The public never had the chance to say, 'When are we going to have another Abbott and Costello film?' The films were there all the time. Their films kept the studio running. Nate Blumberg, the president, said, 'Thank God for Abbott and Costello!'"

ONE NIGHT IN THE TROPICS

SYNOPSIS

Steve Harper's upcoming marriage to Cynthia Merrick is jeopardized by his tenacious former girlfriend, Mickey Fitzgerald, and Cynthia's disapproving Aunt Kitty. So Steve's best man, an innovative insurance agent named Jim Moore, issues a "love insurance" policy that will pay Steve $1,000,000 if the wedding doesn't come off. Half of the policy is underwritten by a nightclub operator named Roscoe, who warns Jim to protect his interests or else. Roscoe also assigns two of his boys, Abbott and Costello, to oversee Jim.

Cynthia, Aunt Kitty, and Jim set sail for the Caribbean island of San Marcos, where the wedding is to take place, but Mickey prevents Steve from making the boat. Roscoe manages to rescue Steve and ship him off to the island. He orders Abbott and Costello to escort Mickey to Kansas City, but she easily dupes the boys into taking her to San Marcos. Steve arrives to make an uncomfortable threesome, since Jim and Cynthia seem to be falling in love. But when Mickey shows Cynthia the "love insurance" policy, Cynthia calls off her wedding to Steve and is furious with Jim. Roscoe arrives in time to coerce the Mayor, Señor Escobar, into performing the wedding at gun point. Jim disarms Roscoe, and Mickey grabs the gun, forcing Escobar to marry her and Steve. Steve decides that Mickey is indeed the girl for him after all. Jim announces that Steve's marriage has made the policy void, and Cynthia agrees to marry him.

BACKGROUND

Early in 1940, Universal signed Allan Jones to a two-picture deal that granted him story approval, cast approval, and director approval. For the first film, producer Jules Levey offered Jones the screen version of George Abbott's Broadway hit, *The Boys From Syracuse*, and cast Jones' wife, Irene Hervey, Alan Mowbray, Martha Raye, and Joe Penner in support. Leonard Spigelgass and Charles Grayson wrote the adaptation, and A. Edward Sutherland directed. Levey also wanted Abbott and Costello for small roles in the picture, but at the time Bud and Lou were obligated to the Kate Smith program in New York. Levey did manage to bring the team along when the film opened in Syracuse, New York, on July 18, 1940. In fact, Bud and Lou's first screen appearance is in the July 23, 1940 Universal Newsreel covering the premiere.

After *Syracuse*, screenwriter Leonard Spigelgass was promoted to producer and began looking for another project for Allan Jones. He found two promising properties languishing on the shelves at Universal. The first was a treatment based on Earl Derr Biggers' 1914 novel, *Love*

Earliest Draft: 1937

Production Start:
August 26, 1940

Production Completed:
September 30, 1940

Copyright Date:
November 14, 1940

Release Date:
November 15, 1940

Reissued: June 15, 1950
(with *The Naughty Nineties*); 1954 (with *Little Giant*)

Running Time: 83 minutes in original release; 69 minutes in rerelease

Directed By:
A. Edward Sutherland

Produced By:
Leonard Spigelgass

Screenplay By:
Gertrude Purcell & Charles Grayson

Adapted By:
Kathryn Scola and Francis Martin from the novel *Love Insurance* By Earl Derr Biggers

Music By: Jerome Kern

"You and Your Kiss,"
"Simple Philosophy,"
"Remind Me," and
"Farandola" Lyrics By:
Dorothy Fields

"Your Dream" Lyrics By:
Oscar Hammerstein II

Director of Photography:
Joseph Valentine

Art Director:
Jack Otterson

Associate: Martina Obzina

Film Editor:
Milton Carruth

Gowns: Vera West

Set Decoration:
R.A. Gausman

Insurance. (Biggers is perhaps best remembered as the creator of Charlie Chan.) The scenario, called "Riviera," was intended for French import Danielle Darrieux in 1937. Spigelgass's second find was the musical score. The great Jerome Kern (1885–1945) had collaborated with Dorothy Fields (1904–1974) on four songs for the production. Kern and Fields wrote the scores for *Swing Time* (with Fred Astaire and Ginger Rogers), "Riviera," *When You're In Love* and *High, Wide and Handsome* in quick succession in 1936. *Swing Time* is by far the best of the lot, yielding "A Fine Romance, "Pick Yourself Up," and the Oscar-winning "The Way You Look Tonight."

But Universal was in dire straights from 1936 through 1938, and while many productions were planned, not all of them found budgets. The studio lost $1.8 million in 1936, and another million in 1937. New management swept in, and projects initiated by the old guard were scrutinized warily. "Riviera" was officially "put in mothballs," according to a studio memo, on August 22, 1938.

Now in 1940, Kern authorized use of his score for "Riviera" for a substantial additional payment. It was also agreed that another song, "Your Dream," which Kern had written with Oscar Hammerstein II (1895–1960) in 1938 for a prospective Broadway musical, "Gentlemen Unafraid," would also be included. Spigelgass recalled that "Remind Me" was not initially conceived in a Latin beat, but that the film's new setting suggested the change. To Spigelgass' surprise, Kern was delighted by the new arrangement.

Meanwhile, in New York, Abbott and Costello were fielding offers from three studios to appear in upcoming musicals. William Morris had set up a deal with MGM for the team to do a couple of routines in the studio's massive *Ziegfeld Girl* for $17,500. But Eddie Sherman thought Bud and Lou could do better. On their own initiative, they made a deal with Universal executive Matty Fox to appear in a musical for $35,000. Eddie correctly reasoned that Bud and Lou would have a far better chance of being noticed at the smaller studio. (MGM was notorious for signing talent and then having it sit idle. By the time MGM released *Ziegfeld Girl* in April 1941, Abbott and Costello were shooting their fourth film at Universal.) The musical Universal had on the boards was "Riviera" (later retitled *One Night in the Tropics*), and Bud and Lou signed for the picture on July 24, 1940.

THE SCRIPT

By then, Spigelgass and screenwriter Charles Grayson had been wrestling with the script for nearly three months. Just when they thought they were done, word came down from the front office to integrate two radio comedians into the story. This couldn't have been a complete surprise, however, since an early Spigelgass memo suggests using George Burns and Gracie Allen for comic relief.

Director Eddie Sutherland's haircut is supervised by Bud and Lou.

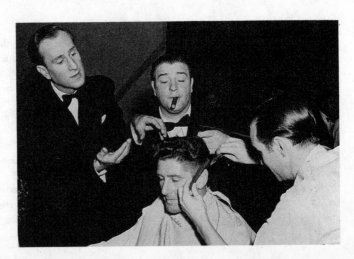

Spigelgass was compelled to ask the film's star, Allan Jones, if he approved of the addition of Abbott and Costello. "I had seen them in *Streets of Paris* on Broadway," Jones recalled. "I thought they were brilliant in it, and that's how I remembered them when the producer mentioned them. I said, 'What'll they do?' And he said, 'They'll do one of their routines in the casino. We'll make them henchmen to Bill Frawley.' So I said, 'Fine.' "

"It was absurd to put Abbott and Costello in the picture," Spigelgass groused. "You had a story, you had all that Jerome Kern music. You add a third external element, and the story just disappears. I had to work with the writers all night to try to give them some semblance of a reason for being in the picture—and there wasn't any." About this time, Eddie Sutherland signed on as director, and to Spigelgass's further distress, asked for changes in the script. The producer brought in screenwriters Kathryn Scola and Frances Martin for a fresh perspective, and on August 15 they delivered a treatment that is very close to the final film. Grayson and Gertrude Purcell (mostly Purcell) executed the final draft, which was delivered on August 22. Curiously, even though the locale had long since been changed to the Caribbean, the project was still being called "Riviera."

John Grant meanwhile had been following the various drafts and suggesting the appropriate Abbott and Costello routines. In the final shooting script, Bud and Lou's scenes are merely titled, "Two Tens for a Five," "The Baseball Routine," "Jonah and the Whale," "365 Days—Firing Routine," and "Mustard." (Evidently the "Smoking" routine was added later.)

THE CAST

Allan Jones (b. 1907) had appeared with the Marx Brothers in *A Night at the Opera* (1935) and *A Day at the Races* (1937). He was seen to better advantage in *Showboat* (1936) and *The Firefly* (1937). Jones selected Robert Cummings (1908–1990) and Nancy Kelly (b. 1921) for the cast. They had been paired earlier in the year in the Hugh Herbert comedy *Private Affairs*. Since both Nancy Kelly and Peggy Moran were brunettes, Kelly, to give more contrast to the characters, dyed her hair blonde.

Tropics was just one of *nine* films twenty-one-year-old Peggy Moran did in 1940, including *The Mummy's Hand, Argentine Nights,* and *Oh Johnny, How You Can Love!* "I was there two and a half years," Peggy recalled, "and did something like 30 pictures. I remember coming out of one picture and two days later they handed me another script." After *Tropics* she and Cummings appeared in Deanna Durbin's *Spring Parade*. Like most of the Durbin films, it was directed by Henry Koster, whom Peggy married in 1942. Peggy recalled that Henry had seen Bud and Lou perform in New York at a nightclub (either the Versailles or the Casa Mañana) and recommended them to Universal's executives.

William Frawley (1887–1966) was signed to play Roscoe. (An earlier draft suggests George Raft for the role.) A veteran of hundreds of films and television shows, Frawley worked with Bud and Lou again in *Abbott and Costello Meet the Invisible Man* in 1951.

THE PRODUCTION

Eddie Sutherland was Jones' choice for director. Sutherland (1895–1974) broke into films as a stuntman in 1914 and appeared in Keystone comedies before becoming Charlie Chaplin's assistant director on *A Woman of Paris* (1923). His credits include Mae West's *Every Day's a Holiday* (1938); the Laurel and Hardy classic *The Flying Deuces* (1939); and W.C. Fields' *Mississippi* (1935) and *Poppy* (1936).

When shooting commenced on August 26, Bud and Lou were appearing as Fred Allen's summer replacement on NBC radio. The team uprooted the show and moved it to Hollywood while they worked on the film. Co-stars Allan Jones and Robert Cummings were guests on the program on August 21, 1940. The team's final broadcast was on September 25, while "Riviera" was still in production.

As Robert Cummings remembered it, much of *Tropics* had been shot before he met Abbott and Costello. "We finished the picture and went home. Then the studio said there are certain parts of the picture that drag. I said I can believe that. So Abbott and Costello were brought in, and we shot little connecting scenes with them so they didn't have to reshoot the whole picture. It was a funny, strange arrangement."

Yet Bud and Lou had been fully integrated into the script some weeks before shooting began. Lou's brother Pat Costello remembers Bud and Lou being at the studio every day that the picture was shooting. Peggy Moran Koster concurred. "It's my impression that they were on the set from the first day; they were going to be in the picture from the beginning. I remember them being around a lot. I remember that Lou was such a sweet fellow and I felt like a pal with him. I didn't get the feeling I knew Bud as well. He mostly kept to himself."

There also seems to be some dispute over whether the team was nervous making its film debut. Spigelgass said, "They were scared to death. Lou used to come into my office and say, 'What are we supposed to do? I don't know how to work without an audience.' That was his chief concern. But you see they did have an audience—the crew—and they did laugh and we had terrible problems when they laughed. We had to tell everybody, 'Stop laughing!' " Robert Cummings, however, recalled, "They didn't seem to be a bit nervous because they were doing the routines they knew backwards. They were very calm and sweet and kind when they worked with me." Peggy Moran laughed and added, "They weren't half as nervous as I was."

Robert Cummings also remembered that the team was on its best behavior. "I didn't see any poker games. They were so careful not to do anything wrong on their first picture. They practically took their hats off and kneeled before Allan Jones, because he was such a well-known star. If they did any ad-libbing we didn't notice it, because both Allan and I were from the stage; we ad-libbed right back."

Allan Jones recalled, "When we finished the picture, my director called me and said, 'Do you have cutting approval?' And I said no; why? He said they cut out most of the good parts of the picture and put seven Abbott and Costello routines in. When you think you have yourself protected, something always comes up you didn't think about." Years later, in South America, Jones spotted a theater marquee that read *Abbott and Costello in One Night in The Tropics.* "I thought, 'Where the hell am I?' " Jones said. "So I don't have any fond memories of Abbott and Costello. They weren't supposed to take over the picture; the idea was one routine. They double-crossed me on that [laughs]."

BUD AND LOU'S SCENES

Abbott and Costello's first movie moments are off-camera, when they are heard but not seen, in the casino. It was a clever way of introducing two radio comedians to filmgoers. This sequence has other firsts: the first time Costello gets slapped, and the first (and second) time he says, "I'm a baaad boy!" The boys quickly launch into their "Money Changing" routine. Lou discussed this routine in a *New York Times* interview in 1940. "Me and Bud always pull a lot of 'skulls' on the stage," Lou explained. "Now for a 'skull,' Bud feeds me a piece of business [like, 'Have you got two tens for a five?']. I fall for it, start to walk away, and then stop short, making out like I'm just wising up that something's wrong. When I say, 'Hey, what's the idea?,' that's the 'skull'; that's where we get the laugh, for the piece of business becomes entrenched in the minds of the people in the audience during the few seconds I leave Bud. We build this up to a terrific situation simply by repeating this business, with me being gypped in each exchange. When I come back for my money, Bud gets mad and says, 'I shouldn't have done business with you in the first place. Here's your five, give me back my two tens.' We keep this up. It's screwy, but it gets laughs."

Pat Costello recalled, "The first scene Bud and Lou shot was on the pier, where they did 'Who's On First?' " This was a good idea on Sutherland's part; it was the boys' signature routine, and starting with it probably helped relax them if they were nervous. The boys never

FAR LEFT: Peggy Moran with Leo Carillo, Lou, and Bud. LEFT: Cut scene of the street brawl that opened the film, with Allan Jones and Bob Cummings.

leave the infield, with Who, What, and I Don't Know, because of time constraints. Their performing instincts were remarkable. All they needed to know was how long a director wanted a sketch to run and they could break it off on the button. "Who's On First?" could run six, seven, nine, ten minutes if they wished.

In their next routine, Costello claims to have written a new joke about "Jonah and the Whale," but has a difficult time telling it because Abbott incessantly interrupts with ludicrous questions—"What kind of whale?," "What ocean?," and so on. Costello is marvelous to watch for his increasing irritability, which Abbott finally deflates by offhandedly exposing the punch-line. The team reprised the routine in *Here Come the Co-Eds* (1945) and applied the same basic formula to another story, "Little Red Riding Hood," in *Abbott and Costello In Hollywood* (1945).

In another routine, Costello has failed his assignment to guard Mickey, so Abbott fires him, launching into a burlesque chestnut known as "Paid in Full." Costello is to receive $1 for every day he worked, and he demands one year's salary, $365. But, Abbott reasons, since Lou only worked eight hours a day, or a third of each day, he's really only entitled to $121. But before Costello can accept that, Bud proceeds to further deduct $52 for the Sundays he didn't work; $26 for half days on Saturdays; $15 for all his lunch hours; $14 for vacations; and $13 for holidays. This leaves the bewildered Costello with $1, which a passing waiter snatches for a tip. For some reason, the team never did the routine again, which is a shame, because the material is great, and they perform it flawlessly.

Their final routine is their most popular after "Who's On First?" In "Mustard," Abbott rebukes Costello for not putting mustard on his hotdog. "The hotdog and the mustard go together," Abbott tells him. "Let 'em go together," snaps Lou. "I don't want to spoil any romance!" Abbott is outraged. "Don't you know they spend millions of dollars every year to put up factories *just* to manufacture mustard? Do you know those factories employ thousands and thousands of men, *just* to manufacture mustard? Do you know those men take care of thousands of families and homes—all on account of mustard? And you—just because you don't like mustard—what do you want them to do? Close those factories and put all those people out of work?!" Costello responds, "Wait a minute. Do you mean to stand there and tell me just because I don't eat mustard that I'm closing down the mustard factories? Are you trying to tell me that those thousands of people are making one little jar of mustard just for *me?* Well if they are, you can tell 'em not to make it any more 'cause I'm not gonna eat it! You can lay 'em off! Who am I to support thousands?!"

DELETED SCENES

The film's opening credits roll over scenes of Steve and Jim, dapper in top hats and tails, walking the streets of New York. Then there's an abrupt cut to Steve in his apartment the next morning, attemping to write an apology to Cynthia. For what, we never knew.

When *Tropics* was reissued in 1950, Realart lopped fourteen minutes off the picture, reducing it to its present length of sixty-nine minutes. The bulk of this was at the opening. Since the original negative was actually cut, those missing minutes were thought to be lost forever. When we brought this to Universal's attention, Mike Fitzgerald and Dave Oakden initiated a worldwide search and located a full-length print in the British Film Archives.

We are also able to reconstruct the missing minutes through the continuity script. After the opening titles, Steve and Jim inadvertently provoke a street brawl on their way to pick up Cynthia for a night on the town. Fleeing around a corner, Steve bowls over Aunt Kitty outside Cynthia's apartment building. Still unaware that she is his fiancée's aunt, Steve clashes with Kitty again in the building's elevator. When she finds him in Cynthia's apartment, she throws him out and calls the wedding off. Meanwhile, Jim has landed in night court, but he charms the judge into dropping the charges by insuring her upcoming election to Superior Court.

REVIEWS

Universal planned to premiere *Tropics* (which was alternately titled "Riviera," "Caribbean Holiday," and "Moonlight in the Tropics") in New Orleans. But when Lou mentioned that he was going back to Paterson for an annual benefit for his parish church, St. Anthony's, arrangements were made for the world premiere of the first Abbott and Costello film to be in Paterson. The city declared October 30, 1940, a holiday, held a parade, and renamed the street in front of Lou's parent's house "Costello Square." Universal refused to take any rental fee for the film, and Bud, Lou, Red Skelton, and Henny Youngman appeared live before the packed house that turned out to see it. The first installment on the new St. Anthony's was raised, and the next day Lou took the first spadeful of dirt from the site where the new church would rise.

Virtually every critic panned the story, and most were divided over Kern's score. "The picture was absolutely ghastly," Spigelgass said. "We had three disparate elements. You would do a bit of the story, then you would do Kern, then you would do Abbott and Costello. Then you had to tell the audience the story all over again. We also had an absolute maniac named Jerome Kern who went out of his mind whenever he saw Abbott and Costello. I don't think he ever met them, but oh God, he did not approve of them. He almost tore my hair off. It's the only Jerome Kern score that never had a hit. It had a semi-hit in 'Remind Me,' but it really wasn't very good at all. It was the only picture I ever produced and I didn't do that very well [laughs]."

Peggy Moran Koster explained with a laugh, "Bob Cummings and I always refer to it as *One Night in the Flopics.*"

But Bud and Lou received unanimous praise.

"It made stars of them," Allan Jones said. "They'd have become stars in any picture they put them in. It just happened to be *my* picture."

Time: "Actually, *One Night in the Tropics* was designed as a major film operetta. Jerome Kern, aided by Lyricists Dorothy Fields and Oscar Hammerstein II, wrote five not-so-melodious tunes for Allan Jones' piercing tenor. Short, jaunty, oldtime Musical Director A. Edward Sutherland conducted the actors through the story by the late Earl Derr Biggers. Top-flight Cinematographer Joseph Valentine ran the camera. Yet together, this combination of Hollywood's ablest backstage talent accomplished no more than a jumbled exaggeration of the Boy Meets Girl Motif with scattered comic turns by Radio Zanies Abbott and Costello."

Variety: "It's a slim story that fails to hold together with any sustaining degree, and the music by Jerome Kern fails to reveal one tune that will be remembered. Only the comedy of Abbott and Costello, neatly spotted for periodic appearances, saves the picture from general tediousness.... Fast-talking and slapsticky in turn, the team clicks solidly with six specialties for solid laughs in each instance."

The New York Times: "After the first five minutes the plot becomes as dizzying as a ride on a merry-go-round. It's a pity, too, because Allan Jones ... can sing a romantic stanza with persuasion and Jerome Kern's lilting melodies, especially 'You and Your Kiss' and 'Your Dream,' sound entrancing under a prop moon.

"The Messrs. Abbott and Costello, as a pair of undercover men, account for whatever hilarity there is in the film—and that is strange because the plot stalls in its tracks when they appear. When Costello is rooked out of a year's salary by a series of logical deductions for holidays and lunch hours, or he and Abbott become involved in cosmic issues over the question of eating a hot dog with or without mustard, 'One Night in the Tropics' becomes a riotous excursion. For the rest, it is merely a mild sedative."

Despite the raves, Bud and Lou preferred to ignore *One Night in the Tropics* and call *Buck Privates* their first film.

Lou with brother Pat on the set.

POSTSCRIPT

Clearly, Bud and Lou were headed for stardom. When the picture was completed, they started a ten-week vaudeville tour commencing October 12 at the Orpheum Theater in Los Angeles. When they returned to New York, Matty Fox summoned them to his office and asked what their plans were. Lou bluffed that they had a meeting coming up with Paramount to discuss doing an Army picture, since they had a couple of great routines that would fit right in. Fox asked for a demonstration, and Lou and Bud performed the "Drill Routine," the "Dice Game," and "Packing and Unpacking" for him. Fox was hooked. Lou suggested that they could follow with a ghost picture, and they auditioned their "Moving Candle" scene. Fox was convulsed with laughter. He offered them a two-picture deal to start, with options up to seven years.

In an interview, Eddie Sherman explained how the deal was made. "We sat down, Abe Lastfogel and Sam Weisbrod from the William Morris agency, Bud and Lou and myself, and the studio executives, and I think they started off at $35,000 a picture, four pictures per year. Then there was a question of either $5,000 or $10,000 more per picture, and I said, 'I will forgo that and rather have 10 percent of the profits.' It was up to $40,000 or $45,000, and I said, 'No. We'll take the 10 percent.' Well, nobody ever heard of percentage deals in those days. But I had a crazy idea about it because I thought those pictures would be great.

"Now, Abbott and Costello were adding this up in their heads and saw maybe $40,000 more a year if we took the higher salary. Lou called me out into the hall. I said, 'Look, Lou, take the deal I suggest. I think those pictures will make you a hell of a lot of money percentage-wise. I'll make you a deal right now. If you don't make at least the $10,000 difference on each picture, you don't have to pay my commission.' Lou said, 'If you feel that strongly about it, I've got to go along with you.'

Composer Jerome Kern (left) with musical director Charles Previn.

"Universal was tickled to death to take the percentage deal rather than pay the extra money. As it turned out, the *least* Abbott and Costello made on any of the first four pictures was $250,000—their percentage amounted to that much. So it was a difference of almost $1,000,000 a year."

And so, on November 6, Bud and Lou signed a contract to make two pictures. The team would receive a flat $70,000, plus "10 percent of the gross proceeds in excess of 170 percent of production cost." After the two pictures, if the studio wished to exercise its option, the contract would be extended to one year, with options for six more. Bud and Lou would make four pictures per year, starting at $35,000 per picture, plus 10 percent of the profits, the first year.

BUCK PRIVATES

Earliest Draft:
November 5, 1940

Production Start:
December 13, 1940

Production End:
January 11, 1941

Copyright Date:
January 28, 1941

Released:
January 31, 1941

Running Time:
82 minutes

Reissued: November
1948 and October 1953
(with *Keep 'Em Flying*)

Directed By: Arthur Lubin

Produced By:
Alex Gottlieb

Screenplay By:
Arthur T. Horman

Special Material for
Abbott & Costello By:
John Grant

Director of Photography:
Milton Krasner ASC,
Jerry Ash ASC

Art Director:
Jack Otterson

Associate:
Ralph M. DeLacy

Film Editor: Philip Cahn

Dance Director:
Nick Castle

Sound Supervisor:
Bernard B. Brown

Technician: Paul Neal

Gowns: Vera West

Set Decorator:
R. A. Gausman

Assistant Director:
Gil Valle

Military Advisor:
Captain Jack Voglin

Musical Director:
Charles Previn

SYNOPSIS

Sidewalk tie salesman Slicker Smith and his shill, Herbie Brown, elude their nemesis, Patrolman Collins, by ducking into the movies. But the theater has been converted into an Army enlistment center, and before they know it the boys have become involuntary volunteers. Bound for boot camp with them are Randolph Parker III, a spoiled playboy; Bob Martin, his long-suffering valet; the Andrews Sisters and Judy Gray, who will serve as camp hostesses.

Slicker and Herbie discover to their dismay that Collins is now their sergeant, but along with Bob they try their best to become good soldiers. Herbie, however, can't seem to do anything right. The snooty Parker, meanwhile, greets the Army with disdain and fully expects his influential father to wangle him a discharge. Despite her fondness for Bob, Judy finds herself falling for Parker, and it is she who shames Parker into reforming. Parker redeems himself by winning the war games for his outfit.

BACKGROUND

Two months after Congress passed the Draft Bill, the November 17 *New York Times* reported that six studios planned to use the draft as an inspiration for comedies. Paramount was readying *Caught in the Draft* for Bob Hope, while two studios were bickering over the title, *You're in the Army Now*. Warners wanted it for Kay Kyser and his orchestra, and RKO wanted it for Phil Silvers and Jimmy Durante. And out at Universal, Milton Feld and Alex Gottlieb were in the midst of preparing *Buck Privates* for Abbott and Costello.

Gottlieb (1906–1988) had started out as a reporter for the *Brooklyn Eagle*. In 1929 he ghostwrote an article as a favor to a classmate, and the byline led to a job for the girl. In appreciation, the girl's brother, Milton Feld, an executive at Paramount in New York, offered Gottlieb a job as publicity director of the Rialto Theater, even though Alex knew nothing about publicity. In 1936, Feld left Parmount to join Universal. "His friends had bought Universal, and they wanted him to be one of five executive producers there," Gottlieb recalled. "I came out in 1937. I'd been advertising director for United Artists, and then Columbia. I was publicity director for Walter Wanger, until he went broke. I went to work as a screenwriter at Republic, then Universal."

One day, Gottlieb was summoned to Feld's office. "Milton said, 'How'd you like to be a producer?'" Gottlieb recalled. "Naturally I said I'd like to move up from writer to producer. He said, 'We've just signed a comedy team from burlesque, Abbott and Costello. They were on radio with Kate Smith. Have you ever heard of them?' I said, 'Yes, I saw them in *Streets of Paris* and laughed my fool head off.' He said, 'We want to make a series of B pictures with them, and we want a writer/producer, somebody who can write scripts behind John Grant.'

42

I asked why he picked me. He said, 'You are the twenty-seventh writer I've talked to. Everyone else turned it down. They all want to be producers, too. But they all said that these are a couple of cheap burlesque comics who will never get *anywhere*.' I told Milton, 'Those twenty-seven writers are all wrong, and the studio is all wrong. I saw Abbott and Costello on Broadway, with a crowd that paid a lot of money to see them, and those people never stopped laughing. I couldn't believe the amount of laughter. I kept looking around. They appealed to every kind of audience. They had found a common denominator of humor. Milton, I will bet you that within a year they rate number one at the box office. You can make the pictures cheap, but I guarantee that they will be that popular.' And Milton said, 'We don't want that. We just want to make a series of B pictures to round out our program.' I said, 'You can plan anything you like. But I will be the star producer on your lot, I will make Universal rich, and I'll make stars of Abbott and Costello.' Milton thought I was crazy. Later I told Nate Blumberg, the head of the studio, the same thing. He thought I was crazy, too. He said, 'Do anything you want with them, just make the pictures and don't spend too much money.' "

Gottlieb was already at work on the script when he had his first meeting with Lou. "He told me a little bit of his history and then he got real serious. He said, 'Alex, I only have one ambition in life. If you help me fulfill that ambition, I'll do anything you want me to do.' I asked him what it was, and he said, as if he was a little boy, 'I wanna be a *star*.' "

While Gottlieb was offered his job as producer, director Arthur Lubin wasn't given the option. He was baffled by his new assignment. "I was honest. I said, 'I'm sorry, but I just don't feel I'm the right director for this project. I'm not a dance director.' They all looked at me in the executive office with puzzled expressions. One of the men said, 'Dancing? What do you mean?' I replied, 'There's a troupe at the Figueroa Theater called the Abbott Dancers. Isn't that what we're talking about?' Everybody laughed. Then they explained who Abbott and Costello were."

There was never any question that *Buck Privates* would be a comedy with music. Fortunately, Universal had another cultural icon under contract, and their style was as unique as Abbott and Costello's. Added to the cast were the popular Andrews Sisters, Patty (b. 1920), Maxene (b. 1918) and LaVerne (1915–1967). Maxene recalled, "We had made a picture called *Argentine Nights* (1940) with the Ritz Brothers. The studio was so sure it was a flop that they dropped our contract; they didn't want us anymore. But when the picture played in Argentina, the Castillo regime took it as a personal affront and banned the picture. Well, from all the publicity, the picture caught on in the states. So Universal started chasing after us to pick up our option, and foolishly we let them. Universal was terrible. They never spent any money on our pictures, and we had to do them in ten days, which is ridiculous. You just worked your tail off and you got nothing, not even a thanks. At that point, Universal still wasn't sure if Abbott and Costello could carry a picture alone—or whether the Andrews Sisters could either. But they knew with the two commodities they had something. That's how we got into *Buck Privates* with Bud and Lou."

THE SCRIPT

Screenwriter Harold Shumate had first crack at the service comedy, and his treatment, clinically titled "Abbott and Costello Conscription Story," was turned in on November 11, 1940. The title "Sons O' Guns" was briefly affixed, but replaced almost instantly by *Buck Privates*. The only similarity to the final film is the title. Bud, Lou, and the Andrews Sisters are struggling vaudevillians befriended by a would-be songwriter who turns out to be a wealthy outcast.

Gottlieb and Milton Feld passed on Shumate's scenario and handed the assignment to Arthur T. Horman, who had worked on *Argentine Nights*. Over the next four weeks, Horman and Gottlieb wrote three drafts, with the final shooting script completed on December 10, 1940. This set the format—for better or worse—of all the A&C films. The script would be

"Boogie Woogie Bugle Boy," "Bounce Me Brother With a Solid Four," and "When Private Brown Becomes a Captain" By: Don Raye, Hughie Prince, and Sonny Burke

"I Wish You Were Here" By: Don Raye, Hughie Prince, and Vic Schoen

"I'll Be With You When It's Apple Blossom Time" By: Albert Von Tilzer and Neville Fleeson

Vocal Arrangements By: Vic Schoen

Music Supervisor: Ted Cain

Slicker Smith
.... Bud Abbott
Herbie Brown
.... Lou Costello
Andrews Sisters
.... Themselves
Randolph Parker III
.... Lee Bowman
Bob Martin.... Alan Curtis
Judy Gray....Jane Frazee
Sergeant Michael Collins
.... Nat Pendleton
Dick Burnette.. Don Raye
Miss Durling
.... Dora Clemant
Captain Williams
.... J. Anthony Hughes
Henry...... Hughie Prince
Briggs .... Leonard Elliott
Hostesses .. Jeanne Kelly
Elaine Morey
Kay Leslie
Nina Orla
Dorothy Darrell
Sergeant Callahan
.... Harry Strang
Harmonica Player
.... Frank Cook
Major General Emerson
.... Samuel S. Hinds
Cook..... Shemp Howard
Mrs. Parker
.... Nella Walker
Mr. Parker
.... Douglas Wood
Announcer
.... Mike Frankovich
Tough Fighter.. Al Billings
Sergeant Marks
.... Frank Penny
Small Boxer
.... Frank Grandetta
and The World Champion Boogie Woogie Dancers as Themselves

built around several key routines, which, like Bud and Lou themselves, were not necessarily tied to the plot. The "Drill" routine and the "Dice Game" were obligatory for *Buck Privates;* John Grant added "Go Ahead and Sing," "You're Forty, She's Ten," and the "Boxing" scene. Gottlieb and his collaborators also made an attempt to redefine the Abbott and Costello screen characterizations, making Bud more devious and Lou more innocent than they had been in *Tropics.* It was decided to minimize Costello's ubiquitous cigar, which somehow always seemed at odds with his "I'm a baaad boy" catchphrase. It can be glimpsed briefly in two scenes in *Buck Privates,* but was eliminated in all subsequent films. To further polarize them, they would receive descriptive character names; Abbott would be "Slicker" and Costello the more nebbish "Herbie."

Lubin was puzzled when he received his script. John Grant had integrated the boys' routines simply by writing, "The Drill Routine Here" or "An Abbott and Costello routine here." Since Bud and Lou knew the routines by heart, Grant didn't bother writing them out. "*Buck Privates* was very strange to shoot because they didn't go by much of a shooting script," Lubin explained. "Being burlesque comedians, they just did their old routines. . . . I'd say, 'We'll put a camera here, and a camera there.' I couldn't tell them how to do comedy, because it was their forte."

While John Grant was providing material for Bud and Lou, Don Raye and Hughie Prince were working on equally memorable material for the Andrews Sisters. They had previously composed the hits "Rhumboogie" and "Beat Me Daddy, Eight to the Bar." For *Buck Privates,* they wrote "Boogie Woogie Bugle Boy of Company B," "You're a Lucky Fellow, Mr. Smith," and "Bounce Me Brother With a Solid Four." Another song that would become an Andrews' staple, "Apple Blossom Time," barely made it into the picture. The music publisher wanted the studio to pay a $200 usage fee. Feld refused because he didn't want the song in the picture. The Andrews Sisters paid the fee themselves.

Patty Andrews further explained, "When Don and Hughie wrote 'Boogie Woogie Bugle Boy' for us, we had to learn the dance routines at night! We were busy shooting during the daytime, and we were not allowed to learn dancing on Universal's time. We begged the executives to bring in Nick Castle from Twentieth Century-Fox to choreograph that song for the film. Universal didn't want a choreographer. So, in spite of the studio, we all made *Buck Privates* big." All concerned felt vindicated when "Boogie-Woogie Bugle Boy of Company B" was nominated for an Oscar for best song, and Charles Previn's score for *Buck Privates* was nominated for best score.

The Breen Office urged Feld to "secure competent technical advice as to the military angles involved in this story in view of the present critical conditions and the situations of this country involving the Army. It would be especially important that the finished picture not be subject to unfavorable criticism or possible legal action by the War Department." As for specific points of the script, Breen expressed concern over the draftees bodies being overexposed in the physical examination scenes (hence the T-shirts); cautioned against "undue brutality in the boxing match"; and asked that Lubin "avoid the more extreme moves of the 'jitterbug dance.'"

Turning to Abbott and Costello's scenes, Breen reminded Feld that some local censor boards deleted scenes with money in connection with gambling, and advised that "the money should be suggested rather than actually shown." Breen thought Costello's hotfoot during the boxing scene should be treated in a similar manner. Costello's line in the medical examination, "Brother, you got a very poor sense of direction," according to Breen, "must be read carefully and without vulgar suggestiveness, if it is to be approved." Breen suggested omitting Herbie actually kissing Collins in the scene with the radio, "since such action will undoubtedly prove offensive to many people."

THE CAST

Lee Bowman (1914–1979) was on loan from MGM for two pictures at Universal, *Model Wife* being the second. Alan Curtis (1909–1953) had just completed *High Sierra* at Warner Bros. Curtis would work with the boys again in 1945 in *The Naughty Nineties*. Jane Frazee (1918–1985) was making her second screen appearance. Jane would work with Universal's other comedy team, Olsen and Johnson, in *Hellzapoppin'* (1941). She was married to Glenn Tryon, a former cowboy star who co-produced *Hold That Ghost* and *Keep 'Em Flying* later in the year. Jane also turned up in an episode of Bud and Lou's TV series in the 1950s. Nat Pendleton (1895–1967) was a perfect foil for Costello. A former professional wrestler, he had just completed another service film, *Flight Command,* at MGM. His role in *Buck Privates* earned him the lead role in Monogram's *Top Sergeant Mulligan* (1941). Pendleton reprised his role as Collins in the sequel, *Buck Privates Come Home* (1947).

THE PRODUCTION

Legend has it that *Buck Privates* cost just $180,000 to make. That may have been the original intention, but by the time shooting started on Friday, December 13, 1940, the picture was budgeted at $233,000 on a twenty-day schedule. "The studio warned me it didn't want to spend much money on the picture because they weren't quite sure how Abbott and Costello were going to act," Lubin explained. "Nothing was built for *Buck Privates.* We used sets that were already standing. The big staircase in the Grand Central Station scene was built for a musical Charlie Rogers had made. The camp was set up on the back lot. There was nothing at Universal in those days but a hillside." The little location work was done at Providencia Ranch and Lake Elinor. The second unit also took some establishing shots at Camp Ord. In all, *Buck Privates* ran four days over schedule and $12,000 over budget.

During filming, there were no problems between Bud and Lou nor between them and Lubin. "They were like Alice in Wonderland," Lubin recalled. "From the first day of shooting they were on the set *hours* ahead of time. They would walk around the set, watch us change scenery, or move the camera; point up at a grip and say, 'What's he doing?' or 'Why is that person doing that.' Everything was new and strange to them."

Lubin explained, "I found it very difficult to direct them at first. They were naive as far as filmmaking was concerned. They played to the people on the set instead of the camera. They were used to having a live audience and missed getting laughs. But they learned quickly and we had a lot of fun on that picture. Both men took direction well. I cannot ever remember Lou having a temper tantrum on the set because he couldn't shoot a scene correctly on the first take.

"There was nothing I could tell Lou when it came to his routines. He knew exactly every move to make, right down to the split-second timing. I would just say, 'We'll take a close-up here and a two-shot here.' I never interfered. There was nothing I could do, because these were tried and true old burlesque routines. My biggest problem was when Lou became very spontaneous and would begin to ad-lib a great deal. It was sometimes difficult to keep him within camera range."

Lou's brother Pat became his stunt double on this film. His first stunt was to be tossed over Bud's shoulder and into Nat Pendleton's lap. He made $31 that day. Frankie Van, who ran the studio gym, was originally supposed to double for Lou. Van can be spotted in the "Drill Routine": he is the stocky soldier who marches with Lou.

Patty Andrews loved working with Bud and Lou, particularly Lou. She described him as the Peck's Bad Boy of the Universal lot, since he delighted in playing practical jokes. "The remarkable person was Bud Abbott," Patty says. "At the time I was not aware of these things because I was more concerned with our numbers and the things we were going to do in the picture. But seeing their pictures now, you realize that Bud Abbott was the greatest straight man that ever lived. I mean, to be able to keep it all together with Lou, when you never knew what Lou was going to do. Bud was fantastic."

TOP: "The Dice Game"
TOP CENTER: "The Drill Routine" TOP RIGHT: "The Boxing Scene"

BUD AND LOU'S SCENES

A good example of how Bud and Lou's characters were tuned comes in the scene at Grand Central Station. Bob tenders his resignation to Randoph with a sock on the jaw, and Herbie is inspired to do the same to Smitty. In the script, Herbie was actually supposed to floor Smitty. In the film, however, Herbie barely raises his hand when Smitty smacks him. Herbie pleads with his fist, "Well what are you waiting for?"

The hilarious "Dice Game" sequence is much shorter in scripted form than in the finished film. Smitty lures Herbie into the game, but is astonished when Herbie begins dropping gambling phrases like "Fade that," or "Let it ride" at the right moments. Here is where Abbott and Costello's remarkable teamwork shines. The boys embellish the routine with repetition, slaps, pauses, and overlapping dialogue. Rhythm is so crucial to the team's interplay; you not only laugh at what Bud and Lou say, but how they say it. In the shooting script, Herbie claims he learned the jargon at "the Cigar Counter." Instinctively the boys changed it to "Clubhouse," which affords more humor in its rhythm. When Smitty inquires if Herbie ever played the game at the Clubhouse, Herbie says the other boys wouldn't let him, he's too young. Then, in an aside, Costello adds, "Startin' Tuesday I'm going out with girls." Without missing a beat, Bud replies, "Well, I don't blame you," and keeps the routine moving along. In the end, of course, Herbie fleeces Smitty by turning his own "rules" against him. This device would be used in several other Abbott and Costello gambling routines.

Incredibly, the "Drill" routine was scripted for Pendleton and Costello, which is absurd since Bud and Lou had been performing it on stage for years. There are several quick lines to listen for. "Get your chins up!" Abbott barks at Costello. When Bud says, "Order, arms," Costello cracks, "I'll have a cap pistol." At one point, Lou suddenly asks, "What time is it," which has nothing to do with the routine. Instantly, Abbott snaps back, "None of your business!," and Lou says, "Okay." The lines were left in the picture. That's because Gottlieb realized that the routine was the funniest thing in the film and used every piece of footage he could to extend it. Arthur Lubin remembered doing several takes because whenever Lou was hit in the head by the rifle, he would break up. (Keen-eyed obervers can spot the burly soldier on the end stifle a laugh more than once during the routine.) "I said to the cutter, Phil Cahn, 'I want you to dig out every take—print up everything,'" Gottlieb explained. "You know, we ran that 'Drill' routine a dozen times, and Lou did it differently each time. I said, 'I want you to recut that routine and make it *at least* twice as long. Everybody said that the "Drill" routine is the best-cut, greatest routine they've ever seen. When I took Lou into the projection room and ran it, he laughed his head off. He said, 'We never did it like that before.' I said, 'You're damn right you didn't,' and I told him what we did. He said, 'You can do *that*? You can take it and stretch it out?' I said, 'You're just lucky you made so many mistakes!' That 'Drill' routine made him a star."

"You're Forty, She's Ten" is another quintessential Abbott and Costello confrontation with logic. It is a classic piece of burlesque patter called "Handful of Nickels" that really is a showcase for the straight man. It was originally designed not only to get laughs, but to stall for time while the next act scrambled backstage. The straight man could add other routines onto it, such as "Hole in the Wall," to keep it going indefinitely. This in fact was how it was scripted, but only the first routine was used. Smitty poses a hypothetical question to Herbie. "Suppose you're forty and you're in love with a little girl who's ten years old." "This one's gonna be a pip," Herbie cracks, "now I'm goin' around with a ten-year-old girl. You got a good idea where I'm gonna wind up!" Smitty continues, "You're forty, and she's ten. You're four times as old as that girl. Now you couldn't marry her, so you wait five years. Now the little girl is fifteen, you're forty-five. You're only *three* times as old as that little girl. So you wait fifteen years more. Now the little girl is thirty, you're sixty. You're only *twice* as old as that little girl." "She's catchin' up," Herbie realizes. "Now here's the question," Smitty says. "How long do you have to wait before you and the little girl are the same age?" "What kind of question is that?!" Herbie bleats. "That's ridiculous! If I keep waitin' for that girl, she'll pass me up—she'll wind up older than I am. Then she'll have to wait for me!" "Why should she wait for you?" wonders Smitty. "I was nice enough to wait for her!" Herbie reasons.

The scene ends with Herbie accidentally tossing a basin of water in Collins' face. Laurel and Hardy nearly repeated the gag in their own service comedy, *Great Guns* (1941), but caught themselves: "They did that in *Buck Privates!*" says Ollie.

One night, Herbie absent-mindedly turns on a radio in the tent. Collins bursts in and demands, "Who's playing that radio?" "Nobody," cracks Herbie. "It's playin' by itself." Collins orders him to turn the radio off and keep it off. Smitty, however, goads Herbie into turning it on, and Collins returns to manhandle Herbie for disobeying orders. The boys repeat this simple yet hilarious business, which is a variation of the burlesque routine "Go Ahead and Sing," without wearing it out.

The "Boxing" scene is a low-comedy masterpiece, expertly staged by Bud, Lou, and John Grant. Abbott and Costello once performed the scene at the Eltinge Theater on 42nd Street before they teamed up; Bud was the referee, Lou and Joe Lyons the boxers. Lubin recalled, "Not being a boxer, I let them do what they wanted to do. They rehearsed the broad things like the boxing."

REVIEWS

Editor Phil Cahn was assembling *Buck Privates* as it was being shot, since Universal was rushing to be first on the market with a draft comedy. Bob Hope's *Caught in the Draft* was still in production. On Tuesday, January 28, 1941, five months after the Draft Bill was passed, *Buck Privates* was previewed in Inglewood, California. Alex Gottlieb recalled that night: "We went to preview the picture at the Alexander Theater. Alexander is my real name, so I figured it was going to be good luck. But I was afraid we wouldn't get any audience because this wasn't a big, important preview—Bud and Lou were two unknowns. Well, this picture goes on and the audience started laughing and they never stopped! When we came out of the theater into the lobby, Milton Feld said to me, 'You son of a bitch, you were right. They're going to be big stars.' I said, 'Costello will be a big star. Abbott will be what he needs to work with.' That was never meant to be a malicious statement. I think the facts bear me out."

Lubin explains, "*Buck Privates* was a very, very funny show. And, actually, I must say it was very little credit to the director. It consisted mainly of fabulous gags that these two wonderful guys knew from years and years of being in burlesque."

The success of *Buck Privates* was legendary. It was held over in New Orleans for eight weeks, and in St. Paul for five. In Toronto, Shea's ran *Buck Privates* for ten weeks, then was picketed by other exhibitors. Not until three more weeks had passed did Shea's end the run. Patty Andrews explained, "People kept going back to see it because the laughs were so loud that you missed half the dialogue the first time around."

The reviews were fabulous. The story was panned, of course, but Abbott and Costello were hailed as the comedy find of the decade.

Variety was there at the preview on January 28, 1941: "Picture has a good chance to skyrocket the former burlesk and radio team of Bud Abbott and Lou Costello into topflight starring ranks. . . . Picture is studded with several Abbott and Costello routines that are particularly effective for sustained laughs. Tops is the sequence in which Costello is a member of the awkward squad for special rifle drill. Running about five minutes, episode builds quickly for continuous hilarity—with dialog drowned in the audience uproar. A new angle on the oldie money changing routine and a particularly funny dice game also hit high marks for comedy reaction.

" 'Buck Privates' needs special exploitation to get started in the key spots, but will get immediate word-of-mouth to zoom it to profitable b.o."

Dallas Morning News: "The squad drill, with Costello taking the rifle barrel on his kisser, threw us in the aisle. There is a wonderful crapshooting game, followed by the sharp money count-up over the bar. None of it is too new, which is just as well. Suffice to say that Abbott and Costello truck out the oldies for the most irresistible humor seen on the screen in some months. . . . Unless they are badly messed up by corny handling, they will take a place among movie greats."

Philadelphia Evening Ledger: ". . . 'Buck Privates' is one long chuckle and can be classed as a perfect anodyne for the alarums and excursions of the headlines. Not since Chaplin interrupted the grim business of Mars with his 'Shoulder Arms' in World War I has the hapless rookie been exposed so merrily. And speaking of Chaplin, he has a rival in pantomime and gorgeous helplessness in Lou Costello, the 'bad boy' of radio and burlesque fame who is presented as Rookie Number One in the new opera."

The New York Times: "If the real thing is at all like this preview of Army life—with the Messrs. A. & C. dropping gags once a minute and the Andrews Sisters crooning patriotic boogie-woogie airs—well, it's going to be a merry war, folks. For 'Buck Privates' is an hour and a half of uproarious monkeyshines. Army humor isn't apt to be subtle, and neither are Abbott and Costello. Their antics have as much innuendo as a 1,000-pound bomb but nearly as much explosive force."

More amazed were the studio executives. *Buck Privates* outdrew such films as *How Green Was My Valley, Citizen Kane, Here Comes Mr. Jordan,* and *Sergeant York.* The critics embraced Bud and Lou as few comedians ever before. But perhaps the most satisfying review for Lou came from his idol, Charlie Chaplin, who called Lou "the best comic working in the business today."

POSTSCRIPT

Buck Privates was the studio's biggest money-maker to date, eventually grossing $4 million at a time when movie admission prices were 25¢. But poor Universal had rented *Buck Privates* to exhibitors at B-picture rates; the millions of dollars in profit went largely to the theaters and theater chains. It was a blunder Universal was certain not to repeat. Subsequent Abbott and Costello films were offered at the higher, A-rental rate.

During the war, *Buck Privates* landed in the Smithsonian as an example of prebattle entertainment. It was shown to troops on eight battlefronts: Russian, Chinese, Atlantic, Mediterranean, Middle East, South Pacific, Alaskan, and Western Europe. Meanwhile, the Japanese were using the film for their own propaganda purposes as proof of how inept the American soldiers were! Bud and Lou performed a radio version of *Buck Privates* for the Lux Radio Theater on October 13, 1941. The following year, a terrible clone called *Tramp, Tramp, Tramp* was made at Monogram and starred Jackie Gleason and Jack Durant. Ironically it was directed by future Abbott and Costello auteur Charles Barton.

Arthur Lubin, who was earning $350 a week, was given a $5,000 bonus. Ten days after completing *Buck Privates,* Lubin began shooting the boys' haunted house comedy, "Oh, Charlie!" (later titled *Hold That Ghost*). Meanwhile, two more Abbott and Costello films were already on the drawing board—*In the Navy* and *Ride 'Em Cowboy.*

IN THE NAVY

SYNOPSIS

Radio's number one crooner, Russ Raymond, decides to abandon his career and his swooning fans to join the navy under an assumed name, Tommy Halstead. But he is spotted in San Diego by a newspaper photographer, Dorothy Roberts, who relentlessly pursues him in hopes of getting candid photographs of the rookie seaman.

Tommy is assigned to the *Alabama* with Smoky, Pomeroy, and hard-boiled chief petty officer Dynamite Dugan. Dorothy manages to stow away aboard the ship and get her scoop, but falls in love with Tommy. Meanwhile, the bumbling Pomeroy has been writing love letters to Patty Andrews of the Andrews Sisters, building himself up as an officer. Patty is disappointed to discover that Pomeroy is only a baker. During Visitor's Day, Pomeroy, in an effort to impress Patty, impersonates the captain and puts the battleship through a series of spectacular maneuvers. Unfortunately for Pomeroy, however, the whole thing turns out to be a dream.

BACKGROUND

Abbott and Costello were well into production on "Oh, Charlie!" when the returns from *Buck Privates* began pouring in. Alex Gottlieb recalled, "Milton Feld called me and said, '*Buck Privates* is doing sensational business. We've got to make another picture with Abbott and Costello right away.' I said, 'Well, we've made an army picture—how about a navy picture?'" Universal decided to shelve "Oh, Charlie!" while the studio whipped up a navy comedy. When that was completed, "Oh, Charlie!" would go back into production to add the obligatory musical numbers.

THE SCRIPT

In fact, according to studio memos, Gottlieb began working on an outline for *In the Navy* even before *Buck Privates* was previewed. Arthur Horman was officially assigned to write the screenplay on February 9, and he turned in his first draft exactly one month later on March 9.

Gottlieb not only had to contend with criticism from the Breen censors, but from the navy department as well. The script was forwarded first to Commander A.J. Bolton, U.S.N. Retired, a technical advisor at Fox, for an unofficial critique. Bolton confided that "if [the picture] can be kept in the spirit of good, clean fun, you will probably avoid the wrath of the powers that be. Naturally it is a lampoon from start to finish and must be kept in that spirit. This you carefully achieved in *Buck Privates,* and I see no reason why you shouldn't be able to do it here with a few minor changes." Bolton suggested that the officers be played with more dignity than indicated in the script, and that Pomeroy's run-ins be with a chief petty officer rather than an admiral.

Earliest Draft:
February 3, 1941

Production Start:
April 8, 1941

Production End:
May 9, 1941

Copyright Date:
June 2, 1941

Released: May 27, 1941

Running Time:
85 minutes

Reissued: January 1949
with *Who Done It?*

Directed By: Arthur Lubin

Produced By:
Alex Gottlieb

Screenplay By:
Arthur T. Horman,
John Grant

Original Story:
Arthur T. Horman

Director of Photography:
Joseph Valentine ASC

Special Effects:
John P. Fulton ASC

Art Director:
Jack Otterson

Associate:
Harold H. MacArthur

Film Editor: Philip Cahn

Musical Numbers Staged
By: Nick Castle

Sound Supervisor:
Bernard B. Brown

Technician: Charles Carroll

Gowns: Vera West

Set Decoration:
R.A. Gausman

Dialogue Director:
Joan Hathaway

Assistant Director:
Philip P. Karlstein

Technical Advisor:
H.F. Harris, USN Ret.

Musical Director:
Charles Previn

Words and Music:
Don Raye,
Gene de Paul

Music Supervisor:
Ted Cain

Arrangements:
Vic Schoen

Smoky Adams
.... Bud Abbott

Pomeroy Watson
.... Lou Costello

Tommy Halstead
.... Dick Powell

Dorothy Roberts
.... Claire Dodd

Andrews Sisters
.... Themselves

Dynamite Dugan
.... Dick Foran

Dizzy .... Shemp Howard

Butch....... Billy Lenhart

Buddy ...Kenneth Brown

Condos Brothers
.... Themselves

Captain Richards
.... William Davidson

Head of Committee
.... Thurston Hall

Travers .. Robert Emmett
Keane

Commander
........Edward Fielding

Admiral Stacey
.... Douglas Wood

Floor Manager
.... Don Terry

Dancer......Sunny O'Dea

Ticket Taker
.... Eddie Dunn

Announcer
.... Gary Breckner

Lieutenant Martin
.... J. Anthony Hughes

Traffic Cop... Ralph Dunn

Bos'n .... Frank Penny

The Breen Office, meanwhile, cited another potential trouble spot: "It is especially important that the navy department approve these concluding scenes which involve the comedy business of the captain, the showing of the secretary of the navy, the congressman, and the various comedy business involving these characters." Breen warned the producers that the navy would require five copies of the script for review. "Please keep in mind that the naval authorities, in such matters, appear to move slowly," Breen wrote. "Our experience indicates it is hardly likely you will get any response from the navy, after you have submitted your scripts, until at least three weeks have gone by."

Universal didn't have that much time. After Horman and Gottlieb made the changes Bolton had suggested, but kept the film's climactic battleship sequence intact, the script was sent to Washington. "Fortunately," Arthur Lubin recalled, "the studio knew a Lieutenant Commander Herman Spitzel. He was able to speed things along." Spitzel managed to get a navy board to review the script in just two weeks. (They would have been done sooner, Spitzel said, if Universal had sent more than *one* copy of the script.) Spitzel also arranged for Lubin to shoot establishing scenes at the naval base in San Diego on just two days' notice.

John Grant had integrated a few Abbott and Costello routines into the script, but informed executive producer Milton Feld that the rights to one other routine would cost around $300. Since the studio memo is not specific, we can only speculate which routine Grant meant. A fair guess would be the "7 × 13 = 28" or "Sons of Neptune" scenes, since they had not yet been incorporated into the script. Of course, it could have been some other routine entirely.

Subsequent revisions of the script were of course reviewed by the Production Code Administration, and several criticisms stand out:

"Scene 123 [Palomine Dance Hall]. There must be no 'pansy' reaction where Pomeroy starts to dance with the floor manager."

"Scene 150. Pomeroy's speech, 'And I'd say knots right back to him,' should be rephrased to get away from the unacceptable play on the phrase dealing with 'nuts'."

"Scene 153A [Sons of Neptune]. As now written, this scene suggests that Smoky will spit water on Pomeroy. This is highly objectionable and must be deleted or changed."

"Scene 156 [Sailors prepare to wash down]. There should be no unacceptable exposure of the persons of the sailors when they peel off their blouses, and care must be exercised as to Dorothy's reaction."

These concerns were addressed, and the final shooting script, now titled "Hello Sailor," was completed on April 5, and shooting began on April 8.

THE CAST

Still not sure if Abbott and Costello could carry a picture themselves, and closely adhering to the formula established with *Buck Privates,* the studio overloaded *Navy* not only with the Andrews Sisters, but Dick Powell and Dick Foran. Alex Gottlieb recalled, "We needed a star to play the singer's part, and I thought of Dick Powell, because he was about finished in pictures. Dick was a very nice guy. He said, 'I'll do it, but I've never gotten anything but star billing. But how can you do that? You can't have my name above Abbott and Costello.' I said, 'Why don't we call the picture, "Abbott and Costello and Dick Powell in the Navy." Then Bud and Lou can't say you're getting top billing.' He agreed, and when I told Bud and Lou, they said, 'That's fair enough with us.'" That indeed was the film's official title, but it was commonly referred to as *In the Navy* after release.

Powell was signed on April 4, for five weeks' work at $6,000 per week. The role was strangely autobiographical. At seventeen, Powell (1904–1963) ran away from home in Little Rock, Arkansas, to join the navy. Powell had worked steadily in Warners musicals of the 1930s. In 1939, when he announced he was through with singing roles, his stock at the box office dropped. He manages to croon two songs for this film, which helped rejuvenate his career. Powell finally moved on to tough guy roles in the mid-1940s, then turned to producing in the 1950s. For many years he was head of Four Star Productions.

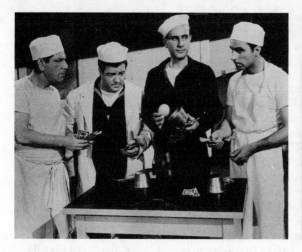 

ABOVE LEFT: The "Lemon Bit" with Shemp Howard (left) and Joe LaCava (right), Bud's stunt double. ABOVE: "The Sons of Neptune"

Dick Foran (1910–1979) had been a star on Princeton's football team. An old friend, Lew Brown, was producing musicals and, recalling Foran's days with the Princeton Glee Club, induced Dick to take a screen test. Foran was soon signed to a contract as a singing cowboy. (In some cities, Foran's twelve-part serial, *Riders of Death Valley,* opened on the same bill with *In the Navy.*)

Claire Dodd (1908–1973) had just completed *The Black Cat* (1941) at Universal. A former Ziegfeld showgirl, she appeared as Della Street in several of the Perry Mason mysteries of the 1930s. Following *In the Navy,* she went into the serial, *Don Winslow of the Navy.*

THE PRODUCTION

Studio production manager Martin Murphy and producer Alex Gottlieb prepared a shooting schedule of twenty-six days, commencing April 8, with a $335,000 budget. Two of the largest indoor sets ever used at Universal were built for the film. On Stage 12 was a reproduction of a section of the grounds surrounding the Royal Palms Hotel in Honolulu, requiring more than two hundred truckloads of dirt and sod, sixty palm trees, scores of banana trees and hundreds of flowering shrubs and plants. Forty hula dancers and sixty Hawaiian singers and musicians worked in support of the Andrews Sisters in this sequence. Over on the studio's process stage, a portion of a 600-foot battleship was constructed, complete with hull, decks, superstructure and gun turrets. Art director Jack Otterson worked from blueprints provided by the navy department. Up to three hundred extras were used in some of these sequences. To expedite production, the film relied heavily on process shots and miniatures. About half of the days were spent on the process stage.

Bud and Lou were visited on the set of *In the Navy* by a D. Lowrence, from *Everyweek* magazine on April 10, when Lubin shot the scenes in Tommy's hotel room. Pomeroy and Smoky push open the door and see Tommy spanking Dorothy. The shot is a tight reaction by Abbott and Costello:

> Staring straight at the camera, they screw their faces into shock, bewilderment, amazement, and embarrasssment in rapid succession. Then Costello squinges his mouth up and says, "Maybe you two would like some ice water?"
>
> "That's not the way you rehearsed it," prompts a gentle, feminine voice—dialogue director Joan Hathaway.
>
> "Cut!" says director Arthur Lubin. "Want to try it again, boys?"
>
> "Sure," they say together, retreating behind the closing door. They do it again, again, and still again. Each time, it's entirely different.

51

Later, back in a far corner of the huge stage, the boys are tracked down, face to face across a card table, looking like anything but funnymen. Intensely they stare at their hands, fling down a card, mark the score. Other actors and stage hands crowd around. The stakes are high, though they swear they come out even year by year. You draw near and watch. Costello looks up. "No, it's not gin rummy," he says. "It's old fashioned knock rummy."

The morning speeds past. Up from the card table they get, as if pulled by the same set of strings. Off to the set, through one short rehearsal, at least six takes—all quite different. At 12:30 the company breaks for lunch. But first, the dailies. The top cast members—long-legged blond Claire Dodd and affable Dick Powell, the romantic team—and the boys lead the march. Lubin, Joan Hathaway, the sound man, both assistant directors, troop across the lot to the projection room, settle themselves for a look at the rushes of the previous days' shooting. You'd expect it to be an ordeal—tense and critical—but the boys won't let it be. They clap and laugh constantly at the bits and pieces that will end up as a picture.

Bursting with lunch and back on the set, there's a mild, two-man revolt in progress. Six scenes with Dick Powell and Claire Dodd have to be shot before Abbott and Costello are asked to work again. "Why can't we go home?" they wheedle.

"To play rummy, I suppose?" Lubin says.

"Yes."

"Well, play it here. We've got to hold your scenes because Powell is shaving off his mustache for the first time, and there's no good way of putting it back on." They grumble, but settle back at the cards again. Every so often one or the other bursts out with a wild cry or a snatch of a song, or a whoop of laughter, and the revolt simmers. "Have to waste all this time because of a few hairs on the top lip of a crooner," says Costello grimly. "Better not hold us after six. It's fight night. We're off at six."

As you sneak off the set, that familiar cry for silence follows you. "Quiet everyone! Lou, Bud—quiet. Ready. Roll 'em!"

Lubin wrapped on May 9, then shot a few additional scenes on May 13. In all, the production ran three days over and cost $379,207.42. "We sent a rough cut of the picture to Washington after it was all done," Alex Gottlieb explained, "and the navy wouldn't allow it to be released." Somehow the battleship sequence—which had been in the script all along—now offended the navy brass on the screen. "Universal was stuck—no second Abbott and Costello picture," Gottlieb continued. "Cliff Work said we've got to do something. I said I'll come up with something. So I ran the picture and I got an idea. I called Cliff up and said, 'Will you give me half the film's budget if I save this picture for you?' [laughs] You know, he wouldn't give it to me?" Gottlieb proposed two options: eliminate the sequence entirely, or make it Pomeroy's dream. Everyone agreed that the sequence had to be saved. "We called Washington and said, 'The whole thing's going to be a dream; is there anything wrong with that?' They said, 'No, that's fine. As long as it doesn't really happen.' "

Gottlieb rewrote on May 17, Lubin shot with Bud and Lou on the 18th (during retakes on "Oh, Charlie!"), and the picture was recut on the 19th. The following day, Maurice Pivar, the head of Universal's editorial department, took a print to Washington, and on May 21, Lubin received a wire from the navy department: "Your picture passed 100 percent. Have accomplished three weeks work in one day. Congratulations." Commander Bolton wired Milton Feld that he found the finished film "delightful" and that "the ingenious twist of having Costello drink the sleeping potion eliminated the only possible objectionable material."

BUD AND LOU'S SCENES

A marvel of timing is the team's "Lemon Bit," a variation on the old shell game. (Lemons are easier for a theater audience to see.) Bud had performed the routine years before with its originator, Harry Steppe. When Bud and Lou crossed paths in burlesque in the mid-1930s, Bud staged the routine for Lou. After the boys teamed up, they reprised the "Lemon Bit" in live appearances at the Roxy Theater. An addition to the routine was a clever money-counting bit. Smoky, making change for Pomeroy, counts it off, "One, two three—how many years have you been in the navy?" "Six," replies Pomeroy, "but what's that got to do with countin' out my change?" "Six? Six?" repeats Smokey, then resumes counting, "Seven, eight, nine, ten." Pomeroy wises up and tries unsuccessfully to put the gag over on Dizzy. (Lynne Overman performed the same routine in the Carole Lombard film *Rumba* [1935].) The other sailor in this scene is Joe LaCava, who usually performed as Bud's stunt double.

Patty Andrews remembered watching the team work in other scenes. "I remember they used to do a lot of huddling with John Grant, setting up their scenes the same way Nick Castle would set up our production numbers. Then, when they went into a scene, and it was *funny,* because they'd get on a roll, Arthur wouldn't yell 'Cut!'—he'd keep the cameras going."

Pat Costello doubled for Lou when Smoky, Pomeroy, and Tommy are sent crashing through a window in the nightclub. Pat also recalled standing by for the hammock scene. "I had been in the navy in the First World War," he explained. "I tried to show Lou how to stay in the hammock; it's the most comfortable thing in the world to sleep in, after you get used to it. But he said, "Pat, nobody's gonna laugh if I stay *in* the hammock; they'll laugh if I fall *out* of it! I said, 'Well, I guess you got a point there!' " The scripted routine is more contrived than need be. On Pomeroy's third attempt to climb into the hammock, the ropes were supposed to break, dropping him to the floor. When Smoky tells him to get new ropes, Pomeroy spots Dynamite's elastic exerciser and uses the bands to fasten the hammock to the ceiling. He climbs in easily, but just when he seems set for the night, the elastic bands at the head end of his hammock begin to stretch. Pomeroy's head sinks from sight, leaving only his feet in frame. He glances over at the floor, puts his hands down on either side, and gives a gentle push to raise himself. Nothing happens. He pushes a little harder. Still nothing. On his third try, the hammock abruptly snaps him up and out of frame. The thunderous crash gets the oblivious Smoky's attention. He looks over to Pomeroy's empty hammock, then up to the ceiling, where he sees a Pomeroy-shaped hole in the steel deck!

BOTTOM LEFT: In a sequence shortened in the film, Pomeroy stops to play with a baby (Lou's 2½-year-old daughter Carole). BOTTOM: The Andrews Sisters visit Captain Watson in his quarters.

But Lou Costello didn't need the elastic gag at all. He turned the simple act of climbing into a hammock into a heroic struggle. He tackled it, clung to it by his toes, rode it like a bucking bronco, swung it back and forth like a jump rope, crooned to it, and patted it. But he couldn't conquer it. It was a scene that rivaled the "Drill" routine for deft timing. Two funny quips were in the script. The first—"How you gonna sleep in a snood?"—was used. The other—"Elephants don't roost!"—was omitted.

Lou reprised the routine almost eleven years to the day later on a *Colgate Comedy Hour* in 1952.

During the "Sons of Neptune" scene, director Lubin started laughing uncontrollably. "We started shooting and I started to laugh, and Lou broke down in the middle of the second take and started to laugh and the whole company laughed." A look at the script reveals that Costello's break up was not that spontaneous; it is, in fact, in the script. Proof positive is that years later, whenever Abbott and Costello performed the routine (which is actually called "Buzzing the Bee"), they broke up in the exact same places. This doesn't detract from the effectiveness of the scene, however, which Costello plays wonderfully.

Another popular Abbott and Costello routine was added to the script during production. Through quirky addition, multiplication, and division, Pomeroy proves to Smoky that 7×13 is indeed 28. The boys reprised the surefire routine in *Little Giant* (1946).

DELETIONS AND ADDITIONS

An early scene cut from the picture introduces Dorothy on the job, photographing two models for a fashion layout at the San Diego airport. Russ Raymond, traveling incognito, accidentally bowls her over. She recognizes him and follows him to his hotel.

In a sequence shortened in the film, Pomeroy stops to play with a baby (Lou's two-and-a-half-year-old daughter Carole), who snatches the captain's letter from him. When Pomeroy takes it back, the baby cries. In a panic, Pomeroy picks her up, and is caught by the baby's mother. Her screams for the police bring Dynamite. Whenever Dynamite roughs up Pomeroy, the baby stops crying. Each time Dynamite stops, the baby cries.

In an omitted scene very similar to the team's "Jonah and the Whale" routine, Pomeroy attempts to read Butch and Buddy the story of Little Red Riding Hood, but the obnoxious pair interrupt him with inane questions. (The routine turns up in *Abbott and Costello in Hollywood* [1945].)

The ship's band concert was supposed to include a musical routine by Abbott and Costello. Smoky attempts to lead the band through "Poet and the Peasant," but Pomeroy's drum playing is hopelessly off beat. So Smoky switches to a simpler number, "Stars and Stripes Forever." Pomeroy has a difficult time keeping up with the increasing tempo and winds up sending his drumstick and his head through the drum.

Another deleted song, "Oceana Roll," is a "Boogie Woogie Bugle Boy" clone about a sailor on the *Alabama* who plays syncopated piano.

Patty Andrews recalled working on the sequence where Pomeroy poses as the captain and misdirects the battleship through a series of wild maneuvers. "I had more bruises from Lou Costello! He played that scene with energy. To have a heavyweight like him bump into you like that—it turned out great—but it was rough." In the original version, Captain Richards wakes up in the next room, and pounds furiously on the locked door. As the ship pitches and turns, Tommy and Dorothy become buried under the potatoes in the food locker. After Pomeroy nearly rams the flagship, the scene dissolves to Captain Richards' cabin. Two lieutenants have completed an inquiry and have discovered that only three men weren't at their battle stations throughout the entire maneuver—Tommy, Smoky, and Pomeroy. Captain Richards asks Smoky where he was. "I was looking for a lifeboat. I was nervous, sir." The captain says he can understand why. As Tommy explains that he was trapped in a food locker, Dorothy breaks into the inquiry. She whispers something to the captain, whose crusty attitude melts into a smile. "Seaman Halstead," he announces, "you are remanded into the custody of this young lady until further notice." Now Richards turns his attention to Pomeroy. But before he can reprimand him, the admiral and the committee chairman arrive to congratulate Captain Richards on the magnificent display they just witnessed. The captain looks at Pomeroy, breaks into a grin and slaps him on the back, presumably forgiving him. It was this version that offended the navy brass.

REVIEWS

The New York Times: ". . . [T]he boys are herein aboard a vehicle almost as ponderous, though not as deadly, as a battleship for their second starring trip upon the screen. Yessir, they are really traveling in an overloaded hulk, weighted down by such nonbuoyant ballast as the Andrews Sisters, Dick Powell, and a bleakly unfunny plot. . . . And yet the Messrs. Abbott and Costello, who appear as a pair of seafaring dogs, make it skim and cavort like a surfboard when they are undisputed at the helm. Maybe they aren't quite as funny as they were in 'Buck Privates,' but even fair with Abbott and Costello is good enough for now."

Baltimore Sun: "Abbott & Costello provide enough mad comedy to last at least a week. Abbott feeds the harassed and puzzled Costello with gags that are hoary with age and stem from the old burlesque shows, but the technique of this pair is such that one doesn't mind the antiquity of their jokes. Quite to the contrary. Everyone within hearing in the audience of which we were a part were laughing fit to bust their gussets. And the laughter was as prolonged as it was loud."

New York Morning Telegraph: "The boys . . . are reaching for their gags already in this second starring appearance. They're running short of the rapid-fire dialogue that was so entrancing in their previous appearance. . . . Now they're turning to straight slapstick, shooting water at each other, falling over ropes, even . . . having a love affair with one of the Andrews Sisters. This is not Abbott and Costello, indeed. It's more along the line of a two-reel comedy. The boys are worthy of better treatment.

"To be fair about it, however, it must also be reported that so far there seems to be no indication of running short of laughs. The crowds that poured into the Criterion yesterday received 'In the Navy' with the greatest approval, laughing themselves sick over the two boys. . . ."

New York Post: "Often the riotous laughter drowned out gags which might have been just as funny—if one could have heard them. But, on the whole, one hears enough, and it's all grand and goofy, and tuneful, too, and respectful, in spite of its slapstick, to the fleet.

". . . Unless Laurel and Hardy come along with a picture pretty soon, it's going to be Abbott and Costello for keeps; for prat-falls, for slaps in the face, for the kind of unsubtle humor that sophisticates simply adore."

POSTSCRIPT

In the Navy was a bigger hit than *Buck Privates;* in fact, it was the sixth biggest grossing picture of 1941. It broke every record at Loew's Criterion in New York, playing to 49,947 persons during its first seven days. In order to accommodate the crowds, the theater remained open until five o'clock Sunday morning! Bud and Lou appeared in person at the New York premiere on June 11. Universal threw a big bash at the Hotel Astor the night of the opening.

Predictably, Arthur Lubin received another $5,000 bonus, and began work on *Ride 'Em Cowboy* at the end of June. Another service comedy, set in the air corps, was already on the boards.

On the Sunday before production began on *In the Navy,* Bud and Lou made their first appearance as regulars on the *Chase and Sanborn Hour* with Edgar Bergen and Charlie McCarthy. They would continue on this program until the fall of 1942, when they opened their own series, *The Abbott and Costello Show,* on NBC.

HOLD THAT GHOST

Earliest Draft:
October 23, 1940

Production Start:
January 21, 1941

Production End:
February 24, 1941

Copyright Date:
July 30, 1941

Released: August 6, 1941

Running Time:
85 minutes

Reissued: August 19,
1948 and December
1949 (with Hit the Ice)

Directed By: Arthur Lubin

Screenplay By:
Robert Lees, Fred
Rinaldo, John Grant

Original Story:
Robert Lees,
Fred Rinaldo

Associate Producers:
Burt Kelly, Glenn Tryon

Director of Photography:
Elwood Bredell ASC

Art Director:
Jack Otterson

Associate:
Harold M. MacArthur

Film Editor: Philip Cahn

Musical Director:
H. J. Salter

Musical Numbers Staged
By: Nick Castle

Dialogue Director:
Joan Hathaway

Assistant Director:
Gilbert J. Valle

Sound Supervisor:
Bernard M. Brown

Technician: William Fox

Gowns: Vera West

Set Decoration:
R. A. Gausman

Chuck Murray
.... Bud Abbott

Ferdinand Jones
.... Lou Costello

SYNOPSIS

Chuck Murray and Ferdie Jones are gas station attendants who aspire to better jobs—waiting tables at Chez Glamour. But on their first night on the job, they disrupt the club and promptly land back at the gas station. The boys are accidentally kidnapped while servicing gangster Moose Matson's car when Matson flees from the police. Matson is killed during the chase, and through his strange will, Chuck and Ferdie inherit his abandoned tavern.

Chuck and Ferdie hire a wildcat bus to take them to their new property. The unscrupulous driver maroons the boys and the other passengers—Dr. Jackson, Norma Lind, Camille Brewster, and Charlie Smith—at the old tavern. Smith, a member of Matson's gang, searches the cellar for Moose's bankroll. Although Matson always claimed that he kept his money "in his head," the gang believes it's hidden somewhere in the tavern. Smith is murdered by other gang members who are also after the loot. Their attempts to scare off the intruders and locate the money fail, however, and Ferdie discovers the booty in a moose head. After thwarting the criminals, Chuck and Ferdie transform the tavern into a swank health resort with Dr. Jackson, Norma, and Camille on staff, and hire Ted Lewis and the Andrews Sisters to entertain.

BACKGROUND

Since the original Abbott and Costello contract was for two pictures in twelve weeks, executive producer Milton Feld, to expedite matters, divided the pictures between associate producers Alex Gottlieb and Burt Kelly. Kelly assigned two young screenwriters to the haunted house comedy.

Robert Lees and Fred Rinaldo were junior writers at MGM in the early 1930s. In 1936 they got into the shorts department, where they wrote 35 shorts, including *Crime Doesn't Pay* and the Pete Smith series. For one wonderful year they wrote the Robert Benchley shorts. The team's first full-length feature was *Street of Memories* (1940). "That was the biggest disappointment of our careers," Robert Lees recalled. "But now we had a feature credit, and that led to our contract at Universal." Lees and Rinaldo's first credit at Universal was *The Invisible Woman* (1941) for producer Burt Kelly. "Burt liked us," Lees explained, "and he was producing *Hold That Ghost,* so that's how we got our first Abbott and Costello assignment. In fact, I think he was going to do *Buck Privates,* and we got involved with that picture, too. I can't recall what we did, but we didn't get any credit on it."

THE SCRIPT

"As I recall," Robert Lees said, "the whole reason for the haunted house thing was that they wanted to use the "Moving Candle" routine. That was something that they did in burlesque.

But *Hold That Ghost* started with a very strong idea—which was Fred's—that there's this gangster who's so distrustful of those around him, he wills everything to whoever is with him when he dies. And, of course, that's where we had Abbott and Costello come in." It represented a step forward for the team: the story centered on *them,* and the comedy came out of situations as well as routines. "Fred and I were screenwriters, not gagwriters," Lees said. "We wanted to write stories that held up, had character, and developed." In one respect *Buck Privates* was too successful, since it stymied any potential for growth or experimentation early in the series. Its formula, which made Bud and Lou subordinate to a hackneyed plot and frequently mediocre music, was imposed on the next five Abbott and Costello films.

Lees and Rinaldo began working on *Hold That Ghost* (original titles: "Don't Look Now"; "Oh, Charlie!") while Gottlieb and Horman were writing *Buck Privates.* The final shooting script, titled "Oh, Charlie!," was completed on January 14, 1941, a few days after Lubin wrapped *Buck Privates.*

Generally, the Breen Office was more concerned with the gangsters and the violence in "Oh, Charlie!" than the comedy. Some of the caveats:

"Please have in mind the special regulations re: Crime in Motion Pictures, which prohibit the showing of gun battles between criminals and the police," a memo states. "With this thought in mind, Moose should not fire over two or three shots at the police, but the police may fire unlimited times at Moose. Please avoid gruesomeness in Scene 46, where Moose is shot, and in Scene 52 where he dies."

In an early draft, Ferdie asks Chuck why ethyl is more expensive. Chuck replies, "You can go farther with ethyl." Breen suggested deleting the exchange because of its suggestiveness.

There's one unintentionally funny caveat that even Lou would have appreciated: "Scene 191: Care must be exercised to avoid vulgarity where Costello undresses for bed."

In a funny exchange, Ferdie tells Camille that he enjoys playing post office. When Camille dismisses it as a kid's game, Ferdie assures her, "Not the way I play it!" The Ohio censor board deleted the line from the finished film. The board also excised Ferdie's wolf whistle when Camille, surveying the bedrooms, says, "Looks like we're going to sleep together."

Song lyrics also had to be submitted to the Production Code Administration (PCA). Breen objected to one line in "Aurora"—"I'll give you this and give you that"—as being unacceptable due to sexual suggestiveness. Another line, "Is it me or just my money," would prove offensive to Latin Americans, according to the PCA's South American expert, Addison Durland. Executive producer Milton Feld assured the PCA that no salaciousness was intended, and that the song was already a popular hit in South America.

THE CAST

Richard Carlson (1912–1977) had appeared in Bob Hope's haunted house comedy, *The Ghost Breakers,* in 1940. In the 1950s, Carlson would star in the sci-fi classics *It Came From Outer Space, Riders to the Stars,* and *Creature From the Black Lagoon.*

Joan Davis (1907–1961) was on loan to Universal from Fox. A vaudevillian since childhood, Joan made her film debut in Mack Sennett two-reelers. In the 1940s she starred in the very popular radio series, *I Married Joan,* which successfully made the transition to television in the 1950s.

Evelyn Ankers (1918–1985) was born in Valparaiso, Chile, to British parents, and educated in England. *Hold That Ghost,* her second American film, was a portent of things to come: later in 1941 she was cast in *The Wolf Man* and *The Ghost of Frankenstein,* earning her the dubious title, "Queen of the Horrors."

THE PRODUCTION

Lubin began shooting "Oh, Charlie!" ten days after completing *Buck Privates.* The budget was just $190,000, with a twenty-day shooting schedule. Most of the film takes place in the

Doctor Jackson
.... Richard Carlson
Camille Brewster
.... Joan Davis
Gregory..... Mischa Auer
Norman Lind
.... Evelyn Ankers
Charlie Smith
.... Marc Lawrence
Soda Jerk
.... Shemp Howard
Bannister .. Russell Hicks
Moose Matson
.... William Davidson
Harry Hoskins
.... Milton Parsons
Snake-Eyes
.... Frank Penny
Irondome .. Edgar Dearing
Strangler....... Don Terry
High Collar
.... Edward Pawley
Glum .... Nestor Paiva
Lefty .... Paul Fix
Judge...Howard Hickman
Mr. Jenkins
.... Harry Hayden
State Trooper
.... William Forrest
Big Fink .... Paul Newlan
Little Fink ... Joe LaCava
Bit Waiter.. Bobby Barber
Ted Lewis and His
Orchestra
Andrews Sisters

abandoned roadhouse, and art director Jack Otterson built sets on several stages. It was an ambitious schedule that had Lubin shooting well into the evening to keep pace. During the second week of shooting, the production began to fall behind because Lou was ill and had to leave early on three days. He missed another day on doctor's orders. The second half of production was hampered by bad weather and a fruitless location search for a gas station. Ultimately, the studio built Chuck and Ferdie's gas station on the back lot at a cost of $2500. (It turns up in several Universal films, including Abbott and Costello's *Pardon My Sarong* in 1942.) In all, the picture ran seven days over, and although studio correspondence indicates it was only $3,000 over budget, one has to believe that the final cost of "Oh, Charlie!" in its original form exceeded $200,000.

Meanwhile, *Buck Privates* had become a huge success, and Universal, to its dismay, realized that "Oh, Charlie!" bore no resemblance whatsoever to the previous hit. According to Maxene Andrews, a preview audience confirmed Universal's fears. "They asked everybody in the audience to fill out these cards and say what they thought of the picture. Well, everybody wrote on the cards, 'Where are the Andrews Sisters?'" Studio president Nate Blumberg demanded a *Buck Privates* clone as quickly as possible. Head of production Cliff Work decided to shelve "Oh, Charlie!" and crank out a navy comedy. In the meantime, Lees and Rinaldo set to work integrating musical interludes into "Oh, Charlie!" while salvaging as much of the original footage as possible. Universal hoped to get *In the Navy* in theaters by late May, and the revised "Oh, Charlie!" out by late summer.

Lubin finished shooting *In the Navy* on May 13, and three days later the company returned to finish "Oh, Charlie!" To accommodate the new nightclub footage, many scenes in the original version were dropped. When these were omitted, other sequences had to be reshot to preserve continuity. The original shooting script was 136 pages and 326 scenes; the retake script exceeded 60 pages and 120 scenes. By now, Burt Kelly had gone to Paramount, so Glenn Tryon picked up the reigns as producer. Joan Davis was back at Fox working on *Sun*

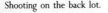
Shooting on the back lot.

Valley Serenade, so her part had to be written out of the retakes. The Andrews Sisters had completed their work on *In the Navy* weeks earlier and were performing in New York. "The studio brought us back and we shot two songs for the nightclub scenes," Patty recalled. Ted Lewis was also signed to perform in the film, and while the nightclub set was standing, the studio shot several additional Lewis numbers for a short release that summer. A clipping states that revamping "Oh, Charlie!"—now retitled *Hold That Ghost*—cost Universal an additional $200,000.

DELETIONS AND ADDITIONS

It was during retakes that the boys first met Bobby Barber, hired for a bit part as a waiter in the opening sequence. Though his scene was cut, Bobby was hired for bits in many of their pictures and later became the team's "court jester" off-screen.

In a sequence cut from the original version, a probate court judge rules that Chuck and Ferdie are the legal heirs to Matson's estate. Ferdie still doesn't understand what an inheritance is, so Chuck tries to explain. "Look," Chuck says, "suppose I died and left you some money. What would you call it?" "A miracle," Ferdie cracks.

Bannister shows the boys a beautiful architect's rendering of the Forrester's Club, and explains that it was once a speakeasy. "What kind of place was it?" Ferdie inquires. "Speakeasy," answers Chuck. So Ferdie whispers, "Okay. What kind of place was it?" Chuck snaps back, "I just told you—speakeasy!" Ferdie gasps, "I am speaking easy—whaddaya want me to do? Talk with my fingers!?"

The two detectives who arrive at the tavern turn out to be Irondome and Strangler, members of Matson's gang. In a deleted scene, they are joined in the cellar by Rosy, Snake-Eyes, Glum, and High Collar. Snake-Eyes suggests that they scare off the intruders and find the money fast because Lefty and his boys have escaped from prison and are bound to be heading their way. In the original film, Moose's entire gang convenes to take the money away from Chuck and Ferdie. As the gangsters begin tying everyone up, Lefty, Big Fink, and Little Fink arrive, and the two factions begin fighting it out until the police arrive.

BUD AND LOU'S SCENES

Ferdie and Camille do a hilarious comic dance routine that is one of the highlights of the film. One of Joan's specialties was a comic ballet. "A lot of people think they just improvised that," explains Robert Lees. "But it's in the script. Otherwise, how could they have built the set and had that rain puddle and everything?" Davis, according to the pressbook, had to be "measured" for a custom-made pail to fit her derriere. "I remember being in the projection room," Lees continued, "looking at this dance scene, and it's hysterical. *Literally.* And from the back of the room we hear a voice that is obviously Costello's saying, 'Who's the star of this film?' He felt he was being upstaged by Joan Davis. But what he didn't realize yet was that, when he had a good comedienne to play off, it made him funnier, too."

One of the all-time best sequences in any Abbott and Costello film is the "Changing Room," where Ferdie's bedroom transforms into a gambling casino. "The 'Changing Room' scene was very, very carefully worked out," Robert Lees recalled. "Of course, the 'Changing Room' is really a variation of their 'Moving Candle' routine: something happens to Costello that Abbott doesn't see. Fred and I knew that the chandelier would come down and be the roulette table; we knew the beds would turn over and be the crap table. We knew all these things would happen. Now, Abbott and Costello managed to work it out pretty well. They could have done much more with it, but it called for a tremendous amount of rehearsal and they didn't have that rehearsal time. They also were never very sure of visual gags; they were more sure of their own routines. But what Fred and I *never* expected was how big a laugh there was in *anticipation*. When Costello is washing up, dabbing water in his eyes, the audience *knows* he's going to go crazy because the room has changed—and they were laughing all through that scene. They went crazy on *Hold That Ghost*." One line was omitted at the end of the sequence. Ferdie, sobbing, can't understand why everything happens to him. "I'm a baaad boy!" he wails.

The "Moving Candle" gag is the film's centerpiece. In it Chuck orders Ferdie to study a map to find the easiest way back to town. As Ferdie reads the map, two candles mysteriously levitate or slide back and forth. Every time he summons Chuck or Camille, the candles stop moving. Costello's pantomime elaborates on the loosely written scene. He uses everything—gasping breath, hand gestures, etc.—to convey sputtering fear. He knows exactly how long to keep this up before giving birth to an audible "Oh, Chuck!" each time. Bud also expands on the bare bones of the script, and knows when to throw Costello a plum line. After Camille has missed seeing the candle move for a second time, further infuriating Ferdie, Chuck reasons, "Take it easy, don't get excited about this thing. Everything's all right. You have company here—you're not alone." To which Ferdie can sarcastically retort, "No, not much." Universal's other comedy team, Olsen and Johnson, paid homage to this sequence in their own horror comedy, *Ghost Catchers* (1944).

Costello ad-libs his lines throughout the sequence where Ferdie searches the moose head, and they're some of the funniest in the film. "I'm going to put my hand in your mouth," he informs the stuffed animal. "*Don't* bite it. This one's going in. This is the one I eat with." In an aside to Chuck and Camille, he confides, "I have a way with animals." For a moment his hand gets stuck as he pulls wads of cash out of the head. "I'll never join your lodge!" he howls.

Pat Costello recalled his stuntwork on the picture. "I only did one stunt—where I go flying down the bannister with the bag of money. I rolled down the bannister on a flat board. The only thing was, I went down so fast the first time that I went flying off the bannister about fifteen feet and bounced into a wall on the other side of the room!"

REVIEWS

Motion Picture Herald: "Yes, Ladies and Gentlemen, they've done it again. In fact, by count and with witnesses, the Messrs. Abbott and Costello got more, louder, and longer laughs in 'Hold That Ghost' at its Hollywood preview than they did in 'Buck Privates' or 'In the Navy.' Veritably, it is to be doubted if any two comedians ever got so many laughs in one picture any time anywhere."

Motion Picture Daily: " 'Hold That Ghost' is, in the vernacular, hot as a firecracker. It is, to use some more vernacular, by far the corniest comedy the Abbott and Costello duo has committed, but don't get me wrong—for 'corniest' is, in this case, a synonym for best. On the evidence provided by a capacity preview audience, this is the screamingest riot the boys have turned in—and I mean screams, not just guffaws, blurts and haw-haws, but screams!"

The New York Times: "The arrival of 'Hold That Ghost' at the Capitol yesterday makes it three straight hits in a row for Abbott and Costello, judging by the gales of laughter which greeted their every turn. An accomplishment that is all the more remarkable because their present caper is freighted with practically all of the whiskered antics that go with a ghost-house setting. Yes, the boys are immensely funny as they romp through a ramshackle house abounding in secret passageways, sliding panels, clutching hands, eerie sound effects and all sorts of trick contraptions. An ideal background, to be sure, but the boys linger in it a little too long. For while their bag of tricks is considerable, it is by no means inexhaustible.

"But while [the musical] interludes are entertaining of themselves, they tend to slow up the film's pace and before the final fade-out one is all too conscious that 'Hold That Ghost' runs 86 minutes."

New York Morning Telegraph: "To an impartial observer (of which there are admittedly only a few in the world), it does seem that the boys are running short on material. 'Buck Privates'

was a howl, principally because Abbott and Costello went through their routines with that split-second timing, that rapid fire precision that has brought them to where they are today. 'In the Navy' had a little less routine and a little more slapstick, which the Three Stooges could have done equally as well, and now 'Hold That Ghost' only occasionally has the two boys firing the question and answer business at each other, with much more of the sliding door business thrown in than they really need.

'Hold That Ghost' is good, rowdy, risible slapstick. But it should have been better Abbott and Costello."

POSTSCRIPT

"When we saw the first cut of *Hold That Ghost* in the projection room," Robert Lees confessed, "we were almost so upset that we considered taking our names off it. You see, in writing it, you visualize it, and you visualize it much funnier or much better than what they did. I said to Fred, 'Damn it, if we were on the set, we would have done this, we'd do that.' All writers go through this. Now, a lot of things can happen logistically to change what you wrote; maybe the set didn't work, or the light wasn't right. But you have a concept of what it is going to be when you put it in the script. And in many cases we could be wrong. But when we saw the picture with an audience, we were rolling in the aisles along with everyone else. You see, it was all in their timing. Something absolutely happens with an audience and Abbott and Costello. So Fred and I said to ourselves, 'We must have been crazy. We didn't realize how funny this thing really is!' "

Lou Costello found his specialty in the scare take. He was second to none. Realizing how sure-fire and profitable this was, the studio tried to scare him at least once in every film, whether there was a place for it or not. In *Keep 'Em Flying,* Lou treads into an amusement park's haunted house—"a sequence dragged in by its heels," according to one critic. Of course, Costello's masterpiece would come seven years later in *Abbott and Costello Meet Frankenstein.*

With *Buck Privates* taking the country by storm, Universal immediately picked up the team's option for one year, commencing February 12, 1941. The boys would continue to earn a salary of $35,000 per film, plus 10 percent of the profits. They were scheduled for four films per year, one of which the studio agreed to budget at $450,000—about double what the current films cost.

On August 1, 1941, Abbott and Costello recreated *Hold That Ghost* for radio audiences on Louella Parsons' *Hollywood Premiere.*

TOP: A deleted scene from the original cut: Richard Carlson, Bud, Evelyn Ankers, Joan Davis, and Lou keep the gansters at bay by slinging phonograph records at them. TOP CENTER: Even though Moose's money turns out to be counterfeit, Chuck and Ferdie manage to turn the hotel into a posh rest home with their new friends on staff. In the final scene, Ferdie and Chuck tell a guest, Mrs. Giltedge, to just pull the bell cord if she needs anything. Ferdie demonstrates, but the curtain parts to reveal the closet. "Oops, wrong rope," Ferdie says. He opens the closet and Charlie Smith's body drops out once more. The film ends on a close-up of Camille screaming. TOP LEFT: "The Moving Candle," with Joan Davis.

KEEP 'EM FLYING

Earliest Draft:
  May 9, 1941

Production Start:
  September 5, 1941

Production End:
  October 29, 1941

Copyright Date:
  November 27, 1941

Released:
  November 28, 1941

Running Time:
  86 minutes

Reissued: May 30, 1949
  with *Ride 'Em Cowboy*
  and October 1953 with
  Buck Privates

Directed By: Arthur Lubin

Produced By: Glenn Tryon

Screenplay By:
  True Boardman, Nat
  Perrin, John Grant

Original Story:
  Edmund L. Hartmann

Director of Photography:
  Joseph Valentine ASC

Special Photographic
  Effects: John P. Fulton
  ASC

Aerial Photography:
  Elmer Dyer ASC

Art Director:
  Jack Otterson

Associate:
  Harold H. MacArthur

Film Editor: Philip Cahn

Sound Director:
  Bernard B. Brown

Technician:
  William Hedgcock

Gowns: Vera West

Set Decoration:
  R. A. Gausman

Dialogue Director:
  Joan Hathaway

Assistant Director:
  Gil Valle

SYNOPSIS

Daredevil stunt pilot Jinx Roberts and his assistants, Blackie and Heathcliff, are fired from McGonigle's Carnival and Air Show after an argument with the boss. Jinx decides to enlist in the army air corps at Cal-Aero Academy, and the boys celebrate at a nightclub, where Jinx falls for the club's beautiful singer, Linda Joyce. Linda becomes a USO hostess at Cal-Aero, where her brother, Jimmy, is enrolled as a cadet. Jinx clashes with his instructor at the academy, Craig Morrison. Years before, Morrison was Roberts' co-pilot on a commercial airliner. Heathcliff and Blackie sign up as ground crewmen and fall for twin sisters Barbara and Gloria Phelps, who are also USO hostesses.

Jinx, in a botched effort to help Jimmy solo, breaks all regulations and nearly gets the boy killed. Jinx is washed out of the corps, along with Blackie and Heathcliff. But as they leave the base, Morrison, during a parachute-jumping demonstration, gets his chute caught on the transport plane's fuselage. He dangles precariously until Jinx, in a spectacular maneuver, rescues him with his plane. Jinx is reinstated, and Linda forgives him.

BACKGROUND

With the United States edging toward war—but still pre-Pearl Harbor—the War Department contracted twenty-eight privately owned flying schools to train cadets for the Army Air Corps. The idea of Abbott and Costello run amok in flight school was rife with possibilities. During production, the War Department coincidentally initiated a drive for volunteers using the slogan of the cadet air corps, "Keep 'Em Flying." As Arthur Lubin explained in 1941, "We were going to release their cowboy picture at this time and save *Keep 'Em Flying* for February. Then 'Keep 'Em Flying Week' was announced. We had to take advantage of that, so we changed around the two pictures."

THE SCRIPT

With Gottlieb finishing up *Ride 'Em Cowboy*, Glenn Tryon was elected to produce *Keep 'Em Flying* (working title: "Up in the Air") Tryon assigned the scripting chores to Edmund Hartmann, who had come up with the story for *Cowboy*, as well as Robert Lees and Fred Rinaldo. After several rewrites, Hartmann's story was finally selected in July, and Nat Perrin, True Boardman, and John Grant independently contributed to the screenplay. The final shooting script was delivered August 22. According to *Look* magazine, the film's heroic rescue of a parachutist was based on a real incident.

As the script was being developed, executive producer Milton Feld sent a memo to Tryon detailing the placement of the musical interludes in the previous Abbott and Costello films. Feld's memo precisely broke them down to page and scene number. "It has been my attempt," Feld wrote, "to keep them as well spaced as possible so that at no time do we lose sight of the fact that we are doing a comedy with music. This may be a guide to you in preparation of the script."

According to the pressbook, Lou's character, Heathcliff, was named after the role Laurence Olivier played in *Wuthering Heights* (1939). Lou apparently was so impressed with Olivier's performance, it became a running gag between him and Lubin. The director finally suggested Lou play the role of Heathcliff . . . but in *Keep 'Em Flying*.

THE CAST

It was a busy year for Dick Foran. In addition to three Abbott and Costello films, he appeared in *Horror Island, The Kid from Kansas, Mob Town,* and *Unfinished Business* in 1941.

William Gargan (1905–1979) had completed *Flying Cadets* (1941) just two days before beginning work on *Keep 'Em Flying*. Gargan, who was nominated for an Academy Award for *They Knew What They Wanted* (1940), worked with Bud and Lou again in *Who Done It?* (1942).

Martha Raye (b. 1916) joined her parents' vaudeville act when she was only three years old. At sixteen, she joined Paul Ash's orchestra as a singing comedian. Director Norman Taurog discovered her in 1936 and she debuted in Bing Crosby's *Rhythm on the Range*. Her previous films included *The Boys From Syracuse* (1940); *Navy Blues* (1941); and *Hellzapoppin'* (1941), with Olsen and Johnson. Martha's song "Pig Foot Pete" was nominated for an Oscar—but erroneously credited to *Hellzapoppin'* in the Academy's official record. Orchestra leader Freddie Slack plays piano on the number.

Keep 'Em Flying was Carol Bruce's second film. Born in Great Neck, New York, Carol was seventeen when she became a vocalist with Lloyd Huntley's orchestra. Irving Berlin discovered her singing in a New York nightclub and promptly put her in *Louisiana Purchase* on Broadway. She made her film debut in *This Woman Is Mine* (1941).

THE PRODUCTION

The air corps' largest training facility was the Cal-Aero school in Ontario, California, near Chino. Universal received permission to shoot there as long as the production didn't interfere with training. A cast and crew of 150 spent twelve days on location. After they left, the second unit, led by director Ralph Ceder and cinematographer John Boyle, stayed on to shoot the flying stunts. Ceder was a veteran of the Mack Sennett thrill-comedy days. The stunt planes were owned by Paul Mantz, generally regarded as the best stunt pilot in the business.

Lou's brother Pat continued to do stunt work in Lou's place, and his resemblance to Lou caused a problem one day. "I get to Cal-Aero early one day, around seven-thirty or so, and Lou has a call for something like eight or eight-thirty," Pat recounts. "Well, eight-thirty comes and no Lou. Nine o'clock. Nine-thirty. Still no Lou. So Arthur Lubin sends the assistants to look for him. They get to the front gate and there's Lou, having an argument with two soldiers. Lou is saying, 'Dammit, *I'm* Costello!' And this guard very calmly says, 'No, you are not. He's been here since seven-thirty.' Lou says, 'Whaddaya mean he's been here?' The guard says, 'He drove up, said, "Costello," and I let him in. I've had no problems until you showed up.' They had the damndest time. Arthur Lubin had to go to the gate, and the colonel finally straightened it out."

Carol Bruce remembers the film affectionately. "I think I just sat there kind of agape, watching their antics, laughing, and saying to myself, 'For this I'm getting *paid?*' Lou really was the nut to me; Bud was the straight man, not given to as much spontaneity or extemporaneous humor as Lou was. But there was such horseplay, and they did break up the other

Musical Director:
  Charles Previn

"Let's Keep 'Em Flying,"
  "Pig Foot Pete," "The
  Boy With The Wistful
  Eyes"; Words and
  Music By: Don Raye
  and Gene de Paul

"I'm Getting Sentimental
  Over You"; Words By:
  Ned Washington; Music
  By: George Bassman

Music Supervisor:
  Ted Cain

Musical Score:
  Frank Skinner

Musical Numbers Staged
  By: Edward Prinz

Torpedo chase and flying
  sequences directed by
  Ralph Ceder

Assistant: Fred Frank;
  Chief Pilot: Paul Mantz

Technical Advisors:
  Major Robert L. Scott
  Jr., Lieutenant David L.
  Jones

Flying school sequences
  photographed at Cal-
  Aero Academy, Ontario,
  California

Blackie Benson
 . . . . Bud Abbott

Heathcliff
 . . . . Lou Costello

Barbara and Gloria Phelps
 . . . . Martha Raye

Linda Joyce . . Carol Bruce

Craig Morrison
 . . . . William Gargan

Jinx Roberts . . Dick Foran

Jim Joyce . . . Charles Lang

McGonigle
 . . . . William Davidson

Spealer . . . . . Frank Penny

Butch . . . . Truman Bradley

Major Barstow
 . . . . Loring Smith

Colonel . . . William Forrest

Cadets . . . . . Stanley Smith
  James Horne, Jr.
  Charlie King, Jr.
  Regis Parton
  Scotty Groves

USO Hostesses
 . . . . Dorothy Darrell
  Elaine Morey
  Marcia Ralston

Pianist . . . . . Freddie Slack
  and The Six Hits

63

people. God knows I was glad I wasn't in their place. Bud and Lou realized I was frightened and they just couldn't have been more gracious and more welcoming. Lou would come over and put his arm around me and say, 'Hey kid, relax, we're having a ball.' I have nothing but positive and warm, affectionate things to say about them. To me it *was* Alice in Wonderland—I was in Hollywood, working with Abbott and Costello, and Martha Raye, who is still a friend of mine. Arthur Lubin was the most helpful to me. There was a camaraderie on the set due a lot to Arthur, and we remained friends for years. Bill Gargan was an absolute doll to me—he gave me more confidence and courage. But I guess it's the best time I had in my short, easily forgotten film career."

Carol has special memories of Dick Foran. "I was not a naive kid; I knew when somebody had the hots for me. And one day Dick Foran said to me, 'Carol, on the lunch break, you want to come back to my dressing room?' And I gave him one of those eyebrow lifts and said, 'Oh really? Are you gonna do the etchings bit?' He said, 'No! We'll play jacks.' I said, 'Oh now I've heard everything.' But I said to myself, what the hell, I gotta see this; after all, I'm a big girl and if he tries anything I'll run or whatever. I went back to his dressing room and, son of a bitch, he got the jacks out! [laughs] And we sat down on the floor and we played jacks. And I thought, 'This I will tell my grandkids.' And I have told my grandsons. Because it's bizarre: this big hunk—yes, he had eyes for me—but he really wanted to play jacks."

Carol was delighted to sing "I'm Getting Sentimental Over You" in the film. "It's one of my very favorite things of all time because Tommy Dorsey was one of my best friends in the world. I was so thrilled, and Tommy was, too. I still like my rendition from that time."

During production, Major Robert Lee Scott, the commanding officer at Cal-Aero, presented Bud and Lou with honorary titles as "Flying Cadets, US Army Air Corps."

BUD AND LOU'S SCENES

Bud and Lou's memorable scene with Martha Raye as twin waitresses was actually expanded on the set. Originally, according to the script, the scene did not include the opening "Go Ahead, Order Something" routine. The boys only have a quarter to their name. "I'll order a turkey sandwich and a cup of coffee," Blackie explains, "and I'll give you half. But if she asks you if you want anything, you say no, I don't care for anything." Heathcliff dutifully follows instructions, but Blackie, suddenly benevolent, urges, "Oh, go ahead, have something." When Heathcliff orders, Blackie slaps him for disobeying him. This business is repeated several times and builds steadily. Bud's masterful coaxing, and Lou's weighty deliberations (all conveyed on his face) are wonderfully funny.

One of the broadest sequences in the film is Heathcliff's wild ride on a runaway air torpedo. That was brother Pat in the long shots. Pat explained, "It was driven from inside. The driver, however, wasn't a stunt driver. At first he went about five miles an hour, so slow I kept sliding off. Then we tried it at fifteen miles an hour and when we finally got it up to forty, I did it without falling off. When we were ready, Arthur Lubin, the director, said, 'Let's see how it's gonna look for the camera.' I got on the torpedo, Lubin yelled 'Action,' and away we went. One thing went wrong, however. Instead of just riding out of camera range and then slowing down until it stopped, the driver made a turn and flung me in the air.

"Lubin wanted to retake the shot, so I pounded on the shell and said to the guy, 'Keep the damn thing straight this time. No turns. Okay?' Okay. We started over and somehow I just knew this guy was going to make a left turn out of camera range, but instead he turned right and off I go again. I got up, brushed myself off, and went up to the assistant director and said, 'Either you get somebody else to drive that thing or get somebody else to ride it!" It was useless. Every time we did it, he either went left or right—never straight. They brought in a professional stuntman from Hollywood to take the driver's place. I explained it to the stuntman: drive it out of the picture, slow down, and just stop. The stuntman said, 'No problem.' Then he said to me, 'You know, Pat, if we can get this torpedo to go another five miles an hour faster I think it'll look great. Then we can go to the assistant and bargain for more money.'

"Well, at forty-five miles per hour the steel prop on the end (for visual effect only) was spinning up a storm and looked really authentic. God certainly must've been on my side because my nose couldn't have been more than one inch away from that twirling propeller. (In the film, Lou appears to be riding it backwards.) After he brought it to a stop, I got off the thing and said, 'Let's go back to forty miles an hour. I can do with less money.'"

Lou, meanwhile, was standing on the sidelines, doubled over in laughter.

Pat also doubled for Lou in all the acrobatic and stunt flying sequences. As Pat discovered, the pay scale was negotiable. "The assistant director comes over and says to Paul Mantz, 'We want you to go through the four hangars.' Mantz says okay. Of course, he thought they wanted us to *taxi* through the hangars. The assistant says, 'How much are you going to charge us for that?' Mantz says $200 per hanger. Now the assistant comes to me. 'How much do you want to go up in the plane?' I said $200. He said, 'Two hundred! Christ, Pat, I can't give you that much!' I said, 'How much are you giving the guy in front?' He said, *'But that's Paul Mantz!'* I said, 'I don't give a shit who it is; if I'm in the same plane and he's making $200, *I'm* gonna get $200!' [laughs] So now they explain that they want us to fly through the hangars. And I'm expecting Mantz to ask for a couple of hundred more dollars, but he didn't. Now, I have to be very honest. We flew through four hangars. But I don't remember anything after the first one—I passed out!"

Mantz's Stearman had to be specially outfitted for the belly landing stunt at a cost of a whopping $250. "The assistant director told me, 'When you get up there, Mantz will give you the signal, and then you pull this wire and this wheel will drop off, and pull that wire and the other wheel will drop off,'" Pat recalled. "The first wire was easy to pull, but when I looked over the side and saw that first wheel fall away, it was awful hard to pull the wire on the left hand side! [laughs] But he landed the plane as easy as I put this glass down on the table." A week later, Mantz submitted an invoice for repairs to his ship: $66.35 for damages to the landing gear tires; $90.00 to repair the propeller blade.

DELETIONS AND ADDITIONS

Blackie runs the "Hit the Umpire" concession at the carnival and installs Heathcliff as the umpire. When Heathcliff objects that he'll be hurt, Blackie explains that he'll control the mechanical batter to swing and hit the ball before it hits Heathcliff. All Heathcliff has to do is cue Blackie by saying, "Ready." In the omitted scenes, three girls take their turns and throw wildly, never coming close to Heathcliff. This suddenly makes him very brave, and he takes

BOTTOM LEFT: With Martha Raye in the "Go Ahead, Order Something" scene. BOTTOM: A cut sequence: Blackie attempts to perform a magic act only to have his tricks exposed by his bumbling assistant, Heathcliff. Since the boys' air corps uniforms closely resembled their bus driver uniforms in *Pardon My Sarong*, Gottlieb briefly considered salvaging this footage in the latter film. The routine finally turned up in one of their MGM releases, *Lost in a Harem* (1944).

up Blackie's spiel, "Come on, hit the umpire over the head! Knock his block off! Break his bean! C'mon, hit me right here!" Now three men step up and, with pinpoint accuracy, nail Heathcliff in the head three times. He staggers out in front of the mechanical batter. "Why didn't you make the guy hit the ball?" Heathcliff asks Blackie. "I was waiting for you to say, 'Ready,'" Blackie replies. Heathcliff protests, "I didn't have a *chance* to say 'Ready'!" On cue, Blackie pushes the button and the mechanical batter whacks Heathcliff in the back of the head. The film picks up here, with Heathcliff battling the mechanical man.

In another deleted scene, Heathcliff dresses up as a little boy and pretends to be Jinx's son to scare off his marriage-minded female fans.

The lovely ballad "I'll Remember April" was originally written for Carol Bruce in *Keep 'Em Flying.* But Alex Gottlieb and Milton Feld liked it so much, they had Dick Foran record it for *Ride 'Em Cowboy,* which was already in production. "The frustrating thing about 'I'll Remember April' was that it was written for *me,*" Carol explained. "I recorded it with Charlie Previn for the film, and it was never used. I guess it was a case of 'Cut here and use more Abbott and Costello.' So I wound up not the face on the cutting room floor but the song on the cutting room floor. That kind of broke my heart, because I loved that song. And then we tried it again for my ill-fated, last film, *Behind the Eight Ball* (1942)—God knows that title was apropos—and again it was deleted."

Each of the team's previous films had placed Costello in a gambling situation where at first he appeared inept but ultimately triumphed. *Flying's* game, a comic billiard match at the USO club, was dropped from the finished film. Heathcliff assures Blackie that he can beat Butch, the base champion, so Blackie bets $50 on his pal. Blackie begins to worry when Heathcliff selects the most warped cue stick, and Butch proceeds to sink every ball on the break. But Heathcliff replaces the chalk with soap, and Butch miscues on his second break. As Heathcliff draws back his cue, a player shooting at the next table inadvertently jabs him several times in the back of the head. Blackie snaps, "Stop stalling and shoot! Pick up that cue and get busy!" Butch also substitutes the soap for the chalk, and Heathcliff miscues, tearing a hole in the table. Now Blackie complains, "Listen, I've got $50 invested here, and I better get it back!" Heathcliff says, "Gimme a chance—I ain't warmed up yet!" Heathcliff is about to shoot when the cue stick of the player behind him hits his stick and sends the cue ball into the pack. It bounces off, catches Heathcliff in the head, and bounces back onto the table, scattering every ball into the pockets. Butch burns. On the next break, Heathcliff puts a topspin on the ball, and it travels around the table knocking each of the balls into a pocket.

Cut from the film was a wild sequence at a roller skating rink, where Martha Raye sang "We Oughta Dance" and Heathcliff wound up as the end man on a crack-the-whip line. Pat reprised many of the same stunts on ice skates in *Hit the Ice* (1943).

A second Carol Bruce number was deleted. After Linda confronts Jinx outside the base hospital, she sings "You Don't Know What Love Is." Carol sighed, "That's the song that I truly *adored.* I mean, it was my kind of torch song. Years later I did that song in cafe work. I had to get it out of my system someplace. [laughs] But it was very ironic and frustrating that those two songs were both written for me and never made it into the film."

Lubin was troubled by the rough cut he screened on October 17 and wrote a memo to Glenn Tryon. The director felt that the ending was far too long and suggested the sequence be recut. In the original, the parachute jump sequence was not part of the graduation exercises, but a separate exhibition that preceded them. The finale didn't begin until after Heathcliff and Blackie parachuted safely into the girls' arms. The sequence intercut between Linda singing, planes taking off, and parading cadets, and it didn't return to Heathcliff and Blackie until the end of the song, when Heathcliff is hauled skyward for the fadeout. "The audience will be halfway out of the theater before we get to Lou's laugh line," Lubin warned. And so the finished film was successfully recut to consolidate all three elements while maintaining the pace of the picture.

But it was rare for Lubin to get involved at all in cutting the film. "I no sooner finished an Abbott and Costello when I was pushed immediately into another one," he explained. "In

The World Premier for *Keep 'Em Flying* at the Fox Theater in Detroit.

fact, in those days, the director had no rights. I had so little time to even see the dailies, unless it was very late at night. I had nothing to do with the casting. The head of the music department selected the music. A director had no right to even see his picture cut until it was finished. You had no choice. Either take it, or go on suspension."

One slip-up wasn't caught in the re-edit. Watch the inserts of the ignition switch during Jim's solo flight. When Jinx instructs him to cut the engine, we see the ignition being turned *on*. When Jinx tells him to turn it on, he turns it *off*. Heathcliff has the same problem with his plane; he also starts it by turning the ignition off!

REVIEWS

Bud, Lou, and Carol Bruce were dispatched on an all-expenses paid promotional tour for *Keep 'Em Flying* that culminated with the film's world premiere in Detroit on November 19. Mayor Edward Jeffries proclaimed it "Keep 'Em Flying Day," and the festivities began with a rally at City Hall, followed by a parade and tours of production plants. That night the Mutual radio network broadcast the premiere from the lobby of the Fox Theater. Carol Bruce sang, and Bud and Lou performed "Who's On First?"

The tour moved on to other cities, including Chicago, Cleveland, New York, Washington, and Baltimore. "That's when it really got to be fun, when we went out on the promotional tour," Carol recalled, "because we spent more time together. Bud was a dear man, and Lou— all I had to do was look at him and I'd start to laugh. They played a lot of poker, and I had such a good time watching them. They allowed me to kind of be one of the guys, kibitzing. *That* was like a film unto itself."

The New York premiere on November 26 was particularly sweet for Carol. "Being a kid from Brooklyn, the New York premier was probably my second greatest thrill. I showed up in my white fox coat—which we didn't charge to Universal. That was my big glamour night as the young Hollywood star."

In an interview published at the time, Arthur Lubin said he was interested in watching audience reaction to an experiment in *Keep 'Em Flying*. He thought it was important that the team's films develop a dramatic as well as a comic side. "I think that Lou should have funny parts with a pathetic twist. That's the sort of thing that kept Chaplin going so long. They'll get tired of him eventually unless he offers more than comedy. There aren't that many gags. And Lou has that quality. He is an appealing little fellow. He can put pathos into a scene when he's allowed. This time he makes a serious speech for the first time, sort of a flag-waving speech. It's the first time we've let him be serious. The audiences seem to like it. Now we try to build up that side of his acting."

67

In spite of the experiment, *Keep 'Em Flying* adhered to the formula begun with *Buck Privates*. By now, however, that formula began to receive a critical backlash.

The New York Times: ". . . [C]halk up another mad antic for these two harum-scarum clowns, and give Universal credit for the third in its series of rowdy service films. But don't give too much credit to the producers for anything else. For 'Keep 'Em Flying' is not exactly a triumph in the field of comic art. . . . But whenever the starring gentlemen have the screen more or less to themselves, they push out from it enough hilarity to brighten the darker spots."

Time: "Little Lou Costello, fat and funny, is a great clown. Bud Abbott, skinny and sour, is a first-rate straight man. On their own, the two can be counted on to supply plenty of low-comedy guffaws. But greedy Universal has almost squeezed the last laugh out of them before their first cinema year's end."

Variety: " 'Keep 'Em Flying' is the fourth release starring A&C within a 10-month stretch. It indicates the boys are appearing too often with their burleycue type of roustabout comedy to remain in public popularity for any length of time, unless new material is provided for their screen appearances. Too many of the numerous laugh routines displayed here are only slight variations of previous material, with resultant loss of audience reaction."

New York Morning Telegraph: "The fat little clown is one of the funniest comics that ever lived, and the wonder is that Universal insists on confining him to slapstick and surrounding him with unfunny formula plots and supporting players who could be improved on by throwing a stone in any direction and placing what it hits before the camera.

"It may be treason, yet I suggest that Costello's logical partner and foil, after seeing her work with him in this film, is not Abbott but Miss Martha Raye. . . . [S]ome of his sequences with Miss Raye are the funniest since Chaplin was at his best.

Hollywood Reporter: "A lot of topnotch flying features the show, the thrill highlight an air rescue of a parachutist caught foul of his plane. And, of course, it is a riot when Abbott and Costello take off in a craft they do not know how to pilot. Another physical gag has Costello riding a torpedo on wheels. The boys are adept at milking every situation dry of laughs, and Lubin is again to be congratulated for not prolonging a scene after its topper is delivered. He switches attention instantly, yet this is a technique demanding a surrounding plot worthy of attention."

POSTSCRIPT

While *Flying* was in production, Bud and Lou began their second season as regulars on the Chase and Sanborn program with Edgar Bergen and Charlie McCarthy. On October 13, 1941, the team presented a radio adaptation of *Buck Privates* on Lux Radio Theater.

Although it was released before *Ride 'Em Cowboy, Keep 'Em Flying* was the last Abbott and Costello film Arthur Lubin directed. "I asked to be released after the fifth picture because they came on the set late, they didn't know their lines, and I think they were beginning to get tired of one another. They were bored. And for the first time they were beginning to complain about the scripts. But it was five fabulous pictures with those boys. They were very good for me. They gave me a reputation. I learned everything about timing from them. And I think I was very good for them, in this respect: not in their routines, but in trying to give them some class. Whenever they got crude or rude, I'd try to soften it. And I tried in all my set-ups to keep a balance of refinement against the earthiness of some of their routines."

However he did it, the Lubin touch was perfect for Abbott and Costello. None of the team's subsequent films have the happy vitality of these initial five. Which is all the more remarkable considering they were shot over a grueling period of just eleven months. Very few of the directors that followed would have the same rapport with the team. Lubin remained good friends with them, and continued to see them often. Universal recruited other B-picture directors on the lot like Erle C. Kenton, Charles Lamont, and Jean Yarbrough to take over the series.

RIDE 'EM COWBOY

SYNOPSIS

Bronco Bob Mitchell is the author of best-selling western novels and songs, yet according to a newspaper exposé he has never been west of the Hudson River. To bolster his flagging image, Bob makes an appearance at a Long Island charity rodeo. When a steer escapes, Bob panics and is thrown from his horse. One of the cowgirls, Anne Shaw, quickly bulldogs the steer and saves Bob's life. But she is injured and must forgo the competition and a chance to win the $10,000 prize. Bob is grateful, but Anne is angry and disillusioned. She returns to her father's dude ranch in Arizona, followed by Bob, who is eager to make amends and learn how to be a real cowboy.

Duke and Willoughby are two inept vendors at the rodeo. Hiding from their boss, they accidentally stow away in a cattle car and find themselves on the same westbound train as Anne and Bob. Soon after arriving in Gower Gulch, Willoughby accidentally shoots an arrow through the tepee of a plump Indian maiden, which she takes as a proposal of marriage. Willoughby and Duke flee to the ranch, where they are given jobs by the foreman, Alabam, but are still menaced by the angry Indians. Anne secretly teaches Bob how to ride and rope. Alabam has included Bob on the Lazy S team for the state rodeo championships. But a local gambler, Ace Henderson, has bet against the Lazy S, and to ensure his bet he kidnaps Bob and Alabam. Willoughby and Duke, fleeing the Indians once more, come to the rescue, and deliver Bob to the rodeo in the nick of time. Bob manages to stay on a bucking bronco long enough to win the championship for the ranch.

BACKGROUND

Ride 'Em Cowboy was originally intended to be Abbott and Costello's third film, following *Buck Privates* and *Hold That Ghost*, but the team's other two service comedies intervened. Its production was pushed back to accommodate *In the Navy,* and its release was held up in favor of *Keep 'Em Flying*. By the time it was released in February 1942, Bud and Lou had been voted the number-three box office attractions of 1941 by exhibitors. *Look* magazine offered three explanations why Abbott and Costello were so popular: "(1) Their comedy is psychologically fundamental. Almost everybody can understand it, and almost nobody can resist laughing at it. (2) Abbott and Costello are new to the younger group of moviegoers. They are a refreshing change from old familiar comics. (3) Their comedy is clean."

THE SCRIPT

Robert Lees and Fred Rinaldo began working on a treatment for *Ride 'Em Cowboy* late in February as production on *Hold That Ghost* drew to a close. In their scenario, Costello is a

Earliest Draft:
February 26, 1941

Production Start:
June 30, 1941

Production End:
August 9, 1941

Copyright Date:
December 4, 1941

Released:
February 20, 1942

Running Time:
86 minutes

Reissued: May 30, 1949
with *Keep 'Em Flying*
and 1954 with *Who
Done It?*

Directed By: Arthur Lubin

Produced By:
Alex Gottlieb

Screenplay By:
True Boardman,
John Grant

Adapted By:
Harold Shumate

Original Story By:
Edmund L. Hartmann

Director of Photography:
John W. Boyle ASC

Art Director:
Jack Otterson

Associate:
Ralph M. DeLacy

Film Editor: Philip Cahn

Sound Supervisor:
Bernard B. Brown

Technician:
Hal Bumbaugh

Gowns: Vera West

Set Decoration:
R. A. Gausman

Assistant Director:
Gil Valle

Dialogue Director:
Joan Hathaway

clever New York newsboy who wins an all-expense-paid vacation at a dude ranch and takes his supervisor, Abbott, along.

Gottlieb and Feld liked some of the situations Lees and Rinaldo created, particularly the business of Willoughby's arrow piercing Moonbeam's tent, roping a bucking bronco, and driving a jalopy in a wild chase. But they felt that the story wasn't right. The project was reassigned to Edmund Hartmann, and it is his treatment, more or less, that became the final film. Hartmann's script centered on Jim Hill, a cowboy movie star who'd never been on a real horse. When Harold Shumate adapted the story, he turned Jim into Bronco Bob Mitchell. True Boardman and John Grant completed the final screenplay on June 27.

The Breen Office had a considerable effect on the comedy scenes in *Ride 'Em Cowboy,* causing one sequence at the Indian village to be deleted, and the classic "Crazy House" sketch to be muddled unforgivably (see pages 72–73). In another scene, Willoughby and Duke, anxious to use the pool, run to the dressing rooms to change into their swimsuits. Willoughby opens the door marked "Men" and a woman's scream is heard. Willoughby gulps, "Pardon me, mister!" "There certainly must be no suggestion," Breen wrote, "either that there's a woman in the men's dressing room, or that this is a 'pansy' gag." The bit never made it into the film, and an attempt to put it in *Rio Rita* failed as well. Breen was also quite concerned with how the animals would be treated during production and directed the producers to have a representative of the American Humane Society supervise those scenes.

THE CAST

For Dick Foran (1910–1979), the part was almost typecasting. A graduate of Princeton, Foran starred as a singing cowboy in a series of low budget westerns at Warner Bros. in the mid-1930s. In 1941 he continued the tradition at Universal in a serial, *Riders of Death Valley.*

Anne Gwynne (b. 1918) seemed to divide her time at Universal between thrillers such as *House of Frankenstein* and westerns such as *Frontier Badmen.* Before *Ride 'Em Cowboy,* she appeared in the Johnny Mack Brown westerns *Oklahoma Frontier* (1939) and *Bad Man from Red Butte* (1940). "I think Arthur Lubin wanted Shirley Ross for *Ride 'Em Cowboy,*" Anne recalled, "but they thought that she was too old. I heard this years afterward. He had to take me because I was under contract. But we got along fine. Arthur was a very good director, actually. When I was there I never dreamed he had someone else in mind for the part; fortunately I didn't know it and it didn't bother me." Anne recalled preparing for her role. "I was tutored by Sam Garrett to do the trick roping, but that was cut out of the picture. [Garrett was seven-time winner of the world's roping championship and longtime pal of Will Rogers.] They gave me a pretty Palomino and I rode him on the studio ranch for three weeks to get comfortable. I did a lot more riding in *Frontier Badmen.*"

Johnny Mack Brown (1904–1974) was an All-American halfback and a Rose Bowl hero in 1926, but turned down professional football offers for Hollywood. He was a star at MGM in the late 1920s, and played opposite Greta Garbo, Joan Crawford, Marion Davies, Norma Shearer, Mary Pickford, and Mae West. In 1930 he made *Billy the Kid,* and became a perennial western film hero.

Ella Fitzgerald (b. 1918) made her screen debut in *Ride 'Em Cowboy.* Ella was born in Newport News, Virginia, but reared in Harlem by her mother. She was discovered on the amateur circuit by Chick Webb, who signed her to sing with his band. Ella took over the orchestra when Webb died. She co-wrote "A Tisket, A Tasket," which was a number one hit in 1938. But a second Fitzgerald song, "Cow-Cow Boogie," was deleted from the finished film. It was a hit for Ella in 1944.

Curiously, a newspaper clipping dated May 7 reported that the Andrews Sisters were scheduled for *Ride 'Em Cowboy.* Patty Andrews couldn't recall anything about it, and has no explanation why the trio didn't make more films with Bud and Lou. The sisters did move on to their own series at Universal, which included *Private Buckaroo* (1942) and *How's About It?* (1943). The Merry Macs, regulars on the Fred Allen program, inherited the singing chores.

THE PRODUCTION

Two dude ranches in Southern California—the B-Bar A near Newhall and Rancho Chihuahua in Solemint Canyon—were among the location sites Lubin used. He explained, "The studio didn't want to spend any money building sets, so we went on location to the canyon."

Anne Gwynne recalled, "We never stayed overnight on location. They would take a busload out early in the morning; from here to Newhall is only about a forty-five-minute or an hour trip. And then we'd come back in the evening. The interiors were done at the studio."

One of Anne's first scenes was bulldogging the escaped steer at the rodeo. "The only thing that was a little frightening for me was when I had to take the horns of the bull and I was lifted off the ground. We did that about seven o'clock one night. I did the close-ups of this scene and the bull lifted me up about four feet from the ground. They were going to take the next shot and the bull started huffing and scraping his hoof. I told the assistant director, Gil Valle, 'Gil, he looks mad!' And Gil said, 'You are so right—we're not going to do it.' They had saved that for the last scene of the day, and I was tired and the bull was tired and the whole crew was tired. So they got a medium shot and a close-up of me, but a double did the long shot."

Anne remembers Bud and Lou with great fondness. "Universal was like a little town—everyone knew one another. I had seen Bud and Lou many times when they were making their other pictures. I'd even take my grandmother to see them. So I knew them, but I didn't *know* them. I never had a problem working with them because they were real professionals, and they were so natural and so funny—especially Lou—you felt right at home with them. These two fellows were old burlesque boys; they knew the ropes. They were so fresh and delightful and funny. They weren't burned out and they *loved* doing what they were doing. Every time somebody laughed, they were in ecstasy. There was a genuineness about them. If they had to do a scene three or four times, there was never any arguing or getting uptight. I don't recall them playing cards much; no swearing; no gambling. They could have done it when I wasn't there. [laughs] Even when I saw them working on other pictures, they were delightful."

One of the best songs to ever come out of an Abbott and Costello film was "I'll Remember April." The ballad was originally intended for *Keep 'Em Flying,* which was then in preproduction. Songwriters Don Raye and Gene de Paul didn't know Alex Gottlieb made the switch until they saw the preview:

"One of the scenes involved a midnight horseback ride," de Paul explained, "and it opened with a beautiful long shot of the horses on a winding trail. Dick Foran and Anne Gwynne were riding at the back of the pack. (Remember, this takes place at midnight.) Dick proposes

BOTTOM LEFT: With Anne Gwynne on location in Solemint Canyon. BOTTOM: Ella Fitzgerald's deleted song, "Cow-Cow Boogie."

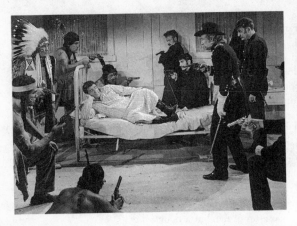

TOP: "Crazy House" TOP RIGHT: Part of a sequence deleted from the "Poker Game."

to Anne that they go off on their own. She gets his point and they turn off and ride to a secluded spot. They dismount and Anne sits down on a log very conveniently placed there by the prop department. Dick, without taking off his cowboy hat, puts his boot on the log and begins to sing. The opening words of 'I'll Remember April' are: 'This lovely day will lengthen into evening.' Don and I nearly fell out of our chairs. It's midnight and here he is singing about this lovely day. We went to Alex Gottlieb and asked him if he was trying to crucify us. His response was, 'Well, we thought it was so beautiful we had to use it in this scene.'"

BUD AND LOU'S SCENES

A dude ranch was a perfect setting for Bud and Lou to perform the "Heard of Cows" routine that was cut from *Hold That Ghost*. "Hey," says Willoughby, "look at that bunch of cows!" "Not 'bunch'—herd," corrects Duke. "Heard what?" asks Willoughby. "Herd of cows," says Duke. "Certainly I heard of cows! Whaddaya think I am, a dummy?" Sure, it's ancient and obvious. But Abbott and Costello make you laugh in spite of yourself. Their delivery is flawless. Costello has more memorable moments attempting to milk a cow. Duke instructs him to put the bucket under the cow's udder. "The cow's udder what?" he wonders.

The boys also offer a weak variation on the "Moving Candle" routine from *Hold That Ghost*. Practical jokers place a dummy of Jake Rainwater in Willoughby's cabin. Willoughby is terrified until Duke proves to him that it's only wood. But the real Jake exchanges places with the dummy and comes to life only when Duke leaves the room.

One of the greatest burlesque sketches of all was "Crazy House." Its original premise was that an applicant for a job in a mental institution is mistaken for one of the patients. Since he encounters a bewildering array of lunatics, virtually any old gag could be inserted in the sketch and not appear incongruous. When Abbott and Costello performed the sketch in *Streets of Paris*, Lou was not a new employee at an asylum, but simply someone who checked into what he thought was a rest home for some peace and quiet. The uproarious scene stopped the show every night at the Broadhurst Theater.

The cinematic translation of "Crazy House," however, isn't effective. To give some rationale for the lunacy, it was decided to turn the sketch into a dream. Why not—it had worked for *In the Navy*. But two things make the routine funny—first, the idea that this is really happening, and second, that the stream of intruders is relentless. The intercuts of Willoughby tossing and turning, as if this is all a nightmare, work directly against these points. The routine also suffers from several omissions. Early on, when Willoughby requests a room, Duke checks to see if one is available. He knocks on the door of the stable and asks, "Fellas, do you mind giving up this room for the night?" He steps aside and we cut to Willoughby, watching *something* pass by, we're never shown what. In the original script, ten head of cattle poured out of the little room, followed by four whooping Indians on horseback! In another cut bit, Duke warns Willoughby about another patient, General Custer. "He still thinks he's chasing Indians," Duke explains. "Be very careful around him. The very word 'Indian' arouses him to a fury!" That would have set up the recurring outbursts of the general, which, in the final film, seem to be irrational rather than cued. The Breen Office censors nixed two other segments: "The entire sequence from where Ruby enters like an Indian carrying a can marked 'red paint,' as well as the following gag about 'Would you like to have your palm read?' and the business of Moonbeam sprinkling Willoughby while he is lying there in his nightgown, is unacceptable on account of its vulgar suggestiveness," they decreed. The most glaring omission, for burlesque afficionados, is the routine's blackout. An Indian maiden enters and picks imaginary apples off an invisible tree. Intrigued, Willoughby shakes the phantom tree and is promptly conked on the head by a bushel of real apples.

The team later presented the sketch to better advantage in an episode of their television series and on a live broadcast of the *Colgate Comedy Hour*.

If "Crazy House" is a disappointment, the team's first elaborate movie chase makes up for it. It proved such a hit with audiences that chases were added to the formula of burlesque routines and boogie-woogie in their future films. The script includes two gags that weren't used. In one, the boys' jalopy splits in two to avoid a telegraph pole, then rejoins. In another, Willoughby falls out of the car, tumbles down a hill, and lands back in the driver's seat as if nothing happened. Of course, all of this was shot with doubles, then Bud and Lou matched scenes on the process stage, adding dialogue. They were visited during one late session by a reporter from *Collier's:*

It was ten o'clock at night and the boys were still whooping it up on Stage Eight at Universal. They had been there since six in the morning and still had four scenes to shoot but the gags were flying fast. Another Abbott & Costello comedy, this one *Ride 'Em Cowboy,* and it would be like all the others—funny and full of old memories.

"All right boys, let's go!" yells Arthur Lubin, the director.

"What's this one about?" asks Abbott.

"Haven't you read the script?" demands Lubin.

"To hell with the script," squeaks Costello. "What's it about?"

"You're in a jalopy and the Indians are chasing you. You lose your hat."

They get set in the car and stagehands begin jiggling the old crate to give the illusion of a wild ride. Costello nods at one of the stagehands and speaks out of the corner of his mouth to Abbott.

"Fame. Think of going home and telling the kids, 'I jiggle the car for Costello and Abbott.' "

"*Abbott* and Costello," Abbott corrects him sternly.

"An error in printin'," says Costello.

"Never mind. You lose your hat. Don't forget that."

"I lose my hat," admits Costello, getting adjusted in the seat. "Why?"

"Just because you're dumb."

"Smart guys don't lose hats?"

"No."

"You're a smart guy?"

"Yes."

"So you're expectin' me to knock your hat off?"

"Yes. Why don't you?"—threateningly.

"I'm not so dumb."

"Come on, boys; let's go," Lubin says easily.

"He wants me to knock his hat off," says Costello, nodding at Abbott.

"I do not."

"You said you was expectin' it."

"I said you were dumb."

"That's different," says Costello, relieved.

"Alright, boys; we're turning," says Lubin. "Just the one line . . . 'Where's my hat?' "

They bounced up and down on the seat of the jalopy, the wind machine blows furiously, the Indians appear on another projection screen behind them and gallop madly in pursuit. Lou grasps the wheel with desperation and tries to hold his hat. He loses it. The dialogue starts. Instead of one line, the loss of the hat becomes an epic event.

"Where's my hat? Who stole my hat? Who's got that hat? Gimme the hat!" squeaks Costello endlessly, grabbing at the wheel, grabbing for his hat.

Abbott is just as steadily howling:

"What hat? Where'd you lose it? I ain't got no hat! What hat?"

Lubin looks on complacently. In the early days of his association with the wacks, he learned never to yell "Cut," never to worry about the script, never to worry about the dialogue, never to worry about the picture.

In the excitement, Costello loses control of the wheel and Abbott grabs it. Costello grabs it right back, yelling:

"Who the hell's drivin' this crib!"

That breaks it up.

"The movies," Abbott says breathlessly. "Just like a blood transfusion in reverse. They draw it out of you in quarts."

During the chase, a newspaper flies into Willoughby's face. Before he discards it, he notices, "Hey, DiMaggio got another hit!," referring to the Yankee Clipper's incredible fifty-six game hitting streak during that summer. DiMaggio and Costello were good friends. In fact, DiMaggio gave Lou the bat he used when he set the record.

Pat Costello, of course, doubled Lou for the dangerous stunts, including the bronco-busting scene. Pat recalled, "Lou said, 'Pat, even I wouldn't be afraid to ride this horse.' So I got on it, and he started bucking and jumping all over the place like he was crazy. Off I went. I said, 'Lou, what the hell are they doing to this horse?' He said, 'Nothin', Pat.' Well, they get me back on again and they get an idea to tie my feet underneath the horse and tie my belt to the saddle horn. I was on and off that horse for about two hours, and, Oh Jesus, I want to tell you, I had the sorest back and sorest butt of anybody around!"

DELETIONS AND ADDITIONS

In the prelude to the poker game, Willoughby confesses that he's a novice when it comes to playing cards. "Is this anything like dice?" he asks hopefully, referring to that classic routine from *Buck Privates*. According to the script, the poker game routine is indeed very much like the "Dice Game," although very little of it made it into the finished film.

"How many cards?" Duke asks Willoughby. "How many do I want?" wonders Willoughby. Duke surveys his hand and sees Willoughby is holding four aces and a deuce. "Aces are no good," Duke explains. "Throw 'em away." Willoughby complies, and Duke deals him another four cards. "Hey," Willoughby inquires, "what do you call it when all my cards are one color?" "A misdeal," snaps Duke. Everyone at the table tosses in their cards. "Who wins?" Willoughby inquires. "I do. I dealt, didn't I?" says Duke, raking in the pot. Willoughby understands, "Oh, when there's a misdeal, the dealer gets the money." "Naturally," affirms Duke, who's already dealing another hand. Willoughby picks up his cards, then disgustedly tosses four of them away, complaining, "I got those darn aces again!" He draws three cards, and ends up holding four deuces. Duke has a pair of eights. Willoughby starts to gather the pot, but Duke stops him, explaining that two eights beat four deuces because two eights are sixteen, and four twos are only eight. "When am I gonna deal?" Willoughby grouses. "You can't deal until you win," Duke explains. "And I can't win until I deal," cracks Willoughby. After another hand, Duke lets him deal, and Willoughby draws four kings. He is about to pull in the pot when the train lurches and two additional cards get mixed into his hand. Duke claims a misdeal, but Willoughby triumphs: "You said misdeal wins—haha!"

The boys' first meeting with the shrewd Jake Rainwater contained a quintessential Abbott and Costello routine that was cut out of the picture:

Jake: How.
Duke: How. (*To Willoughby:*) Tell the man 'How.'
Willoughby: I don't know how.
Duke: 'How' is the Indians' salutation.
Willoughby: How do I know? I never met the guy before.
Duke: Stop getting silly and greet the man.
Willoughby: How?
Duke: That's right.
Willoughby: What's right?
Duke: 'How!'
Willoughby: Are you asking me or telling me?
Duke: Telling you what?
Willoughby: How.
Duke: That's perfect.
Willoughby: What's perfect? I don't even know what I'm talkin' about!

A long sequence at the Indian village was also cut by the Breen Office because of its mildly risque ending. The scene begins at the ranch barbecue, where Duke and Willoughby, feeding a baby pig, are ambushed by Indians. In the finished film, the Indians appear only to threaten the boys. But in the script, they actually carry Willoughby and Duke off to the Indian village, where poor Willoughby is tied to a post to be burned at the stake. Thinking fast, Duke makes the piglet a peace offering to Moonbeam. He asks her to call off the wedding and save his pal. Moonbeam says she has to consult her grandfather, Jake. She places the pig in a basket inside her tepee, then heads over to where Jake is about to ignite Willoughby. Moonbeam asks Jake to spare him because something has happened to soften her heart. As she leads Jake to her tepee, Duke whispers to Willoughby that he's fixed everything and unties him. The little pig, meanwhile, has run off, and a squaw has placed a baby in the empty basket. Moonbeam directs Jake to look inside her tepee. Jake—and only Jake—peers in and sees the infant. He is startled. "When you get married?" he asks. "Why grandfather," Moonbeam gasps, "I'm not married!" "Then where you get *that?*" Jake demands, pointing at the tepee. "I gave it to her," pipes up Willoughby. Jake gives out a war whoop, and the tribe chases after the boys. They barely make it back to the barbecue, where the film resumes with Duke's line, "That was a close one!"

Willoughby and Duke are captured by Indians in a deleted scene.

REVIEWS

New York Journal American: "It's Abbott and Costello at the Criterion this week, which means that the theater is jammed and that the audience howls whenever the two are within camera range.... But, as was the case in their previous offerings, the film sags each time the two step aside for routine story complications ..."

Baltimore Evening Sun: "Say what you will about the mustiness of their material, Abbott and Costello are far from being slouches in peddling it for more than it's worth. The overripe age of a gag never gives them pause, and they will repeat and illustrate it, if an illustration is deemed necessary, with all the enthusiasm of pioneers uncovering a nugget of new and authentic wit. This enthusiasm for the relics of humor is contagious; so contagious, indeed, that it appears, heaven forfend, they might go on forever."

New York Morning Telegraph: "For my part, the familiar A. and C. antics are by far the best moments of the film—as they should be. Such as the poker game ... the wild bronc busting sequence ... the business with the Indians.... And, also, the inevitable dream sequence (all these Abbott and Costello pictures seem to have dream sequences these days), which looks as if it came straight from the boys' old burlesque routine, but, in the hands of Lou Costello, still manages to make you hold your sides."

New York Daily News: "I know that devotion to comedians is a purely personal matter. You either like 'em, or you don't. But, take it from one who wouldn't go out of her way to see this particular team in action, they are funny; much funnier, I think, than they were in the preceding 'Keep 'Em Flying.' It's Costello, the plump, shy, coy fellow, who gets the laughs as he does everything backward on the ranch.... Of course, Bud Abbott deserves credit for feeding the gags to his partner."

The New York Times was concerned enough to offer some advice to the boys in a separate editorial on March 8, 1942: "Bud Abbott and Lou Costello have been seen in enough pictures now to give every one an opportunity to decide just how funny they are. For a fact which is becoming more apparent is that they alter but hardly change their routines, and if you like them in one picture you will like them for the same reasons in the next.... But a further fact—which is now growing painful—is that a picture must have more than Bud and Lou to keep it continually entertaining. And 'Ride 'Em Cowboy' hasn't. The Merry Macs, a bevy of girls and Dick Foran are poor company when the boys are off the screen. Bud and Lou—particularly Lou—are genial comics. But even they can't live long in vacuums."

The *Hollywood Reporter* concurred: "It might be well for Universal and particularly associate producer Alex Gottlieb to experiment with a picture for Abbott and Costello that is about Abbott and Costello. There was once another high-ranking team of film comics named Laurel and Hardy whose producer wore thin their welcome with features that were never about them."

POSTSCRIPT

The admonitions of the critics notwithstanding, Universal's bank account said that *Ride 'Em Cowboy* and the Abbott and Costello formula were doing just fine, thank you: *Cowboy* was the eighth biggest grossing film of 1942.

Before Bud and Lou completed the film, Universal took up two years' option in place of one on the boys' contract. According to *Variety,* "Studio spokesmen said the two-year option, taken up a year in advance on the term, was to assure A&C's security, to give them a sense of confidence in the company, and to enable them to make contracts for homes and other comforts in line with their position in the industry as a matter of company policy." The boys also received a $25,000 bonus for *Buck Privates* and *In the Navy.* (*Hold That Ghost* hadn't been released yet.)

Bud and Lou were raking it in from all sides. They renewed their contract to appear on the Edgar Bergen and Charlie McCarthy program, and they signed a deal to perform some of their jokes on an RCA Victor recording called, "Laugh, Laugh, Laugh."

RIO RITA

SYNOPSIS

Rita Winslow, owner of the Hotel Vista del Rio, awaits the arrival of her childhood sweetheart, Ricardo Montera, now a popular radio star. Also looking forward to his arrival are Maurice, Jake, Trask, and Gus—Nazi agents who plan to use Montera's national radio broadcast to transmit coded messages to their fellow saboteurs. When Montera arrives, he carries two stowaways in the rumble seat of his car, Doc and Wishy. Half-starved, the boys steal a basket of apples from the hotel manager's desk, but the apples turn out to be miniature radios, to be distributed to other foreign agents for the broadcast.

Rita hires Doc and Wishy as house detectives, and they soon discover that the place is crawling with spies. They recover the Nazi's codebook and hand it over to Ricardo. Doc and Wishy are captured, tied up, and left in a room with a time bomb. Wishy, however, manages to slip the bomb into Jake's pocket. Craindall and Trask force Ricardo and Rita to begin their broadcast, but Ricardo fights them off until the spies hear the Texas Rangers approaching. Wishy has fooled them with a parade of donkeys carrying blaring radios. As the spies attempt to escape by car, the time bomb in Jake's pocket explodes.

BACKGROUND

The phenomenal success of *Buck Privates* and *In the Navy* embittered MGM's Louis B. Mayer, who had the team all but signed for *Ziegfeld Girl* back in 1940. Eddie Sherman explained, "Early in our relationship with Universal we found that there was a lot of ill feeling between Metro and them, particularly after the first two pictures came out and were such smashes. It's possible that Abe Lastfogel at William Morris may have promised Abbott and Costello to Louis B. Mayer, but couldn't deliver them. So Universal, not to have any trouble with Metro, which was the big power in Hollywood, loaned them Abbott and Costello for one picture a year. The loan-out deal was based on their getting double the salary that they were getting at Universal, but no percentages. MGM wasn't giving anybody any percentages."

According to the contract, signed September 16, 1941, Universal agreed to loan Abbott and Costello to MGM on a year-by-year basis. For the first year, MGM would pay Bud and Lou $70,000 and Universal $70,000.

THE SCRIPT

Rio Rita was originally a Broadway musical produced by Flo Ziegfeld in 1927. Comedians Bert Wheeler and Robert Woolsey teamed up during the show, and reprised their supporting roles in RKO's 1929 film version. The film, virtually a documentation of the two-act stage play, originally ran two hours and twenty minutes, with the second half in Technicolor.

Earliest Draft:
September 22, 1941

Production Start:
November 10, 1941

Production End:
January 14, 1942

Copyright Date:
March 24, 1942

Released: March 11, 1942

Running Time:
91 minutes

Directed By:
S. Sylvan Simon

Produced By:
Pandro S. Berman

Screenplay By:
Richard Connell and
Gladys Lehman

Special Material for
Abbott and Costello By:
John Grant

Musical Direction:
Herbert Stothart

"Rio Rita," "The
Ranger's Song" By:
Harry Tierney and
Joseph McCarthy

"Long Before You Came
Along" By: Harold Arlen
and E. Y. Harburg

Vocals and Orchestrations
By: Murray Cutter, Leo
Arnaud, Paul Marquardt

Director of Photography:
George Folsey ASC

Recording Director:
Douglas Schearer

Art Director:
Cedric Gibbons

Associate: Eddie Imazu

Set Decorations:
Edwin B. Willis

Special Effects:
Warren Newcombe

Gowns By: Kalloch

Men's Wardrobe By:
Gile Steele

Film Editor: Ben Lewis

MGM bought the property and updated it for Abbott and Costello. Practically nothing remains of the original story. Screenwriters Gladys Lehman and Richard Connell substituted Nazi spies for Mexican bandits, and only two of the original eighteen songs—"Rio Rita" and "The Ranger's Song"—were retained. One comedy scene survived: Costello, after drinking pulque, imagines he sees a girl taking off her clothes. Abbott grabs the bottle shouting, "Give me a drink of that!"

Rio Rita also had the largest file of Breen Office correspondence of any of the team's pictures we examined. The Production Code's Latin American expert, Addison Durland, successfully lobbied to have the locale shifted from Mexico to Texas, since some Latin American countries "might react poorly to the film's depiction of Nazi activity in South America." (We wonder how Texans felt about it.) Durland objected to the disparaging depiction of Mexican peasants in Kathryn Grayson's opening musical number, "Most Unusual Day," so the sequence was replaced by Bud and Lou's "Pike's Peke" routine. Durland also cited Ricardo's quirky accent. "The excessive use of broken English invariably used by Latin American characters in American motion pictures has been the cause of much resentment in Latin America. May we suggest that Ricardo speak fluent English with, of course, a Mexican accent?"

As for Bud and Lou's scenes, Durland challenged the pulque episode. "When Abbott and Costello drink it, they reach the heights of delirium tremens and begin to see owls, nude women, etc. In real life, not even opium or marijuana can produce such effects," Durland protested. One exchange was eliminated in the scene where Lucette mistakes Wishy for the laundry boy: Lucette asks, "Do you work by hand or by machine?" Wishy looks into the camera and cracks, "Is she kiddin'?"

THE CAST

Kathryn Grayson (b. 1922) made her screen debut in *Andy Hardy's Private Secretary* (1941), then followed up with *The Vanishing Virginian* (1942) before being assigned to *Rio Rita*. At the time, Kathryn had just married John Shelton, who later appeared with the team in *The Time of Their Lives* (1946). Kathryn later went on to memorable performances in *Show Boat* (1951) and *Kiss Me Kate* (1953).

John Carroll (1905–1979) had come off two excellent musicals, *Sunny* and *Lady Be Good*. Earlier in 1941, he appeared with Carol Bruce in *This Woman Is Mine*.

Tom Conway (1904–1967), brother of George Sanders, had a busy year in 1942. He appeared in *Mr. and Mrs. North*, *Grand Central Murder*, and *Cat People*, and began his recurring role as The Falcon in *The Falcon's Brother*.

Eros Volusia (1913–?) was making her film debut in *Rio Rita*. Born in Rio de Janeiro, Volusia rehearsed her routines with Vincente Minnelli, who was apprenticing at MGM at the time. Her dance was recut after the Production Code Administration objected to the "bumps." (Volusia's dance was eliminated entirely when *Rio Rita* played in India in 1953.)

The cast also includes Lou's future brother-in-law, Joe Kirk (1904–1975). Kirk, best known as Mr. Bacciagalupe on the team's classic television series, had bit parts in most of the features.

THE PRODUCTION

Reportedly, the budgets on the MGM films were triple those at Universal, which would put *Rio Rita's* anywhere from $600,000 to $900,000. The studio assigned the project to the distinguished Pandro S. Berman (b. 1905), who had produced the Astaire and Rogers hits, as well as *Stage Door*, *Gunga Din* and *The Hunchback of Notre Dame* at RKO. Joining Metro in 1940, Berman produced *Ziegfeld Girl* and *Love Crazy* before *Rio Rita*.

Berman selected S. Sylvan Simon (1910–1951) to direct. Simon had recently directed the Red Skelton comedy *Whistling in the Dark*, and would later do its two sequels, as well as *The Fuller Brush Man*. In an interview published in the film's pressbook, Simon talked about working with Bud and Lou: "You don't have rules with them. You just have two cameras shooting from different angles. The director just has a seat on the aisle—and a handkerchief ready to stuff in his mouth. Some day a director is going to shoot A&C in rehearsals without their knowledge. If it can't be used on the screen, it'll be great stuff for private showings—like Red Skelton's screen test. They're still showing that to visitors on the lot as a special treat.

"It's always impossible to guess what they'll do next. Sometimes they follow the script, but they're just as likely to throw in their own stuff. More so, in fact. They may do something in a rehearsal that's funny enough, but when we're shooting they'll elaborate on it unexpectedly. I've discovered this—making a picture with them is like being in the audience at a theater. You can never anticipate what they're going to do or say."

One of the most influential cinematographers in the industry, George Folsey, had the difficult task of keeping the boys in frame. "You might say that every take was a double take," Folsey is quoted in the pressbook. "We discovered early in the picture that with one camera and one set of lights focused on either Abbott or Costello, we'd be likely to lose something from the other. So we doubled up on them. As a result, neither was ever out of range of a camera and a microphone at any time. We still had our troubles, but they were laughing difficulties. The crew had to learn to restrain itself. Once, I fell off my camera seat. That meant a retake. Simon finally solved his problem by stuffing a handkerchief in his mouth."

BUD AND LOU'S SCENES

Bud and Lou's pet shop scene was added after the picture was completed. It accomplished two things for the producers: it established the locale as Texas, and replaced a potentially offensive musical sequence with Mexican peasants. Doc receives a call from a Mrs. Pike, who wants someone to pick up her dog, which happens to be a Pekingese. "Wishy, go over and get a Peke at Mrs. Pike's," he says. "Why can't I take a good look?" Wishy asks.

On December 22, a reporter from United Press International visited the set when the boys were shooting what was originally their first appearance in the film:

> Messrs. A&C this afternoon on Stage Eight woke up from a nap they were supposed to have been taking in an automobile in which they hitched a ride and found themselves marooned in the car atop one of those hydraulic lifts that filling stations use for greasing jobs.
>
> The floor beneath was spread plentifully with thick mattresses in case they tumbled off, and they wrestled on the rear deck and teetered on the hood, while the car started to spin atop its steel pillar. As the car went faster and faster, like a merry-go-round, Costello was supposed to fall off. He was ready to do it, but director S. Sylvan Simon said not on his life would he do any falling. A double would fill in for him. "A fine thing," moaned Costello. "A little drop of maybe eight feet and you won't let me do it. Why, not many years ago I fell off the top of the administration building and nobody cared whether I broke my neck or not." Simon explained that Metro's interest in Costello remained strictly business. Let him break an ankle, the picture suspends, and the loss mounts to thousands of dollars. The double took the fall.

Later, a *New York Times* reporter dropped by while Lou was shooting scenes on the process stage, and he talked candidly about his growing displeasure with Universal:

> [Costello] was being strapped into a corset by a stalwart, and his conversation was punctuated by complaints to which the stalwart paid no attention. Between grunts, Mr. Costello made invidious comparisons between Metro and Universal. He and his partner feel that Universal does not treat them with sufficient respect after making a profit of $4 million on their first three starring pictures. Having disclosed the figures, he added ominously that Universal had better be nice to them. He said that everyone at MGM is very nice and that he does not want to go back to Universal. The latter studio attributes the comedians' unrest to new-found self-importance and calmly disregards their plaints,

Lou takes a dunk in a giant washing machine.

which have been going on for some time. It is even said at Universal that Costello takes himself so seriously that he wants to do a dramatic picture. Confronted with this canard, Mr. Costello commented that, like Charles Chaplin, he puts serious acting—drama and pathos, as well as slapstick—into all his performances, even if Universal doesn't appreciate it. Therewith he permitted himself to be led away and hoisted into the air by wires attached to the corset. Behind him, on a process screen, a landscape whirled round and round, while he uttered pathetic and dramatic cries for help.

Pat Costello thought MGM was a nice place to visit. "We had a lot more time to shoot a picture at Metro. I think we had something like a fifty-two day schedule, but shot it in thirty-nine or forty-one days. That was one thing that was nicer. But I think we were treated better at Universal."

Pat doubled for Lou in the film's best sequence with the giant washing machine. (The hotel laundry boy who dumps Lou into the chute is Bud's nephew, Norman Abbott, who also served as his stand-in.) Pat recalled, "Coming down the laundry chute, I got knocked out. Then we did the scene in the washing machine. I said to Harry Raven, who was doing extra work on the picture, 'Stand by with an axe, and if anything goes wrong, bust the glass.' That scene was shot over several days, and this one day, I didn't know it, but the assistant threw in this heavy blanket. It was wool, and with all the soap and water, it weighed a ton. And of course I'm in this washing machine going around, and I get under this blanket, and I couldn't get the goddamn thing up off my head to breathe! I finally make it, get a nice belly full of air, and I see Harry just about to come down with the axe!"

The washing machine sequence was included in Robert Youngson's compilation film, *MGM's Big Parade of Comedy* (1964).

DELETIONS AND ADDITIONS

In the pulque sequence, Doc and Wishy imagine they see a girl take off her clothes. In a cut scene, a real girl enters, but the boys think she is also a mirage. "All right—do your stuff," says Wishy. "Take off your clothes and fade away!" Wishy attempts to pass his hat through her, but catches her on the fanny. She hauls off and gives him a terrific slap.

Kathryn Grayson had another song cut, "Whip-Poor-Will," after Doc and Wishy show Ricardo the code book.

In the film's original ending, Wishy steps up to the microphone and broadcasts a message to the Nazis. "This is Wishy Dunn, announcing for Maurice Craindall. I got a message for certain parties that is expectin' a message!" Several Nazis, gathered around a radio somewhere, draw close and anxiously write down every word. "The secret of my message," Wishy continues, "lies in your inkwell. Take the inkwell and place it in front of you." The Nazis comply. "Now place a piece of ice in the ink." They do. "Now, all of you stand up, and tell me what's in the inkwell." The Nazis stand, peer into the inkwell, and in chorus, announce, "Iced ink!" Wishy's voice comes over the radio: "You're telling me!"

Brother Pat doubled for Lou in the wash cycle.

REVIEWS

Abbott and Costello requested that the preview of *Rio Rita* be switched from Inglewood to Glendale because all of their previous hits were previewed at the same theater, the Alexander.

Hollywood Reporter: "A&C are even more hysterical in MGM's 'Rio Rita' than they have ever been before. They have the best comedy material they've had to date. The audience at the picture's Glendale preview simply roared, which should mean that the box office all over the country should roar also. However . . . the script was poorly written, badly directed, and impossible to follow with any interest . . . [it] can be classed as a pretty poor effort on the part of Pandro Berman, the picture's producer, for it could and should have been entirely in the upper brackets in every department."

FAR LEFT: Shooting the scene with the spies' apple radios. LEFT: Show business pundits theorized that Bud and Lou's popularity was a result of the country's anxiety over the looming war. It was ironic, then, that Abbott and Costello had their footprints enshrined at Grauman's Chinese Theater on Dec. 8, 1941. That same night they recorded their record, "Laugh, Laugh, Laugh."

Variety: "Like all Abbott and Costello pictures to date, on their home Universal lot and on borrowed time (this one for Metro), the stars carry it to big box office results. And, like all A. & C. entries, without them it would be so much celluloid."

Time: "Rootin', shootin' pals Abbott and Costello provide about two reels' worth of good slapstickery. Fatso Costello puts bombs in Nazi pockets, converses hilariously with a dog which has swallowed a radio, for the most part stands around with hands in pockets wondering what to do next. Apparently both Producer Pandro Berman and Director Sylvan Simon were in the same predicament."

PM: "There is something ever-fresh and bouncy and impervious-to-old-gags about [Abbott and Costello]. Even when their routines are only ordinary—as they often are in 'Rio Rita'— they still can knock an audience in the aisles. . . . It will be a great day when Hollywood, which has assimilated so many comedians with no trouble at all, learns how to put these boys in a movie that's as good as they are."

POSTSCRIPT

Bud and Lou hadn't had a respite since starting on *Buck Privates* in December 1940. In thirteen months, they had churned out six features. Sundays, their only day off from filming, were reserved for their regular appearances on the Chase and Sanborn program. Lou told *The New York Times,* "Universal has us scheduled to start another one immediately. They don't know it out at Universal City, but we're going to start nothing for a while. I'm going to Florida and spend about three months there, resting. Then I'm coming back and make movies again. But not before. Bud and I have been working hard ever since we got here, with hardly a day off between pictures, and we need some rest. We're going to get it, no matter what Universal thinks."

Working so closely and relentlessly under such great pressure put a serious strain on the boys' relationship that came to a head after *Rio Rita* finished production. According to manager Eddie Sherman, when the team signed to play the Steel Pier in 1936, Bud was reluctant to accept the engagement. Lou, on the other hand, was eager to move out of burlesque. "Lou asked Bud what he'd take to do the engagement," Sherman recalled. "Bud said, 'Ten dollars more a week.' So Lou said, 'Okay, take it out of my half.' And they did. For a while after that, any deal they signed, Lou was required to give Bud an extra $10." Lou resented Bud's obstinance, and as production wound down on *Rio Rita,* Lou demanded that the team's weekly salary now be split sixty-forty in his favor. Rather than break up the team, Bud submitted. On January 9, 1942, they signed an agreement to that effect. However, Abbott and Costello continued to split the earnings of their earlier films fifty-fifty, and fifty-five–forty-five on all subsequent pictures.

According to clippings, MGM's next A&C film would be "The People's Choice," reportedly written by Lou and Gene Schrott. Costello would play a streetcleaner involuntarily chosen by the people of Chaos City to clean up the mess left by Abbott's administration. No other information is available on it.

PARDON MY SARONG

Earliest Draft:
July 19, 1941

Production Start:
March 2, 1942

Production End:
April 28, 1942

Copyright Date:
July 21, 1942

Released: August 7, 1942

Running Time:
84 minutes

Reissued: 1948 (?)

Directed By:
Erle C. Kenton

Produced By:
Alex Gottlieb

Screenplay By:
True Boardman,
Nat Perrin, John Grant

Director of Photography:
Milton Krasner ASC

Art Director:
Jack Otterson

Associate: Martina Obzina

Film Editor: Arthur Hilton

Set Decorations:
R. A. Gausman

Associate: E. R. Robinson

Sound Director:
Bernard B. Brown

Technician:
Robert Pritchard

Gowns: Vera West

Assistant Director:
Howard Christie

"Lovely Luana," "Vingo
Jingo" Words and
Music By: Don Raye,
Gene de Paul

Musical Director:
Charles Previn

Musical Supervisor:
Ted Cain

SYNOPSIS

Playboy Tommy Layton charters a Chicago city bus for a ride to Los Angeles, where he is due to compete in a yacht race to Honolulu. The errant bus drivers, Algy and Wellington, are pursued by Detective Kendall, hired by the bus company. The boys escape Kendall by accidentally driving the bus off a pier. They are rescued by Layton on his yacht and become his crew for the race. Layton also shanghais Joan Marshall, a competitor in the race who dismissed his original crew.

Blown off course by a hurricane, the party lands on an uncharted island in the South Pacific, inhabited by innocent natives and the mysterious Dr. Varnoff. Wellington is mistaken for a legendary hero and betrothed to Luana, the beautiful princess. Varnoff's men have rigged the volcano to erupt in an effort to wangle the tribe's sacred jewel. When Wellington is sent to vanquish the evil spirit that resides in the volcano, he carries the priceless jewel as a talisman. Varnoff and his men converge to chase him all over the island. Finally Wellington and Algy thwart the gang and leave the natives to their peaceful island.

BACKGROUND

Executive producer Jules Levey had been an Abbott and Costello booster since the team's early days in New York. He wanted Bud and Lou for his production of *The Boys From Syracuse* in 1940, but the film's shooting schedule conflicted with the team's commitment to the Kate Smith radio program. Bud and Lou never forgot Levey's support, and they agreed to make *Pardon My Sarong* for his independent company, Mayfair Productions. Bud and Lou were paid $52,500, plus 10 percent of the gross over 170 percent of the production costs, and the film was released through Universal.

With Arthur Lubin assigned to *Eagle Squadron*, director Erle C. Kenton (1896–1980) came in to plot the next three A&C films. Kenton had just wrapped *The Ghost of Frankenstein* (1942).

THE SCRIPT

Veteran comedy writer Nat Perrin recalled how *Pardon My Sarong* came about. "I wasn't under contract to Universal, but I knew their producer, Alex Gottlieb, very well, so that's how I got the assignment. I knew that the studios had catalogues of properties that they owned—pictures that were made in the past, with certain backgrounds, or unproduced pictures. And my recollection is going through these synopses and finding some story that had to do with diving for pearls—that was the springboard. I don't remember working with John Grant or True Boardman. I would discuss the script with Gottlieb."

Perrin's original (dated July 19, 1941, and titled "Road to Montezuma") had Tommy, the boys, and the chorus girls sail to the South Seas in search of the black pearls of Montua. They arrive to find white men plundering the sea beds and preying on the natives' superstitions. Perrin's script suggested Martha Raye for the role of the chief's daughter. The part went to Nan Wynn. "If the part went to Nan Wynn," Perrin chuckled, "I must have suggested that, too, because I liked her personally. She was cute as could be."

Gottlieb worked with Perrin on the next two drafts, which brought the story closer to the finished picture, and retitled it *Pardon My Sarong*. Screenwriter True Boardman made contributions as well. Boardman once offered an explanation why the plot doesn't always make much sense. He would carefully work out a plot sequence of about twelve pages, then submit the pages to John Grant, who would make changes. When Boardman saw his treatment again, the plot sequence had been reduced to about three pages, and the rest contained gags and routines devised by Grant. John probably couldn't resist piling on so many gags. There were a host of burlesque "jungle" sketches, most with white explorers and sarong-clad native princesses, going back to skits performed as early as 1910 on the Eastern Burlesque Wheel. Legitimate Broadway shows like *White Cargo* and *Rain* inspired more. In fact, the script for *Pardon My Sarong* was crammed with more gags and routines than any other Abbott and Costello film we examined.

Sarong contains an excellent chase sequence for its finale. "Fundamentally, a chase represents the life struggle of an individual," Kenton explained in the pressbook. "A chase is therefore the most sure-fire act in the motion picture bag of tricks. The elements haven't changed in 25 years, and they're likely never to change." According to the pressbook, the sequence was the result of six months' planning, incorporating ideas and suggestions from three other directors. Many of the gags came from Charles Lamont.

THE CAST

Virginia Bruce (1910–1982), who had appeared in Lees and Rinaldo's *The Invisible Woman* (1941), just completed *Butch Minds the Baby* (1942) with Dick Foran. Later in 1942, Virginia's second husband, director J. Walter Ruben, died, and Virginia's film appearances became more sparse.

Robert Paige (1910–1988) came to Universal from Paramount in 1941 and frequently found himself paired with Jane Frazee in musicals directed by Charles Lamont. In 1941 he appeared in *Hellzapoppin'*, with Olsen and Johnson. Paige worked with Bud and Lou eleven years later in *Abbott and Costello Go to Mars* (1953).

Lionel Atwill (1885–1946), one of Hollywood's best villains, had just completed *The Ghost of Frankenstein* for director Erle Kenton. Atwill's other memorable appearances in 1942 include *The Mad Doctor of Market Street* (as an insane doctor on a remote Pacific island); *Night Monster;* and *Sherlock Holmes and the Secret Weapon* (as Professor Moriarity).

Leif Erickson (1911–1986) had just finished a role in *Eagle Squadron*. Later in 1942, after making *Night Monster* and *Arabian Nights,* Erickson served in World War II, during which he was twice wounded in action. He met up with Bud and Lou again in *Abbott and Costello Meet Captain Kidd* (1952).

Maria Montez was originally cast for *Sarong,* but replaced by Marie McDonald. Montez went into Poe's *The Mystery of Marie Roget* (1942) instead.

PRODUCTION

Sarong seems to be more lavish than the team's previous Universal fare, and easily topped $400,000, considering the eight-week shooting schedule and the cast of extras. There are several elaborate sets, including a water-tank for the yacht sequences and an island set dressed

Dances Originated and
  Staged By:
  Katherine Dunham

Algy Shaw . . . Bud Abbott
Wellington Phlug
  . . . . Lou Costello
Joan Marshall
  . . . . Virginia Bruce
Tommy Layton
  . . . . Robert Paige
Varnoff . . . . . Lionel Atwill
Whaba . . . . . Leif Erickson
Detective Kendall
  . . . . . . William Demarest
Chief Kolua
  . . . . Samuel S. Hinds
Ink Spots . . . . Themselves
Tip, Tap, Toe
  . . . . Themselves
Proprietor . . . Irving Bacon
Luana . . . . Nan Wynn
Ferna . . . . Marie McDonald
Amo . . . . Elaine Morey
Tagalong . . . Susan Levine
Tabor . . . . Jack LaRue
Moss . . . . . Hans Schumm
Henchman . . . . . . Joe Kirk
Henchman . . Frank Penny
Superintendent
  . . . . Charles Lane
Sven . . . . Tom Fadden
Marco . . . . Sig Arno

83

with 20,000 plants, date and cocoa palms, magnolia trees, and ferns. The cast and crew also went on location to Salton Sea for many of the intricate chase scenes. However, according to the pressbook, Abbott and Costello were costumed for a total of just $39.80. The bus driver's outfits cost a total of $10.95 each, plus rental of caps at 75¢ each. The sailors' outfits cost $6.95 each. Bud's sarong cost $1, and Lou's cost $1.50, because there was that much more material.

Bud's nephew, Norman Abbott, recalled the filming of the hurricane sequence. "There was a big process stage at Universal where they had a big yacht in a wet tank with millions of gallons of water. And in the scene, Lou just got drenched! Oh, was he *soaked!* And I remember Lou didn't want to go back and do it a second time. Mr. Gottlieb came down to the set and practically pleaded on his knees with Lou. I've never seen such begging. 'Please,' Alex said, 'dry off and go back and do it one more time.' What a time that was. But Lou went back and did it again."

"By now," Alex Gottlieb recalled, "Bud and Lou had a beautiful trailer of their own, and they wanted to play poker between shots. This is the first time they began to get a little bit difficult. The minute a shot was done, Erle Kenton might say, 'I think you could do that a little better, Lou.' And Lou would say, 'That's good enough. Come on, Bud.' They'd go to the trailer and play until they were needed for another scene. Mike Potson was with them every day. But they never held up a scene because of the game."

A Hollywood columnist named Harrison paid a visit to the *Sarong* set and recorded the boys at work:

Around the edges of the set lolled a tribe of south sea islanders, most of them playing gin rummy. The men wore bathrobes over their sarongs and would have looked like prize fighters except that they had flowers in their hair. The women were pretty well wrapped in mink coats against the chill of the soundstage. When they stepped out in costumes of startling skimpiness, you knew at once the picture must be a comedy; the Hayes office is much more tolerant with comedies.

In production, Abbott and Costello pictures are unlike any others. For sequences in which the stars appear, the scriptwriters do little more than indicate the eventful course of action. The comics work out the lines and business after they take their places on the set. This time the scene was a native feast following a ceremony in which Costello unknowingly becomes betrothed to the beautiful princess. Costello sat next to the furiously jealous chief, whom he addresses as "Stinker," after explaining it means "great man." The chief, Leif Erickson, wore a tall headdress apparently made of enormous pearls, and as they sat down, Costello remarked, "That's a nice head of ping pong balls you've got."

Director Erle Kenton said, "That's funny, Lou; use it." The scene-building proceeded. Costello took off his yachting cap, looked around hesitantly, and finally hung it on a spiked shoulder ornament worn by the chief. A number of on-lookers snickered, so that piece of business was included. After considerable experimentation, the feast was begun, with Costello picking up a whole fowl. It was snatched from his teeth by the chief, who ran his sword through it, and then calmly speared a fish on the table. The fat comic grabbed a banana, impaled it on the sword too, saying, "Here's dessert."

When they got to the wine-drinking part, with Costello knowing his cup was poisoned, he and Erickson went into the old burlesque routine in which each distracts the other's attention while switching the cups. Eventually, by moving the cups but not switching them, Costello got the chief to drink the Mickey Finn. "Goodnight, Stinker," he said, placing a lily in the prostrate native's fist.

During production, Robert Paige was knocked unconscious by a breakaway vase that wasn't breakaway. Paige suffered a cut scalp, and Kenton shot around him. He returned to work the next day. Bud Abbott, meanwhile, was nursing a lacerated right hand, which he injured while trying to reset the mechanism of a slot machine in his home.

Although two songs shot for the film were cut, there's still too much music in *Sarong*. The

Ink Spots perform "Do I Worry" and "Shout, Brother, Shout," while their big hit, "Java Jive," was omitted. Two production numbers by the natives, "Lovely Luana" and "Vingo Jingo," are tedious, but caused a stir in 1942. The censor boards in Pennsylvania, Massachusetts, and Ohio pruned some of the more suggestive dance movements. Another deleted number was "Island of the Moon," sung by Paige and Bruce.

BUD AND LOU'S SCENES

One of the funniest scenes in the picture comes when Kendall commandeers the bus and the boys drive it to the edge of the pier. "Go ahead and back up," is the seemingly contradictory command Algy gives Wellington. Bud and Lou know exactly how long to keep this up before it gets boring. Then Wellington drives the bus into the Pacific Ocean. A great special effect follows, showing the bus sitting on the ocean floor. Algy and Kendall swim away, but Wellington, still at the wheel, turns on the windshield wipers, as if that would do any good! This "tank" effect was used memorably during *Ride 'Em Cowboy*'s chase as well.

Two grim scenes were scripted when the boys are lost at sea. In one the crew hears a radio newscast announcing that their bodies haven't been recovered yet. This aimless, humorless scene was deleted. But a second, where Algy hands Wellington a pistol and intimates that he should do away with himself to save the others, was, for some reason, retained. The scene pushed the Abbott and Costello caricatures to extremes, and, in retrospect, is too oppressive to be funny. Yet, it remained in the film, suggesting that preview audiences in 1942 laughed their way through it.

On the other hand, the "Tree of Truth" scene is still quite funny. Luana warns Wellington that if he tells a lie under the tree something will happen to him. When he boasts, "Well, I got nothing to worry about; I never tell any lies," he is conked on the head by a coconut. He can't seem to open his mouth without getting plunked, so Algy suggests that he simply tell Luana a story. He begins to tell her a traveling salesman joke. (Notice that Lou refers to a "merchandising agent." That's because the term "traveling salesman" was on the Breen Office list of forbidden phrases.) Algy stops him because the story is unfit for a young girl. But every other story Wellington knows somehow leads into a traveling salesman joke. Finally Luana asks, "What did the man want?" Wellington replies, "He—he wanted a glass of milk," and is instantly pelted by a shower of coconuts! Later, a quick reprise of the gag was deleted. Luana kisses Wellington just before he heads for the volcano. "I'll always remember your last kiss," he swoons. A big coconut flies in and catches him on the back of the head. "How do you like that? That darned tree even *throws* 'em at you!" he complains.

A variation on the "Tree of Truth" scene was performed with Mari Blanchard, the beautiful Venusian queen in *Abbott and Costello Go to Mars* (1953).

BOTTOM LEFT: With Nan Wynn and Lief Erikson.
BOTTOM: "The Tree of Truth" with Nan Wynn.

FAR RIGHT: In the original ending, Luana joins Wellington on the yacht.
RIGHT: In this cut sequence, Wellington is held captive the night before the great sacrifice.

DELETIONS AND ADDITIONS

A funny exchange was omitted as the boys career in the bus. Wellington complains that the brakes aren't working very well. "Well, use the hand brake," Algy says. "The what?" "The hand brake," Algy says. "What do you put on in an emergency?" "My bathrobe," cracks Wellington.

A classic Abbott and Costello bit was deleted from the sequence in which Kendall corrals the boys at the nightclub. When he roughs up Wellington, Algy warns him not to hurt his pal or he'll report him. "Oh you will?" Kendall snarls; "Well, brother, you gotta have a witness. My word is as good as yours." Algy seeks a witness, but his first candidate, an old-timer, misses the trouncing because he wasn't wearing his glasses. Next, Algy recruits a burly wrestler and dares Kendall to thrash Wellington again. Kendall happily obliges. "Did you see the way he tossed him around?" Algy asks hopefully. "Yeah," confirms the wrestler, "but he didn't do it right. He shoulda used a hold like this." He proceeds to hoist poor Wellington in an airplane spin and drop him. Now Algy is more determined than ever. He snatches a camera from a passing girl and snaps a picture as Kendall manhandles Wellington once more. Algy is triumphant—until he discovers that there isn't any film in the camera. The boys reworked this routine in *Abbott and Costello in Hollywood* (1945) and *Abbott and Costello Meet Frankenstein* (1948).

In addition to Wellington's shaving scene, another routine was scripted for the hurricane sequence on the boat. As Wellington attempts to wash some dishes, the soap flies out of his hand and lands on a high shelf. Retrieving it becomes a comedy of errors. He climbs up on the counter and steps into a sinkful of water, some flypaper, a basin of dough, and then a mousetrap. Algy finally comes to his rescue. The scene was later redone in *Here Come the Co-Eds* (1945).

There were more deletions once the boys reached the tropical island. The night before Wellington is to encounter the evil spirit of the volcano, he is imprisoned by the tribe. But Algy has a plan to rescue him: he'll put on a lion suit to scare off the guard. Of course, a real lion shows up in Algy's place, but Wellington still thinks it's Algy. Gradually, he realizes his mistake and faints. Back in his cell, Wellington is asked by the tribesmen to convey messages to the gods. "Tell gods Tonwala want catch more fish," says one man. "Sanu want three sons," says another. "How do you like that," muses Wellington, "now I'm Western Union!" This gives Algy an idea. "Okay, boys," he announces to the natives, "it'll cost you ten cents a word. Moolah take message to gods, you pay gold, silver, bracelets." Each native pays Algy a trinket in exchange for his message. "Wellington, you're gonna clean up at this racket," Algy says, massaging his palms. "A lot of good it'll do me," sighs Wellington. "Don't be silly," Algy responds. "When I get home, I'll use this to buy you a beautiful tombstone." Wellington is touched. "Algy, you're too good to me."

The film originally ended with Tommy, Joan, Wellington, and Algy on the yacht. Piled high near Wellington is a treasure from the grateful natives. Tommy and Joan kiss, and Wellington, embarrassed, inadvertently pulls the canvas covering off the dinghy—revealing Luana as a stowaway. Wellington closes his eyes to kiss her, but Sharkey slips in between them. Wellington kisses the seal, opens his eyes, reels, and falls down the open hatchway. The film ends on Sharkey applauding happily.

The ending was reshot while Abbott and Costello were working on their next picture, *Who Done It?*

REVIEWS

The New York Times: "Fortunately, the writers have been generous in their dishing out of situations and gags. And, although they build to little more than blackouts, a string of such with Abbott and Costello is good enough—provided, as in this case, they are good. Thus, Bud and Lou spoofing a magician, or Lou trying to shave on a storm-tossed boat, or the same gentlemen making a monkey out of Lief Erickson as a native blow-hard, are the sort of nonsensical business out of which 'Pardon My Sarong' is contrived. Nan Wynn, as a grass-bordered lady, does moan a couple of songs, and the screen is occasionally agitated by many young females grinding their hips. But Bud and Lou are the show, as usual. They don't make sense, but they make 80 minutes fly."

New York Post: "It seems regrettable that Costello especially should be subject to the laws of diminishing returns from an act repeated. He is such an ingratiating clown that he might have a long comic life if he could vary his material sufficiently. . . . It might even be that Abbott and Costello are not fading, only that their picture is too great a handicap even for them. That question will be answered in their next picture, which should be a matter of moments if they continue at their present rate of production. They have been gold mines for their company, Universal, and it is high time that Universal ploughed back a little of the gold with a superior script. This is intended as a warning from one who has giggled incessantly at the two men in their past endeavors."

New York Herald Tribune: "The opening reels have all the zest and comic excitement inherent in an antic screen chase. Unfortunately the gagmen have tired before the proceedings are over. . . . Abbott and Costello fans will probably be satisfied that the two clowns turn in some funny cavorting in the course of *Pardon My Sarong,* but even they would do well to see only the first half of the offering."

PM: "The production staff apparently got a bit embarrassed about half-way through the film, and started to hoke the whole thing up with a spate of zooming imagination. If you could arrange to drop in for just the last half-hour, say, you'd see Costello's brush with a surfboard and a swordfish; his grunt-and-groan wrestling scene with the villain; his brief entanglement with a runaway outboard motor. This portion might be worth your while, if you like to see cinema fancy running free."

POSTSCRIPT

Pardon My Sarong premiered in Paterson for the benefit of St. Anthony's church. The picture became the team's biggest hit to date, and the second biggest moneymaker of 1942 behind *Mrs. Miniver.* In New York, Loews Criterion remained open until five am to accommodate the crowds.

Bud and Lou made the first of several tours on behalf of the war effort upon completion of *Pardon My Sarong.* During production, the team announced that they were going on an eight-week personal appearance tour, starting May 6, to raise $350,000 to buy a bomber for the government. However, Under Secretary of War Robert Patterson requested Abbott and Costello tour in support of the Army Emergency Relief Fund. According to a press release, "Although Congress has appropriated billions for bombers, not a penny has been allotted to dependents of soldiers. Since financial emergencies arise each day for the wives, mothers and sisters of men now on Bataan or heading for Australia, Ireland or Iceland, Abbott and Costello feel that the Army Emergency Relief Fund is obviously a far more worthy cause." The team raised their goal to $500,000 and paid traveling expenses out of their own pockets.

WHO DONE IT?

Earliest Draft:
   April 26, 1941

Production Start:
   May 25, 1942

Production End:
   June 29, 1942

Copyright Date:
   October 26, 1942

Released:
   November 6, 1942

Running Time:
   76 minutes

Reissued: January 1949
   with *In the Navy*; 1954
   with *Ride 'Em Cowboy*

Directed By:
   Erle C. Kenton

Produced By:
   Alex Gottlieb

Screenplay By: Stanley
   Roberts, Edmund
   Joseph, John Grant

Original Story By:
   Stanley Roberts

Director of Photography:
   Charles Van Enger ASC

Art Director:
   Jack Otterson

Associate: Robert Boyle

Set Decorations:
   R. A. Gausman

Associate:
   A.J. Gilmore

Costumes: Vera West

Assistant Director:
   Howard Christie

Musical Director:
   Charles Previn

Music By Frank Skinner

Film Editor: Arthur Hilton

Sound Director:
   Bernard B. Brown

SYNOPSIS

Chick Larkin and Mervyn Milgrim are soda jerks at Radio Center, but yearn to become radio mystery writers. Along with Jimmy Turner, a new writer, and Jane Little, the program's producer, the boys attend a broadcast of the *Murder at Midnight* program. As he is about to introduce the show, the network president, Colonel J. R. Andrews, is electrocuted. Hoping to solve the crime—and get their own radio show—Chick and Mervyn impersonate detectives. They question the suspects, which include Andrews' personal physician, Dr. Marek, and the show's writer, Marco Heller.

But real detectives Moran and Brannigan arrive to unmask Chick and Mervyn, considering them prime suspects. During a chase through the studio offices, the boys discover that Dr. Marek has also been murdered. The boys are briefly chased out of the building, but learn that Mervyn has won $10,000 on the *Wheel of Fortune* program. When they return to the studio to claim the prize, Moran and Brannigan arrest them. But Jimmy and Jane convince the detectives to trap the real murderer by staging a reenactment of the events leading up to the crime. It seems that a spy has been using one of the network's programs to relay information to his homeland. Colonel Andrews and Dr. Marek were about to unmask the foreign agent when they were murdered. As the reenactment reaches a climax, Art Fraser betrays himself as the killer. He races to the roof, where Chick and Mervyn manage to subdue him.

BACKGROUND

Who Done It? was scheduled to follow *Ride 'Em Cowboy* as the fifth Abbott and Costello film. Alex Gottlieb consulted his hallowed list of Wheeler and Woolsey backgrounds in the spring of 1941 and assigned *The Nitwits* (1935) premise to writer Stanley Roberts. By the time the picture was produced a year later, Roberts was working at MGM. He recalled, "I was quite friendly with John Grant, whom I liked enormously, and he got me a job at Metro when they went over to do *Rio Rita*. He recommended me to Sylvan Simon for a Red Skelton picture."

THE SCRIPT

Roberts initially had the boys as groundskeepers at Radio City who aspire to be mystery writers. Their adventures at the station easily integrated musical numbers by the Andrews Sisters and Phil Spitalny and His All-Girl Orchestra. Over the next few months, Roberts and

Edmund Joseph developed the screenplay. "In one sense, we really didn't write for Abbott and Costello," Roberts explained. "We wrote the story, the action scenes; but when it came to the jokes and the routines, that was John Grant. Lou wouldn't trust anything that hadn't been done before. Even if John wrote a brand-new routine, he would have to convince Lou that it was done at the Palace in 1912."

Work continued on the script, however, for some months to follow. It was passed along to Hugh Wedlock and Howard Snyder, who, among other changes, made the boys soda jerks, and True Boardman, who added the memorable rooftop finale. But for all the plot construction, *Who Done It?* is a prop-driven comedy: John Grant devised hilarious encounters with a wedge of Limburger cheese; a water fountain; a record turntable; an elevator; an acrobatic troupe; a telephone; a radio; a pair of handcuffs; and a flagpole. They were as incidental to this story as the burlesque routines had been to the previous scenarios.

From the Breen Office correspondence available, it appears that *Who Done It?* was rather chaste. Incredibly, the censors missed the name of the acrobatic troupe Mervyn encounters— the Flying Bordellos!

THE CAST

Patric Knowles (b. 1911) appeared in a few British films before making his Hollywood debut in 1936. That same year he played with Errol Flynn and Olivia de Havilland in *The Charge of the Light Brigade* and, in 1938, *The Adventures of Robin Hood.* His first film for Universal was *The Wolf Man* (1941). Knowles also appeared in *Hit the Ice* (1943) with Bud and Lou.

William Gargan (1905–1979) had worked with Bud and Lou in *Keep 'Em Flying* (1941). Since then, he had starred in three *Ellery Queen* mysteries at Columbia. In the 1950s he starred on TV as private eye "Martin Kane." In 1960 he was diagnosed with cancer of the larynx and had his voice box removed, forcing his retirement. He became a spokesman for The American Cancer Society in a campaign against smoking.

Louise Allbritton (1920–1979) later appeared in *Son of Dracula* (1943) and *The Egg and I* (1947). She retired from the screen several years after her marriage to CBS news correspondent Charles Collingwood.

William Bendix (1906–1964) made his Broadway debut in 1939 as an Irish cop in William Saroyan's *The Time of Your Life.* His first year in films, 1942, was a busy one: *Woman of the Year, Wake Island, The Glass Key, Brooklyn Orchid,* and *Who Done It?* His memorable appearances later include *Lifeboat* (1944), *The Hairy Ape* (1944), *A Bell for Adano* (1945), and *The Babe Ruth Story* (1948). In 1947 Bill appeared in a short, *10,000 Kids and a Cop,* that publicized the Lou Costello Jr. Youth Center in Los Angeles.

Mary Wickes (b. 1916) played the heckled nurse in the stage and screen version of *The Man Who Came to Dinner* (1941), then was signed by Universal to a term contract following her performance in *Private Buckaroo* (1942). Mary also appeared in *Now Voyager* in 1942. She is in Bud and Lou's final film, *Dance with Me, Henry* (1956).

Don Porter (b. 1912) had been in *Eagle Squadron* and *Madame Spy* before being assigned *Who Done It?* "I was under contract. In those days, it was kind of a family studio, not like the factories today. They handed me a script and said, 'Here's where you go to work Monday.' [laughs] I don't remember having a choice of roles. When I went to Universal, the first part I did was with Leo Carillo and Andy Devine in *Top Sergeant* (1942). I played a soldier who was the killer. I guess *Who Done It?* was the first comedy film I had done, and I enjoyed it— but I still was the killer." [laughs]

PRODUCTION

Who Done It? provided Abbott and Costello with their best supporting cast to date. No musical numbers shot for the production, probably in deference to the mood of the film. Kenton's direction, combined with Charles Van Enger's atmospheric camera work, give the film an

Technician:
  Robert Pritchard

Chick Larkin
.... Bud Abbott
Mervyn Milgrim
.... Lou Costello
Lieutenant Moran
.... William Gargan
Jane Little
.... Louise Allbritton
Jimmy Turner
.... Patric Knowles
Art Fraser .... Don Porter
Marco Heller
.........Jerome Cowan
Brannigan. William Bendix
Juliet Collins
.... Mary Wickes
Colonel J.R. Andrews
.... Thomas Gomez
Dr. Anton Marek
.... Ludwig Stossel
Jenkins
.... Edmund MacDonald
Thompson ...... Joe Kirk
Elevator Boy
.... Walter Tetley
Radio Actors
.... Crane Whitley
  Margaret Brayton
  Gene O'Donnell
  Paul Dubov
Acrobats....... The Pinas
Coroner... Milton Parsons
Telephone Operator
.... Gladys Blake
Spinelli...... Frank Penny
Technician
.... Bobby Barber

With the murderer, Don Porter, on the rooftop.

appropriately sinister ambiance. Reportedly, the production was scheduled for forty days, including a week in New York to shoot exteriors around Radio City. But the crew never left Universal City.

Pat Costello recalled the first day of shooting. "Pat Knowles was a good friend of mine. I suggested that he have his agent contact Alex Gottlieb, and he got the job. He was so nervous his first day on the set, his hands were shaking. He told me, 'I've never been so nervous in my life.' I said, 'What are you nervous about? These guys are burlesque comics, they're not actors! No matter what you do, they'll think you're great.' But he was still nervous. So I went to Lou and I told him, 'You gotta do something for Pat. He's so nervous, he's going to blow his lines. I don't want that to happen because he's a nice guy.' Lou said he'd take care of it, and he talked to Bud. Now in their first scene with him, Pat Knowles starts to talk with that British accent, and Lou yells, 'Cut! Cut!' Lou goes over to Erle Kenton and says, so everybody can hear him, 'How the hell do you expect me to get laughs—look how funny this guy talks! Everyone will be laughing at him and I'll be standing there like a damn fool! Listen to him! Go on, Pat, say somethin'!' Well, Pat Knowles started to laugh, and that broke it up. He did so well that he did another picture with them."

Don Porter also remembers Bud and Lou as good-humored, affable men. "Lou used to use me as a straight man when Bud wasn't around if there were visitors on the set. He'd yell old gags to me from vaudeville and I would straight—'I don't know, Lou; who was that lady in the bushes?'—things like that. Then he'd deliver the punchline. This one day, Lou was gabbing with fifteen or twenty people on the set, and I was in front of the camera. He called over to me, 'Hey Don, what did one bedbug say to the other?' And I said, 'Meet you in the spring.' Well, I'd done the punchline! [laughs] He never threw me another straight line again! [laughs] We had a lot of fun on *Who Done It?* Patric Knowles, Eddie MacDonald, Thomas Gomez, and I were drinking buddies. We had a lot of laughs."

Don offered some insights into Bud and Lou's working methods: "We worked fast; their rhythm demanded that. They preferred to do their scenes off the cuff and see what happened. I don't remember any difficulties. The remembrance I have of Erle Kenton was that he was an awfully nice guy, very laid back, and very forbearing with them, and, as a result, he got more out of them I imagine than if he'd been antagonistic. I enjoyed watching their technique, watching them work in certain scenes.

"One of the big things, as far as speed was concerned—or the lack of it—was getting them in front of the camera sometimes. They paid no attention to the assistant director. They had a running poker game with Nick the Greek in their trailer outside the stage, and they were *terrible* poker players. I got in the game a couple of times, but I really didn't have enough money to play with them. When I got even, I got *out*. The standard bet as I remember it was about $40—then raised. It got kind of expensive. Bill Gargan was standing behind me, watching, and he said, 'This is easy!' So he got in the game, and he was doing very well. Then finally he stood up and quit. I asked him, 'Why'd you quit? You were doing great!' He said, 'I just bought a ranch, and every time I put $40 on the table I say to myself, "There's another calf!" And that's no way to play poker.' "

The scene in which Mervyn claims his *Wheel of Fortune* prize contains a piece of Abbott and Costello memorabilia—the microphone from their first Kate Smith radio appearance in 1938. They asked for the mike after the broadcast and kept it ever since.

Pat Costello doubled for Lou in the sequence where Mervyn gets mixed up with the acrobatic troupe, and he was injured doing a stunt in the rooftop finale. "I had to jump on the flagpole," he recalls. "It was a jump of eight or ten feet, and you have to hit the pole just right. I had done it about five times and I was getting a little bit tired. Erle Kenton said, 'Just one more,' and I hurt my groin. Everybody said I busted my 'thing,' but of course there's nothing to break. They took my pants down and I was bleeding. God love Lou. I never thought Lou was going to get over that. One thing Lou couldn't stand was blood."

Don Porter explains there was some authenticity in the rooftop gun fight. "The big scene I had with them was up on the roof, when I chased Lou out on the flagpole with a pistol. Then Bud picked up some light bulbs and started to throw them down. I thought it was a gun and I turned around, but didn't see him. He did it again, and I didn't see him. The third time, I saw him and shot the light bulb out of his hand. Well, they had to shoot the close-up of Bud holding the light bulb and the light bulb exploding. They didn't have the sophisticated equipment they have now. The prop man had an ordinary BB gun. But in practice, he kept missing. Well, as a kid I had been in the National Guard up in Oregon. So I kiddingly said, 'Let an old rifleman try it.' So I took the BB gun and hit the light bulb. Bud saw this and said, 'I don't do the scene unless Don shoots it out of my hand.' [laughs] So I'm off-camera with the BB gun and he's holding the light bulb. Now I get Bud Fever—I don't want to hit *him*. I missed it twice, and then hit it on the third shot. So I actually shot the light bulb out of his hand in the film *and* off camera."

BUD AND LOU'S SCENES

Lou's amusing encounter with a noxious wedge of Limburger cheese was actually expanded on the set. In the original script, he prepares the sandwich off-camera, then makes his first appearance, wearing a gas mask.

Another priceless bit is Lou's scuffle with a temperamental water fountain. Most of the action is in the script, but he has an inspired moment when he thrusts his hand in his pockets and impishly feigns indifference to the fountain. "Make out like I don't want a drink" he says to Bud, as if he could fool the contraption.

One of the best segments of the film is the sequence in the transcription room, where Mervyn is frightened by recordings of gangster programs. Only one recording was indicated in the original script. But the premise was too good to pass up, and others were added.

"Alexander 2222" is one of Costello's finest solo routines. Mervyn attempts to telephone the *Wheel of Fortune* program to claim his prize. But each time he asks the operator for the number, she drones, "The lion is bizzy." Meanwhile, a parade of characters make a series of long-distance calls that are instantly connected. Lou's mounting frustration is hilarious. (The Smithsonian Institution included this sequence in a recent exhibit on the Communication Age.)

DELETIONS AND ADDITIONS

Don Porter remembered Bud and Lou ad-libbing a new routine on the spot. "There was one scene where Thomas Gomez took hold of the microphone and was electrocuted. I forget what the exact lines were in the script, but Bud said, 'He got 10,000 volts.' Lou said, 'That's enough to be elected.' Bud said, 'Not votes—*volts*. And Lou said, 'What's volts?' So Bud came back with electrical terms, and they went into the 'Who's On First?' routine with electrical things. [laughs] Everyone behind the camera was breaking up."

A whimsical sequence was deleted from the transcription room scene. As Mervyn struggles with the killer, Juliet accidentally clobbers him with a stack of records. In the film, a dream sequence effect begins, but ends aimlessly. In the original script, Mervyn dreams that he is Romeo, and Juliet is, well, Juliet. Mervyn is dressed in tights, cap, doublet, and long cape. A ridiculously long sword drags on the ground. He sets a ladder against Juliet's balcony, but inadvertently plants it on his feet. When Juliet starts to climb down the ladder, he sputters in pain. Juliet quickly scrambles back to her balcony, and Mervyn readjusts the ladder. As he clambers up, however, the ladder sinks into the soft ground, so that by the end of his climb he's still at ground level. Now Chick enters, similarly dressed, to challenge Mervyn to a duel for Juliet's hand. Their duel, according to the script, is a "burlesque of Fairbanks in *The Corsican Brothers*." Juliet attempts to help by dropping a flower pot on Chick, but she crowns Mervyn instead. That brings the sequence full circle and back to the transcription room.

The boys tried unsuccessfully to exhume the "Romeo and Juliet" scene in *Buck Privates Come Home* (1947). The ladder gag, however, turned up in *It Ain't Hay* (1943).

REVIEWS

New York Herald Tribune: ". . . ['Who Done It?'] gives full scope to the antics of the stars. . . . I would still like to see Costello in a film which would exploit his fine sense of comedy, rather than his ability to make gags, double takes and slapstick stand up in a production."

Variety: "The two comedians are on for practically all of the footage, with spotlight focused on their combined adventures. There's no supporting singing, dancing or production numbers inserted to partially break up the A&C straight line presentation on their own—although such material would have helped better space the comedians' appearances. . . . Gags include plenty of physical and dialog efforts for laughs, with several that have been presented with slight

Who Done It? originally had a different ending. As the police lead Fraser away, Jimmy explains that Fraser disposed of Dr. Marek's body in an air-conditioning outlet in the Transcription Room. The outlets, Jimmy says, lead to the giant air-conditioning unit in the building's basement. Mervyn curiously peaks into an open outlet on the roof, loses his balance, and falls in. Everyone rushes down to the basement, where they find him frozen in a block of ice.

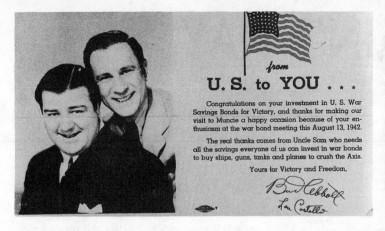

variations in previous A&C pictures. Although laughs are neatly paced, scripters fail to hit roaring toppers to many of the situations that could have been improved by greater care on the writing side."

The New York Times critic Bosley Crowther made the boys the subject of his editorial the following Sunday: "[*Who Done It?*] is the sort of threadbare nonsense that two of the most amiable clowns to come along in a coon's age are given to play in their eighth film. It is, to this watcher's way of thinking, a distressing and inordinate waste. For here are two lovable zanies—one of them is lovable, anyhow—who could, with some fresh and fast material, make the liveliest pictures anyone could wish. The fact that they still manage to be funny and make the audiences laugh with gags of the moldiest nature is the token of their talents and appeal."

New York Morning Telegraph: "For the most part, the two comical knockabouts depend on physical activity in *Who Done It?* . . . It was not always thus. Abbott and Costello had a give and take act that stood them in good stead for many years. They had the timing of their dialogue, their pat routines of questions and answers, their own peculiar manner of laying an audience in the aisles that corresponded to nothing else on the screen. That they should now be reduced to imitating the Three Stooges shows lamentable paucity of invention behind them."

New York Daily Mirror: "You see them first as soda clerks in a luncheonette, and one of the funniest bits is right there when Costello has to fill an order for a Limburger sandwich. His facial work here as he takes the cover off the cheese elicited howls of glee from the customers. Anyone who can still put a Limburger laugh over is a genius."

POSTSCRIPT

With the release of *Who Done It?* late in 1942, Bud and Lou ranked as the country's top box office attractions of the year, more popular than stalwarts such as Clark Gable and Mickey Rooney.

After completing the film, Bud and Lou began a whirlwind tour to sell War Bonds. The boys visited seventy-eight cities and one hundred war production plants in just thirty-four days. The Treasury Department credited Abbott and Costello with selling a record $85,000,000 worth of bonds and stamps on the tour. Not all of the venues were theaters or army camps, however. In Omaha, Nebraska, a twelve-year-old boy named Jerry Young sneaked up to Bud and Lou's suite at the Fontenelle Hotel and asked the team to appear in a benefit show he was staging in his backyard. He offered them 70¢ for their efforts, and Bud and Lou consented. That night, police roped off the streets near Jerry's house as a crowd overflowed the boys' backyard. Bud and Lou arrived by special motorcade, fresh from an appearance in Lincoln, fifty-five miles away. After performing a couple of routines, Bud put Costello's shirt up for auction. When the bids were closing at $10, Lou protested and bid $12 himself so he could keep it.

ABOVE: *Who Done It?* was supposed to be dedicated to Charlie Chaplin, Lou's idol. Before production began, Lou was guest of honor at Chaplin's Beverly Hills home. According to a newspaper clipping, Chaplin entertained his guests with his own impersonation of Abbott and Costello, and the two great comics discussed the possibility of doing a film together. Lou asked about buying the rights to *The Kid*. Later, in 1958, Lou explained, "Charlie told me he planned to remake *The Kid*, with me playing the role he created. Then I guess the whole thing was dropped because he got involved in this political situation, and left the country."

ABOVE LEFT: A souvenir from the team's first War Bond Tour in the summer of 1942.

93

IT AIN'T HAY

Earliest Draft:
  February 20, 1942

Production Start:
  September 28, 1942

Production End:
  November 11, 1942

Copyright Date:
  March 25, 1943

Released: March 19, 1943

Running Time:
  81 minutes

Reissued: 1949

Directed By:
  Erle C. Kenton

Produced By:
  Alex Gottlieb

Screenplay By: Allen
  Boretz, John Grant

Based on *Princess O'Hara*
  By: Damon Runyon

Director of Photography:
  Charles Van Enger ASC

Art Director:
  John Goodman

Associate:
  Harold H. MacArthur

Film Editor: Frank Gross

Gowns: Vera West

Sound Director:
  Bernard B. Brown

Technician: Jesse Moulin

Set Decorations:
  R. A. Gausman

Associate: A. J. Gilmore

Assistant Director:
  Howard Christie

Musical Director:
  Charles Previn

Orchestrations:
  Frank Skinner

Musical Numbers Staged
  By: Danny Dare

Words and Music By:
  Harry Revel and
  Paul Francis Webster

Grover Mockridge
  . . . . Bud Abbott

Wilbur Hoolihan
  . . . . Lou Costello

SYNOPSIS

Wilbur Hoolihan feeds candy to a hack horse belonging to King O'Hara and his daughter, Princess, and the horse dies. Anxious to replace it, Wilbur and his friend Grover visit a gambling parlor and win enough money to buy a new horse, but Wilbur is duped out of the bankroll by a con man. Three touts, Umbrella Sam, Harry the Horse, and Chauncey the Eye, inform the boys that an old nag is available at the Empire track. But that night at the stables, Grover and Wilbur unwittingly steal the champion, Tea Biscuit, and give him to King O'Hara.

Tea Biscuit's owner, Colonel Brainard, posts a reward for the return of the horse. King, meanwhile, drives a fare up to Saratoga, and the boys, realizing their error, follow him. They are pursued by Sam, Harry, and Chauncey, who also realize what happened and seek the reward. Wilbur and Grover recover Tea Biscuit and conceal him in their hotel room, but the hotel's new manager, Warner, discovers the ruse. Fleeing Warner, Wilbur rides Tea Biscuit to the track in time for the big race. Colonel Brainard has entered the missing thoroughbred as a sentimental gesture. Wilbur inadvertently switches horses with another jockey, and Tea Biscuit actually wins the race. Sam, Harry, Chauncey, and Warner hastily buy Wilbur's horse for $500, believing it to be Tea Biscuit. When they attempt to collect the reward, however, Colonel Brainard withdraws it, since it appears that Tea Biscuit was never really missing. Grover holds the only winning ticket, and with their windfall, the boys buy King a new horse and carriage, and finance a camp show for their friend Joe.

BACKGROUND

Bud and Lou returned from their record-breaking bond tour a few weeks before starting *It Ain't Hay*. The picture was originally titled "Hold Your Horses," but renamed in honor of the tremendous sum of money Bud and Lou had just raised.

When Bud and Betty Abbott returned from the tour, it was with a new addition to the family. They adopted a three-year-old boy in New York, and named him Bud Abbott, Jr. "This is my reward for helping Uncle Sam," Bud Sr. told the press.

THE SCRIPT

It Ain't Hay is based on the Damon Runyon short story, "Princess O'Hara," originally published in *Collier's* on March 3, 1934. Universal bought the screen rights, and the studio's first version, *Princess O'Hara* was released in 1935. It was produced by Leonard Spigelgass and starred Chester Morris, Jean Parker, and Leon Errol.

Alex Gottlieb assigned the screenwriting chores to Allen Boretz in February 1942. Boretz worked on the script (tentatively titled "The Sky's the Limit," then "Hold Your Horses") several months before John Grant made his amendments. Although Grant added numerous stock routines, he tried to maintain the flavor of the story. "I bought a small book of Runyon's stories," he explained in a letter to Gottlieb, "and in reading them I noticed that most of his characters are touts, chiselers, con-men, etc. Therefore, I feel that the more of these fellows we can put into the scenes with Costello, the more comedy we can get out of it." To that end, Grant also added the backroom betting parlor sequence with Big Hearted Charlie and his boys.

THE CAST

Grace McDonald (b. 1919) and her brother Ray had been a song-and-dance team in vaudeville. Ray signed with MGM, and Grace with Universal, where she appeared in seventeen musicals betwen 1941 and 1945, including *Crazy House* (1944) with Olsen and Johnson.

Eugene Pallette (1889–1954) lent his impressive talents and waistline to numerous classic films, including *My Man Godfrey* (1936) and *The Adventures of Robin Hood* (1938). Like Lou, he was a former stunt man.

Cecil Kellaway (1893–1973) was on loan from Paramount. He had just completed one of his most memorable roles in *I Married a Witch* (1942). Cecil was later nominated for Oscars in *The Luck of the Irish* (1948) and *Guess Who's Coming to Dinner* (1967).

Patsy O'Connor (b. 1931) was a third-generation vaudevillian. "We knew Bud and Lou from vaudeville," Patsy explained. "My father, Jack, had run into them in burlesque. I remember we went to see them at the Paramount Theater in Los Angeles just before they went to Universal. My uncle, Donald O'Connor, had come out first and gone under contract. I had just come from New York, where I was doing a play with Ethel Merman, 'Panama Hattie.' I tested for the role of Princess. They felt Gloria Jean was too old. The first day that I met Bud and Lou as Princess O'Hara, Lou came over and put his hand on my cheek and said, 'Who said she's not pretty?' *That* made me feel terrible, because I thought somebody had said, 'She's ugly.' I guess from the look on my face—because he was such a sensitive man—Lou went to great lengths for the next week to make me feel like the most beautiful thing that ever walked the face of the earth. He was a very kind man."

Eddie Quillan (1907–1990), a veteran comic actor, adds to the Runyonesque flavor. "I was a freelance actor at the time, and it surprised me how often I was used, not being under contract to Universal. My younger brother, Joe, wrote for Abbott and Costello on the Kate Smith show in New York. He also wrote for Eddie Cantor, and *Our Miss Brooks,* on radio and television. So I knew them, and of course they knew me, because by that time I had been in the business about 15 years. As soon as I heard they were on the lot at Universal, I went over to see Bud and Lou. I liked them both very, very much."

THE PRODUCTION

Director Erle Kenton was allotted thirty-eight days to shoot the picture and spent a fair amount of that time on exteriors and on location. "The opening scene was shot at Griffith Park," Patsy recalled. "That was an interesting story. They had gotten a circus horse to pull my cab, and every time they started the playback of my song, "Sunbeam Serenade," the horse reared. He was trained to do that every time he heard music! Now, I was quite a horsewoman from the time I was three years old, so I was able to contain him. But it was hysterical; we'd have to stop every two seconds because he'd rear up."

Perhaps the horse was a better judge of music than he was given credit for. Both the music and the choreography for the film are below par, which is surprising given the talents of songwriters Harry Revel and Paul Francis Webster, and choreographer Danny Dare. Broadway and movie veterans, Revel and Webster each had numerous hits with other writing partners, but had only recently begun collaborating. Their songs are much better in their next Abbott and Costello assignment, *Hit the Ice*. While much of Danny Dare's work in the finale was cut from the picture, it can't begin to compare with his choreography for *Holiday Inn* earlier in 1942. The Step-Brothers' acrobatic routine with Costello, however, remains delightful.

Kitty McCloin .... Grace McDonald

Gregory Warner .... Eugene Pallett

Private Joe Collins .... Leighton Noble

King O'Hara .... Cecil Kellaway

Peggy, Princess O'Hara .... Patsy O'Connor

Umbrella Sam .... Shemp Howard

Harry the Horse .... Eddie Quillan

Chauncey the Eye .... David Hacker

Slicker ...... Richard Lane

Colonel Brainard .... Samuel S. Hinds

Roller Skate Specialty .... Three Hollywood Blondes

Musical Specialty .... The Vagabonds

Big-Hearted Charlie .... Andrew Tombes

Major Harper .... Pierre Watkin

Banker ... William Forrest

Reilly ...... Wade Boteler

Grant .... Selmer Jackson

Bouncers .. Mike Mazurki Sammy Stein

and The Four Step-Brothers

95

A Universal Newsreel crew shot footage of the opening of Saratoga's summer season on July 27, 1942, specifically for inclusion in the film. They also covered the racetrack and the town for establishing shots and process shots. But the film's actual racing footage was shot at Pomona, according to Patsy. "The hotel was actually Carl Laemmle, Jr.'s estate, which I think was also in Pomona."

Pat Costello remembers doubling Lou in the "Headless Horseman" sequence. In the scene, Grover pulls Wilbur onto the horse so they can make their getaway. Pat was rigged up in a body harness to achieve the effect. Each time Kenton yelled "Cut!" Pat rang up another $75 in stunt pay. During a break, Pat asked Lou, "See how long you can keep this thing going." Lou said okay, and Pat went back to work. The next time he was yanked into the air, Pat heard a loud "ping!" and the wire broke. He came crashing to the ground. "I had made my last $75 for that day!" he laughed.

Patsy O'Connor remembers another blooper. "We were on the process stage, and a train was supposed to be coming at us. It hits our carriage, cuts it in half, and we're sent spinning around. [laughs] Well the carriage spun around so fast, I went flying out! Lou reached out to catch me, and he got a hold of my panties, and my panties ripped! [laughs] Then he grabbed my dress, and it ripped a little bit. He finally hauled me back in, and he gave me a big hug. Then he shook his finger at me and said, 'Don't you ever do that again!' " [laughs]

Lou's clowning with Patsy held up at least one scene. "I know one day Erle got a little upset with Lou because Lou loved to kid around. He was always joking with me. I had this scene where I was supposed to overhear something and burst into tears. But Lou had me in such hysterics that Erle came over and said, 'Lou, would you stop it! This girl has to *cry!*' And Lou just gave a pout, like a little boy, and walked away. The make-up man said he had to use more stuff in my eyes for tears than he'd ever used on anybody else. It was *impossible* to be sad with Lou around."

BUD AND LOU'S SCENES

The boys revive their "Mudder/Fodder" routine when Wilbur feeds candy to the horse. "You'll spoil the horse's appetite," Grover admonishes Wilbur. "Now he won't eat his fodder." Wilbur is confused. "Eat his father? What do you think Finnegan is, a cannibal!" Later, Sam, Harry, and Chauncey clarify a racing form for Wilbur. "If a horse has an 'x' in front of his name, that shows he's a mudder," explains Sam. "How can a *he* be a mudder?" wonders Wilbur. "Ain't a she always a mudder?" "No," answers Grover. "Sometimes a he is a better mudder than a she." Finally, in Finnegan's stable, Wilbur tries to take the ailing horse's pulse. Grover instructs him to examine the horse's forelegs. "The horse's forelegs are in front," he explains. "The horse's four legs are in front? What's those things in the back—crutches?" cracks Wilbur. The routines turned up again in *The Noose Hangs High* (1948).

It Ain't Hay contains an unusual number of inside jokes. Early in the film, you may spot a restaurant called, "Windsor House Band Box." This is a hybrid of the names of the two restaurants Bud and Lou owned. Abbott later changed the name of the "Windsor House" to "Abbott's Backstage." Eagle-eyed fans will notice that the restaurant where Wilbur runs up a tab is named "Grant's Cafeteria," after John. The little boy who blames Wilbur for Finnegan's death is Alex Gottlieb's son, Stephen. At the back room betting parlor, Grover gives the password, "Stinky Fields sent us." "Yeah, he's a good friend of Shorty McAllister's," adds Wilbur. These are the names of a popular burlesque team, Harry Katz Fields and Richie McAllister. Another inside gag comes later in the film, when there's a knock on a door and Grover says, "Answer the door, it might be Warner." "It won't do no good," says Wilbur. "We're signed up with Universal."

Grant was wrestling with the restaurant sequence for some time. In his earlier letter to Alex Gottlieb, John wrote, "I want to revise the restaurant scene, but just can't get the idea clear yet. But I'll have it sooner or later." As Eddie Quillan remembers it, John finally worked

it out on the set. "John Grant was on the set all the time. We were going to do that cafeteria scene. Shemp, David, and myself were sitting at a table and Bud, Lou, and John were over in a corner, talking for I don't know how long. I went by once and overheard them talking about some bit they did in Detroit. But I didn't know what they were talking about it for. I went back to the table, and Bud and Lou came on the set. Most of the scene that we had in the script was eliminated because they were going to do this thing that they did in Detroit." [laughs]

The crooked betting parlor is the best sequence in the film. Wilbur and Grover place their bet, then listen to the call of the race over a loudspeaker. The races are "broadcast," with all the appropriate effects, from the very next room. The track announcer, without pausing for breath, shouts, "They're off, the race is over, you lose!" Each successive race has a smaller field of entrants but Wilbur still can't win. Finally, Wilbur bets on a one-horse race. "They're off in a bunch!" blurts the announcer. Wilbur's horse is beat out by a sluggish horse finishing the previous race! Grover manages to work his way to the back room, however, and change the outcome of the race in Wilbur's favor.

Lou has his most poignant scene to date when he discovers that Finnegan has died. He handles it quite well, and audience reaction seemed to be favorable. Scenes of pathos like this would be included in the next several Abbott and Costello scripts, but not all of them made it to the screen.

TOP LEFT: The restaurant sequence with Shemp Howard, Eddie Quillan (back to camera), and Dave Hacker. TOP CENTER: With Patsy O'Connor. TOP: In a deleted sequence at Saratoga, Grover and Wilbur are chased through a spa. Wilbur stops for a drink at a fountain that dispenses Hawthorne #6, a bitter-tasting iron tonic. He spits it out in a curve that just misses Grover. At the next fountain, Wilbur inadvertently samples Hawthorne #4, an astringent. His mouth puckers up until he can barely speak.

DELETIONS AND ADDITIONS

After the boys steal Tea Biscuit, an early draft of the script indicated a very funny sight gag: "Shot of subway train in tunnel. Crowded. Wilbur and Grover standing, holding straps. Camera reveals Tea Biscuit standing beside them. When train stops, fat man gets up. There is a scramble for his seat, obscuring Grover, Wilbur, and Tea Biscuit. When smoke clears, Wilbur and Grover are still holding straps, but Tea Biscuit is seated."

The film's finale was drastically cut, according to Patsy O'Connor. "There was a big, fabulous ending, that took two days to shoot. There was a cast of thousands. It really was something. But the picture ended up being very long with all the musical numbers. So people like myself and Grace were cut out, because they wanted to keep all the Abbott and Costello stuff in."

According to the script, "Hang Your Troubles On a Rainbow" had several additional verses that were deleted, most of them innocuous referrals to war time shortages. But there was one particularly heavy-handed verse:

Grover: Come on let's all sing a toast
      To the ones we hate the most
Wilbur: Let Heinie and Fritz'll
      Choke to death on Weiner Schnitzel

CHORUS: Hats off to Old Glory
         To Hell with the Heil!
         Hang Your Troubles on a Rainbow
         And rally round a smile!

The Breen Office wouldn't permit the line, "To Hell with the Heil."

REVIEWS

New York Sun: "A&C, Damon Runyon, and a sizeable hunk of straight vaudeville are stirred together in 'It Ain't Hay.' The result is a stew more palatable than the more recent Costello-Abbott frolics. The gags are usually fresh. The story, sentimental as any Runyon yarn, at least is a story. The comics find plenty to do."

New York World-Telegram: "A&C have skidded dangerously close to the margin of bad pictures several times, and finally they have gotten just a little too negligent. 'It Ain't Hay' ain't doing right by the A&C admirers. . . . It's not Lou Costello who is letting his followers down. He is piling up confusion as energetically as ever, but his writers fail to come through with a reasonable number of gags. The boys have been rushing A&C pictures through too fast. . . ."

New York Daily Mirror: "Considering the rate at which Universal is grinding out A&C films, it is not surprising that their quality is not keeping pace. 'It Ain't Hay' is not as funny as the team's early pictures. . . . But their fans will probably confound us by going for it in a big way."

New York Morning Telegraph: "Back in the old days, the two boys bounced around in a give-and-take act that for speed, timing and nonsensical effects had no match anywhere. Now their studio has been compelled to turn to, of all people, Damon Runyon, to bolster them up, and the result is somewhat less than happy. Runyon is good. A&C are good. But the two brands of comedy should never be blended into the same picture. . . . [The] manner of handling the picture is straight slapstick, and that's no way to treat the lads who gave us that baseball routine when they first started out. . . . [T]he emphasis is laid not so much on the quick firing dialogue that should distinguish A&C from all others, as it is on Costello's own muggings, burpings, and allegedly highly comical close-ups."

PM: "The title of their new movie is 'It Ain't Hay,' and the title really says a mouthful; not only ain't it hay, it ain't even good corn."

POSTSCRIPT

In some cities, *It Ain't Hay* played on a double bill with *Frankenstein Meets the Wolf Man,* thus anticipating *Abbott and Costello Meet Frankenstein* by five years.

This was Erle Kenton's last film with Bud and Lou, and his least effective. But his previous two, *Pardon My Sarong* and *Who Done It?,* are among the team's best. Alex Gottlieb explained, "Erle Kenton was a pretty good director, and a very conscientious director. He got fed up with Bud and Lou, because they wouldn't listen to him as much as he wanted them to. And the director really is the guy who makes the picture work. He tries to get the most out of the actors. Kenton was a very dedicated fellow."

Early in the production, Abbott and Costello initiated their own NBC radio series on Thursday night, October 8. Their guest on the opening program was Veronica Lake, and in the weeks that followed, stars such as Marlene Dietrich, John Garfield, Basil Rathbone, Merle Oberon, and Adolphe Menjou appeared on the show. The boys were required to leave Universal at noon every Thursday in order to prepare for the broadcasts.

Near the end of production, on November 6, 1942, Anne Costello gave birth to their third child, Lou Costello, Jr., known as "Butch." "We got a call on the set that the baby was born," Alex Gottlieb recalled. "We stopped shooting for the day and he went home to see the baby. He was in heaven—a son. He thought it was the greatest thing in the world that ever happened to him."

HIT THE ICE

SYNOPSIS

Flash Fulton and Tubby McCoy are sidewalk photographers who hope to land a job on a newspaper. A childhood friend, Dr. Bill Burns, takes them with him on an emergency call to a building fire. Tubby is hurt taking photographs of the fire and brought to a hospital. A gangster named Silky Fellowsby has checked into the hospital to establish an alibi while he and his men rob a nearby bank. They mistake Flash and Tubby for two gunmen from Detroit, and the criminals expect them to participate in the robbery. Flash and Tubby think they've just been hired to take pictures. But when the bank is robbed, they are accused of the crime.

Fellowsby plans to "recuperate" at Sun Valley, and he hires Dr. Burns and nurse Peggy Osborne to attend him. To clear themselves, Flash and Tubby follow the gangsters to the resort, where they take jobs as waiters. Tubby develops a crush on Marcia Manning, a singer at the resort. The boys attempt to recover the money by blackmailing the gangsters, but their photograph proves worthless. After a fight, the boys escape on skis with the loot, and after the chase the gangsters are captured.

BACKGROUND

Bud and Lou started on *Hit the Ice* just two weeks after completing *It Ain't Hay*. The team looked forward to working with its new director, Charles Lamont. According to Charles, they had demanded his services: "I was under contract to Universal at the time. One of my little pictures [possibly *Don't Get Personal* or *You're Telling Me*] was playing at the bottom half of a double bill at the Pantages Theater where they were previewing *Ride 'Em Cowboy*. My picture got ten times as many laughs as their film did. They were furious and went back to the studio screaming, 'Who the hell is this guy? He makes a little situation comedy and gets all the laughs. We want him to direct our pictures!'

"But I didn't want to. I wasn't making those kinds of pictures. I was making situation comedies. I loved doing them. I was told at the time that I had 'the Capra touch.' I knew that if I directed them I'd be considered an Abbott and Costello–type director. All I'd ever get to make would be those kinds of slapstick comedies. Universal, however, was insistent. At that time the Abbott and Costello pictures were making millions of dollars; they were the top box office attraction throughout the world. The studio offered me a deal I just couldn't turn down. So, after much talking, I finally agreed to do just *one* picture."

Lamont, however, worked on an Abbott and Costello film previous to *Hit the Ice*. He devised gags for the memorable chase sequence in *Pardon My Sarong*—many of which came out of his experience as a director for the Christie and Sennett comedies.

Earliest Draft:
February 23, 1942

Production Start:
November 23, 1942

Production End:
December 31, 1942

Copyright Date:
June 24, 1943

Released: July 2, 1943

Running Time: 82 minutes

Reissued: December 1949 with *Hold That Ghost*

Directed By:
Charles Lamont

Produced By:
Alex Gottlieb

Screenplay By:
Robert Lees, Frederic Rinaldo, John Grant

Original Story By:
True Boardman

Director of Photography:
Charles Van Enger ASC

Art Direction:
John B. Goodman, Harold MacArthur

Director of Sound:
Bernard B. Brown

Technician:
Robert Pritchard

Set Decorations: R. A. Gausman, A. J. Gilmore

Film Editor: Frank Gross

Gowns: Vera West

Assistant Director:
Howard Christie

Musical Director:
Charles Previn

Music Supervisor:
Ted Cain

Words and Music By:
Harry Revel, Paul Francis Webster

THE SCRIPT

True Boardman submitted a treatment (titled "Oh Doctor") in February 1942 that is a slightly more complicated version of the same story. Bud and Lou are newspaper photographers staking out a hospital maternity ward because a European princess is about to give birth. Lou's character is a hypochondriac who carries pills in a cartridge belt around his waist and in a conductor's changemaker. After robbing the bank, Fellowsby decides to follow the royal family to Sun Valley to steal the crown jewels. Bud and Lou follow the gangsters to try to clear themselves and save the jewels. Alex Gottlieb felt that the scenario needed to be simplified, and he handed it over to Robert Lees and Fred Rinaldo.

THE CAST

Ginny Simms (b. 1916) had been the featured vocalist with Kay Kyser's band. "I joined Kay Kyser's band when I left high school," Ginny explained. "We made three pictures at RKO, and, by the way, Sheldon played a gangster in all three!" Ginny left the band late in 1941 to star on her own radio program. "I was very surprised to get Hit the Ice," she confessed. She remembers Bud and Lou fondly: "I remember them with great love. They made me feel very, very comfortable. I don't remember any problems on the film. It was a happy, happy set. They were charming people, and we remained friends. Every time I'd see them in Hollywood at a function, they were always so lovely to me. Bud Abbott was great friends with my father."

Patric Knowles (b. 1911) was making his second film with the boys. He wrapped Frankenstein Meets the Wolf Man (1943) two weeks before starting on Hit the Ice.

Elyse Knox (b. 1917) is the daughter of William Franklin Knox, who was Secretary of the Navy under Roosevelt. Elyse, a former model, married football star Tom Harmon. Her son is actor Mark Harmon. She later appeared in a film produced by Lou, A Wave, a Wac, and a Marine (1944).

Sheldon Leonard (b. 1907), a perpetual movie gangster, later became one of television's most successful producers. He worked with the boys again in Abbott and Costello Meet the Invisible Man in 1951. Director Lamont called him, "My favorite heavy."

Joe Sawyer (1901–1982) made the first of three appearances in Abbott and Costello films. He later appeared in The Naughty Nineties (1945) and Comin' Round the Mountain (1951).

THE PRODUCTION

Exteriors for Hit the Ice were to be shot in Sun Valley in Idaho, but the resort was conscripted by the Army Ski Troops just before any sequences could be shot. Lamont ultimately shot the ski chase with doubles at Sode Springs, California, in January 1943.

Lamont's production spent the week of December 20 on location at Sonja Henie's skating rink in Westwood, where the studio built a set on the ice. Pat Costello doubled for Lou on skates. "I was on the tail end of the crack the whip line," he explained. "I had never been on skates, so I was funny without trying to be." Many of the gags were developed for a roller rink sequence that was cut from Keep 'Em Flying.

Most of the production, however, was on a soundstage at Universal, dressed to match the Sun Valley resort. Hollywood correspondent Ed Schallert documented a visit to the Ice set:

"If we want to quit work at 4 o'clock, we want to quit work at 4 o'clock," said Lou. "Comedy is hard work. We get tired. We need relaxation." I gathered that the boys get their relaxation, too. He and Bud Abbott had a game of cards lined up when I left them on the set of Oh Doctor. They were relaxing, but they weren't eating up the company's time because the set wasn't ready for the next shot, anyway.

It's this way, you see. Comedians can't simply sit around doing nothing. They're a nervous lot. And if they don't do gags on the set, then they'll do them off the set. And if they don't do gags they'll play cards, kid the girls, ride a scooter around the lot, or something. I rode with Lou in his scooter. It's got a sidecar and you can be as comfortable as might be expected. It's not a dull ride that you get. I thought at one point that Lou was going to go right through a big sliding door onto one of the stages. I hoped it was a breakaway. Lou yelled as we approached at what seemed like 60 mph, "Open the door! Open the door!" Never slowed his speed. Somehow, though only one man was moving it, it opened magically and we literally glided onto the set: a snow scene showing Sun Valley.

Abbott was on the set herding people around with a gun. I remarked on that. "Aw, you should have seen me with the gun," exclaimed Costello, "just an hour ago." A comic can't afford to be topped by a straight man, no matter how good the straight man, and not even with a gun.

That four o'clock quitting gag is no mere gag, either. They'd like to know that this may be the deadline, although if they're interested in the scenes and not tired and struggling, they may go on until much later. "I like it when things are happy and everybody feels good on the set," said Lou, who happened, because I met him first, to be my chief source of information that day. "You see, I never go into a scene myself unless I do some little gag first to make people laugh. Maybe just some old routine like bumping into a post unexpectedly, and saying 'Pardon me.' We don't want the scene 'cold' when it starts. We'll warm it up, if we have to give somebody a hotfoot. We work best by ourselves, undisturbed, and with an understanding director. We generally know the corn when we see it, and you need a little corn once in a while in any comedy."

One of Lou's legendary acts of thievery occurred during production on *Hit the Ice*. One morning the crew showed up on the indoor swimming pool set to discover all the furniture missing. Gottlieb immediately thought of Lou, and called him at home. "How does the furniture look around your pool?" Alex asked. At first, Lou feigned ignorance, but admitted, "It looks great, and it's gonna stay there." Gottlieb negotiated with Lou for the loan of the furniture until the production was completed; then Lou could have it back.

BUD AND LOU'S SCENES

There are two classic burlesque routines in *Hit the Ice*. The first is the "Pack/Unpack" scene. Now fugitives, Flash and Tubby pack to leave town. But Flash repeatedly changes his mind about running away, causing Tubby to frantically pack, unpack, and repack their grip several times. "I told the studio, 'It's going to take a lot of film,'" recalled Lamont. "I knew you couldn't do it with cuts; it's continuous dialogue and action. So I put *seven* cameras on it. When the call went into the production office, someone asked me what the hell I was going to do with all those cameras. But Jim Pratt, the production manager, said, 'Look, when Lamont asks for anything, don't ask him why. If he wants seven cameras, give him seven cameras. Anything he asks for, he gets.' That's the reputation I had. My plan worked, and I was able to get it all in the first take."

"The Piano Scene" with Ginny Simms.

Nothing in the final cut would indicate Lamont used more than two cameras. In addition, Lamont's blocking places Bud and Lou so far apart that his two-shots are too wide to show the action. Jean Yarbrough staged the routine perfectly for one of the team's television episodes, placing Costello downstage and Abbott upstage. His widest shot was easily able to hold both comedians while catching all of Costello's facial expressions.

The second classic routine was known in burlesque as the "Piano" scene or "Alright." To impress Marcia, Tubby pretends to play the piano. Flash, hidden behind the piano, provides the music with a record player. But Flash falls asleep on the job and misses his cues. Tubby must frantically try to cope. Ginny Simms recalled, "Being new to the game, I studied my lines so I knew them perfectly. Then Bud and Lou would ad-lib and mess me up! [laughs] I

101

RIGHT: Lou tools around the Universal back lot on his scooter. FAR RIGHT: New York Mayor Fiorello H. La Guardia crowns Bud and Lou as the nation's box office champs at the Waldorf Astoria (February 1943).

laughed my way through that picture. Remember the scene where Lou plays the piano to impress me? Well, they were ad-libbing all over the place. I started laughing and laughed through the scene." [laughs]

DELETIONS AND ADDITIONS

Lamont kept *Hit the Ice* remarkably close to the final shooting script. Throughout his career the director rarely indulged in superfluous material. "I knew every frame of a picture before I made the picture," he explained. Still, Lamont was always given a reserve fund for spontaneous additions on the set. "The studio used to give me a budget, plus an additional $5,000 to shoot ad-libs. I used to drift away from the script and then come back to it. But it was all within the story."

Lamont's additions are more likely to be physical gags than jokes, such as having Tubby's pants smolder after Marcia kisses him or having a little girl out-skate him. Generally, Lamont disregarded Bud and Lou's ad-libs. "I never paid any attention to what they said or what they offered. I'd tell them, 'Yeah, that's great. We'll leave it in.' But when I got the film in the cutting room, I cut it out." One funny Costello ad-lib that remained occurs in the bank, when he pretends that the vault door handle is a ship's wheel. Lou also reprises a neat bit from the chase in *Pardon My Sarong*. As he flees from a cop, Lou stops, turns, and asks the cop to hold for a picture. The policeman obliges, then resumes the chase.

REVIEWS

New York Post: "It is a weak plot and weak entertainment. Only Abbott and Costello are strong. But their strength is both intermittent and overly familiar. The laughs depend more than ever on pure slapstick, which is all right if you still laugh, but not so good if you're getting a little tired of their particular brand."

New York Morning Telegraph: "[A]s is usual with an Abbott and Costello picture, their antics were received with much approbation on the part of the audience that came to pay homage. This, of course, does not always indicate that the picture being shown to the audience is strictly first flight. Some cynics present in said audience yesterday may have detected a note of forced laugher every once in a while, as if the spectators felt they had to like Abbott and Costello whether they wanted to or not. In some instances the laughter, indeed, was much below the decibel volume of the previous efforts of the boys, a sure indication that they're not what they used to be."

Variety: "Utilizing the comedic abilities of Bud Abbott and Lou Costello in a compact script, in contrast to previous Abbott and Costello features, this one carries more than passing semblance of story credulity. . . . Not to be overlooked, in addition to the script by Lees, Rinaldo, and Grant, is the expert direction by Charles Lamont. Latter, with extensive experience in two-reel field of silent comedy, rounds out every comedy sequence with tailored precision. . . . Abbott and Costello romp in their usual top style, with strong support from Miss Simms, Knowles, Miss Knox, Long and orch. and gang trio of Leonard, Marc Lawrence and Joseph Sawyer. . . . Production is of 'A' rating throughout, with photography by far the best provided for the comedy team at Universal. There's class to the settings and general technical contributions."

Hollywood Reporter: ". . . Lou Costello makes one of his happiest appearances in 'Hit the Ice.' The rotund comic, who has lifted frustration to a fine art of hilarity, and his valuable partner, Bud Abbott, seem to be working more carefully on routines that have visual comedy impact. . . . There appears to be a choicer selection of gags in 'Hit the Ice' than ever before. The story is solid as Abbott and Costello sell it, and the Alex Gottlieb production is smartly directed by Charles Lamont."

POSTSCRIPT

Charles Lamont fulfilled his contract and moved on to *Mister Big* (1943), a lively musical with Gloria Jean, Donald O'Connor and Peggy Ryan. "After I finished *Hit the Ice,* Lamont explained, "I told the studio I didn't want to do any more of their pictures . . . and I meant it."

Lamont wrapped on December 31, 1942. That evening, on the Abbott and Costello radio show, Walter Wanger, President of the Academy of Motion Picture Arts and Sciences, presented Abbott and Costello with the Motion Picture Herald scroll proclaiming them the Number One Box Office Stars of the Year. Six weeks later, Mayor Fiorello La Guardia officially crowned them at a testimonial luncheon at the Waldorf Astoria in New York.

As 1943 dawned, Lou talked about the team's future projects. "A stage show on Broadway. That's what we really want to do. Sometime in the future. Comedians need new audiences. We get a lot of them on our bond tours. We sold $80 million worth, you know, since we started, we put a lot of industries right over the top when we visited their plants. But we'd like to have that fling at Broadway in a big show."

The show, according to a clipping, would be a musical, and would include the Frankenstein monster, Dracula, and probably Dracula's daughters, the Wolf Man, and various other horror personalities. The idea was probably inspired by *Frankenstein Meets the Wolf Man,* which was shooting on the same lot at the same time as *It Ain't Hay.* After its Broadway run, the boys would turn the horror-comedy into a film. "But we want to give a year to the show, and there's no chance of it right now," Lou continued. "The best we might be able to do is five months. That's not enough for Broadway if you have a really successful comedy show. Well, maybe after the war is over."

Instead, Bud and Lou began an extensive two-month tour of army camps with their radio show cast. When they returned to California on March 3, 1943, the pace had caught up with Lou. He was burning up with fever and his joints were painfully swollen. He had contracted rheumatic fever. His doctor ordered him bedridden, and word quickly spread that Lou Costello was gravely ill.

THE LOST YEAR

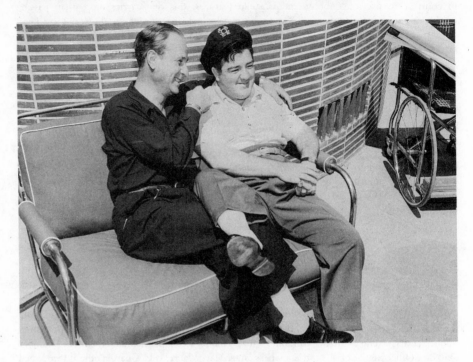

Bud on one of his daily visits to Lou's home during his convalescence.

Ironically, Lou had collapsed on his thirty-seventh birthday. He was driven home by Milt Bronson, who had only arrived in California the month before to manage Costello's nightclub, The Bandbox. Milt put Lou to bed and began applying hot compresses to his legs to relieve the pain. The doctor later told Milt that he probably had saved Lou's life.

The most critical period for Lou was that first month. Specialists from the Mayo Clinic flew in to examine him. The only cure for rheumatic fever, they told him, was bed rest, and Lou was confined to bed for months. Universal's carpenters built a special bed for him that could be wheeled out beside the pool so Lou could enjoy the air and watch his children play.

During his illness Lou received a constant stream of visitors, from Hollywood royalty like Charlie Chaplin and Clark Gable, to humble studio workers. Lou was thoroughly democratic about it. Everyone was welcome.

Abbott and Costello, meanwhile, were still before the public since Universal had only just released *It Ain't Hay,* and the team's follow-up picture, *Hit the Ice,* was held up until July. Astonishingly, although only two of their films were released, the team managed to place third on the list of Top Ten box office attractions of 1943.

Most of the team's movie projects were simply put on hold until Lou became available. One film, however, seems to have slipped through the cracks and was never made. It is significant because it was written by Robert Lees and Fred Rinaldo, the screenwriters previously responsible for *Hold That Ghost* (1941) and *Hit the Ice* (1943).

Early in 1942, Lees and Rinaldo submitted a bizarre horror-comedy titled "By Candlelight" (later retitled "You Hypnotize Me"). In the story, Bud and Lou run afoul of the sinister Dr. Ayoff (Basil Rathbone), who uses an incredible machine to tap into the preserved brains of his former clients! Ayoff learns all the intimate details of their lives and, more importantly, their finances. Lees and Rinaldo were able to salvage some of the situations and atmosphere for their later masterpiece, *Abbott and Costello Meet Frankenstein,* in 1948.

As he began to recover, Lou marked his progress by Butch's development. When Butch began to crawl, so did Lou. Finally, when the baby took his first steps in October, so did Lou. But other children began to concern Lou. He had received hundreds of letters from other rheumatic fever sufferers, mostly children, all wishing him well and wondering if a rich and famous man like himself had found a cure. He hadn't. The only cure, he'd write back, was months of bed rest. The letters made Lou aware of just how widespread the disease was and how many children suffered from it. "I can't fail those poor kids who've been rooting for me more than for themselves," he told an interviewer. "There's a reason why I got ill. The Man Upstairs wants someone down here to help those youngsters. I'm sure he means me." Stirred by the letters, Lou and Bud decided to establish the Abbott and Costello Rheumatic Fever Foundation to help young victims who couldn't afford expensive treatment and care. A 300-patient hospital research center was planned for Palm Springs, and the team agreed to split the $500,000 construction cost. Bud and Lou would raise the money to keep it going through personal appearance tours.

On a visit to the studio, Lou meets up with W.C. Fields on the set of *Follow the Boys* (1943).

By late October Lou was pronounced fit for work, and MGM rescheduled production on *Lost in a Harem* to begin in November 1944. On Thursday afternoon, November 4, Abbott and Costello reported to NBC studios to rehearse their first radio show broadcast since Lou's illness. The festivities were shattered by an urgent phone call that informed Eddie Sherman that Butch had drowned. The baby somehow had shaken loose a slat in his playpen, crawled across the patio, and fallen into the pool. Sherman drove Lou home, where they found Anne in shock and the rest of the family grieving. That morning Lou had asked Anne to keep Butch up so he could hear his father on the radio. Lou decided to go on with the show that night, reasoning, "Wherever Butch is tonight, I want him to hear me." Only the studio audience sensed something was amiss. To listeners at home, however, it was the same old Abbott and Costello—loud, fast, and foolish. At the close of the broadcast, Bud stepped up to the microphone and, choking back his own tears, addressed a national audience:

"Ladies and gentlemen, now that our program is over and we have done our best to entertain you, I would like to take a moment to pay tribute to my best friend and a man who has more courage than I have ever seen displayed in the theater. Tonight, the old expression, 'The show must go on,' was brought home to all of us on this program more clearly then ever before. Just a short time before our broadcast started, Lou Costello was told that his baby son—who would have been one year old in a couple of days— had died. In the face of the greatest tragedy which can come to any man, Lou Costello went on tonight so that you, the radio audience, would not be disappointed. There is nothing more I can say except I know you all join me in expressing our deepest sympathy to a great trouper. Good night."

The morning of the show, Anne had given Lou a bracelet with the baby's name inscribed on it. Lou had the bracelet welded around his right wrist so it couldn't be removed. It can be spotted in every subsequent film he made.

After the baby's death, plans for the Rheumatic Fever Foundation were postponed. The following year, they were amended. The team would sponsor a Youth Foundation for under-privileged kids in Los Angeles. However, wartime shortages would force the postponement of construction until after the war. Meanwhile, MGM pushed back the start of *Lost in a Harem* to the spring of 1944.

Many say that Lou was not the same man after Butch's death. He was less patient, less gregarious, and, some say, less conscientious about his work, which must have seemed rather unimportant in the wake of the tragedy. The team's new producer at Universal, Edmund L. Hartmann, was the first to encounter Lou's initial indifference. Gradually, time helped heal the wound, and although there were moments in the team's later films where Lou recaptured the original spirit and vibrance of the early work, it was never the same. Much of the little boy in Lou Costello died with his son.

105

IN SOCIETY

Earliest Draft:
March 11, 1943

Production Start:
June 12, 1944

Production End:
July 21, 1944

Copyright Date:
August 30, 1944

Released:
August 18, 1944

Running Time:
74 minutes

Reissued: March 1953

Directed By:
Jean Yarbrough

Produced By:
Edmund L. Hartmann

Screenplay By: John
Grant, Edmund L.
Hartmann, Hal Fimberg

Original Story:
Hugh Wedlock Jr.,
Howard Snyder

Director of Photography:
Jerome Ash ASC

Art Direction:
John B. Goodman,
Eugene Lourie

Director of Sound:
Bernard B. Brown

Technician:
Robert Pritchard

Set Decoration:
R. A. Gausman,
Leigh Smith

Film Editor: Philip Cahn

Gowns: Vera West

Dialogue Director:
Carter DeHaven

Assistant Director:
Howard DeHaven

Assistant Director:
Howard Christie

Special Photography By:
John P. Fulton ASC

Musical Director:
Edgar Fairchild

"What a Change In The
Weather" By: Kim
Gannon and Walter
Kent

SYNOPSIS

Plumbers Eddie and Albert are called to repair a leak in the bathroom of wealthy Mr. Van Cleve, whose wife is giving a costume ball. The plumbers arrive at the Van Cleve mansion in a taxi driven by Elsie Hammerdingle. Playboy Peter Evans mistakes Elsie for a costumed guest, and a romance begins. He invites her to spend the weekend at Mrs. Winthrop's estate, Briarwood. Meanwhile, Eddie and Albert devastate the upstairs bathroom and flood the master bedroom. Mrs. Van Cleve writes an indignant letter to the plumbers, but accidentally mails them her own invitation to Mrs. Winthrop's society weekend.

Eddie and Albert are delighted at the prospect of meeting so many new and wealthy customers. Drexel, a loanshark, demands that the boys help him steal the Winthrop's valuable painting, "The Plunger," but the boys refuse. Eddie, Albert, and Elsie arrive at Briarwood, and the boys spend a riotous weekend putting on airs, confounding the butler, and participating in a fox hunt. Drexel shows up and enlists Marlow, a shady chauffeur, in his scheme to steal the painting. Gloria Winthrop, jealous of Elsie, denounces her, Eddie, and Albert as the thieves. As Drexel and Marlow flee, Albert and Eddie pursue them in a firetruck, capture them, and return the painting.

BACKGROUND

Not long after Lou collapsed, Alex Gottlieb accepted a job at Warner Bros. "I finally realized I was going to be marked as just making Abbott and Costello pictures," he explained. "They had just taken up my option at Universal, and I had gone from $350 a week up to $800 a week, which was not a lot of money. I told my agent, 'See if you can get me a good job at another studio. I want to make different kinds of pictures.' I wanted to get away from Abbott and Costello, because when they go down, I'd go down with them. Warners gave me everything I wanted and I became quite successful over there."

Milton Feld selected screenwriter Edmund L. Hartmann as the boys' next producer. Hartmann had just finished writing and producing Olsen and Johnson's *Ghost Catchers* (1944), and had written the stories for *Keep 'Em Flying, Ride 'Em Cowboy,* and *Here Come the Co-Eds.* Hartmann recalled his first meeting with Bud and Lou as their new producer. "I'll never forget this because it never happened to me before or since. They had just come from Metro, where they'd made *Lost in a Harem.* There they had been given the Metro treatment of stars being royalty. That was a little different than the Universal treatment. Lou said, 'We just made a picture at Metro, and this is the way you make movies. We come in at ten and we leave at three. If you're in the middle of a shot, it's just too bad. We do one take, and if you don't get it, that's your hard luck.' Well, I thought to myself, this is nonsense; when we get on the set it's not going to be like this at all. Well, it *was.*"

From the assistant director's reports filed every day during production, it seems that Bud and Lou were probably no less cooperative than they had been before Lou's illness. Out of the thirty-two days they were scheduled to work, Bud and Lou quit at three pm or earlier on just nine days. Some of those days were scheduled half-days, and on other days their call was for eight am.

This expeditiousness was a boon. Hartmann had to have the picture in theaters before September. "Metro had finished their picture," he recalled, "and it very well could have been the first picture out after Bud and Lou's absence from the screen. But they very graciously offered to hold their picture back if we could finish a picture and release it by September. So we had to write fast, shoot fast, and cut fast. We had four sets of cutters cutting the film as we went along. It was a tremendous logistical job."

THE SCRIPT

Fortunately, several scripts had piled up in the interim. Hugh Wedlock and Howard Snyder, former gag writers for Jack Benny, were writing *In Society* when Lou became ill in March 1943. Their third draft was delivered on April 20, 1943.

John Grant wrote a two-page memo to executive producer Milton Feld, citing his dissatisfaction with the screenplay. He wrote, "The treatment of Abbott and Costello in the story does not follow our handling of them in previous pictures. It is my feeling that with the exception of the bathroom plumbing scene, the tennis match, the fox hunt, and the boat chase, the other scenes are static—that is, they simply stand still and tell jokes. In former Abbott and Costello pictures, we have used innumerable jokes. However, we also tried to use the jokes in action, such as the betting-room scene in 'It Ain't Hay,' the packing-the-grip routine in 'Hit the Ice,' the bank scene in 'Hit the Ice,' and others of similar caliber." John went on to point out that many of the situations had been exploited in earlier films, and therefore needed to be changed.

Hal Fimberg and Edmund Hartmann revised the screenplay, adding Elsie as a love interest for Lou; the priceless painting, "The Plunger"; and a chase finale at a horse show. Ultimately, however, the film's ending utilized a firetruck chase sequence from W.C. Fields' *Never Give a Sucker an Even Break* (1941). "The ending was done just to have an exciting last reel," Edmund Hartmann explained. "It was also something Lou wanted to do, and it seemed like a pretty good idea. He was a marvelous athlete."

Lou had more suggestions for the screenplay. He insisted on hiring Sid Fields (1898–1975) to "punch up" the script. Fields wrote three routines, none of which made it into the finished film. However, Sid stayed on in Hollywood to join the writing staff of the Abbott and Costello radio show and, later, appear as the irascible landlord on the team's television series. Another uncredited contributor to the screenplay was veteran comedy writer Clyde Bruckman.

Edmund Hartmann remembers another of Lou's additions to the script. "About two-thirds of the way through the picture, Lou came to me and said, 'We're going to do "Fleugel Street." ' I said, 'But there's nothing in this picture that has anything to do with "Fleugel Street." ' He said, 'Well, we're going to do it.' And they did. I tried to make sense of it. The one thing I was able to do as a writer was, whatever they did that day, I would change the script to make it as rational as possible. I rewrote the other characters' scenes to set up what Lou and Bud had already done. I was constantly rewriting. The wonder was not whether it was good or bad, but that there was a picture."

THE CAST

Marion Hutton (1919–1987) was a vocalist with the Glenn Miller orchestra, and introduced such classics as "Kalamazoo," "Chattanooga Choo Choo," and "Don't Sit Under the Apple Tree." Her sister is Betty Hutton.

Kirby Grant (1911–1985) had been a child prodigy violinist, and later, a radio singer. He

"No Bout Adoubt It" and "My Dreams Are Getting Better All The Time": Music By: Vic Mizzy; Lyrics By: Mann Curtis

"Rehearsin' " By: Bobby Worth, Stanley Cowan

Musical Numbers Devised and Staged By: George Dobbs

Eddie Harrington .... Bud Abbott

Albert Mansfield .... Lou Costello

Elsie Hammerdingle .... Marion Hutton

Peter Evans .... Kirby Grant

Mrs. Winthrop .... Margaret Irving

Gloria Winthrop .... Ann Gillis

Pipps the Butler .... Arthur Treacher

Drexel ... Thomas Gomez

Baron Sergei .... George Dolenz

Count Alexis .... Steven Geray

Marlow .. Murray Leonard

Mr. Van Cleve .... Thurston Hall

Mrs. Van Cleve .... Nella Walker

Parker .... William B. Davidson

Drunk........ Don Barclay

Cop .... Edgar Dearing

Policeman ...... Charles Sherlock

Bit Man ...... Tom Dugan

Bit Woman .... Dorothy Granger

Cop .... Ralph Dunn

Luigi .... Luis Alberni

Bit Man ..... Leon DeVoe

Bit Man ..... Milt Bronson

Bit Woman ... Elvia Allman

Fire Chief ... Tom Fadden

Three Sisters ... Marge, Bea, and Geri

Will Osborne and Orchestra

107

had just finished *Ghost Catchers* with Olsen and Johnson. In the 1950s, he starred in "Sky King" on television. He worked with Bud and Lou again in *Comin' Round the Mountain* (1951).

Arthur Treacher (1894–1975) had portrayed the title role of a butler in *Thank You, Jeeves* (1936) so flawlessly that he became Hollywood's perennial butler.

THE PRODUCTION

The film began Abbott and Costello's long association with director Jean Yarbrough, who directed five of their features and produced and directed their television series in the 1950s. Yarbrough began his career in 1921 as a prop man on the Hal Roach lot, then quickly graduated to assistant director. His first full-fledged directorial assignment was making the Leon Errol shorts at RKO in the 1930s.

"Jean was a very able director," recalled Hartmann. "He had practically no sense of humor; he was very straight. But we worked together well and were pretty good friends. He pretty much took what I said as being true as far as comedy was concerned, and I accepted what he said as far as what camera angles to use."

Fully two-thirds of *In Society* was shot on location, primarily at the Jewett Estate on Arden Road in Pasadena. Erle Kenton directed two production numbers on location: "Rehearsin'," at the Janns estate in Beverly Hills, and "Change in the Weather" at Reuss Lake. "Erle was shooting those scenes at the same time as we were shooting something else in order to finish the picture on time," Hartmann explained. "We would have used whatever means necessary to get it done."

The picture became Universal's most expensive Abbott and Costello production to date. Originally scheduled for thirty-one days, *In Society* ran three days over. Bud and Lou's salary was $80,000, plus a percentage. The final cost was $659,526.14.

Bud and Lou were visited by a reporter from *The New York Times* on the costume ball set. They were having a labor dispute with assistant director Howard Christie. A newspaper clipping reports:

> Christie refused to let either of the team's $3,000 luxury house trailers on the sound stage where the lavish costume ball was being staged. "There's not enough room for both trailers," Christie said. "I want to be fair, so there's only one thing to do. Neither of the trailers can be brought in."
>
> Abbott and Costello, being creative artists, declared they needed a quiet place of their own on the set where they could retire between scenes and create. Their artistic feelings were touched by the cold, impartial judgment of the a.d. which denied them what they felt to be their due as actors, scholars and gentlemen. So, the two comedians picketed back and forth in front of a table where Christie, onetime University of California football ace, eats in the commissary. They carried banners stating Christie was unfair to them. Christie, being a paid up member of the guild, couldn't cross the picket line. He was in danger of going without lunch. Finally he negotiated, and the grievance was settled: one trailer was moved onto the stage. "We are agreeable," said Lou. "After all, there's a war on, and anybody who can't get along with one trailer is not patriotic."

BUD AND LOU'S SCENES

The bathroom plumbing sequence was shot over two days. While stunt man Irving Gregg had to spin the tool bag over his head and fall six times, most of Bud and Lou's scenes were done in one take, or two at the most. "The bathtub sequence was done in a big tank," Edmund Hartmann explained. "The special effects department set it up and there were no problems with it at all."

The classic "Fleugel Street" routine was not done in one continuous take. In fact, counting the fifteen different set-ups and variations filmed, there were some thirty-eight takes! The script refers to the Pioneer Hat Company on Beagle Street, but during shooting this was changed to the Susquehanna Hat Company. The zanies Lou encounters are played by some familiar faces: Elvia Allman (a regular on their radio show); Milt Bronson (an old pal from burlesque, and Lou's stand-in); Dorothy Granger (a bit player in a few films and TV episodes); Leon DeVoe (a burlesquer); Tom Dugan (Hollywood's perennial cop); and Luis Alberni (a prolific character actor).

There is an alternate ending in the script that was not used. When the last man explains that he was killed by a falling safe, Lou says, "Wait a minute, mister; I was just talking to your wife." The lunatic exclaims, "So *that's* why you let the safe drop on me! You wanted to steal my wife!" Lou explains that he's only trying to deliver hats to the Pioneer Hat Company. "Give me that hat!" the man shouts, crumpling it. "I'm not going to have another poor man killed because of one of those hats! It's the *cheapest, worst grade of straw I ever saw!*" Just then, Elvia Allman re-enters the scene. "Hey lady," Lou bleats, "here's your husband. Please get him away from me!" She's incensed. "My husband? How *dare* you bring him back! Now I'll have to give back all the insurance money—and I've already *spent it!* It's all your fault!" She flails Lou with a hat. After the man and woman take parting swipes at Lou, they leave in opposite directions. Now Bud berates Lou, "Well, I hope you're satisfied. It wasn't enough that you were breaking up hats—now you're breaking up happy homes! You should be ashamed of yourself!" Bud pushes Lou into the shelves full of pottery for the blackout.

Edmund Hartmann was fascinated by "Fleugel Street." He explained, "Here a man is going to 'Fleugel Street' to deliver some hats, and every person he asks breaks up his hats and beats him up. Well, now, these are *lunatics.* I figured there's got to be a rationale somewhere, and I did a lot of research on it. I finally found out what it was. It originally made a lot of sense. It was the story of a strike at a hat company, and this fellow is hired without knowing it as a strikebreaker. He's delivering this box of straw hats through the picket line to the struck hat company. So when he's got all the hats and he says, 'Where's Fleugel Street,' and the strikers beat him up and break up his hats, they have a reason to. But the comics in burlesque realized that people don't laugh when you talk about a strike; they laugh when you beat a guy up and break his hats."

Despite the fact that "Fluegel Street" was written in 1918 by Billy K. Wells, burlesque's most proficient writer, many comics tried to claim it. "When the picture was released," Hartmann continued, "we were sued by eight different comics who said that they had initiated it."

BELOW: With director Jean Yarbrough on the set of *In Society* (1944). Yarbrough later directed the team's classic TV series in the early 1950s. BELOW LEFT: The "Beagle Street" scene, a.k.a. "Susquehanna Hat Company."

DELETIONS AND ADDITIONS

One sequence followed in the tradition of *It Ain't Hay* and *Hit the Ice* in giving Lou a scene for pathos. After Elsie sings "My Dreams Are Getting Better All The Time," she and Peter embrace, depressing Albert. "I'm the unhappiest boy in the world," he confides to Eddie. "All my life I've loved Elsie Hammerdingle—and now she's in love with somebody else. I've loved her ever since we were kids together. I'll never forget the first time I met her . . . It was in the seventh grade. She was nine and I was nineteen. I was so much in love with her. Every minute of the day—no matter what I was doing—there was only one word I kept hearing. All the time it was 'Hammerdingle, Hammerdingle, Hammerdingle.' I used to take jobs shoveling snow, selling papers and running errands so I could get enough money to buy Elsie a chocolate soda. We used to drink with two straws. I let her sip faster so she could get more of the soda. I'll never forget the first time I bought her a box of chocolates and took her to see a movie. We sat in the box. Crushed every chocolate. Now she's in love with somebody else . . ."

Sid Fields was signed to perform his character Professor Mellonhead in "The Language Scene." Albert asks the Professor to make him a gentleman so he can compete with Peter for Elsie's affections. "Make you a gentleman?" Fields muses. "A gentleman is a person of refinement and culture—the antithesis of everything you have displayed thus far!" "I resemble that remark!" exclaims Albert." "Resemble?" sneers Fields. "You see? The moment I use polysyllabic conversation, you're at a loss. Resemble! Why do you attempt intelligent repartee when your intelligence quotient is obviously minus nil?" This scene was deleted, but Fields returned to perform a similar routine in *Mexican Hayride* (1948).

In the "Garden Party" sequence, Albert inadvertently rings a bell that summons Pipps, who brings a bottle of champagne and charges him $5. Pipps explains that whenever the bell rings, it means he's ordered a bottle of champagne. Of course, Albert continues to accidently ring the bell—his hat hits it, he tries to hide it, etc.—until he collects a dozen bottles. Although the bulk of the scene was cut, listen carefully and you can hear the bell ring the first time and then see A&C suddenly with a table full of bottles.

REVIEWS

"If there was any doubt that Abbott and Costello might not be the same magical draw as before, the first preview took care of that," Hartmann explained. "When the Universal logo appeared, the audience started laughing, whistling and stamping their feet. By the time it said, 'Abbott and Costello,' you couldn't hear anything for the noise. And the first shot back then [since changed] was a dripping faucet. Nothing had happened yet—but that got the biggest laugh I've ever heard. It was an enormous laugh."

Variety: "This is probably the most uproarious in the successful string of comedy vehicles the team's turned out. . . . Costello works in his old stride, while Abbott is more efficient, smooth-working than ever as straight man in the laugh combo. . . . Jean Yarbrough distinguishes himself with his swiftly paced direction. . . . Edmund L. Hartmann's production bespeaks care for details, some of the sets being lavish."

New York Post: " 'In Society' is perhaps a little quieter than some of the more boisterous madhouses Abbott and Costello have been in during the past. But it is substantially the same. You laugh at the same kind of situations and once again you marvel at Lou Costello's ability to extract merriment from repetitious business. He is an underslung genius with a face that conquers all. Assuming that you can stand Abbott and Costello again, 'In Society' goes on your comedy list beneath, but a long way beneath, 'Hail the Conquering Hero.' "

Los Angeles Examiner: "That lull we just passed through was due to the absence of Bud Abbott and Lou Costello from the screen. The lads could have done with fresher, newer material, that we admit. Too much is entirely too much and Universal should realize a change of pace is needed along about now if this team of funny men are to survive."

PM: "[It brings] back all my memories of Harold Loyd and the Marx Brothers, but unfortunately not all my enjoyment. Although the Abbott & Costello devotees at the Criterion

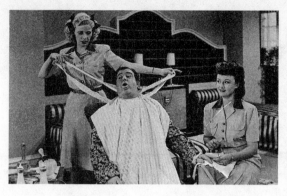

yesterday morning appeared to be getting what they came for, there seemed to me something more forced than funny about a lot of the custard-pyrotechnics, and something familiar about even the best of them. . . . [Costello] needs a scriptwriter who can think of something more waggish than mispronouncing 'etiquette' or capping 'Your bath is drawn' with 'Erase it.' And though something like burlesque's ancient 'Begel St.' routine may still be good for the movies, there's no need to take it and ruin it."

The New York Times: "Ordinarily the past, present and future status of a comedy team isn't of Page One importance to others than the comedians themselves, their contract holders and their next of kin. In this particular case, however, a rather interesting phase of the screen industry seems to be involved. How long can even the sturdiest comedy team stand up under plotless pictures in which rehashes of well-worn pieces of business provide the only relief? True enough the A-C team has been able, as in their latest picture, to keep the pace rolling through their own energy. But the thickest bag of tricks grows thin when on display several times a year.

"Thus we find a team generally accredited with having all the qualifications of a long-enduring comedy and money-earning combination being bled white, so to speak, in pieces below their abilities. . . . Now, in 1944, there is one picture which furnishes little or no departure from the previous five. 'In Society' will undoubtedly make money for the studio and quite probably a few more just like it will continue to make money for the studio, too. But what will they do for Abbott and Costello? That's the thought for today!"

Letter to the Times Film Editor: "In your analysis of the current and future appeal of Abbott and Costello, you made two points which I think are open to question. One is that great clowns must vary their routines in order to hold the affections of their audiences. Where does the Chaplin of 'Easy Street' differ from the Chaplin of 'Gold Rush'? In fact, it was only when Chaplin attempted to change that characterization in 'The Great Dictator' that any members of his vast army of followers found cause for complaint. As to point number two—that the public is tiring of Abbott and Costello—just take a look at the Criterion Theater. . . . In its first five days, 'In Society' topped grosses for pictures like Deanna Durbin and Gene Kelly in 'Christmas Holiday,' 'Gung Ho,' 'Cabin in the Sky,' and, incidentally, all the other Abbott and Costello hits. Let me put this on record. If Universal will promise faithfully to produce picture after picture with Abbott and Costello just as funny, and just as much in the Abbott and Costello groove as 'In Society,' my patrons and I will be very happy indeed."—*Charles B. Moss, Managing Director, Loew's Criterion.*

POSTSCRIPT

In six months, Bud and Lou completed two pictures. It seemed as if the old pace was about to start again. But Bud and Lou enjoyed some time off during the summer of 1944 before resuming their radio program that fall. Lou was also busy planning the rheumatic fever foundation.

ABOVE: Albert has another run-in with the Professor at the buffet table. "I'm supposed to make a gentleman out of you," Fields sneers. "You are obviously the complete vindication of the Darwinian theory of evolution. I'll prove it. First there was the primeval ooze, then the amoeba, then the pithcanthrupus erectus, the Neanderthal man, then the missing link, then you, and then the human race!" (Arthur Treacher on left.) ABOVE LEFT: Arthur requests a shave and a manicure, but the barberette (Mabel Todd) and manicurist (Gladys Blake) are more interested in gossiping about the guests than noticing his predicament. When the barberette nicks him, Lou protests. She replies, "A woman has as much right to be a barber as a man. This business needs new blood." Lou cracks, "Well, you don't have to take mine!" She continues to nick him, and apply huge bandages to his face until finally he is totally masked. "Help! Help! I've disappeared! I'm the Invisible Man!" he cries.

LOST IN A HAREM

Earliest Draft:
August 13, 1941

Production Start:
March 22, 1944

Production End:
June 3, 1944

Copyright Date:
August 22, 1944

Released:
August 31, 1944

Running Time:
89 minutes

Directed By:
Charles Riesner

Produced By:
George Haight

Screenplay By:
Harry Ruskin, John
Grant and Harry Crane

Musical Supervision:
Johnny Green

Musical Direction:
David Snell

"It is Written," "I Know
It's Wrong," and
"Destiny" By: Don
Raye and Gene de Paul

"Sons of The Desert"
By: Sammy Fain and
Ralph Freed

"John Silver" By:
Toots Camarata

"Noche de Ronda" By:
Maria Terese Lara

Orchestrations:
Sonny Burke, Ted
Duncan, Wally Heglin

Musical Production
Directed By:
Jack Donohoe

Director of Photography:
Lester White ASC

Recording Director:
Douglas Shearer

Art Direction:
Cedric Gibbons,
Daniel C. Cathcart

Set Decorations:
Edwin B. Willis

SYNOPSIS

When the "International Review," a small vaudeville show, becomes stranded in Port Inferno, a bizarre city in the mystic East, singer Hazel Moon lands a job at the Cafe of All Nations. She persuades the owner to hire the revue's prop men, Harvey Garvey and Pete Johnson, as a comedy team. Their magic act starts a brawl in the club, and Hazel and the boys are thrown in jail. Ramo, a desert shiek, offers to help Hazel and the boys escape if they help him regain the throne of Barabeeha, which his wicked uncle, Nimativ, has usurped with the aid of two hypnotic rings. Pete, Harvey, and Hazel escape and join Ramo's band of desert riders. Ramo explains that his uncle is susceptible to blondes. With Hazel to distract him, Pete and Harvey can steal the rings.

Posing as Hollywood talent scouts, the boys enter the capital city with Hazel. Nimativ is captivated by Hazel, but he quickly hypnotizes Pete and Harvey and learns of Ramo's plan. The boys are tossed in jail, and Hazel is hypnotized to become wife number thirty-eight. Ramo rescues the boys and smuggles them into the palace, where Harvey wins the cooperation of Teema, the chief wife of the harem, by promising to get her into movies. Harvey disguises himself as Teema, and Pete impersonates Nimativ. During a great celebration, the boys steal the rings and hypnotize Nimativ into abdicating. Ramo is restored to the throne, Hazel becomes his wife, and our heroes are off for America.

BACKGROUND

While Bud and Lou received $70,000 for their first MGM effort, *Rio Rita,* and were to be paid $80,000 for *Lost in a Harem,* each of their Universal features earned them three times those amounts. The team plainly resented Universal's agreement with Metro. Eddie Sherman recalled, "I took into account the fact that we were not earning the same money as we were at Universal. I felt that we were no party to Universal's deal with Metro. I notified Universal that we weren't going to report to *Lost in a Harem;* it was their headache. I got a call from Bennie Thau of MGM. He said, 'Mr. L. B. is going to be very mad.' I said 'Well, that's just too bad. I don't do any business with him anyway. So he can be as mad as he wants to be.'

"The next day I got a call from L. B. Mayer, and I went over to see him. I made my point, that we were giving up one of four pictures a year at Universal to go to Metro, where we'd be earning less money because we were losing our percentage. Mayer said, 'What will you take for the next two pictures?' I figured the least I would want not to have too much difficulty. I said, 'I'll take double the salary—$150,000. But double the salary goes entirely to us.' He said okay. I said, 'That isn't all of it. It's retroactive to *Rio Rita.* You'll have to give me $450,000 for three pictures.' Well, he blew his stack. He said, 'Even if I wanted to give it to you, I couldn't. Salary Stabilization won't permit it.' I said, 'Are you willing to pay this money if we can clear it with Salary Stabilization?' He said yes.

"There were two wonderful fellows working at Universal, Morrie Davis and Ed Muhl. I sat with them and worked it out. They wanted to keep me satisfied because they didn't want any problems with Abbott and Costello." Bud and Lou signed their new contract on February 18. Universal collected $300,000 from MGM for *Lost in a Harem,* which included the studio's loan out fee, plus $225,000 for Bud and Lou. Universal agreed to pay the salary out over a period of twelve months to satisfy Salary Stabilization. The same arrangement was made the following year for their third MGM production, *Abbott and Costello in Hollywood.*

THE SCRIPT

Harem was originally intended as Abbott and Costello's first picture for MGM. Earl Baldwin submitted a first draft on August 13, 1941, pre-dating any of the *Rio Rita* material by a month. Baldwin's script had the boys, named Doc and Cozy, thwart Nazi spies who steal the formula for a powerful explosive developed by an Oxford-educated Arab prince. The basic idea of a Nazi spy background was appropriated for the plot of *Rio Rita.*

A new *Harem* script was prepared by Harry Ruskin, ostensibly for filming in the spring of 1943. Of course, Lou's illness and his son's death precluded production before the following year. By then, Harry Crane and John Grant had added to the screenplay, now titled "Harem Scare 'Em." (One working title, "Two Nights in a Harem," was deemed "too sexy" for kid fans of the team.)

Veteran comedy writer Harry Crane met Bud and Lou when they worked on the Edgar Bergen program in 1941. He had seen them perform in burlesque back in New York. "It was the same act in burlesque, just a little tackier," Crane recalled. Crane was working at Metro when *Harem* was in development, and Bud and Lou endorsed his participation as a screenwriter. "While they were doing the picture," Harry explained, "they had a radio show. Eddie Sherman called me and said, 'How would you like to do the radio show?' I said I can't, I'm working for MGM. He said, 'We'll work it out.' And so I wrote for their radio show, too."

Crane appreciated Lou's wit. "One day somebody asked Lou why he played the horses. And Lou said, 'Because it increased my appetite. I started playing the races ten years ago, and I've been hungry ever since!' [laughs] Another time Lou and I went down to the races at Del Mar. We went to the window to place a bet, and Harry James came up to Lou and asked, 'What looks good?' Lou turned to me and said, 'He's married to Betty Grable and he asks me what looks good!' Lou was truly a funny man."

Of course the Breen Office was concerned about the costuming of the dancing and harem girls, frequently referred to as "revealing" in the script. "We urge that you advise the costume department to use extreme care in the designing of these costumes. In this connection, please make certain that the dance routines performed by these lightly costumed girls be watched closely in order to avoid any suggestive or sensuous body movements. Otherwise they could not be approved under the provisions of the Code."

Breen was particularly sensitive about foreign reaction to the film. "Please make sure you avoid any use of the expression, 'Allah be praised,' or any like religious expression that may be taken as a derogatory reference to the religion of the Mohammedans. This is very important." Producer George Haight hit on the idea of "scrambled research" so that the locale could not be narrowed down to any one place or any one nationality. Characteristics of different lands were blended together, from the choreography to the architecture. Yet the film was rejected for showing in Morocco, while several cuts had to be made for showing in Syria.

One Abbott and Costello exchange had to be deleted from the script. An Arab fruit seller asks Harvey, "Would you like a date?" Pete says, "Answer the man. He wants to give you a date." "He don't appeal to me," replies Harvey. The Breen Office wrote, "This scene is unacceptable because of a 'pansy' flavor."

Associate:
  Richard Pefferle

Costume Supervision:
  Irene

Associate: Kay Dean

Men's Costumes: Valles

Make-Up Created By:
  Jack Dawn

Film Editor: George Hively

Peter Johnson
  .... Bud Abbott

Harvey Garvey
  .... Lou Costello

Hazel Moon
  .... Marilyn Maxwell

Prince Ramo
  .... John Conte

Nimativ
  ...... Douglas Dumbrille

Jimmy Dorsey ... Himself

Teema .... Lottie Harrison

Bobo .. J. Lockard Martin

The Derelict
  .... Murray Leonard

Chief Ghamu
  .... Adia Kuznetzoff

Mr. Ormulu
  .... Ralph Sanford

Chase Guards
  .... Bud Wolfe
            Cary Loftin

Police Chief
  .... Harry Cording

Native Jailor
  .... Sammy Stein

Jailor .... Duke York

Beautiful Girl
  .... Katharine Booth

Bearded Vendor
  .... Frank Penny

Majordomo .. Tor Johnson

Laundry Woman
  .... Jody Gilbert

Guard ...... Tiny Newland

Sentry .... Eddie Dunn

Zaida, Maid
  .... Sondra Rogers

Natives in Cafe
  .... Heinie Conklin
          Ernest Brenck

Slave Girls ... Toni LaRue
        Francis Ramsden
        Margaret Savage
            Jan Bryant
        Margaret Kelly
            Elinor Troy
        Symona Boniface

Acrobats .... The Pinas

THE CAST

Marilyn Maxwell (1921–1972) sang with various big bands before becoming a contract player at MGM in 1942. She was a regular in the *Dr. Kildare* series of films starring Van Johnson, and had just come off *Three Men in White* when production began on *Harem*. During filming, Marilyn became engaged to co-star John Conte. They were divorced in 1946. That year, Marilyn joined the Abbott and Costello radio program as vocalist. She later appeared with Bob Hope in *The Lemon Drop Kid* (1951).

John Conte appeared on radio with comedian Frank Morgan, who played the title role in *The Wizard of Oz* (1939). Conte recalled being assigned *Lost in a Harem*. "I was under contract to Metro, and they had tested a few people and they weren't happy with them. I think Peter Lawford tested, but he came across as too British. So, somebody at the studio asked me if I would be interested in doing the test, and I said yes. They wrapped me in a turban and I did the test with Marilyn. They liked what they saw and signed me for the film.

"I felt rather elated to be in an Abbott and Costello picture because I knew that these guys had a tremendous following and that the picture was going to be seen. It's like being in a picture with Clark Gable. You knew that everybody was going to see it."

Douglas Dumbrille (1890–1974) was one of Hollywood's ablest character actors, and a favorite foil for comedians like the Marx Brothers (*A Day at the Races, The Big Store*) or Bob Hope (*Road to Utopia, Monsieur Beaucaire, Son of Paleface*). He had previously appeared with Bud and Lou in *Ride 'Em Cowboy* (1941).

Murray Leonard (1898–1970) was an old pal from burlesque who worked with the boys in *In Society, The Noose Hangs High,* and *The Wistful Widow of Wagon Gap,* as well as the team's television series.

THE PRODUCTION

Director Charles Riesner (1887–1962) had been a vaudevillian and comedian at Keystone and Vitagraph during World War I. He was Chaplin's associate director on *A Dog's Life* (1918), *The Kid* (1921), *The Pilgrim* (1923), and *The Gold Rush* (1925), while playing nasty villains in the first three. He became a director in the mid-1920s, and worked with Keaton, W.C. Fields, and the Marx Brothers. John Conte recalled, "Our director, Chuck Riesner, was a dream. Because he'd just sit back and he'd say, 'Roll 'em. Everybody ready? Action.' Even in the scenes I had with Marilyn, Chuck was almost noncommittal in what he wanted us to do. He'd say, 'Get out there and do it.' He'd just let Bud and Lou go. That was it. I never saw Chuck direct one inch of that film. The guys did it all themselves.

"They were thoroughly professional. Bud and Lou were so in tune to each other—which we all knew and realized. They had worked together for so long, they lived and breathed each other's rhythm. They were known as the greatest non-rehearsers of all time; they hated to rehearse. They were both such quick studies that the director would walk them through the mechanics of the scene and they'd always say, 'Okay, let's go!' They wanted to get back to their dressing room. But in spite of the limited time that they would want to give to rehearsals, they'd have all the moves and all the lines down. It was just no big deal; after all, they weren't playing character parts, they were playing themselves. Just one take and the director would say, 'Okay, next set-up.' "

Harem's budget was reportedly $1,225,000, but this is debatable considering the studio utilized standing sets from its production of *Kismet* (1944). Ten thousand square feet of sand covered the floor of one of the studio's biggest stages. Twenty-five date palms, hauled from Indio, California, were transplanted in pits on the set. Bedouin tents, Arabian horses, and camels were added. There were over 100 bit parts in the film, not including extras. It looked as if the studio had raided every west coast vaudeville and side show.

A correspondent was on hand for Bud and Lou's first day back on a soundstage:

ABOVE LEFT: Lottie Harrison, Lou, and Lou's stunt double, Irving Gregg.
ABOVE:
Co-stars John Conte and Marilyn Maxwell were engaged during the production.

Before shooting on the first day, Riesner, a former actor, held up his hand for silence and addressed the crowd that had been gathered to watch. 'These boys haven't faced a camera for a year and a half. Let's give them a big hand.' Everyone applauded enthusiastically. Then Bud and Lou, beaming, played a flawless scene. Riesner nudged me. 'It works every time,' he chuckled. 'Give an actor a hand and he'll go overboard to give you a good performance.' "

On the harem set were dozens of very large, colorful stuffed pillows. After shooting was completed, Lou was caught tossing pillows into the back of a delivery truck. Nobody said anything to him, but the following day the prop department frantically searched for its pillows—they were needed for another scene. Someone tipped off the front office, and Lou was asked, "Please bring them back so we can complete shooting. Then you can have them!"

Lou's daughter Paddy remembers another souvenir from the picture. "Dad brought home the dress he wore in the film—he had it hanging in the closet! It was so big and *heavy*. Oh, was that a funny dress!"

BUD AND LOU'S SCENES

"It was a joy to watch them," John Conte said. "I recall that whenever they went into one of their classic bits in the film, the entire company would gather around behind the cameras and watch. There was a lot of interest in Bud and Lou, and it was a sort of a built-in habit of the actors who were not busy working on films of their own who could get away and visit the various working sets. I recall a number of visitors would love to come and be contained on the sidelines and watch these guys go to work. It was a treat."

Bud and Lou's first scene in the film is a comic magic act, exhumed from *Keep 'Em Flying*. Pete attempts to perform some simple tricks, but Harvey inadvertently exposes them all.

Bud and Lou, going over the script, noticed that John Grant had included "Slowly I Turned." They told Haight, "About the only actor who could do it with us is Murray Leonard." Leonard was contacted in New York and signed to re-create the routine. When *Lost in a Harem* was released late in 1944, a Three Stooges short that also featured the routine, *Gents Without Cents* (1944) was also in theaters. Harry Crane explained, "That's a burlesque classic; all the comics knew it, and there were even several different versions of it."

Lou has a wonderful sequence where he tries to sleep in a crowded tent at Ramo's desert camp, but the chief's flowing beard flies in his face. In a bit reminiscent of the milking scene in *Ride 'Em Cowboy*, Harvey ties a stone to the beard to anchor it. Naturally, the next snore

115

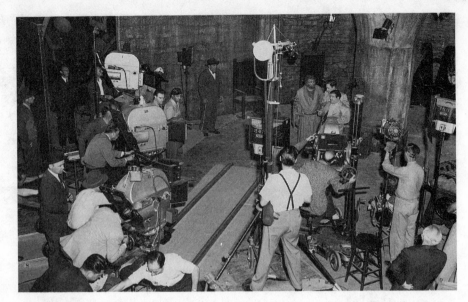

Shooting the second dungeon sequence with Murray Leonard. Riesner followed the boys with four dollying cameras. It was the first time he or cinematographer Lester White could recall using so many mobile cameras on one scene. Two cameras were set for close-ups, two for long-shots, so the sequence could be filmed in one take.

sends both the beard and the rock into Harvey's head. His yelp rouses everyone in the tent. The chief offers to sleep with his back to Harvey, but his scimitar jabs Harvey in the rear. Once again, he wakes everyone in the tent. The scene continues, and Costello's helplessness is hilarious.

DELETIONS AND ADDITIONS

Of course in a desert picture a screenwriter would be remiss if he didn't include a scene where Costello attempts to mount a camel. And the script for *Lost in a Harem* contains just such a scene, in which Lou has to fall or slide off the beast no less than five times. It was not shot, however, perhaps because of the tremendous physical demands it would have made on him.

In another cut segment, the boys hide in an odd room, unaware that it's actually a lion cage. Pete bullies Harvey into facing down the lion. "You've got to bluff him," Pete reasons. "Do everything he does. He's glaring at you—glare back at him." Harvey does. The lion roars. "He's roaring at you—roar back at him." Harvey does. "Now he's lashing his tail," observes Pete. "That let's me out!" cracks Harvey. Pete isn't amused. "We'll never get out of here if you don't do something to get him away from the door. Do something to amuse him," Pete orders. "Okay," says Harvey. "Hey, lion. Would you like to hear our baseball routine, 'Who's On First?'" The lion roars and lashes its tail ferociously. "All right, all right!" bleats Harvey. "Ya don't have to listen to it!"

The film actually ends quite differently than the script. As originally written, Nimativ is about to have Harvey beheaded when his wives mutiny and save the boys. Ramo takes the rings from his uncle, and Harvey, axe in hand, leads Nimativ to the chopping block. Pete pleads with him, "Harvey, you can't do a thing like that! Are you losing your head?" "No," says Harvey, "he's losing his!" Nimativ puts his head on the block, and Harvey raises the axe. But when he puts it down to spit on his hands for a better grip, Nimativ swipes the axe and begins chasing him. As Harvey ducks behind a statue, Nimativ takes a wild swing and hacks the head off the statue. Ramo overpowers Nimativ, but Harvey is distraught. "Pete! He cut off my head! Now I got no head! This is the end. *This is the end!*" Pete slaps him. "Stop yelling! That's a statue's head!" Harvey turns to the camera. "Well," he says, "it's 'The End' anyway!"

116

REVIEWS

Brooklyn Daily Eagle: "[W]e'll just break down and admit we liked it. No particuliar reason. . . . MGM made this film with apparent care, and seems to have spent money on it rather recklessly. It's a smooth production, and comes nearer to adult comedy than anything The Boys have done lately. Of course, if you like Abbott and Costello, and we understand a few do—a few million—we don't have to waste time trying to sell them to you. And if you don't, we know very well you haven't read this far."

Variety: " 'Lost in a Harem' is good standard fare for Abbott and Costello fans. The boys are in the groove, knocking themselves out for laughs in a slapstick bit of nonsense that is plenty corny at times, but is still funny. The plot is thin and the action drags badly at times, but on the whole the boys deliver. . . . Film will also garner some unintended laughs from keen-eyed audiences who recognize some of the sets in 'Harem' as having also been used in 'Kismet.' This isn't a terrible fault, sets fitting in nicely, and the film itself getting lavish-enough production not to be accused of skimping on budget. There is an elaborate ballet scene, for instance, . . . as attractive as any seen in recent films. . . . Murray Leonard, as a wacky derelict, grabs off a wad of laughs himself. One prison scene with Leonard and the boys, however, is much too long, spun out long after the gags are outworn."

The New York Times: "Apparently the people at Metro had nothing more to offer the boys than the set left over from 'Kismet' and their very warmest regards. For 'Lost in a Harem' is just another Abbott and Costello lark—amusing when those pals are in there pitching, but dull in the stretches when they are not. . . . The funniest sequence in the picture is that in which Bud and Lou fall in with a tempestuous crackpot who sees phantoms in the obviously thin air. And there is also another, fairly funny, in which they dress up in harem costumes."

New York World-Telegram: "Right across from *Kismet* in Time Square they have another version without the technicolor, no Marlene Dietrich legs or anything—just Abbott and Costello to supply all those missing elements. A bumper crowd of admirers of these comedians was out to welcome them to Loew's Criterion this morning in *Lost in a Harem*. They laughed appreciatively but not boisterously. From where I sat, the boys sounded a little below par on their latest crop of jokes . . ."

Film Daily: "Sad to relate, almost none of the infinite comic possibilities were realized in this inane, makeshift farce—a decided let-down after their current laugh-filled feature, 'In Society.' This ultra-nonsensical farce finds them working twice as hard as they did in their Universal hit for below-average laugh returns."

POSTSCRIPT

Lost in a Harem wasn't the only production Lou was involved with in the spring of 1944. Even before he started on the picture, Louella Parsons reported that Lou was going to direct an East Side Kids comedy called *Blockbusters* (1944) at Monogram. The series' producer, Sam Katzman, was a neighbor of Lou's. Costello issued a statement through Universal denying the story, but a reporter questioned Katzman, who confirmed that Lou was to direct the film. "Costello will direct a picture for me at some other time, but not this picture," Katzman said.

Not long after, Lou produced a low-budget comedy called *A Wave, a Wac, and a Marine* at Monogram starring Henny Youngman, Red Marshall, Billy Mack, Elyse Knox, and Ann Gillis. Lou formed Biltmore Productions, and put his father, Sebastian, on the payroll. Production began on March 10, 1944, and lasted five weeks. Lou apparently was going to direct the film under the name Lucas Tello, but Universal objected, even to the extent of making its displeasure known in tradepaper advertising. The picture was directed by Phil Karlson (né Karlstein), who had been an assistant director on the first few Abbott and Costello films at Universal.

HERE COME THE CO-EDS

Earliest Draft:
February 15, 1943

Production Start:
October 24, 1944

Production End:
December 6, 1944

Copyright Date:
February 6, 1945

Released:
February 2, 1945

Running Time:
88 minutes

Reissued: 1950

Directed By:
Jean Yarbrough

Produced By: John Grant

Screenplay By: Arthur T.
Horman and John Grant

Original Story:
Edmund L. Hartmann

Director of Photography:
George Robinson ASC

Art Direction:
John B. Goodman,
Richard H. Riedel

Director of Sound:
Bernard B. Brown

Technician:
Robert Pritchard

Set Decoration:
Russell A. Gausman,
A. J. Gilmore

Film Editor: Arthur Hilton

Gowns: Vera West

Assistant Director:
Howard Christie

Special Photography By:
John P. Fulton ASC

Musical Director:
Edgar Fairchild

"I Don't Care If I Never
Dream Again,"
"Jumpin' on Saturday
Night," "Hooray for
Our Side," "Some Day
We Will Remember,"
"A New Day," "The
Head of The Class,"
and "Let's Play House"
By: Jack Brooks and
Edgar Fairchild

Musical Numbers Staged
By: Louis Da Pron

SYNOPSIS

Molly, her brother, Slats, and his pal, Oliver, are taxi dancers at the Miramar Ballroom. As a publicity stunt, Slats plants an article about Molly that proclaims her ambition is to earn enough money to attend staid Bixby College. The progressive dean of Bixby, Larry Benson, reads the article, and offers Molly a scholarship. Molly accepts on the condition that Slats and Oliver come along too. Luckily there are two openings at Bixby for caretakers.

But pompous Chairman Kirkland holds the mortgage on dear old Bixby, and despite the fact that his daughter Diane and her friend Patty are students, he threatens to foreclose if Benson persists in flouting tradition and doesn't expel Molly. Meanwhile, Slats and Oliver can't seem to please their surly supervisor, Mr. Johnson. But the boys scheme with the co-eds to raise the $20,000 necessary to save the school. Slats arranges for Oliver to wrestle the Masked Marvel for $1,000 and although Johnson replaces the Masked Marvel, Oliver manages to win the match. Slats bets the stakes at 20-to-1 on a Bixby basketball game. But the bookie, Honest Dan, recruits a team of professional basketball players to play in place of the girls from Carlton. Oliver joins the game as a ringer for Bixby. Oliver loses the game, but swipes Honest Dan's bankroll, and he and Slats, after a wild cross-town chase, make it to Bixby with the money just in time.

BACKGROUND

Although he wrote the original story, Edmund Hartmann didn't produce *Here Come the Co-Eds*. John Grant was given the assignment after sharing the producing chores on *In Society*. During Lou's illness, John produced a Universal B musical, *Bowery to Broadway*, which was released in 1944. Among the cast: Peggy Ryan and Donald Cook.

THE SCRIPT

Edmund Hartmann's original treatment for *Co-Eds* (submitted February 15, 1943) opened at a burlesque theater, where Bud and Lou are employed as candy butchers. Star stripper Diane Mulligan is set to marry millionaire Phillip Trumbull on the condition that she goes to Bixby College, his mother's alma mater, and acquire enough polish and culture to make her acceptable to the blue bloods. That's okay with Diane, since she wants to better herself, too. Trumbull has promised a $10 million endowment if the school accepts Diane. Not only is Bixby in dire financial straights, but the Governor wants to close the school and make it a reformatory. The dean and faculty fawn over Diane. The boys follow Diane to Bixby, where they are mistaken for two new professors. The endowment vanishes when Phillip marries a dance hall hostess. Bud and Lou propose betting on an upcoming water polo match to win enough money to save the school. The boys play in the match as ringers in drag, but lose to a squad of Amazons. Bixby is all but finished until Diane comes up with an idea to stage the school play for Old

Grad Week. It's a wild burlesque show, with the wealthy alumni bidding on pieces of Diane's costume as she strips. Incredibly, Diane's crazy idea manages to raise the money, and Bixby is saved.

The script, completed by Hartmann, Edmund Joseph, and Hal Fimberg, sat on a shelf for a year. When it was dusted off in the spring of 1944, Arthur Horman and John Grant began reworking it. The burlesque angle was gone. Curiously, Horman's initial drafts were a hybrid between *Co-Eds* as we know it and what will later be *The Noose Hangs High*. Bud and Lou, as messengers hired to deliver $20,000 in gambling winnings, accidently mail the windfall to Diane, a taxi dancer at the Miramar Ballroom who yearns to go to college. The scenario was further simplified during the summer of 1944, and the final shooting script completed on September 26, 1944.

The Breen Office cautioned the producers over the fixed basketball game. "We request that you tone down the idea that these professional girl basketball players intend to cripple the girls on the Bixby team. We recommend that in Scene 198 Bertha's dialogue be modified to something to the effect that they will merely play their usual hard game against the other girls. It would be well to avoid unacceptable brutality or any suggestion that the Bixby girls are injured badly or suffering intensely from their injuries."

THE CAST

Peggy Ryan (b. 1924) was a staple of Universal's minor musicals, almost always teamed with Donald O'Connor. She was a regular on TV's *Hawaii Five-O* (1968–1980) as McGarrett's secretary.

Martha O'Driscoll (b. 1922) had appeared in *Crazy House* (1943) and *Ghost Catchers* (1944) with Olsen and Johnson. After *Co-Eds,* she was cast in *House of Dracula* (1945).

Lon Chaney, Jr. (1906–1973) had also appeared in *Ghost Catchers,* thus broadening his characterizations to comedy. He would later contribute to the success of *Abbott and Costello Meet Frankenstein* (1948). He moved on to *House of Dracula* after *Co-Eds.*

Phil Spitalny's All-Girl Orchestra were popular radio favorites on *The Hour of Charm.* Later in 1945, Spitalny married Evelyn Klein, the orchestra's concertmaster.

Seven of the eight Amazons were portrayed by members of Los Angeles' Tip Toppers Club. The eighth member of the team was actress Dorothy Ford (b. 1923), who would later appear with the team in *Jack and the Beanstalk* (1952).

THE PRODUCTION

Co-Eds was shot in forty-three days, at a cost of $717,621.39 ($15,000 over budget), of which Bud and Lou were paid $102,000 (plus a percentage).

The Bixby campus was represented by North Hollywood Park, while the Shelby home on Universal's backlot served as the school's main building. (It also appears as the manor house in *The Time of Their Lives* [1946].)

The wrestling set is possibly the most spartan ever seen in an Abbott and Costello production. It seems like an afterthought. To stage the sequence, Yarbrough went to a wrestling arena on Hollywood Boulevard and hired two professional wrestlers to double for Chaney and Costello, who appear only in the close-ups.

The most elaborate set was the college gymnasium, built on the studio's giant Phantom Stage (where, obviously, *The Phantom of the Opera* [1925] was made). Lou was delighted to finally play basketball on camera. As Pat Costello recalled, "Lou played on a semi-pro basketball team in Paterson. They played an exhibition game against the Boston Celtics. Lou played against Nat Holman, and he held Holman to very few points and outscored him." A renowned basketball star was hired to stage the game for the film, and he instructed Lou in a condescending manner. Lou played along, asking, "How do I hold the ball?" and "Can't I throw the ball from here?" The player smiled indulgently, then stared unbelievingly as Lou tossed a perfect

Slats . . . . Bud Abbott
Oliver . . . . Lou Costello
Patty . . . . Peggy Ryan
Molly . . . Martha O'Driscoll
Diane . . . . June Vincent
Johnson . Lon Chaney, Jr.
Benson . . . . . Donald Cook
Kirkland . . . . Charles Dingle
Near-Sighted Man
 . . . . Richard Lane
Honest Dan . . . . . Joe Kirk
Bill Stern . . . . Himself
Bertha . . . . . Dorothy Ford
Basketball Coach
 . . . . Carl Knowles
Amazons
 . . . . Martha Garetto
 Naomi Stout
 June Cuendet
 Muriel Stetson
 Marilyn Hoeck
 Margaret Eversole
 Lorna Peterson
Tiger McGurk
 . . . . Sammy Stein
Miss Holford . . . Ruth Lee
Diamond . . . . Don Costello
Women in Ballroom
 . . . . Rebel Randall
 Maxine Gates
 Jean Carlin
 June Hazard
 Dorothy Granger
Flannigan . . . . Ed Dunn
Chief . . . . . . Pierre Watkin

and Phil Spitalny and his
Hour of Charm
All Girl Orchestra
featuring Evelyn
and her magic violin

shot into the basket. Lou did the same thing on *Keep 'Em Flying* at the Cal-Aero school in a pick-up game with the cadets. "A little fat man is the last guy in the world you'd expect to be an athlete," Edmund Hartmann said. "He used to do a thing on the basketball court where he'd stand in the middle of the court and bounce the ball right into the basket. He did that very easily. He was wonderful." Director Jean Yarbrough said Lou made all of the trick shots by himself—and never missed.

The film features one of the oddest chases the team ever did, as a sailboat on a trailer winds its way through traffic and train tunnels. Veteran gagman Felix Adler submitted many of the gags without screen credit. Much of it was shot near the corner of Ventura and Sepulveda Boulevards, as well as the U.C.L.A. campus and Mulholland Drive. It took six days to shoot, with Irving Gregg and Charlie Murray doubling for Lou and Bud.

Lou as Daisy Dimple, the greatest girl basketball player.

BUD AND LOU'S SCENES

Much of the material in *Co-Eds* had either been played by the team before or was cut from earlier films. Even so, they clearly haven't lost their enthusiasm for the routines, and they turned in some of their best renditions in *Co-Eds*.

Bud and Lou's slapstick attempt to clean up the kitchen of the caretaker's quarters was originally scripted for the ship's galley in *Pardon My Sarong*.

The "Oyster" routine was originated by Billy Bevan in a Mack Sennett short, *Wandering Willies* (1926), coincidentally directed by Three Stooges auteur Del Lord. Curly Howard exhumed the bit in the 1941 Stooges short, *Dutiful But Dumb*, also directed by Lord. The Stooges, in fact, did it in three other shorts. The scene was probably added to *Co-Eds* by longtime Stooge gagman Felix Adler. Bud and Lou spent virtually an entire day shooting the routine. Later, they did an even better variation using a frog in *The Wistful Widow of Wagon Gap* (1947).

"Jonah and the Whale" returns to the screen after making its debut in *One Night in the Tropics* (1940).

The wrestling scene was originally scripted for *In the Navy* as a way for Pomeroy to impress Patty Andrews. The sequence took four days to complete. Bud did not have a call on the third and fourth days, which may explain why he suddenly disappears mid-match. The boys re-created the match in an episode of their TV series in the 1950s.

One would think Bud and Lou would steer clear of dice games after doing the classic scene in *Buck Privates*. But the writers managed to invent an interesting companion piece for *Co-Eds*. Oliver accidentally swallows Johnson's custom-made dice, and the janitor confirms his suspicions by examining him with a fluoroscope. Johnson and Slats then begin an impromptu crap game by shaking up Oliver and then checking the dice rolls on the fluoroscope. The inspired dice game in *Co-Eds* reappeared in a variation in *Abbott and Costello Meet the Mummy* (1955).

DELETIONS AND ADDITIONS

Before Slats and Oliver see Honest Dan to place a bet on the Bixby basketball team, the boys were supposed to stroll down a street and launch into a series of routines. Here's the notation in the script:

Scene 164   TRUCKING SHOT—STREET—DAY

Oliver and Slats stop in front of a bank. Through the window in the background we see a large vault. Oliver and Slats argue about boring a hole in the vault. As they continue down the street, a man, wearing a sandwich board advertising BASEBALL GAME TODAY, passes them. Oliver and Slats get into an argument about going to the ballgame, having hot dogs with mustard and worcestershire sauce. Then they continue down the street and stop in front of a restaurant where two signs show SPECIAL TODAY: PORTER-HOUSE STEAK—BLUE PLATE SPECIAL: PORK AND BEANS. Oliver and Slats get into another argument as to which of the specials Oliver would choose. After the argument, they continue down the street to a V-shaped board standing by the curb which advertises RAILROAD, STEAMSHIP, BUS TICKETS. Again Slats gets Oliver into an argument over taking a trip by railroad or bus, etc. From there we go to the EXTERIOR of Honest Dan's ice cream parlor.

Note: The above scene is the Abbott and Costello HOLE IN THE WALL ROUTINE which the boys know and requires no rehearsal.

According to the assistant director's reports, the boys shot the sequence but it was cut from the film.

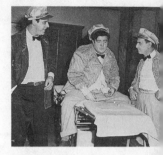

The inventive "Dice Game" with Lon Chaney, Jr.

REVIEWS

The New York Times: "Maybe it's just that Lou Costello has more and funnier scenes in which to play, or maybe thanks are due to Universal for taking some real productive pains. Anyhow, the latest picture in which Bud Abbott and his plump sidekick are starred is plainly the most diverting burlesque that they have tossed in a number of tries. . . . And the hardest thing to say about it is that it rates a high grade for low comedy . . . [Lou's] frightful encounter with the wrestler is a howl; when he plaintively gasps to the audience, 'Boy, am I in a mess!' you can bet that he is. And his basketball playing is delirious. As he says, he can't dribble but he can drool."

Los Angeles Examiner: " 'Here Come the Co-Eds' has the Abbott and Costello fans back in the aisles. . . . The gags are bright, new, and even the few that are more routine have been dressed up and the frayed edges trimmed off. Moreover, A and C go along with the gags in a more restrained fashion which, some way or other, makes everything seem funnier."

New York World-Telegram: "It certainly pays to take a little extra trouble with material for an Abbott and Costello comedy. Given half a chance, those boys can be very funny. They get a full chance in 'Here Come the Co-Eds,' and they pay off double. They have seemed a very tired pair in some of their recent comedies, struggling with worn-out odds and ends from old burlesque shows and radio scripts. Their new picture will re-warm old friendships that have been frigid for the past couple of years. I, for one, am back on strong and I am sure I am part of a long parade."

POSTSCRIPT

Milton Feld's memo to Cliff Work on December 29, 1944 gives us some idea of what the post-production schedules were like on the Abbott and Costello films:

Wed., Jan. 3—Departmental screening	Sat., Jan. 13—Editorial changes
Tues., Jan 9—Music scoring	Mon., Jan. 15—Negative cutting
Wed., Jan 10—Dub	Tues., Jan. 16—Laboratory
Thurs., Jan 11—Dub	Fri., Jan. 19—Ship
Fri., Jan. 12—Sneak preview	Mon., Jan 22—Arrive New York

When we meet Oliver at the Miramar Ballroom, he is delighted to finally sit one dance out. We can understand why from this cut scene. A rather large woman (Maxine Gates) has purchased several hours' worth of tickets to dance with him. There was a funny sight gag showing Lou's shoes smoking.

THE NAUGHTY NINETIES

Earliest Draft:
January 16, 1943

Production Start:
January 15, 1945

Production End:
March 1, 1945

Copyright Date:
June 27, 1945

Released: July 6, 1945

Running Time:
76 minutes

Reissued: June 15, 1950
with *One Night in the Tropics*

Directed by:
Jean Yarbrough

Produced By:
Edmund L. Hartmann
and John Grant

Screenplay By:
Edmund L. Hartmann,
John Grant, Edmund
Joseph, Hal Fimberg

Additional Comedy
Sequences By:
Felix Adler

Director of Photography:
George Robinson ASC

Musical Director:
Edgar Fairchild

Art Direction:
John B. Goodman,
Harold H. MacArthur

Director of Sound:
Bernard B. Brown

Technician:
Robert Pritchard

Set Decorations:
Russell A. Gausman,
Leigh Smith

Film Editor: Arthur Hilton

Gowns: Vera West

Make-up Director:
Jack P. Pierce

SYNOPSIS

Trouble looms for Captain Sam, owner of the showboat *River Queen,* when he ties up at the Mississippi river town of Ironville. Despite his better judgment and the advice of his lead actor, Dexter, his chief roustabout, Sebastian, and his beautiful daughter Caroline, the kind-hearted Captain Sam befriends three dubious characters. The newcomers—a gentleman gambler named Crawford; his companion, Bonita; and their bodyguard, Bailey—are fugitives from the sheriff, and use the *River Queen* to escape to St. Louis.

In St. Louis, they invite Captain Sam to be their guest at a notorious gambling house, the Gilded Cage. Plying the captain with liquor during a crooked card game, Crawford and Bonita win controlling interest in the *River Queen.* To the despair of the honest captain, Bonita and Crawford install a crooked gambling operation on the riverboat. Sebastian and Dexter start a brawl with Bailey and his men that leads to a frantic chase around the riverboat. The unwelcomed intruders are ousted and ownership of the *River Queen* is finally restored to Captain Sam.

BACKGROUND

Abbott and Costello now began to take an interest in owning more than 10 percent of their films. The team put up $150,000 to buy a 20 percent interest in *The Naughty Nineties.* They would do this again on some of their later films as well.

While the film was in production, Bud and Lou reviewed blueprints and conferred with experts on juvenile delinquency as their efforts to build a youth center in Los Angeles proceeded. "This movement is gonna be strictly for the poor kids," Lou told a reporter. "And we're gonna shoot the works and give 'em an idea what fun in this country really is. It's gonna have everything—swimming pools, athletic equipment, lunches, afternoon snacks. Everything. And all for free." Bud agreed, "We don't want anybody but ragamuffins. This thing is for the kids whose folks don't have extra dimes for Scouts or any of the other children's clubs, the kids who have to play around in the gutter."

THE SCRIPT

The original story for *The Naughty Nineties* was written by Edmund Joseph early in 1943. Joseph and Hal Fimberg wrote the screenplay, supplemented by John Grant, and it was considered ready to produce in the fall of 1943. In fact, at one point, it was reported to be Abbott and Costello's first film back at Universal after Lou's illness. When *Nineties* was pushed back on the itinerary, Edmund Hartmann and Grant reworked the screenplay and delivered the final shooting script on November 30, 1944. Additional scenes and gags were written by Felix Adler and Sid Fields just before production commenced after the new year.

In 1941, a Broadway musical about the gay nineties called *Hold Your Horses* opened at the Winter Garden Theater. It was written by Charles Beahan, Russell Crouse, and Corey Ford. In 1949, Beahan learned from an acquaintance that Universal had made an Abbott and Costello comedy set in that era, and that one gag in the film—where Sebastian uses a magnet on the roulette wheel—was remarkably similar to one in his original show. He wrote Ed Muhl and requested a screening of the film. Universal obliged, and after viewing the picture, Beahan agreed that for $100 he would drop any claims against the studio.

THE CAST

Alan Curtis (1909–1953) had appeared with Bud and Lou in *Buck Privates*. He had just portrayed a San Francisco gambler in *Frisco Sal* (1945).

Henry Travers (1874–1965), a veteran character actor, had appeared in *Mrs. Miniver* (1942) and *The Moon Is Down* (1943). He may be best remembered as the angel, Clarence, in *It's a Wonderful Life* (1946).

Lois Collier (b. 1919) had appeared in *Cobra Woman, Weird Woman, Jungle Woman,* and *Ladies Courageous* in 1944 before being assigned *The Naughty Nineties.* Later in 1945 she appeared in the serial, *Jungle Queen.*

Joe Sawyer (1901–1982), a graduate of Hollywood High School, had menaced the boys in *Hit the Ice* (1942) and would return in 1951 in *Comin' Round The Mountain.*

THE PRODUCTION

Universal had constructed a portion of a riverboat for its opulent musical, *Show Boat* (1936). It remained on the back lot, and it was only a matter of time before the Abbott and Costello writers exploited it for the team. Shots of the *River Queen* in motion were achieved with models. "So many times you think you know what you're doing, but you don't," mused producer Edmund Hartmann. "Jean Yarbrough came up to me and said, 'Do you want the riverboat going from right to left or left to right?' because it's going to New Orleans. I said,

Asistant Director:
Howard Christie

Musical Numbers Staged
By: Jack Doyle

Dexter . . . . Bud Abbott
Sebastian . . . Lou Costello
Crawford . . . . . Alan Curtis
Bonita . . . . . . Rita Johnson
Captain Sam
. . . . Henry Travers
Caroline . . . . Lois Collier
Bailey . . . . Joe Sawyer
Croupier . . . . Joe Kirk
Drunk . . . . Jack Norton
Matt . . . . Sam McDaniel
Minstrel . . . . . . Billy Green
Croupiers . . . . . Bud Wolfe
Henry Russell
Ralph Jones
Bing Conley
Tony Dell
John Indrisano
Bud O'Connor
Charles Phillips
Magician
. . . . . . William W. Larsen
Tight Wire Act
. . . . Dolores Evers
Effie . . . . Lillian Yarbo
Sheriff . . . . John Hamilton
Baxter . . . . Ed Gargan
Croupier . . . . . Donald Kerr
Emery . . . . . . Milt Bronson
Sheriff Wright
. . . . Rex Lease
Singing Specialty
. . . . Torchy Rand
Specialty Dancer
. . . . Ronnie Stanton
Bit Man . . . . Sid Fields

FAR LEFT: "My Bonnie Lies Over the Ocean." LEFT: The film's highlight, "Who's On First?" (See transcription on pp. 268–269.)

'That's ridiculous; of course it's going from right to left—that's down river to New Orleans.' Well, I was born in St. Louis, which is on the east side of the river. So boats going down river traveled from right to left. And Jean looked at me and said, 'But what if you're standing on the other side of the river?' [laughs] I had no answer."

Hartmann found Bud and Lou more cooperative than they had been on *In Society*. "As I remember it, it was much easier," he said. "I remember my daughter, Susie, was about six years old, and sometimes I'd bring her to the set. Lou would stop production, have one of his stooges get his motorcycle, which had a sidecar, and give my daughter a tour of the studio. Meanwhile, the whole company waited for him. He was childlike in so many nice ways."

The team was visited on the set on February 22 by a reporter from UPI.

Today they were trying out an old vaudeville act they did 12 years ago when they were playing one night stands in honky tonks. Abbott was fixing a backdrop and Costello was singing *My Bonnie Lies Over the Ocean.* And everytime Abbott would holler to raise the curtain a little higher, Costello, thinking he meant the song, upped to a falsetto.

"Get it level with the floor," shouted Abbott, his back to Costello.

So his roly-poly partner heaved his bulk on the floor and sang from there.

"Bring it forward," ordered Abbott. "Two or three more feet."

And Costello moved three feet forward and tumbled into the orchestra pit in the middle of "Bring Back My Bonnie . . ."

They did it once. Three cameras got the shot from every angle and that was that.

"There's no sense doing a retake," sighed Yarbrough, a harried veteran of A&C movies. "They don't even rehearse, because neither knows what the other's going to do until they do it. We just shoot the rehearsal and let it go at that."

Once in a while they have to shoot a scene over. But that's because somebody in the crew laughs out loud like the customers are supposed to.

Actually, according to the script supervisor's notes, they did the scene twice; the first take was aborted when the scenery didn't move correctly, and the second take was used in the film.

One of gag writer Felix Adler's signature routines is the "Feathers in the Cake" scene, which he had written for the 1935 Stooges short, *Uncivil Warriors,* and reworked for Lou. Special effects man Carl Lee designed and built special containers, small enough to fit in the mouth, but large enough to hold a handful of feathers, for the cafe patrons to cough up feathers.

BUD AND LOU'S SCENES

"Who's On First?" wasn't originally planned for *The Naughty Nineties;* according to the final draft, Bud and Lou were to perform their "Hole in The Wall" routine, but a few days before production began, the boys decided on the baseball routine. It was originally intended much earlier in the story. Notice that in the scene, Sebastian says, "When we get to St. Louis . . . ," but in the new placement, the riverboat has already reached St. Louis.

On February 27, 1945, forty extras had to sit in stony silence while A&C performed "Who's On First?" According to the pressbook, a laugh track was to be added later so as not to interfere with the dialogue. "I don't want to hear the smallest giggle nor the slightest snicker," Yarbrough instructed them. "You must pretend to laugh and slap your knees, but you must do it quietly." The scene, according to cinematographer George Robinson, took 548 feet of film, the longest in the picture. After the shot, the audience relieved their repressed emotions by applauding loud and long.

The biggest problem Yarbrough had was keeping the studio technicians from laughing out loud while the boys ran through their dialogue. According to the script notes, the routine was done twice. The first take was probably marred by crew laughter. In fact, even on the take that's in the film, listen closely and you can hear the cameramen and grips laughing in the background!

According to Bud Abbott, Jr., "My dad told me once that they never did the baseball routine the same way twice. There was always something put in, something new added, or changed around. And yet, each time they did it, it was like they'd done it exactly the same way for years."

Stan Irwin performed the routine twice at benefits with Lou after Abbott and Costello split up. Lou let him in on the secret. "I memorized the 'Who's on First?' record, word for word, both parts," Stan explained. "When I met Lou backstage, I said, 'I'm all set, Lou. I've got it memorized.' And he said, 'You've got what memorized?' I said, 'The record; I know it by heart.' Lou said, '*I* don't even know the record. What Bud and I would do is, we'd go out there and try and catch each other. That way, we'd keep it fresh.' I said okay, and he said, 'You just stay alert.' "

The rest of *Nineties* is undermined by the repetition of many time-worn gags, including the old "Mirror Scene" which first appears on film in Max Linder's *Seven Years* (1927) and later in the Marx Brothers' *Horse Feathers* (1932). Lou reprises the gag with Joe Sawyer.

DELETIONS AND ADDITIONS

In the film, Dexter and Sebastian attempt to rescue Captain Sam from the crooked gamblers by letting a performing bear loose in the casino. But the original plan was different. Edmund Hartmann explained, "Lou was a great admirer of Harold Lloyd, and he decided he was going to do Lloyd's 'Magic Coat' routine. In the routine, Lloyd is at a party dressed in a dinner jacket. He goes into the bathroom and takes off his coat, and as he comes out, he picks a coat off the rack that he thinks is his, but belongs to a magician that's been hired to work the party. Lloyd puts it on, and as he's dancing with the heroine a rabbit comes out of one pocket, and so on. It's a classic, classic scene. Lou decided we were going to copy it shot for shot. So we hired Clyde Bruckman, who worked with Harold Lloyd and had been in on the creation of that scene. We shot the exact scene, which a lot of people would call thieving, but it really was a homage to Lloyd. Well, somehow the Lloyd company found out about it

The deleted "Magic Coat" scene—Lou's tribute to Harold Lloyd—with Rita Johnson.

and they called the studio and said they were going to sue. The studio got terrified, grabbed all the prints, put them in safe deposit, kept them out of the picture, tore up any reference to it, and it's never been shown."

In the deleted scene, Dexter notices a sign on a door, "Officer 666," and orders Sebastian, "Go in there and get that policeman's uniform and raid the gambling room! We'll save Captain Sam that way!" What the boys don't know is that "Officer 666" is a music hall magician who performs in character as a policeman. Inside the dressing room, the magician finishes reloading his prop uniform by putting a pigeon in an inside pocket, then retires to an adjacent room. Sebastian warily enters, quickly grabs the policeman's coat, hat, and nightstick, and dashes out into the gambling parlor. "It's a raid! Everybody out!" Sebastian shouts. As he waves his arms, the pigeon flies out of the back of his coat and lands on a woman's head. Then he swings his nightstick, and an egg drops out of his sleeve. Sebastian suddenly feels something wriggling inside his coat. He pulls out a rabbit, and deposits it on a platter on a passing tray. Finally Sebastian confronts Bonita and Bailey, but when he bows to Bonita, his boutonniere squirts a stream of water into her face. Bailey seizes Sebastian by the seat of his pants and starts to give him the bum's rush. A white mouse climbs out on Sebastian's shoulder and scampers on top of his hat. As they pass a woman, Bailey gives Sebastian a violent shove, which throws the mouse on to the woman's head. The mouse runs down her back, and she screams. Sebastian reaches into his coat and discovers a box of white mice, and dumps them on the floor. The casino clears out in a panic, and the boys escape.

The scene was replaced on May 13, 1945 (ten weeks after the film was completed) with a perennial Abbott and Costello sketch. Dexter notices the dressing room of "Crestello's Bears" (a play on Lou's real name). He'll slip into a bear costume and scare the patrons out of the casino. Of course, the real bear gets loose, and Sebastian wrestles with it, thinking it's Dexter in costume. Lou's slow realization of his predicament was always surefire, whether the animal skin in question was that of a bear, a lion, or a gorilla.

REVIEWS

The New York Times: "Bud Abbott and Lou Costello have either run out of comedy routines or they have such an affection for their old ones that they figure it is fair to repeat. In either case their latest picture . . . is literally a musty archive of old gags and acts they have played before. . . . But then, apparently, Universal is so anxious to keep them on the screen that it doesn't have any conscience about what sort of script they play."

Los Angeles Examiner: "Fans of Lou's and Bud's, and they come in droves, will probably enjoy every single bit of their corny malarky, which includes the usual chase, falls and slapstick, the kind that comes in the large, economy-sized package. Lou going to heaven as 'Little Eva' is a ridiculous sequence that had people laughing despite themselves. And for us that ageless baseball routine with 'Who's on first,' which they repeat, is worth the price of admission."

New York Herald-Tribune: "The brightest spot in the film is a repeat performance of the famous Abbott and Costello 'Who's on First' baseball routine; this sequence, in which Costello tries to find out the names of a baseball team, is always good for as many laughs as any one can spare. The supporting cast goes along for the sport of 'The Naughty Nineties,' which is, quite naturally, much better for Abbott and Costello enthusiasts than for the casual moviegoer."

POSTSCRIPT

Following *Nineties,* Bud and Lou returned to Metro for what would be their final film there, *Abbott and Costello in Hollywood.* Meanwhile, according to *Daily Variety,* work continued on the scripts of what would be the next two Abbott and Costello pictures at Universal, *She Meant No Harm* and *The Phantom Pirates.*

ABBOTT AND COSTELLO IN HOLLYWOOD

SYNOPSIS

Buzz and Abercrombie, a barber and a porter in a posh Hollywood salon, are dispatched to the office of superagent Norman Royce to administer a haircut and shine. En route, they meet Claire Warren, a former manicurist at the salon, who has landed the lead in a big-budget musical. Her co-star, fading crooner Gregory LeMaise, coincidentally drives up and invites her to lunch but she declines, which angers LeMaise. In the agent's office, Buzz and Abercrombie witness Royce making fantastic deals by simply picking up a phone. A young singer, Jeff Parker, auditions for Royce, and when LeMaise announces that he refuses to work with Claire, Royce offers the part to Jeff. LeMaise quickly reconsiders, and Royce agrees to drop Jeff. Buzz and Abercrombie appoint themselves Jeff's agents, and promise to get him the part by paying a visit to Mr. Kavanaugh, the head of the studio.

But when Buzz and Abercrombie crash into Kavanaugh's car at the studio gate, Kavanaugh orders the boys barred from the lot. They sneak in with a group of extras, and before they know it, the costume department has outfitted Buzz as a cop and Abercrombie as a tramp, and they roam the lot. Claire, meanwhile, introduces Jeff to Kavanaugh, and he agrees to sign the newcomer. But at Ciro's that night, LeMaise tells Kavanaugh that he has decided to take the part after all. Abercrombie and Buzz hatch a plan to get rid of LeMaise. The boys visit LeMaise on his boat and attempt to provoke an argument that will result in a fight with Abercrombie. Buzz will photograph the fight and have LeMaise arrested, keeping him out of the movie. But when LeMaise knocks Abercrombie overboard, it appears as if the little fellow has really drowned. LeMaise panics and drops out of sight, so filming begins with Jeff in the role. Buzz disguises Abercrombie as his East Indian chauffeur, but at a nearby cafe, LeMaise, also incognito, recognizes him and chases him onto the soundstage, where the film's elaborate rollercoaster finale is being shot. After a wild ride, LeMaise is subdued. The picture makes stars of Claire and Jeff, and Buzz and Abercrombie become Hollywood's hottest agents.

BACKGROUND

Abbott and Costello in Hollywood's producer, Martin Gosch, produced the team's radio show on NBC. Screenwriter Nat Perrin recalled, "I can remember that Gosch, who was always a

Earliest Draft:
October 21, 1944

Production Start:
April 10, 1945

Production End:
June 1, 1945

Copyright Date:
August 14, 1945

Released:
August 22, 1945

Running Time:
83 minutes

Directed By:
S. Sylvan Simon

Produced By:
Martin A. Gosch

Screenplay By: Nat Perrin
and Lou Breslow

Original Story: Nat Perrin
and Martin A. Gosch

Songs: Ralph Blane,
Hugh Martin

Dances Directed By:
Charles Walters

Musical Direction:
George Bassman

Orchestrations:
Ted Duncan

Director of Photography:
Charles Schoenbaum
ASC

Film Editor: Ben Lewis

Recording Director:
Douglas Schearer

Art Direction:
Cedric Gibbons,
Wade B. Rubottom

Set Decorations:
Edwin B. Willis

Costume Supervision:
   Irene

Associate: Kay Carter

Men's Costumes: Valles

Make-Up Created By:
   Jack Dawn

Buzz Curtis .. Bud Abbott

Abercrombie
   .... Lou Costello

Claire Warren
   ....Frances Rafferty

Jeff Parker
   .... Robert Stanton

Ruthie .... Jean Porter

Norman Royce
   ...... Warner Anderson

"Rags" Ragland . Himself

Klondike Pete
   .... Mike Mazurki

Gregory LeMaise
   ..... Carleton G. Young

Dennis Kavanaugh
   .... Donald MacBride

Second Studio Cop
   .... Robert Emmet
               O'Connor

Louise .. Katherine Booth

First Studio Cop
   .... Edgar Dearing

Quartette Specialty
   ...... The Lyttle Sisters

Miss Milbane
   .... Marion Martin

Director.... Arthur Space

Child Star
   .... Dean Stockwell

Child Star
   ...... Sharon McManus

Mr. Burvis
   .... Chester Clute

Hard-Boiled Assistant
   .... William Tannen

Wardrobe Man
   .... Skeets Noyes

Prop Man
   .... Dick Alexander

Dr. Snide's Voice
   .... William Tannen

Counterman
   .... Milton Kibbee
           and
      Lucille Ball
     Preston Foster
   Robert Z. Leonard
  Jackie "Butch" Jenkins
     as themselves

128

promotive type of guy, somehow got an interview with Louis B. Mayer and told him that he saw Abbott and Costello as a couple of Hollywood barbers. Now, I'm not saying it's a good idea or a bad idea, but Mayer flipped over it. He hired Gosch to develop the story, and Gosch wanted me to write it. I didn't want to work on it particularly because there was so little to work with and the expectancy was so great. There are a million other things that might get you funnier scenes than barbers; they're such drab characters."

THE SCRIPT

But Perrin forged ahead. "You can't sit and wait for the assignments you really want, or the people you really feel a rapport with," he explained. "Abbott and Costello weren't generally my dish. Now, I'm only telling you my impression, but I thought that Abbott and Costello could have been more conscientious about their work. They would do the general idea of what was written, then throw in whatever came into their heads, just to get it done in one take. I saw that was a terrible waste, because I thought that Costello was an extremely talented guy, as was Abbott in his way. But they weren't fussy about what they were going to do. I don't think that they got the maximum out of themselves. . . . Most comedians I knew would come off a scene worried that maybe they blew it somewhere, and would want to do another take. Or, if the director wanted another take, they'd be concerned about where they blew it. But not Abbott and Costello. I doubt whether they heard the word 'cut' without being glad that they were done with the scene."

Yet Perrin, one of the top writers in the business, wrote several funny scenes for the team, two of which are classics. And from the available records, it seems he did it without John Grant. "I tried my very, very best on that picture. That's my nature. Now, I don't remember how far I'd gotten into it, but I asked Lou Breslow, a very dear friend of mine, to help me with it. I knew John Grant, but I don't ever remember working with him or discussing a scene with him, or his being involved in the writing of a scene. He very well could have, but I don't remember it at all."

THE CAST

Frances Rafferty (b. 1922) made her professional debut as a ballerina but, after suffering a torn cartilage, turned to acting. She appeared in dramas like *Dragon Seed* (1944) and *Mrs. Parkington* (1944). According to the pressbook, *Abbott and Costello In Hollywood* was her first dancing role on screen. Dance director Chuck Walters was her partner for the "Fun on the Midway" number. In the 1950s Frances starred in *December Bride* on television.

Robert Stanton probably identified with his character: he too was making his first film. His brother was singer Dick Haymes, and Robert had been known as Bob Haymes until shortly before making the film. He later had more success as a songwriter.

Carleton Young (1907–1971) had appeared as a bandleader in *Keep 'Em Flying*. A dependable character actor, Young appeared in the *Buck Rogers* and *Dick Tracy* serials, as well as *Smash-Up* (1947), *20,000 Leagues Under the Sea* (1954), and *The Man Who Shot Liberty Valance* (1962).

Rags Ragland (1905–1946) was an old pal from Bud and Lou's burlesque days. Rags became a contract player at Metro, and appeared in *Whistling in the Dark, Panama Hattie, DuBarry Was a Lady, Girl Crazy,* and *Ziegfeld Follies.*

Jean Porter (b. 1925) had appeared in *Babes on Broadway, The Youngest Profession, Andy Hardy's Blonde Trouble,* and *Bathing Beauty.* Jean filmed *Abbott and Costello in Hollywood* while rehearsing *Easy to Wed* with Van Johnson and Esther Williams. Jean worked with the team again in an episode of their TV series in 1953.

"I was a contract player," Porter explained, "and I guess I was the right height for Lou, so they cast me as Ruthie. The first day I met Lou and Bud was the first day of the picture. I had worked with a lot of comedians, and I thought it had to be fun. Well, I didn't know how *much* fun it was going to be! As we got into the film, there was a lot of fooling around. But the jokes were worth it. I think that comforted them. I think when they could play around and fool around and have other people join in—and they had a lot of their old buddies with them on- and off-camera—that made them comfortable."

THE PRODUCTION

By placing the action on the back lot, Metro enjoyed considerable savings on the production. The only extravagance was the mammoth Midway set. An entire street carnival complete with Ferris wheel and rides was constructed. "The Midway set took up a whole stage, and it took a long time for them to build that and get it ready," Jean Porter recalled.

Lou with Edgar Dearing and the great Buster Keaton, who had performed the same routine together in Keaton's *Free and Easy* (1930).

S. Sylvan Simon had directed the team in its first MGM effort, *Rio Rita*. In the interim, he had directed Edger Bergen and W.C. Fields in *Song of the Open Road* (1944), Wallace Beery in *Salute to the Marines* (1943) and two more Red Skelton vehicles, *Whistling in Dixie* (1942) and *Whistling in Brooklyn* (1943). In the pressbook, Simon discussed his experiences with them all. "Beery works from instinct, Skelton works from script, and Abbott and Costello work when they feel like it. When they feel fine they work from stimulation. And that's really just what comedy is—stimulating. As a stimulant it rates one-hundred proof. You can actually see the effect of it on Abbott and Costello. With them it takes the form of ad-libbing. And that's why it's a lot of fun directing them. When I go to work in the morning I never know what's going to happen. The script doesn't mean a thing."

Jean Porter worked with both Bud and Lou and Red Skelton. "Red is wonderful and funny, and you kind of know what you're going to do by the script," she explained. "Red kept to himself a lot. He'd go to his dressing room, work out the next scene and what he was going to do. Lou was very much into working with everybody. I hate to say that Lou was a sweeter man, but Lou *was*—he was a very caring person. He wanted everybody to feel comfortable and he was out on the set a lot. He didn't withdraw into his dressing room— except for gambling. [laughs] Lou and I really got along well together, and I really appreciated his humor. He was so clever and fast, some of it went over some heads. He never did anything off-color, which some comics do. He was really a gentleman. Unfortunately I didn't get to know Bud Abbott as well."

Jean recalled that the team's card games didn't hinder production. "Abbott and Costello were always on call; we didn't have to wait for them. They were very professional, on time, and they knew that every minute counts." Once on the set, Bud and Lou worked out their scenes with Simon. "A film director absolutely has to have a rehearsal with camera to know where everybody's going to be going," Jean explained. "So we always had rehearsals. But that doesn't mean that every rehearsal was going to be what was shot! [laughs] Sometimes they would rehearse a scene as it came out of the script. Or Bud and Lou would come in with ideas before the rehearsal, so that might bring on some changes. The rehearsal might show us something else that could be done with it, and give Sylvan a better idea of what it would turn out to be. Then they would shoot it."

Even so, Simon explained in the pressbook, there was no guarantee that Bud and Lou would stick to what they had rehearsed. "I have to watch myself with Bud and Lou. They're so unpredictable that I'm always on my guard when they're around. And before starting a scene with them I grow terribly stern. I warn the technical and working crews that there's to be no laughing on their part. Meanwhile, I have a handkerchief ready to stuff into my mouth. You see, I break easily. That's the trouble with me. The others are all right, minding their business, and keeping quiet. Then what happens? Suddenly, and forgetting all about my handkerchief, I burst out laughing."

The songs for *In Hollywood* were written by Ralph Blane and Hugh Martin. The year before, they had a huge hit with the score for *Meet Me in St. Louis,* which included "The Trolley Song,"' "Have Yourself a Merry Little Christmas," and "The Boy Next Door."

129

BUD AND LOU'S SCENES

Jean thought that Bud and Lou looked to Sylvan for guidance during the film. "I think Lou and Bud told Sylvan to keep them in line—don't let them go wild. I know a couple of days they were running wild and they knew they were; some of this ad-lib stuff just went on and on too long. I remember at one point they asked Sylvan to really keep a rope on it and let them know if they were going too far with something. So they wanted somebody guiding them."

Early in the film, Abercrombie demands that Buzz allow him to shave the next customer. It turns out to be Rags Ragland, fresh from four weeks on location with a tough beard. (Nat Pendleton was originally scheduled for the scene.) Abercrombie struggles valiantly with the chair, the apron, and other props as he prepares to shave Rags. He finally decides that the safest thing will be to shave Rags with the dull side of the razor. When Abercrombie finishes, Rags asks for a mirror. Thinking fast, Abercrombie holds up a framed publicity portrait of Rags. "I look ten years younger," muses Rags, pleased with the results. Jean Porter recalled, "Rags is one of my favorite people in the world. You can imagine how their scene got going with ad-libs! If you saw it on the screen they probably cut about half of the stuff, too, because it would just go on and on."

While Lou preferred to ad-lib lines, he had to stick close to the script in the "Little Red Riding Hood" scene because the children needed to hear the right cues. According to the pressbook, Costello tried it a few times unsuccessfully, then Sylvan Simon finally had the lines written on a blackboard out of camera range.

Abercrombie hides from a studio guard in a pile of dummies being readied for a stunt sequence in a western saloon. Naturally, he is chosen by the prop man and repeatedly dragged up a stairway and tossed off a balcony in a scene. Of course, Lou's stunt double, Irving Gregg, took the beating, but fifteen years earlier, Costello handled similar chores as an anonymous stuntman at MGM.

The "Insomnia" scene is one of Bud and Lou's best sequences in a Metro picture. In fact, they liked it so much they reprised it effectively on their TV series. Abercrombie is so upset that Jeff has lost the part to LeMaise, he can't sleep. So Buzz gives him a record guaranteed to put anyone to sleep. It works beautifully, but no one is there to turn it off. The needle reaches the last groove and begins skipping incessantly, waking Abercrombie. Buzz offers to wait in Abercrombie's room until the record is over, then turn it off. But the record is so persuasive, Buzz nods off and misses his cue. (In the script, the record also took its toll on the landlord, several tenants, neighbors, and policemen—all in Abercrombie's room! Abercrombie finally falls asleep by listening to the Abbott and Costello radio program! This sequence was shot, but deleted from the finished picture.) In a sequence added later in retakes, Abercrombie hits on an idea to stuff cotton in Buzz's ears, so that his partner won't be affected by the recording. This leads to a very funny exchange with Bud and Lou alternately stuffing their ears to demonstrate the effectiveness of the earplugs. (The sequence was a highlight of the MGM compilation film, *That's Entertainment, Part 2* [1976].) When this fails, Abercrombie ties a string from the phonograph switch to his toe. This keeps his leg raised, but as he falls asleep, his leg will drop, pull the string, and turn off the phonograph. But when Abercrombie dozes off, not only does the string turn off the phonograph, but it turns on the radio, which blares a loud march!

In another memorable sequence, Buzz plans to take a picture of LeMaise attacking Abercrombie, then have the actor arrested for assault. This basic gag had been cut from *Pardon My Sarong*, but Perrin and Breslow managed to build on the idea and play it out to its logical conclusion. Abercrombie falls overboard and appears to have drowned. Buzz is heartbroken. At a waterfront tavern, he tearfully mourns the loss of his little pal. "I wish it had been me instead," Buzz laments. "After the way I've treated him. The sweetest guy that ever lived. The rightest, loyalest pal that ever drew breath." By now, Abercrombie, dripping wet and covered with fish, has entered the tavern. He stands behind Buzz, moved by his touching speech. Buzz continues, "And me—always playin' him for a sucker. I've been cheatin' and

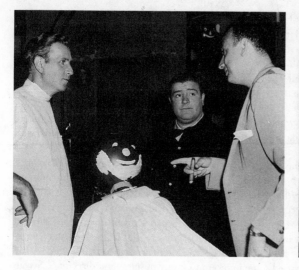

ABOVE LEFT: Director S. Sylvan Simon instructs the boys in the "Barber School" scene. ABOVE: The classic "Insomnia Scene."

shortchangin' the poor kid for years. If he could only come back to life long enough for me to tell him how *sorry* I am—how miserable I feel—how much I'm going to miss him." Abercrombie, feeling sorry for Buzz, taps him timidly on the shoulder. Buzz turns and wham!—slaps Abercrombie across the face. "Where have you been! What's the idea of worrying me like that!" he barks. As funny as the scene was, Bud and Lou improved upon it in *Africa Screams* (1949) and an episode of their television series, with Lou actually sharing a good cry with Bud over the apparent loss of his partner.

DELETIONS AND ADDITIONS

Unfortunately, we were unable to turn up a final shooting script for *In Hollywood*. Any comparisons between the script and the finished film would be based on early drafts and not very useful.

Two production numbers were cut from the film. The first, "Shake Your Salt on the Bluebird's Tail," was performed by Buzz, Abercrombie, Jeff, and Claire at the rehearsal studio. This is where Claire first meets Jeff and discovers what a great singer he is. Jean Porter was disappointed over the second deleted production number, which occurred in the nightclub sequence. "We spent weeks rehearsing a musical number that was cut out of the picture—the "Cocabola Tree." We pre-recorded it, and Bob was the singer, and we had a group—the Lyttle Sisters—that was popular at that time doing backgrounds. It was such fun; Lou was in a tux and I was in an evening dress—we were dancing all over the place, over fences and on drums. It was terrific, and I've often wondered if they saved that somewhere."

REVIEWS

Variety: "An Abbott and Costello picture may not be an artistic triumph, but the duo certainly try hard enough to make audiences laugh. Their latest is no exception; it should do fairly good business. For their final effort at Metro the studio has embellished this A&C production with several sequences that run into important dough. . . . Despite the 83 minutes running time, this one moves rapidly, aided by the direction of S. Sylvan Simon."

The New York Times: "Abbott and Costello still have a lot of friends, people who laugh so long and heartily at their slapstick antics that oftentimes running gags are drowned by gales of mirth before they're half finished. . . . If only their script writers would meet them halfway, everything would be just dandy. . . . Among the real rib-tickling sketches in this film the two high spots are Costello's schooling in the tonsorial art and his desperate battle to overcome

131

insomnia. During these interludes his brilliant pantomimic talents are brought into full play. As for the rest, well, even half a laugh is better than none."

Los Angeles Times: "The funniest single gag in [the picture] is that in which Lou stuffs cotton in Bud's ears and then says something to him—something which, of course, Bud can't hear. I'm afraid it doesn't sound funny in the telling. And that, come to think of it, is the trouble with reviewing almost anything that Abbott and Costello and comics of their ilk do."

Los Angeles Examiner: "It is inevitable the boys should land in cinema city, for heaven knows their writers have had them everywhere else. And maybe their fans will get a kick out of the pair romping all over movieville like a pair of Simple Simons. Maybe they'll laugh louder and longer at the gags obliquely and directly aimed at movie business. And frankly, there's no reason why they shouldn't, for the boys are given punchier material than they've had in a long time and they certainly punch it around. . . . But like olives, you either like Bud and Lou or you don't, and if you do, everything they do is funny, so why quibble?"

Film Bulletin: "Youngsters and confirmed A. & C. addicts will probably have a good time, but this is going to be tough on customers who don't find them a scream. Having long scraped the bottom of the barrel for fresh material, the comedians once again fall back on their time-honored routines, mixed up with some violent slapstick for their laughs. In the case of the former, it appears that the boys started some impromptu funny business and director S. Sylvan Simon hastily summoned the cameraman to record the event. Other sequences give off a strongly suspicious flavor of left-overs from the cutting room floor of their previous pictures. . . . Yet, despite all the handicaps, their comedy talents burst through occasionally to give cause for sincere regret that the pair must work with such poor material."

POSTSCRIPT

In mid-July, a few days after Bud and Lou shot their retakes, MGM announced that it would not renew its contract with the team, which had been on a year-to-year basis. The studio's profits had been dropping steadily during the war, despite an increase in revenue. A top-heavy management structure, plus escalating production costs, were to blame. As we have seen, Bud, Lou, and Eddie Sherman were probably relieved to end their sojourns to Metro, where they literally took a cut in pay and, many feel, a drop in quality. Nat Perrin offered an explanation why the team's Metro films weren't as successful as their Universal releases. "Abbott and Costello came out of burlesque, and they brought with them the routines they had been doing for years, material that had been tested on audiences. By the time they got to the Metro pictures, that was all used up. That, I think, is the reason why their earlier pictures are funnier. You know, in later years the Marx Brothers took scenes out on the road for three or four weeks to try them out on audiences. They tried to do what Abbott and Costello had years to do in honing these things."

Halfway through production on *Hollywood,* Abbott and Costello returned to Universal on May 13 for retakes on *The Naughty Nineties.* Suddenly, on May 24, a United Press story reported that Abbott and Costello had announced that they wouldn't be a team much longer. "The comedians, who have slapsticked their way from cheap burlesque to multi-million dollar movies, said that as soon as they can wind up their current contracts, they will start on separate careers," the report stated. "The big things that stand in the way of the break-up right now are a movie contract that still has two years to run, a radio contract that has even longer to go, and a half-finished picture for Metro."

According to a follow-up report, the row was patched up two days later when the team supposedly signed a new five-year contract with Universal. Meanwhile, back at Metro, everything seemed fine. "I *know* that they did not have a falling out on our film," Jean Porter said. "Lou was very concerned with Bud's health. Bud was pretty ill on that picture at times. Bud, as you know, had a male nurse with him all the time. And Lou was very conscious of this and allowed for anything and everything. I was there all the time. I don't know about the next film, or the film after that. But I know on this film they did not have a falling out."

LITTLE GIANT

SYNOPSIS

Benny Miller, a country bumpkin from Cucamonga, California, takes phonograph lessons in salesmanship from a correspondence school, then leaves his mother and his girlfriend, Martha, to seek a career in Los Angeles. Benny looks up his Uncle Clarence, a bookkeeper for the Hercules vaccum cleaner company. The sales manager, John Morrison, mistakes Benny for a model and orders him to strip down to his underwear to assess his physique. Hazel Temple, the advertising manager, and secretly Morrison's new wife, suggests that they hire Benny to keep him quiet. Morrison agrees, since he can't afford the scandal—he's secretly been juggling the company's books. But after Benny has a disastrous first day on the job, Morrison fires him. Uncle Clarence arranges for Benny to transfer to the company's branch office in Stockton, which is run by Morrison's upright cousin, Tom Chandler.

Chandler's secretary Ruby befriends Benny, but his bad luck continues. One night, the other salesmen play a prank on Benny, convincing him that he can read minds. This gives Benny the confidence he needs, and he actually becomes Hercules' Salesman of the Year and is summoned back to Los Angeles to receive an award. When Benny demonstrates his psychic powers by alluding to Morrison's secret bank account, Morrison dispatches Hazel to coax the information out of Benny at her apartment. But Benny becomes ill smoking a cigar and falls into the bathtub. Hazel attempts to put him to sleep with a sedative, which she inadvertently takes. Inevitably, Martha and Morrison walk in on the sleeping pair and imagine the worst. Martha pleads with Morrison to let her take Benny back to Cucamonga. He agrees, and at the award ceremony that night, Morrison disparages Benny. Benny returns to the farm to find Chandler, Ruby, Martha and the company president, Mr. Van Loon, waiting for him. They explain that Chandler has replaced Morrison, and offer Benny a job as sales manager of the Cucamonga district.

BACKGROUND

Bud and Lou's feuding hit the press in May and remained hot copy all summer. In New York, the press hounded the boys backstage at the Roxy Theater, where they were appearing for the benefit of what would become the Lou Costello Jr. Youth Foundation. Although the newspapers reported that the disagreement was a contractual dispute, Lou explained the real reason for the rift in an interview in 1958: "We split for the first time—in 1945—over a really ridiculous thing. I had fired a maid. I had three maids working for me, and when I refused this one a raise, she held meetings in my home, so I fired her. She went to work for Abbott. I explained to Bud why I let her go, and asked him to fire her, but he wouldn't. So

Earliest Draft:
  November 1940

Production Start:
  November 1, 1945

Production End:
  December 17, 1945

Copyright Date:
  February 21, 1946

Released:
  February 22, 1946

Running Time:
  91 minutes

Reissued: May 1, 1951
  with *The Time of Their Lives*; 1954 (with *One Night in the Tropics*)

Directed By:
  William A. Seiter

Produced By:
  Joe Gershenson

Screenplay By:
  Walter DeLeon

Original Story By:
  Paul Jarrico,
  Richard Collins

Director of Photography:
  Charles Van Enger ASC

Film Editor:
  Fred R. Feitshans, Jr.

Music Score and
Direction:
  Edgar Fairchild

Art Direction:
  John B. Goodman,
  Martin Obzina

Director of Sound:
  Bernard B. Brown

Technician:
  Robert Pritchard

Set Decorations:
  Russell A. Gausman,
  E. R. Robinson

Gowns: Vera West

Hair Stylist: Carmen Dirigo

Assistant Director:
  Seward Webb

Make-Up Director:
  Jack P. Pierce

John Morrison & Tom
   Chandler . . . Bud Abbott

Benny Miller
   . . . . Lou Costello

Ruby . . . . . . Brenda Joyce

Hazel . . Jacqueline de Wit

Uncle Clarence
   . . . . . . George Cleveland

Martha Hill
   . . . . Elena Verdugo

Mom Miller . . Mary Gordon

Mr. Van Loon
   . . . . Pierre Watkins

Conductor
   . . . . . . Donald MacBride

Gus . . . . Victor Kilian

Mrs. Hendrickson
   . . . . . Margaret Dumont

O'Brien
   . . . . George Chandler

Miss King . . Beatrice Gray

Professor Watkins' Voice
   . . . . Milburn Stone

Jim . . . . Ralph Peters

Bartender . . . . Bert Roach

Hercules
   . . . . George Holmes

Secretary . . . . . Mary Field

Man in Lower Berth
   . . . . Ralph Dunn

Wife . . . . . Dorothy Christy

Bit Man . . . Lane Chandler

Tailor . . . . Chester Conklin

Farmer Perkins
   . . . . William ''Red''
                Donahue

we had a fight—just as we were leaving on a personal appearance tour. We wouldn't talk to each other except when we were on stage."

When the team returned to California, Lou announced that their next film wouldn't be built around the usual routines. He and Bud were going to play real characters, not comic and straight man. How much of this change was instigated by the rift is open to debate. *The Naughty Nineties* may be considered the first film to separate Bud and Lou as different characters. At least two other treatments written late in 1944 and early in 1945 suggest that the change was initiated before any schism. In "Once in a Lifetime," Lou is a movie extra who's mistaken for an expert on television and hired by the mammoth B.B.D. & G advertising agency to oversee its programming. Bud is his friend, an assistant director. In another, "Hired Husband," Lou plays a shipping clerk who must marry his boss to save her company from its creditors. Bud plays his supervisor in the shipping department. In an interview in 1946, Lou explained, "Our first ten pictures were very successful. Then the box office returns started dropping. So we got together with the studio and decided to make a switch." It is true that the Abbott and Costello films had lost some of their luster. A change of pace certainly was in order. Assistant director Joe Kenny recalled, "Lou wanted a whole change of pace because he wanted to become another Chaplin. He wanted to become a tragedian. He was so wonderful in so many respects. But I think he really made a big mistake with *Little Giant*." Lou demanded that the studio hire a first-class director, and William A. Seiter agreed to produce and direct *Little Giant* for $100,000, nearly half the cost of the early Abbott and Costello films. Seiter had directed Laurel and Hardy in *Sons of the Desert;* the Marx Brothers in *Room Service;* as well as portions of *If I Had a Million, Roberta,* and *Broadway.*

THE SCRIPT

Screenwriter Paul Jarrico recalled, "My having a screen credit on an Abbott and Costello film was a complete fluke. Richard Collins and I wrote an original screenplay called "Boy Wonder." Our agent, Zeppo Marx, sold the story to Universal in 1941 for $15,000. The casting we had in mind, believe it or not, was Jimmy Stewart and Jean Arthur. Our script was shelved for one reason or another and subsequently (without our participation or even our knowledge), adapted to the talents of Abbott and Costello."

Several writers made false starts on the screenplay until Walter DeLeon was handed the assignment in September 1945. DeLeon spent the eight weeks before production began completing the final shooting script, now titled "On the Carpet." Seiter certainly had greater impact on the script than Bud and Lou's previous directors. John Grant was also on salary during the same period, so there seems to have been some intention to bring the screenplay in line with the previous Abbott and Costello vehicles. However, it appears John was overruled on all but a handful of his amendments.

In previous drafts of the script, Morrison and Hazel were not married, and it was obvious that they were having an affair. The Breen Office frowned on this point and urged that Morrison and Hazel be husband and wife. The censors also cautioned the writers about the scenes between Benny and Hazel in her apartment, and Benny could not say "I'm a baaad boy!" when he is discovered there by Martha and Morrison.

THE CAST

Brenda Joyce (b. 1915) is best known for her role as Jane opposite Johnny Weismuller and Lex Barker in the *Tarzan* series. Before making *Little Giant,* she appeared in *The Enchanted Forest, Pillow of Death* (both 1945), and *The Spider Lady Strikes Back* (1946). Brenda retired in 1949 after *Tarzan's Magic Fountain.* (June Vincent, who appeared in *Here Come the Co-Eds,* was originally cast in the role of Ruby.)

Jacqueline de Wit appeared in three other Universal features in 1946: *Cuban Pete* (with

Desi Arnaz); *She Wrote the Book* (with Joan Davis); and *Wild Beauty*. Jacqueline recalled how she got the part of Hazel in *Little Giant:* "I was having lunch with Bill Seiter one day and I said, 'I hear you're going to do the Abbott and Costello picture.' He said, 'That's right.' I said, 'How will you *stand* those two people!' 'Oh, I'll be able to take care of them.' 'I don't know how you can, Bill. I understand they never give anybody a cue!' 'Well that's right, they just give you the sense.' 'That's no help if you're waiting for a cue. All they ever do is play cards from early morning till late at night. You'll be ready to shoot a scene and they'll keep you waiting.' I painted this bleak picture, you see. I said, 'You have my deepest sympathy.' And we talked a little bit further, and then he twinkled at me and said, 'Oh, by the way, you're going to be the leading lady.' And I let out a screech and I said, 'No, no, no.' [laughs] And he said 'Yes, yes, yes.' I said, 'I can't do that, Bill. I understand those little men play tricks on you, and have jokes all day long. And I'm trained to pick up a cue.' And he just said, 'Well, I guess you'll have to get along as best you can.' He was so wonderful to let me go on that way."

Elena Verdugo (b. 1926) had played a series of tragic roles as gypsies or Spanish dancers in films like *House of Frankenstein* and *The Frozen Ghost* (both 1945). She cheerfully recalled that this was the first time she wasn't required to wear a black wig for a film. She also met her future husband, screen and radio writer Charles Marion, on the set. Marion wrote for the Abbott and Costello radio show. Later, Elena starred in the television series *Meet Millie* and *Marcus Welby, M.D.*

George Cleveland (1887–1957) appeared in over 150 films, including Abbott and Costello's *The Wistful Widow of Wagon Gap* (1947). In the 1950s, Cleveland portrayed "Gramps" on TV's *Lassie*.

THE PRODUCTION

Seiter earned nearly as much as Bud and Lou did on *Little Giant*. The director was paid $100,000 for his services; Bud and Lou, $111,000. The total cost of *Little Giant* was $775,000—even though it was all shot on the lot. The production ran thirty-nine days, with Lou working thirty-six days and Bud twenty-one.

Jacqueline de Wit respected Seiter's talents. "Bill Seiter was fantastic. He was one of the finest directors in Hollywood, the reason being he did something that John Huston always did. We'd come in in the morning and he'd be sitting in his chair talking to the cameraman and so on. And when the actors and actresses came out he would say, 'Just run the lines among yourselves.' You would just sort of rehearse with other people—and he was watching it all the time. You weren't aware of it because you thought he was talking with other people. And consequently the actors were very free, and they would do certain things that they would dream up themselves that were funny. That's what John Huston did; John Huston never really gave anybody a direction."

Assistant director Joe Kenny, however, recalled that Seiter didn't add much to *Little Giant*. "Seiter went by the script. Lou would say, 'No, I'd like to do this and this.' And Seiter would say, 'Well, that's not in the script. It says, "Dolly Shot" here, so we dolly. Where it says "Cut to," we cut to, or "Pull Back," we pull back.' " That's how he shot it—literal to the script. And the picture bombed. Oh, it really did. And it was Lou's fault, it really was, because he wanted to play this little guy who was selling vacuum cleaners door to door and it just didn't work. Abbott wasn't in the picture—he did two little schticks, he played two little parts."

Jacqueline recalled that Bud and Lou seemed to treat the picture like any other Abbott and Costello film. "There was no difficulty at all. In fact I think they rather liked it. Abbott and Costello just did anything they pleased. They ran in in the morning with some routine they had and Bill would say 'Very funny' and go on about his business. They expected great applause right away at eight o'clock in the morning or something. I never saw them at the dailies; they did what they wanted to do or what they had to do and that was it. Well you know some of the biggest stars don't go to the dailies, because it upsets them. But it was just like he was directing two children. They didn't want to rehearse, you know; they had their routines and they were terribly successful, and they would just try to get through it in a hurry so they could go back to playing poker. They never stopped! I don't know how they went home at night. I used to wonder if they got in a car together and had somebody drive them so they could play another game before they got home. It really was amazing."

But working in a scene with Abbott and Costello—particularly Costello—was something else entirely. "I had to adapt; it was that or else," Jacqueline explained. "I found the first two or three days nerve-wracking. You certainly weren't going to get a cue; you'd better speak your line and get on with it. I'll tell you I actually lost weight on that picture because those little men drove you up a wall. Now, they were awfully nice. But they were very mischievous—not Abbott so much, but Costello. You were never quite sure what was going to happen next."

Columnist Omar Ranney visited the team on Bud's last day on the picture, December 4:

Out to Universal Studios on the invitation of ex-burlesque comedians Abbott and Costello and found the two comedians looking at rushes of what had been filmed the previous day in their new movie, 'Little Giant.' And with that, a bit of news.

"We're trying something new for us in this picture," said the fat one, Lou Costello, later in the Universal commissary. "We're laying off the gags and the slapstick, going into straight comedy, and believe me we have our fingers crossed."

Bud Abbott spoke up. "Yes, and you can say that again. This is something no comedy team ever did before that I know of, changing our style, I mean, right when we're at the peak. 'Little Giant' is our seventeenth picture and all together these movies of ours have grossed something like $100 million, foreign and domestic, and now we're going to try a different formula. Maybe we're nuts, but if this works, as we certainly think it will, we expect to stay on top much longer."

Costello at this point took over and went on to explain further that in their screenplays up to now, the stories, such as they were, were woven around Abbott and Costello gags and routines. "But now," he said, "we are letting the story itself go to work, and whatever comedy results will be from the plot situations and from the characterizations."

Costello all during lunch was very much occupied. Besides taking time to explain about the new picture, he had to see to it that his two little girls, Pat and Carole, ate what they should. They wanted nothing but cake. And there was the matter of the Daily Racing Form, which he couldn't put down for more than a minute or two at a time.

While we were walking to the set, Abbott began passing out presents to the director of the picture, and to others who had an important hand in its production. Abbott had a gold currency clip for the director, William Seiter. It was in the shape of a horseshoe and was studded with diamonds, and I would imagine it cost somewhere in the neighborhood of $1,000. The total of all his gifts must have come to two or three times that, and this didn't include quite a few $20 bills which were peeled off the Abbott money roll for various technicians.

Russ Drake was the make-up man assigned to turn Bud Abbott into John Morrison, Tom Chandler, *and* their grandmother. Bud Abbott, Jr., recalled the day his dad came home in full make-up as an old woman. "You would think that the part my dad portrayed as a straight man was what he was like off-screen. But it wasn't. He loved comedy, and he was the biggest prankster in the world. There was a part in *Little Giant* where he played his grandmother. In fact, I still have the oil painting they used in the movie. He was dressed up as a grandma. Well, this one day, my mom came into my room—I was about seven years old—and said, 'Guess who's here, you're long distant grandmother!' And I said, 'Grandmother? I don't have any grandmother I know of.' And mom said, 'Oh yes, on your father's side. You've got to

come meet her.' I walked out there and here was this little grandma sitting there who looked like my dad. My dad was saying, 'Come here, sonny. Let me hold you.' It scared me to death! [laughs] He came home in his costume and full make-up just to do this to me. [laughs]. He loved putting people on."

ABOVE LEFT: Bud in make-up as Grandmother Chandler/Grandmother Morrison. ABOVE: With Jacqueline de Wit.

BUD AND LOU'S SCENES

Generally, Kenny's contention that Seiter slavishly followed the script seems accurate. Many of the supporting actors followed it to the letter, while Bud and Lou stayed unusually close for them, with ab-libbing kept to a minimum. Lou varies his performance from slapstick to pathos with great skill, but, as might be expected, the comedic scenes are more adroitly executed than the numerous straight ones. Much of the fault lies with the script, since *Little Giant* is only middling drama, and in Seiter's subdued direction. Yet Costello and Abbott perform those scenes earnestly if not convincingly.

The early sequence on the Cucamonga farm is helped immensely by Sid Fields' appearance as a contentious motorist. The segment was originally shot with actor Eddie Waller in a much straighter scene. Sid was brought in for retakes and added his own brand of material to the script. Fields had appeared with the team on its tour that summer. Benny attempts to sell him oranges, explaining, "Oranges are very good for you. Everybody should eat 'em." "Everybody should eat them?" sneers Sid. "*My* father owns a lemon grove, but you say everybody should eat *oranges!*" Benny politely explains that oranges are good for you because they contain vitamin C. Sid snarls, "For two years the specialists have been giving me vitamin A, B, and D. But no. *You're* smarter. *You* say I need vitamin C!" Sid keeps this up, as only he can, for sustained laughs.

If there was any doubt about Lou's recovery from rheumatic fever, witness the two spectacular tumbles he takes over the farmhouse's Dutch door. That's not a stuntman.

Jacqueline recalled her major scene with Lou. "There was a scene where he's in the tub and the water's running, and I am supposed to undo his tie and shirt and get him out of the tub. Well, in the scene I had to wear a negligee, and the studio spent thousands on this thing.

137

With director William Seiter.

They said please don't even go to lunch in it, which was all right with me. Bill Seiter said before we began, 'This is a very quiet scene because it's very difficult. This scene will go on until I say "Cut," no matter what happens.' Well the scene started, and the water came on, and the lines began, and I got the cufflinks off, but Lou kept pulling back and I couldn't get his tie. He would lean back, I would lean forward, the water was running all over the place, and our lines were all garbled. I was furious, because I thought, 'What is the matter with this man?!' Finally I heard 'Cut!,' and I turned around and the whole crew was in paroxysms of laughter. Bill said, 'Well, why didn't you take the tie off?' And I said, 'I am not in the habit of undressing men. What's the matter with his silly tie, anyway? It won't come undone.' Well, I didn't know it, but it was on a hook and eye; I had never seen such a thing. And that's what they were laughing at. Because they planned it; they said, 'We're going to do this scene and she's never going to get the tie off.' Which made it funnier and funnier. I'll tell you, I have never been in such a flap in my life. We were both *soaked;* my hair was hanging down like a drowned rat. I finally got to the point where I was so enraged and I said to Lou under my breath, 'Help me, help me.' Then he would put his hand up, but he wouldn't be any help!" [laughs]

DELETIONS AND ADDITIONS

Two scenes were cut showing Benny on sales calls. In one early demonstration, he hardly knows which attachment is which. An amused housewife actually shows *him* how to operate the vacuum cleaner, expounding on each and every feature and attachment. She gives such an eloquent and convincing sales talk that Benny, caught up in it, blurts, "I'll take it!" In another cut scene, Benny proceeds to diligently soil a woman's carpet, unaware that her farmhouse has not yet been wired with electricity!

After a disastrous encounter with Margaret Dumont, Benny sits on an orange crate on the sidewalk, mumbling to himself when a cop saunters by and tells him to move along. As a small crowd gathers, Benny explains that he sells vacuum cleaners and is a graduate of the Record Correspondence School. Coincidentally, so is the policeman, and they recount their "classes" with Professor Watkins. Benny makes his first sale to the cop—but when the crowd clears, he discovers his demonstration model has been stolen.

Bud and Lou's "7x13 = 28" routine in Chandler's office was added several weeks later in retakes and grafted onto the existing scene. (Note the placement of Bud's toupee at the start of the scene, and how it suddenly shifts when the boys begin the routine.)

REVIEWS

The New York Times: "Our affection for Abbott and Costello has been strong and abiding ever since those zanies first faced the cameras some six years ago. But that affection is not enhanced by 'Little Giant,' their latest caper. . . . For, while our team can't be expected to hit the cinema jackpot every time, sluggish and uneven are the words for this yarn about a California country bumpkin who essays the role of salesman. The boys, let it be noted, are in there pitching for Universal, but the laughs are not too frequent."

Los Angeles Times: "There is some attempt to make 'Little Giant' dramatic, too, but it doesn't come off very well. As Benny Miller, a correspondence-course salesman, little Lou has been endowed with a characterization, a mother and a heart. The tragedian in him is coming out, or at any rate peeping over his shoulder. Every so often the comedian in him takes a pratfall, as if to prove this is the same old Lou—and then one doesn't know whether to laugh or cry. It's very confusing. . . . Anyhow, the vaudevillian in him triumphs. Most sure-fire visual gag is Lou's ordeal in an upper berth, while on the verbal side there is nothing to top his demonstration to the incredulous Bud Abbott that seven times 13 is 28. In an effort to keep up with Costello's new dual personality, Abbott takes two parts. That way, Universal keeps both happy and averts another feud."

Hollywood Reporter: " 'Little Giant,' thanks to William A. Seiter, starts Abbott and Costello on the path of a brand-new career. It will go down in the books as the boys' first situation comedy, literally the first in which they play roles that are basically funny rather than depend entirely for laughs upon gag patter. . . . Seiter's handling of the production credited to Joe Gershenson is masterful. Every situation is milked without being exhausted. With all accents unmistakably placed on Costello, it was smart to give Abbott a dual role of cousins to keep him in there pitching. Countless other small touches enliven the proceedings, and only a man of Seiter's experience and talents could have brought matters off so effortlessly. Universal should score a gigantic hit with 'Little Giant.' "

POSTSCRIPT

Jacqueline de Wit had this final thought on *Little Giant:* "I'm glad I did the picture, and I'm awfully glad it's over."[laughs]

The team's next effort would also be a departure into the realm of character comedy, but with far more interesting results.

THE TIME OF THEIR LIVES

Earliest Draft:
December 19, 1944

Production Start:
March 6, 1946

Production End:
May 16, 1946

Copyright Date:
August 21, 1946

Released:
August 16, 1946

Running Time:
82 minutes

Reissued: May 1, 1951
with *Little Giant*

Directed By:
Charles Barton

Produced By: Val Burton

Executive Producer:
Joe Gershenson

Screenplay By: Val
Burton, Walter DeLeon,
Bradford Ropes

Additional Dialogue By:
John Grant

Director of Photography:
Charles Van Enger

Film Editor: Philip Cahn

Musical Score and
Direction: Milton Rosen

Art Direction:
Jack Otterson,
Richard H. Riedel

Director of Sound:
Bernard B. Brown

Technician:
Jack A. Bolger, Jr.

Set Decoration:
Morgan Farley

Gowns: Rosemary Odell

Hair Stylist: Carmen Dirigo

Director of Make-up:
Jack P. Pierce

Assistant Director:
Seward Webb

Special Photography By:
D. S. Horsley ASC and
Jerome Ash ASC

SYNOPSIS

In 1780, master tinker Horatio Prim arrives at the estate of one of his best customers, Tom Danbury. Horatio plans to wed Danbury's housemaid, Nora O'Leary, and he hopes that a letter of commendation from General George Washington will persuade Danbury to permit the marriage. But Horatio has a rival in Cuthbert Greenway, the butler at Danbury Manor. When Nora overhears that Danbury is an accomplice in Benedict Arnold's dastardly plot, Danbury seizes the letter and deposits it in a secret compartment of a mantel clock. Danbury's fiancée, Melody Allen, learns what has happened and sets off to warn the revolutionary army. As she and Horatio ride away, American troops overrun the estate and mistakenly shoot them as traitors. Horatio and Melody are buried in a well, and the soldiers condemn their spirits to remain bound to Danbury Acres unless some evidence proves their innocence. The evidence, of course, is Horatio's letter from Washington, which Danbury hid in the clock. The advancing forces overrun the estate, ransack the house, and burn it down.

One hundred and sixty-six years later the ghosts of Horatio and Melody are still bound to Danbury Acres. But the mansion has been restored by playwright Sheldon Gage, whose psychiatrist, Dr. Ralph Greenway is a descendant of the butler, Cuthbert Greenway. Sheldon, his fiancée, June Prescott, her Aunt Millie, and Dr. Greenway arrive to survey the completed house and spend the night. Their psychic maid, Emily, however, senses that the estate is haunted, and Horatio and Melody eagerly oblige. Horatio takes particular delight in terrorizing Greenway. Finally, Emily contacts Horatio and Melody through a seance and learns of Washington's letter. Sheldon explains that the clock that conceals the letter is in a New York museum. Dr. Greenway steals the clock in an effort to make amends with Horatio. Although Greenway is pursued by the state police, the letter is found, and the curse is broken. Melody and Horatio are finally free to join Tom and Nora in heaven.

BACKGROUND

Seiter had added little to *Little Giant* to justify the enormous salary, so Universal turned to a recently acquired, dependable director, Charles T. Barton, for *The Time of Their Lives*. It would be the start of a long, harmonious, and memorable association. Barton (1902–1981), who had appeared in vaudeville, became a director after apprenticing as a prop boy for James Cruze and as an assistant director for William Wellman. He directed his first feature, *Wagon Wheels,* in 1934, and joined Universal in 1945 after a stint at Columbia. Barton had just piloted *Smooth as Silk* and *White Tie and Tails* (both 1946) to good results before drawing the Abbott and Costello assignment.

Val Burton, who wrote the original story, was assigned to produce the film, with Joe Gershenson elevated to executive producer. Burton later co-wrote the screenplay for *Bedtime for Bonzo* (1951).

THE SCRIPT

Val Burton wrote an original treatment, "The Ghost Steps Out," late in 1944. It is similar to the story we know as *The Time of Their Lives,* except that the ghosts are Gwinette De Rome and Cedric Brown, a dandy and his black valet. By the time Walter DeLeon and Bradford Ropes contributed to the screenplay nearly a year later, the script had been reworked as an Abbott and Costello vehicle. John Grant is credited with writing additional dialogue but again not credited as an associate producer on the picture.

In April 1947, lawyers for playwright John Cecil Holm pointed out alleged similarities between *The Time of Their Lives* and his Broadway play, *The Gramercy Ghost.* According to studio memos, lawyers for both sides reviewed the studio's Assignment File, which disclosed that Burton had written the first treatment in 1944. "We agreed neither party appeared to have cause for action against each other," the memo concludes.

THE CAST

Marjorie Reynolds (b. 1921), an actress since childhood, had appeared in *Holiday Inn* (1942) and *Ministry of Fear* (1944). Marjorie appeared in *Monsieur Beaucaire* (1946) with Bob Hope before being loaned out by Paramount for *The Time of Their Lives.* She followed it with another supernatural comedy, *Heaven Only Knows,* in 1947. Marjorie may be best remembered as "Babs" on TV's *Life of Riley.*

Binnie Barnes (1905–1983) was born in London, and had appeared in shorts and features in England before emigrating to Hollywood. Her credits include *The Private Life of Henry VIII* (1933), *Three Smart Girls* (1937), *The Three Musketeers* (1939), *Three Girls About Town* (1941), *Up in Mabel's Room* (1944) and *It's in the Bag* (1945). She retired in 1955, but returned in 1966 for *The Trouble With Angels* and its later sequel.

John Shelton (1917–1972) had appeared in three prior ghost comedies: *The Ghost Comes Home* (with Frank Morgan, 1940); *Whispering Ghosts* (with Milton Berle, 1942); and *A-Haunting We Will Go* (with Laurel and Hardy, 1942). Married to Kathryn Grayson from 1940–1946, Shelton retired from films in the early 1950s.

Gale Sondergaard (1899–1985) won the very first Oscar in the Best Supporting Actress category for her performance in *Anthony Adverse* (1936). In the 1940s she became Hollywood's premier villainess. In the 1950s she became a victim of the communist witch hunts, and didn't return to films until the late 1960s. Gale replaced Almira Sessions in the role of Emily after Sessions had worked on the picture for three days.

Anne Gillis (b. 1927) had been a child actress, and appeared in *The Adventures of Tom Sawyer* and *Little Orphan Annie* (both 1938). Anne appeared with Bud and Lou in *In Society,* and in Lou's independent production, *A Wave, a Wac and a Marine* (both 1944).

THE PRODUCTION

The Time of Their Lives was the most expensive Abbott and Costello picture to date. It was originally scheduled for forty-eight days, but ran two weeks over, coming in at $830,625. Bud and Lou received $111,000, while director Charles Barton received $15,500, including a provisional bonus of $5,000.

Much of the cost was in the special effects, particularly the opticals to achieve the ghost effects. Today's movie special effects costs are staggering, with some approaching the total cost of *The Time of Their Lives* itself, but a survey of the special effects rigged for this film, made in 1946, can only bring thoughts of a simpler time:

Preparation and test of Heaven, $2,000
Wire gags in library, hallways, and living room, $1,500
Rigging car for blind driving and steering wheel to fly off, $750
Drinking water gag on Costello, $600

Cuthbert and Dr.
  Greenway . Bud Abbott
Horatio . . . . . Lou Costello
Melody
  . . . . . Marjorie Reynolds
Mrs. Prescott
  . . . . Binnie Barnes
Sheldon Gage
  . . . . John Shelton
Tom Danbury
  . . . . Jess Barker
Emily . . Gale Sondergaard
Major Putnam
  . . . . Robert Barrat
Lieutenant Mason
  . . . . Donald MacBride
Nora . . . . Anne Gillis
June Prescott
  . . . . Lynn Baggett
Connors . . . . . . William Hall
Sergeant Makepeace
  . . . . Rex Lease
Motorcycle Rider
  . . . . Harry Woolman
Second Sergeant
  . . . . Harry Brown
Bates . . . . . Walter Baldwin
Curator . . Selmer Jackson
First Guard
  . . . . George Carleton
Leigh . . . Vernon Downing
Cranwell . . . . . . Boyd Irwin
Bessie . . . . Marjorie Eaton
Second Guard
  . . . . Wheaton Chambers
Dandies . . . . Kirk Alyn
  Myron Healey

141

Hay gag in stable, $490
Clock compartment gags, $300
Illumination gag on Costello, $250

Cinematographer Charles Van Enger explained, "To get those ghost effects, we'd first photograph the set with nobody on it and then cover everything with black velvet. Next we photographed the scene with the actors. This was overlapped so that, when somebody sat down in a chair, it looked as if you could see right through them, giving the illusion of ghosts." It cost some $6,000 to dress and redress the set in black velvet. Marjorie Reynolds, who had been blonde for several years, was required to return to her original dark hair color for the film, since light hair hindered the effect.

Van Enger had a bigger problem than Marjorie's hair, however. "We worked practically all day doing one of those ghost sequences and left word that no one was to touch anything on the set when we broke for the day. That night, Lou sneaked back in and took a lot of items off the set that he'd been casing during the daytime. As a result, we had to retake all of those scenes, which was costly, because even when we got the stuff back from Lou, we couldn't put them back exactly as they had been before. I don't think Lou realized what he'd done, or why the things couldn't be moved, but we posted signs all over the set following that incident which read: Now Don't Move Anything!!!"

Charles Barton recalled, "There was the most beautiful grandfather's clock on the mansion's hallway set. Well, the crew went to lunch, and when we came back to shoot in the hall, the clock was gone. Nobody knew where it went. Lou had a truck come to the studio, pick it up, and deliver it to his house."

Barton faced his first serious test a few weeks into the picture. "Lou called me one night, mad as hell. He wanted to switch roles with Bud. I think Lou had been off for two or three days, and he thought we were shooting a lot more with Bud than we were with him—because he never read a script. Neither did Bud. Anyway, Lou wanted to switch parts or else he was not coming to work. That meant scrapping weeks of footage. So we just sat and waited him out. When he did come back, everything was beautiful sailing from then on."

Barton explained that he had to adapt to the team's working methods. "It would take you time to fall into the mold of directing Abbott and Costello. I would always let the cameras run. That on-the-spot creativity added life to their films. Both had equal talent. Both had photographic memories. They could glance at a script once and they'd know it. They were very quick learners who hated rehearsals."

BUD AND LOU'S SCENES

As with *Little Giant*, the team was once again "split up" to portray separate characters. In fact, they never even speak to each other in the film, except briefly at the beginning. But somehow you don't mind. *The Time of Their Lives* is a thoroughly enchanting fantasy, with a sustained plot, and humor is derived from characterizations and situations, rather than routines. Lou may have been funnier in other films, but his performance in this picture is easily the most endearing of his career. Bud's portrayal of a harried psychiatrist was one of the rare instances where he was allowed to be funny, too. It also showed that Bud would have made a fine character actor if given the chance. Perhaps the greatest compliment one can give both performers in this film is that you easily forget that they are Bud Abbott and Lou Costello, comedians, and you become engrossed in the story. It proved that the boys didn't need the old routines to charm us.

DELETIONS AND ADDITIONS

Generally, the film is very close to the final shooting script, but there were some interesting changes.

ABOVE LEFT: Setting up a scene with director Charles Barton (on camera). ABOVE: Paddy Costello recalls, "The first day of filming was Dad's 40th birthday. We came down and surprised him with a cake."

A cut gag has Horatio musing to Melody over who his descendants might be had he lived to have a family. "Ah, I can see them now. George Washington Prim . . . Thomas Jefferson Prim . . . Martha Washington Prim . . . Benjamin Franklin Prim . . . John Hancock Prim . . . and, of course, Horatio Prim Junior." As he mentions each name, the figure of a small boy fades in, dressed exactly as Horatio and with his face. All but Horatio Prim, Jr., who is dressed like Horatio but has Cuthbert's face! Horatio takes a good look at Horatio Jr. and reacts. "And they call *me* a traitor!" This scene was omitted because of objections from the Breen Office and was never filmed.

Most of the additions to the film were the little ghostly gags, including a wonderful sequence where Melody and Horatio run into each other and exchange clothes. Other additions include Melody's ability to float down from the tree; Horatio's head becoming stuck in a bottle; and Horatio pulling Lieutenant Mason's hat down over his eyes. The Breen Office cautioned the producers that Melody's little shimmy to become invisible should not be suggestive.

The film's ending differs from the script. After Melody and Horatio say their good-byes, Horatio continues on, looking for Nora. He spots Cuthbert, in a flowing white robe and clutching a small heavenly harp, pursued by two men, similarly clothed, holding tridents in their hands and shouting, "Stop thief! Bring back that harp!" Horatio shakes his head, "Same old Cuthbert." Then Horatio meets Nora in the mist. They embrace and he asks, "What's it like—in heaven?" Nora says, "I don't know, darlin', I haven't been yet." Horatio is surprised. "You mean you've been waiting out here all this time?" Nora nods. "They gave me special permission to wait. You see, it wouldn't be heaven without you." They embrace, and Lancelot, now equipped with the wings of Pegasus, emerges from the mist and carries Horatio and Nora off into limbo.

REVIEWS

Curiously, none of the film's publicity material indicated that the film was a fantasy, or that Lou played a period character. Posters and advertisements depicted Abbott and Costello in contemporary business suits!

Variety: "This one's a picnic for Abbott & Costello fans. Replete with trowelled-on slapstick, corned-up gags and farcical plot, 'Time Of Their Lives' won't shock the patrons with any unfamiliar novelties. Abbott is still playing straight to Costello and all's well at the b.o. . . . With many of the gags double-tracking on themselves, film could be snipped at a few points for punchier comic effects. Direction is well-aimed at the belly-laugh level, and the trick photography is handled with flawless technique. With production values okay in every other department, film sags only in the script, where A&C could use some fresh, bright material instead of the easy and tired way out."

143

Hollywood Reporter: "Something new is being offered by Abbott and Costello, something gay and riotously brand-new. Long specialists in the borrowed and the blue, Bud and Lou had their first whirl at situation comedy in 'Little Giant,' and they came out so well that Universal really throws the book at them in 'Time of Their Lives.' By long odds, it is the best A&C show to date. Look what it has:

"Marjorie Reynolds is the loveliest leading lady who ever chanced on the same screen with Abbott and Costello. She provides the charm of a clever whimsey which has her teamed as an earth-bound ghost with the wraith of the frustrated Lou. . . .

"Charles Barton, justifying the confidence placed in him by [producers] Gershenson and Burton, directs to mark up a personal smash. Barton never reaches for the howls that come so naturally from terrific material. He doesn't even milk gags. He just points the hilarious situations and gets the next roar from a fresh one. This is crack direction in anyone's book. . . .

"With Costello all over the place and socking hard in his own style, it is a pleasure to record that Abbott doesn't get left out of the show. He is never in there feeding Lou with questions to get funny answers. This is a situation comedy, and Bud has a role to play. As a matter of fact, he has two, for he appears as his own great, great grandfather in the prologue. That motivates [Horatio] to plague him, and he sells reactions for a panic."

POSTSCRIPT

Bud's nephew Norman rejoined the fold after serving in the Navy during the war and served as Bud's stand-in on the film. He recalled Bud's reaction to the new direction the team's films were taking. "Bud didn't like doing them at all. He felt that Lou wanted to go on and be a different kind of comedian, that he didn't want to be a team anymore. So the parts were written that way in a couple of pictures, and it didn't work. The audience didn't want to see that. They wanted to see the comedy team they knew and loved."

The war had interrupted the flow of Abbott and Costello films to Europe. When it resumed, France and Spain snapped up all the old A&C films they could. During the summer of 1947, *The Time of Their Lives* was the only American film making money in Madrid.

Bud had to learn how to drive a car for the film. "That's the only time in his life my dad ever drove a car," Bud Abbott, Jr. recalled. "The studio built an electric car for him to practice on. We had it at the house, and he would drive it down Ventura Boulevard—this is before it was a highway—to his restaurant, Abbott's Backstage. The police would let him go on his way, never bothered him."

BUCK PRIVATES COME HOME

SYNOPSIS

Slicker Smith and Herbie Brown, after serving in World War II, return to the States on board a troop ship. When Sergeant Collins discovers that they have smuggled aboard Evey, a six-year-old French orphan, she is held for the immigration officials by Lieutenant Sylvia Hunter, a nurse. Evey escapes from immigration and heads for Times Square, where Slicker and Herbie are back peddling ties. They are about to be pinched by Collins, now a cop, when Evey helps them escape. Herbie learns that he must be married and have a steady income before he can adopt the girl. Evey suggests "Aunt" Sylvia as a prime candidate, and they seek her help.

Sylvia's boyfriend, Bill Gregory, is a midget car racer. His souped-up vehicle is held in hock by a local garage for unpaid bills. But Bill says the car is a cinch to win the $20,000 first prize in the Gold Cup Stakes. The boys' separation pay and money borrowed from their old Army buddies enable Bill to compete in the race. Collins, who has been thrown off the force for allowing Slicker, Herbie, and Evey to escape, finally catches up with them at the track. But Herbie accidentally starts the midget racer and leads the police and immigration officials on a wild, cross-country chase off the track, onto an airfield, around a horseracing track, down city streets, and finally into a movie theater. The midget car's performance so impresses auto magnate Appleby that he orders twenty cars and two hundred engines. This is enough to set Bill up in business, allow him to marry Sylvia, and adopt Evey. Slicker and Herbie are granted visitation rights on the condition that they land steady jobs. Collins' police captain suggests that the boys train for the police force.

BACKGROUND

Buck Privates Come Home began the team's propitious association with producer Robert Arthur (1909–1986). "How I met Abbott and Costello goes back to a fellow named Ed Muhl, who at that time was the head of the legal department at Universal," Arthur recalled. "I was in the service, and Ed's wife and my wife were good friends. While I was in the service I was still under contract to Metro as a writer. The war had just ended, and Ed was telling me about Abbott and Costello. He said that they had made so much money with some of their pictures during the war, but that *Little Giant* and *The Time of Their Lives* didn't do too well. So I suggested to Ed, 'Why don't you do *Buck Privates Come Home?*' After all, they started out really at their peak in the original *Buck Privates,* and now the war was over.

"At that time, Lou wanted more of a say in the scripts, and at the insistence of Lou, Bud and Eddie Sherman, Universal sought a better type of screenwriter. They hired a writer named Dick Macauley, who had worked at Warner Bros. and been a writing partner with Jerry Wald. They gave Dick the assignment in April or May 1946."

Earliest Draft: July 1945

Production Start: November 18, 1946

Production End: January 23, 1947

Copyright Date: March 25, 1947

Released: April 4, 1947

Running Time: 77 minutes

Directed By: Charles Barton

Produced By: Robert Arthur

Screenplay By: John Grant, Frederic I. Rinaldo, and Robert Lees

Based on a Story By: Richard Macauley and Bradford Ropes

Director of Photography: Charles Van Enger

Art Directors: Bernard Herzbrun, Frank A. Richards

Film Editor: Edward Curtiss

Music By: Walter Schumann

Orchestrations: David Tamkin

Sound: Charles Felstead

Technician: Robert Pritchard

Set Decorations: Russell A. Gausman, Charles Wyrick

Gowns: Yvonne Wood

Hair Stylist: Carmen Dirigo

Make-Up: Jack P. Pierce

Assistant Director: Joseph E. Kenny

Special Photography By: David S. Horsley ASC

THE SCRIPT

In point of fact, Arthur T. Horman, who had written the original *Buck Privates,* had first crack at the project during the summer of 1945 and wrote a treatment called "The Return of the Buck Privates." That fall, both Howard Green and Leo Townsend were also put to work on the idea, but they, too, were superseded by Macauley. Robert Arthur continued, "When I heard that the studio was reaching for another type of writer—Dick's salary at that time, I think, was $2,000 a week, which was pretty good—I thought that it was a good idea. But Macauley was a little sluggish. So Ed Muhl called me and asked me to come to the studio; primarily it was a case of, 'Can you get a script out of this fellow?' I was about to return to Metro, but Universal offered me a chance to produce. Eddie Mannix at Metro was very gracious; he said, 'If it doesn't work out, come back.' So, I went to Universal.

"The first thing I had to do was take Dick Macauley off the project. I hired Bradford Ropes, and we set about to make *Buck Privates Come Home.*" Macauley's original, which introduced the midget car angle, had Slicker and Herbie befriend an American orphan girl they discover living in their new apartment. Among other changes, Arthur and Ropes made the girl a French orphan, smuggled into the country by Herbie.

By now, two screenwriters with previous experience writing for Abbott and Costello had returned to Universal after three years at Paramount. Robert Lees and Fred Rinaldo drew the assignment of writing the screenplay. "We liked working for Robert Arthur better than Alex Gottlieb," Lees recalled. "We never really got along with Gottlieb. I thought Arthur was a fine producer, who didn't try to write your picture, the way Alex did. I think the problem was, Gottlieb had a writer's head, not a producer's head."

THE CAST

Tom Brown (1913–1990) was born to vaudevillian parents, and made his Broadway debut at age ten. In 1932 he had the unique distinction of playing a character with his name in *Tom Brown of Culver.* Brown enlisted in the spring of 1942 after starring in Universal's *Adventures of Smilin' Jack* serial, and served nearly five years before being discharged a captain. One of his first roles back in Hollywood was in *Buck Privates Come Home.* In the 1960s he was a regular on TV's *Gunsmoke.*

Joan Shawlee (1926–1987)—a.k.a. Joan Fulton—was spotted by Lou and Bud at the Copacabana in New York. "They were looking for someone to star in *Buck Privates Come Home,*" Joan explained. At the time, early drafts of the screenplay included a character who was a nightclub performer. Joan continued, "I did my little number, and I'm sure I looked like I had it together, but I was only eighteen, lived with my mother, and was terribly naive. So the two of them sent a card back and I went out to meet them. They said they wanted to bring me out to California under contract. I said, 'That's fine, but you'll have to meet with my mother.' And Lou said, 'Ohhh! Out of 10,000 girls in New York, I find the only yo-yo!' [laughs] I brought my mother in and we sat down, and Lou had another man with him. His name was Dean Martin. Lou said, 'I'm signing Mr. Martin, and I'd like to sign you, too.' I said I have to take my mother with me, and Lou paid for our train fare, and Universal put me under contract." Joan had bit parts in six films before being assigned *Buck Privates Come Home.* She was always grateful to Bud and Lou for starting her on her career and for giving it a second chance. "After two years, I left Universal, I got married, and I had a son. I hadn't worked in two years, and I thought I'd settle down, even though I wanted to work. Well, I heard that Bud and Lou were shooting *Jack and the Beanstalk* (1952) at Hal Roach Studios, and I took my son to say hello. Lou said, 'We're going to be doing a TV series. Why don't you come to work!' In this business you very seldom get a second chance, but I suddenly had a whole new career from it." Joan went on to turn in memorable performances in the Billy Wilder hits *Some Like it Hot* (1959), *The Apartment* (1960) and *Irma La Douce* (1963). On television, aside from *The Abbott and Costello Show,* Joan may be best remembered as Pickles on *The Dick Van Dyke Show.*

In a deleted sequence, Evey and the boys meet a young shoeshine boy in the ferry waiting room. A recent immigrant himself, he explains that he has been adopted and attends school. He reads to them from a pamphlet about the Statue of Liberty. As the young boy begins reciting the famous Emma Lazarus poem, Herbie takes over in a heartfelt reading that inspires him and Slicker to find some way to keep Evey. They disguise her as a boy, and head for the French Consulate. Sebastian Cristillo (Lou's father) sits next to Bud.

Beverly Simmons (b. 1938) won her first movie role over forty hopefuls in *Frontier Gal* (1945) with Yvonne DeCarlo. Her second was *Little Miss Big,* and her third, *Cuban Pete* (1946), was with Desi Arnaz and Joan Fulton. *Buck Privates Come Home* was her fourth film. Not long after starting on the film, Beverly came down with chicken pox and missed a week's work.

Since *Buck Privates Come Home* opened with clips from the original *Buck Privates,* one contingency plan for producer Robert Arthur was to reshoot scenes from the original in the event Nat Pendleton did not reprise his role in the sequel. Fortunately, Pendleton did.

THE PRODUCTION

Robert Arthur recalled his initial meeting with Bud and Lou. "I've always been a rather square fellow. I came into the picture business out of the oil business. I had never produced a picture. I certainly had never been involved with anybody like Abbott and Costello. I had heard all of the stories since they had been the studio's bankroll. Their pictures had done the greatest business of anything Universal had all through the war years. They had saved Universal, and with that came certain demands for more control. Lou's complaint always was that we never put important stars in their films.

"Before we ever started the picture, I had a talk with Lou and Bud. Bud was always a beauty. He never gave you any problems. I started to explain to Lou that I had never done a picture of their type. In fact, this was the first picture I produced. I worked on the Jeanette MacDonald–Nelson Eddy pictures at Metro. I said to Lou, 'If this bothers you, let me know because I can go back to Metro. All I want to know is, are you going to let me make this picture or are you going to give me all kinds of trouble?' And Lou said, 'If you think you can make it, let's make it.' And that was our relationship. We were never terribly close personally, but I had a wonderful relationship with Lou because of the way we had started, being honest with each other."

Buck Privates Come Home was scheduled for 50 days, with a budget of $1,167,500. The film came in three days and $34,500 over budget, making it the most expensive A&C vehicle

147

produced at Universal. Bud and Lou were paid $196,133 for their services, while Barton received $13,000.

Twelve of the country's hottest midget drivers worked for a week at Los Angeles' Gilmore Stadium, one of the best midget tracks in the west. Hollwood's top stuntdriver, Carey Loftin, drove in Costello's place. For point-of-view shots of the high-speed chase sequence, Arthur borrowed a 16mm camera from the Air Corps. The automatic camera, normally used by pursuit planes in combat, was mounted on a midget racer. Because the camera held only about a minute of film, the scenes had to be repeated sixteen times to acquire enough footage.

The company also went on location to Fort MacArthur in San Pedro for the sequence where Slicker and Herbie are separated at Fort Dix.

Buck Privates Come Home grossed $2,365,000 to become the studio's eighth biggest grosser of 1947.

BUD AND LOU'S SCENES

Buck Privates Come Home's scenario afforded much opportunity for pathos, which Lou ultimately achieved quite convincingly in the finished film. The fact that in real life Lou related best to children no doubt contributed to the sincerity of his performance. The world may have been deprived of a great performance when Chaplin's plans to remake *The Kid* with Lou Costello fell through.

"The best gag in *Buck Privates Come Home* almost didn't make it into the picture," Robert Lees recalled. "There's a scene where Costello made a table by putting a board on a sawhorse, so that the table moved up and down like a teeter-totter as Abbott and Costello set the table. Well, the studio came to us and said they had to cut it. It was too expensive and taking too long to shoot. We said, 'Why is it too expensive?' Turns out they built a mechanical table with gears so the director could move it up and down. Well, of course, it never worked out right and they wanted to cut the whole scene. Fred and I went out of our minds. We said, 'Just put a guy under the table and cue him with a light and have him move the table up when the light goes on. You don't need a machine!' They had never thought of this. So they put a guy under the table and the scene's one of the highlights of the picture. But that's what you had to put up with at Universal. They took something so simple and made it so complicated." (Lees and Rinaldo had salvaged the gag from their unproduced Abbott and Costello screenplay, "By Candlelight," written in 1943.)

The scene is masterfully staged. Neither Slicker nor Herbie are aware of the table's true nature. Each time Slicker places an object on one end, Herbie, by sheer and fortunate coincidence deposits an equal object on the other, keeping the table balanced. Finally, the teetering table launches a cake into Sergeant Collins' face. Nat Pendleton had to stand in for four takes of the scene. After each take he had to shower to get all the goo off his face and hair just so he could get popped again.

When Herbie, Evey, and Slicker arrive at Sylvia's apartment, it's obvious that Sylvia is not a good prospect for Herbie to marry. "I'd rather marry a homely girl than a pretty girl anyway," he says. Slicker asks why. "Well, if you marry a pretty girl, she's liable to run away." "But Uncle Herbie, isn't a homely girl liable to run away too?" Evey asks. Herbie cracks, "Yeah, but who cares?" The joke has been ascribed to Benjamin Franklin!

The clothesline sequence is another of the film's memorable scenes. Herbie rigs a hammock by pinning a blanket to Sylvia's clothesline. The next morning, a housewife in a building across the yard begins reeling in her laundry—and with it, Herbie. He wakes up to find himself hanging five stories above the ground. His cries for help draw the woman's jealous husband to the window. "So that's what you mean when you complain about the size of the wash!" he exclaims. "The minute I go out the door, *that* comes in the window!" He begins to pull in the line, just as Slicker emerges from Sylvia's window to begin a hilarious tug of war. In the shooting script, the clothesline breaks from the abuse, sending Herbie swinging into a

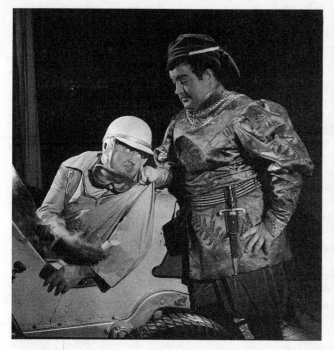

ABOVE LEFT: Lou and his stunt double, Irving Gregg. ABOVE: Bud, Lou, and Betty Alexander in the deleted "Romeo and Juliet" scene.

window on a lower floor. But as the sequence was shot, a verbal battle between Slicker and the husband was added. The husband threatens to cut the line unless Slicker lets go. To Herbie's horror, Slicker challenges, "I'd like to see you do it!" And the man does.

The actual auto race, of course, was shot with doubles, but that doesn't mean that Lou didn't have his share of tight spots. According to the pressbook, he had to be cut out of the midget car after doing several hours' work in front of the process screen. Rescuers from the metal shop arrived armed with hacksaws. Damage to the car—reported in the budget—$250.

DELETIONS AND ADDITIONS

Curiously, the midget car chase was not in the final shooting script. Herbie does accidentally drive the racer, but he manages to stay on the track and win the race after some obvious gags borrowed from *It Ain't Hay*. An undated, eight-page rewrite of the sequence finally takes Herbie off the track, but still differs from the final film. Some of the gags suggested include having the car dash through a warehouse district, knocking poultry crates off a loading dock; tear through a ladies' turkish bath; and execute a double flip over an open drawbridge. The script ends with the car crashing through a nondescript brick wall. At the bottom of the page is this note: "Dear Mr. Grant: Please tell me what's on the other side of the wall."

The ever-reliable John Grant came up with an innovative gag to cap the sequence. Herbie drives the car right through the rear of a movie theater. (Sharp-eyed observers will spot the sign, "Abbott and Costello in 'Romeo Junior' " high up on the wall.) The car stops just as he crashes through the movie screen, on which an Abbott and Costello movie is being shown. Costello-on-screen is in the middle of the balcony scene from *Romeo and Juliet*. Costello looks down at Herbie and demands, "What's the big idea?" Herbie looks up at the giant image of Costello and replies, "Gee, you ain't very pretty, are you." The screen Costello snaps, "Oh, a wise guy! Well, this is gonna hurt me as much as it does you!", and he steps *off the screen* to bop Herbie in the nose! The crash had to be perfectly timed to coincide with the action on the screen. It took sixteen tries to get it right, and yet the scene was omitted from the final print. (Look closely and you'll notice that Herbie is holding his nose when the rest of the cast catches up to him.)

REVIEWS

The New York Times: "It doesn't make much sense—in fact, it doesn't make any sense at all—but the new Abbott and Costello comedy which opened yesterday at the Winter Garden is a lot of fun. 'Buck Privates Come Home' finds the roly-poly one and his straight man in the very best of form. Not having any story line to cramp their zany style they just let themselves go in the broadest kind of slapstick, getting involved in one crazy situation after another. This sort of free clowning may not sit well with every audience but it will satisfy any spectator who is willing to check his inhibitions with the door man. And the small fry—the smaller the better—are hereby guaranteed a noisy, good time."

New York Daily News: "I'm thinking of asking the boss for a bonus for having to sit through, and write a review of, Abbott and Costello's 'Buck Privates Come Home.' Now, I wouldn't feel this way if this new comedy was one of A. and C.'s first half dozen. But, being the 19th since 1940, and being a repetition of the same old monkeyshines that were in the other 18, I can't help it; at this point I'm weary of Abbott and Costello antics."

New York Journal-American: "As one rarely given to audible laughter in a theater, I now swear and depose that I was moved to at least 14 solid cackles by this [picture], all of them the result of the strictly physical nip-ups called 'slapstick.' I depose further that I think the payoff chase is the second funniest sequence Abbott and Costello have ever been involved in (Costello's altercation with an angry oyster in an earlier film will always be my pet!), and that the doings as a whole are the best the boys have yet turned out, and what do you think of that? Inasmuch as it is fashionable to be somewhat defiant about sneaking admiration for Messrs. A. & C., I will be defiant—yaaah!—but my admiration ain't sneaking, it's forthright."

Film Bulletin: "By far the most hilarious comedy ever made by Abbott and Costello, this sidesplitting mirthquake should bring unprecedented returns. It has jet-propulsion pace, uproarious slapstick, time-proven gags and sure-fire heart appeal. At the press screening, an audience of hard-boiled newspaper critics was nearly in hysterics at this 77-minute answer to a showman's prayer."

POSTSCRIPT

Just as all this new creative blood arrived at Universal, many of the studio's old guard were being dismissed. "Just as we were about to begin production," Robert Arthur explained, "Universal merged with International Pictures, and Bill Goetz and Leo Spitz, who ran International, came in to run the studio. Goetz was Louis B. Mayer's son-in-law, and had made pictures that were on a much higher level. They were not particularly interested in Abbott and Costello, Donald O'Connor, Maria Montez, or Yvonne DeCarlo—who were the stars at Universal. Goetz and Spitz wanted to make prestigious pictures. So, almost everybody at Universal was fired. The only reason I was kept was not because of any special ability or anything, but because I had Abbott and Costello—and nobody else wanted anything to do with Abbott and Costello."

Universal-International, as it was now known, would concentrate on highbrow projects at the expense of its bread-and-butter B-movies, westerns and serials. This policy sent the studio careening to a loss of $3.2 million in 1948 after record profits of $4.6 million in 1946. Before long, the second features were back in production.

THE WISTFUL WIDOW OF WAGON GAP

SYNOPSIS

Duke Egan and Chester Wooley, traveling salesmen en route to California, arrive in the tough Montana town of Wagon Gap. One of the infamous citizens, Fred Hawkins, is shot and killed, and Duke and Chester are charged with murder. Jim Simpson, the head of the honest citizen's committee, saves the boys from being lynched by digging up an old Montana law that makes the survivor in a gun duel responsible for the debts and dependents of his victim. The victim's blustery widow, Mrs. Hawkins, and her seven children, become Chester's responsibility. The widow works Chester from dawn till dusk on the farm, trying to wear him down so he'll agree to marry her. Jake Frame, meanwhile, who runs the town's saloon, demands that Chester pay off Hawkins' debt to him by working at the saloon at night.

Chester soon discovers that no one will dare shoot him for fear of inheriting his dreadful responsibilities. Jim realizes that Chester will make an invincible sheriff who can clean up the town once and for all. Armed with a photograph of the widow and her brood to discourage gunslingers, Chester turns Wagon Gap around, foils a hold-up Frame is planning, and even stands up to Duke. While Chester enjoys his new power, Duke longs to move on to California. He tries to persuade Judge Benbow to marry the widow by spreading a rumor that she stands to become rich once the new railroad buys her property. As the rumor spreads, all of the men in Wagon Gap begin gunning for Chester. Finally, the townswomen save Chester, and Frame confesses to the murder of Hawkins. Duke and Chester are free to leave for California, and Judge Benbow is set to marry the widow. The rumor turns out to be true.

BACKGROUND

"Since *Buck Privates Come Home* came off well," Robert Arthur explained, "it was a case of, 'Have you got an idea for another picture?' We did *The Wistful Widow of Wagon Gap*. And the only reason Bill Goetz went for it was because he liked Marjorie Main. She had been in *The Egg and I*, which did tremendous business for Universal."

Off-screen, Lou took great pride in dedicating the Lou Costello Jr. Youth Center in East Los Angeles on May 3, 1947. He and Bud had made several personal appearance tours to raise the $350,000 necessary to build the center.

Less than a week later, on May 9, Lou's father, Sebastian Cristillo, died of a heart attack. The night before, Sebastian had received a telephone call from Eddie Sherman. Lou was being stubborn about something, and Eddie figured the best way to pursuade Lou would be through

Earliest Draft:
February 24, 1947

Production Start:
April 29, 1947

Production End:
June 20, 1947

Copyright Date:
October 31, 1947

Released:
October 8, 1947

Running Time:
78 minutes

Directed By:
Charles Barton

Produced By:
Robert Arthur

Screenplay By: Robert Lees, Frederic I. Rinaldo, and John Grant

Based on a Story By:
D. D. Beauchamp and William Bowers

Director of Photography:
Charles Van Enger

Art Direction:
Bernard Herzbrun and Gabriel Scognamillo

Film Editor: Frank Gross

Sound: Charles Felstead and Robert Pritchard

Set Decorations:
Russell A. Gausman and Charles Wyrick

Associate Producer:
Sebastian Cristillo

Dialogue Director:
Norman Abbott

Costumes:
Rosemary Odell

Hair Stylist: Carmen Dirigo

Make-Up: Bud Westmore

Assistant Director:
Joseph E. Kenny

his father. Sebastian in turn telephoned his son. Lou assured his father that everything was fine. But the next day, when Lou learned that Sebastian had passed away, he blamed Sherman for upsetting him with nonsense. Lou fired Sherman, and the team was without an agent for two years.

THE SCRIPT

The story is based on an obscure Montana law that holds the survivor of a gunfight responsible for the dependents and debts of the victim. Screenwriter D. D. Beauchamp learned of the law thumbing through old law books while snowed in at his ranch near Helena, Montana. He wrote a story for *Collier's* called "The Widow of Wagon Gap," published in May 1947. According to "The Screenwriter Looks at the Screenwriter," Beauchamp and William Bowers wrote a screenplay with Jimmy Stewart in mind, but had to sell the rights when strapped for money. Universal-International bought it for $2,500 on February 19, 1947. (In 1979, Bowers wrote the TV movie *The Wild Wild West Revisited* and set the action in Wagon Gap.)

Ten weeks later, the revised screenplay, by Robert Lees, Fred Rinaldo, and John Grant, was in production. Interestingly, the studio's new management now assigned a budget ceiling to the Abbott and Costello films. *Buck Privates Come Home* slipped through before the decree. Abbott and Costello films were now targeted at $750,000—still "B" movie range.

THE CAST

Marjorie Main (1890–1975) had just come off her memorable performance in *The Egg and I* as Ma Kettle. She and Percy Kilbridge (as Pa Kettle) made such an impression that it led to the popular *Ma and Pa Kettle* series. Previously, Marjorie had a string of dramatic successes on Broadway, culminating in *Dead End,* as the killer's mother. She reprised the role for the 1937 film version. From then on, she appeared in about 100 films, displaying both her formidable comedic and dramatic talents.

Audrey Young literally was in the right place at the right time. Robert Arthur explained, "Patricia Alphin originally played Juanita. One day, about two weeks into the picture, Patricia was perspiring and didn't feel well; but she said she could handle it. Well, her appendix burst, and she was taken to the hospital. Outside the production office I spotted this girl. She told me she didn't think she had much of a future in movies, but that she was going to make somebody a perfect wife. She did—she married Billy Wilder. Of course, she was glib and delightful. But she fit the wardrobe, and that's the only reason she made the picture. Now, this is something you could only do with Bud and Lou. I walked in and explained to them what had happened, and that we had cast another girl. Well they died laughing. Some people would have argued about it, and said, 'No, let's get somebody else.' But Bud and Lou couldn't have been more helpful."

Gordon Jones (1911–1963) had just come off *The Secret Life of Walter Mitty*. Of course, Gordon would later turn up on the Abbott & Costello TV show as Mike The Cop.

William Ching (1912–1989) had appeared as William Brooks in Deanna Durbin's *I'll Be Yours* (1947). He had a bit part in *Buck Privates Come Home*. His most famous film role was in *Pat and Mike* (1952), with Tracy and Hepburn. Ching quit acting in the 1950s to pursue a career in real estate.

THE PRODUCTION

Some exteriors were photographed at Vasquez Rocks, a picturesque area fifty miles from Hollywood where, legend has it, bandits hid in California's pioneer days. Other exteriors were shot at the Iverson Ranch, in the Santa Susanna Pass.

One unique provision in Robert Arthur's $750,000 budget was $800 for the services of a "Comedy Continuity Artist." This was court jester extraordinaire Bobby Barber. Barber, who

The dedication of the Lou Costello Jr. Youth Center, May, 3, 1947.

had bit roles in a handful of the team's films, was hired to clown exclusively off-camera by director Charles Barton. Barton had used Bobby's specialized services in the past, and he brought Bobby in to keep Abbott and Costello amused. It was the beginning of a long, warm friendship.

Bobby proved his value during the second week of production. Bobby's widow, Maxine, explained, "Lou and Bobby weren't close until Lou's father died. Lou's father had a special chair on the set. Lou walked on the set, saw the chair, started to cry, and walked out. They said, 'Bobby, go get him.' So Bobby ran after Lou and walked and talked with him. I don't know what Bobby said to him, but he got Lou to come back. From then on, they were inseparable."

Lou tried to work that morning on the sequence in the saloon where he informs Bud that the stage coach carrying the bullion will come through on Thursday. (Bud instructs Lou to tell Jake that the stage is due on Wednesday, so that the villain's plans to rob it will be foiled.) However, Bud and Lou were dismissed at ten-forty-five am, and the company suspended production for four days. On the day after the funeral, Lou made an unexpected visit to the large western saloon set. He appeared very solemn, and the cast and crew fell silent out of respect. Even Bobby, who was standing at the center of the set, was quiet. Lou walked slowly onto the set and, as he passed Bobby, squirted a mouthful of water on him. The entire soundstage erupted in laughter, and the picture was able to resume in the proper spirit. In tribute to his father, a lifelong fan of westerns, Lou had Sebastian Cristillo listed in the credits as the film's associate producer.

Barber's antics so enlivened the proceedings that Universal's publicity department felt compelled to issue this release about Bobby:

> Bud and Lou rely on Barber to maintain an atmosphere of comedy on their set. That includes not only the players, but also the director and gag writers. Stars have a lot on their minds besides acting, points out Barber in explaining his duties. Production problems, budget, and schedule are worries for players with royalty participating deals. Or it may be income tax, horse races, or the servant headache. Barber explains his job simply: "I help them relax—with laughter."

Here's how Barber does it. When Costello feels the set atmosphere is too depressing for creating comedy, he'll sneak up behind Barber and drop an ice cube down Barber's

153

back. Barber jumps and yells like a man getting an electric shock. The routine varies. Sometimes a rubber frog or a paper bag full of water replaces the ice cube. Pranks are corny, but serve their purpose in amusing the troupe.

"Studios should have somebody like me on all sets," stated Barber. "Film people are tense. Stars muff scenes because they are tense. Fun relaxes them, and saves production time. Even the crew works better. Pictures would turn out better, too."

Barber came from the stage and vaudeville and broke into pictures the same way Vince Barnett did—as a professional ribber. The late director Mark Sandrich first hired Bobby to tease Claudette Colbert and Fred Allen by posing as an ambitious radio writer. Then Barber was put to work on Jack Benny, who, in turn, had Bobby rib Mrs. Benny (Mary Livingston).

Barber used to appear at movie parties as a waiter with garlic breath to annoy guests. Now he is too well known in Hollywood to fool people at parties. Bobby once appeared with Vince Barnett during a banquet for military and plane plant officials. Barnett was introduced as a famous flyer, and Barber as a foreign diplomat. Before the masquerade was dropped, they almost gave several generals and manufacturers apoplexy.

An ABC radio show called *Hollywood Tour* reported this landmark event on May 12, 1947: "Abbott and Costello, who will be boys, had the U-I commissary in convulsions when they went into an ad-lib comedy routine with strawberry shortcakes, custard pies and ice cubes. All free for the spectators.... the boys would probably want stunt pay if they had to take such a plastering in a picture." It was the first known reference to Bud, Lou, and Bobby engaging in their soon-to-be-legendary pie fights.

Maxine Barber explained, "Bobby loved anything that made people laugh. You might say he was the scapegoat, but as long as people laughed, he didn't care. Bobby used to come home and say, 'I really took a beating today.' But he didn't mean it in that respect. He just meant they kept him busy all day. Lou wasn't well even at that time, and he had to keep his mind off of himself. As long as he could use Bobby, Bobby couldn't care less."

Charles Barton recalled, "Lou wanted to get Marjorie Main with a pie, but Bobby told her that he was going to double-cross Lou. Bobby would give her a pie, so she could get Lou first. What Bobby did was, first he told Lou what to do, then he went and told Marjorie what to expect! Everybody on the set was in on it now. The greatest thing that happened was when

Lou plans to surprise Bobby Barber with a rubber frog sandwich during lunch on location.

Lou got hit by that pie. Everybody hollered and roared. Of course, Lou took it so well that he walked up and hugged and kissed Marjorie with pie plastered all over his face. He never got mad—he loved it."

Lou's daughter Paddy recalled how amused her dad was by Marjorie. "She broke him up. He said that before they could do a scene, Marjorie would have to go sit in a corner somewhere and talk to her dead husband and get his permission to do the scene! [laughs] And after the deceased husband gave his permission, she would go out and do the scene! Well, this just blew Dad away."

Robert Arthur remembered one day when Lou came to him with a problem Bobby couldn't solve. "Lou was complaining to me one day that he couldn't pay his bills. I told Ed Muhl and he went to Leo Spitz about it. Muhl was always there for Bud and Lou. He knocked himself out for them. He was primarily responsible for keeping them at Universal for all that time. Anyway, he went to Spitz, and Spitz called me over one day and said he had a check for Lou for $100,000. He said, 'As long as you have to work with him, you give it to him.' It wasn't a loan or anything, just an advance on money he had coming. So I went down to the set and I said, 'Lou, I have a present for you.' And he looked at the check, and he didn't say go to hell, thank you, or anything. He walked right over to the phone, dialed a number, and said, 'I'll take the yacht.'" Lou purchased an eighty-foot, war surplus subchaser, on which he had the engines replaced and the interior gutted and refurbished with luxurious staterooms and a galley. He christened his yacht *Queen Lolly,* after his mother. "It was the most uneconomical boat anybody could ever have, because it cost so much money to run. Now Bud was very sensible about it. He said why pay all the expense of a crew and everything if you don't go out every day. Bud would charter a boat twice a year for ten days and it would only cost him ten or eleven thousand dollars."

With the monkeyshines and the tragedies, *Wistful Widow* finished nearly $28,000 and five days over budget. It was Universal-International's fourth biggest grosser of 1947, taking in $2,625,000.

BUD AND LOU'S SCENES

The showstopper in *Widow* was the "Frog in the Soup" routine, a variation of the "Oyster" gag the team exhumed in *Here Come the Co-Eds*. This, Robert Lees points out, was a John Grant contribution. The widow's eldest child, Matt, surreptitiously deposits a frog in Chester's soup. Of course, the frog only reveals itself to Chester. Comparing the finished sequence to the script, it appears that the entire middle segment, where Chester persuades Duke to trade bowls, was added on the set. The crudeness of the match cut between shots of the boys exchanging bowls would seem to support this notion. Chester thinks the frog is still in the bowl he foisted on Duke, but the toad leaps unnoticed into the bowl in front of Chester. The entire sequence was shot in installments on three separate days. Another funny addition was to have Chester scoop up the frog on his spoon, but not notice it because he's too busy whispering to Duke.

The premise of the story gives Lou a unique chance to wield some power and even turn the tables on Bud. Comparing Chester's timidity at the start of the film, to his later audaciousness as sheriff, one can truly appreciate the effortless range of Lou Costello's performance and abilities. As the new, impregnable sheriff, Chester orders Duke back to the widow's farm to assume his chores. It's something the fans had been waiting to see for quite some time. Chester flaunts his authority over the town's heavies in several scenes. In one scene, he offers to buy drinks for the house. When the denizens of the saloon crowd the bar, Chester prevails upon them to drink milk—or else. Lou screened *The Virginian* (1929) so he could prepare his own interpretation of Gary Cooper's famous walk through a town lined with heavies. Costello deflates his by taking a terrific pratfall. That film also contained the classic line, "Smile when you say that." Robert Lees recalled, "That line, and the business where Lou scratches the match across the guy's beard—that was something I was aching to put in the picture from the beginning. These are the kind of bits of business that were in the script, but nobody realizes it."

While filming one scene, Bud was berated by six-year-old Billy O'Leary, who plays one of the widow's kids. Billy called Bud a bully and told him to stop picking on Lou. This, for Bud, was an occupational hazard. As he explained to an interviewer in 1952, "When I go around the country, lots of kids bawl me out for being so mean to Lou. That's music to my ears, because I know I've done my job well."

DELETIONS AND ADDITIONS

Barton kept the film quite close to the shooting script, but there were several deleted bits and gags.

Chester has a typical run-in with a rusty pump on the farm. In a cut segment, he can't get a drop from the obstinate pump, no matter how vigorously he tries. But the widow's four-year-old daughter, Sarah, effortlessly fills her bucket with just one pump of the handle. Chester tries to duplicate Sarah's technique, but the water spurts out beyond the bucket. He moves the bucket to where the water landed and pumps again. Now the temperamental pump gushes short of the bucket. He quickly tries to move the bucket, but the flow stops. As Chester gives up and starts to walk away, the water spurts again. He rushes back, but it stops. Finally he stands by the spigot, bucket in hand, and makes a noise with his feet as if he were walking away. The water spurts and he quickly gets a bucketful.

A long sequence cut from the film includes character actress Iris Adrian as a dance hall hostess. Duke flirts with her, and offers to buy her a steak dinner—on Chester's tab! As Chester sets the table, another hostess walks by and catches Duke's eye. Iris is furious with Duke for flirting with another girl in her company. She bangs a glass down on the table, breaking it. Duke protests that he didn't flirt, and he also breaks a glass. The bartender observes this, and marks "$10" on a blackboard depicting Chester's tab. The argument escalates, with Iris and Duke alternately breaking more glasses and chinaware. By the end of the scene, the table is littered with rubble, and Chester's "tab" on the blackboard has reached $100.

REVIEWS

The New York Times: "Laughs there are, beyond question, in the spectacle of bashful Lou being forced to take up with a widow-lady whose husband he is alleged to have killed in a Western

Charles Barton offers a suggestion during the shooting of the "Frog in the Soup" scene.

frontier town. And especially since the widow-lady is played by Marjorie Main is his shot-gun bondage to her an explosively risable affair. . . . And the practiced producers of this picture haven't let many angles get by. But when Lou, as Miss Main's unenvied consort, is nominated Sheriff of the town because no one would dare resist him for fear of inheriting his fate, the burlesque becomes a bit too hackneyed and Lou's swaggering becomes a trifle dull. A gun-twirling, stick-'em-up Costello is not an especially funny one even when his hat won't sit straight and his gun-handling fingers are all thumbs. However, we don't want to argue with the Abbott and Costello fans. There's too little laughter in this grave world to be particular about 'The Wistful Widow of Wagon Gap.' "

Los Angeles Times: "As in all Abbott and Costello comedies, gags flow like wine, some good, some otherwise. One audience last night roared at a lengthy sequence in which Costello finds a frog in his soup. The comics continue their familiar formula of making Costello the butt of Abbott's 'ideas.' But when the worm turns, the audience seems doubly satisfied."

Daily Variety: "[Abbott and Costello] team up with their usual success, but have to extend themselves to get an even break with Miss Main on the laughs. Latter scores as the 'wistful widow' with matrimonial designs who won't take no for an answer, and Costello matches her for comedy as the poor guy trying his best to say no. . . . Story doesn't miss a bet in poking fun at the dramatic standbys of the westerns. One of the top scenes is the courageous law-and-order man (Costello) marching slowly and suspensefully down an otherwise deserted street to face the deadly gunplay of the entrenched baddies. Also, merry use is made of the old line, 'When you call me that, smile.' Barton's direction times the gags effectively, points up the sequences for laughs, and keeps the action fortunately paced throughout."

Hollywood Reporter: "As usual, the boys come through with one rather long, beautifully constructed gag sequence so packed with belly laughs that the dialogue is literally unheard. In this instance the sequence involves a frog, a bowl of soup and a glass of milk. Miraculously timed and artfully played it is a low comedy masterpiece—in itself worth the price of admission. . . . Abbott and Costello work with their characteristic energy and, as usual, their years of teaming show advantageously, particularly in the way they build a gag and time it to perfection. Marjorie Main, of course, is a vast help—undoubtedly the best leading lady the boys ever had. The action is divided rather evenly among the three principals, allowing little footage to the supporting cast."

POSTSCRIPT

Abbott and Costello had always been popular in England, but when they started making movies in 1940, the war had already disrupted the market on the European continent. In 1946 and 1947, moviegoers in Europe got their first taste of the team with *Hold That Ghost, Hit the Ice,* and *Pardon My Sarong.* Bud and Lou became instant favorites, and Universal set about to exploit the goldmine. In France, the boys were known as "Les Deux Nigauds"—"The Two Dumbbells." Lou took particular delight in preparing a generic trailer for the Italian market, where fans began referring to them affectionately as Gianni e Pinotto—John and 'Little Pig.' Costello, in Italian, cracked, "Some people call me a pig. But with the price of pork today, I am asking you: Is this an insult?"

Abbott and Costello signed a contract with St. John Publishing in 1947 to produce a series of Abbott and Costello comic books. The first issue would be an adaptation of *The Wistful Widow of Wagon Gap.* Bud and Lou, however, never cleared this deal with Universal-International, which owned the story rights. The comic book was literally about to go to press when the studio first learned of it. Fortunately, U-I permitted the publisher to release the book, but this would be the sole exception. None of the team's other films were allowed to be used in the St. John's series, which ultimately published forty issues between 1948 and 1956.

THE NOOSE HANGS HIGH

Earliest Draft: 1939

Production Start:
November 13, 1947

Production End:
December 10, 1947

Copyright Date:
March 4, 1948

Released: April 5, 1948

Running Time:
77 minutes

Directed By:
Charles Barton

Produced By:
Charles Barton

Screenplay By:
John Grant,
Howard Harris

Adaptation By:
Charles Grayson,
Arthur T. Horman

Original Story By:
Daniel Tradash,
Julian Blaustein,
Bernard Fins

Production Supervision:
James T. Vaughn

Director of Photography:
Charles Van Enger

Film Editor:
Harry Reynolds

Music: Walter Schumann

Orchestrations:
Arthur Morton

Musical Director:
Irving Friedman

Associate Producers:
Lolly Cristillo,
Shirley Feld

Art Direction:
Edward L. Ilou

Set Decorations:
Armor Marlowe

Special Photographic
Effects: George J.
Teague ASC

SYNOPSIS

Ted and Tommy, employees of the Speedy Service Window Washing Company, are mistaken for employees of the Speedy Messenger Service by Nick Craig, a bookie. He sends them to Mr. Stewart's office to collect $50,000 Stewart owes him. Stewart, however, plans to have two of his hoods hold up the boys and take the money back. Chased by the gangsters, Tommy ducks into an office where a corps of girls is mailing face powder samples. He shoves the money in an envelope, which he intends to address to Nick. But his envelope is inadvertently switched with another envelope containing a sample. Meanwhile, Nick discovers his mistake and telephones J. C. MacBride, to whom he owes the windfall, to ask for an extension. Nick orders his gorillas, Chuck and Joe, to find Ted and Tommy, but the boys show up at the office, and explain what happened. The money, they assure Nick, will be delivered tomorrow by the U.S. Mail.

But the next day, a powder sample arrives instead of the money. Nick gives the boys twenty-four hours to contact every prospect on the company's mailing list. They finally locate the recipient, Carol, who has spent most of the money on luxuries. The three of them hope to parlay the remaining $2,000 into $50,000 by betting on a horse race. At the Television Club, Ted, Tommy, and Carol meet an eccentric little man named Julius Caesar, who has never lost a bet. Caesar's horse wins, but Ted, Tommy and Carol lose the rest of their bankroll. With no possible way of repaying Nick, Ted decides that the safest place for them is jail. The boys run up a $500 tab at a swank nightclub and are about to be arrested when Nick and his boys arrive and demand the money. When Ted and Tommy confess that they haven't got it, Nick plans to fit them with cement shoes at a nearby construction warehouse. Carol, meanwhile, wins $50,000 from Caesar betting on fish in the club's aquarium. They arrive at the construction warehouse just in time with the money. Caesar explains that he is J. C. MacBride, and the debt is settled.

BACKGROUND

Abbott and Costello's original contract with Universal, signed in 1940 and extended every year until 1947, expired after completion of *Wistful Widow*. According to Charles Barton, there was never any doubt that the studio would renew. "Goetz and Spitz didn't want to phase them out because they were making pretty good money for the studio. But you had two people in charge of the studio who didn't know anything about comedy at all."

Bud and Lou's popularity was still formidable. That summer the team appeared at the Roxy in New York, at the height of a brutal heat wave and played to $397,637.66 worth of admissions in three weeks. Bosley Crowther of the *Times* fractured tradition by leading off his movie review with the stage presentation rather than the picture: "With Bud Abbott and Lou Costello as the stars of its stage show, the Roxy Theater could be flashing the telephone directory on its screen and still draw the clamoring customers." On August 6, the ABC radio network signed the team to a five-year contract. The prerecorded program was made available to local sponsors in every part of the U. S. and Canada on a revolutionary, cooperative basis.

Universal's new contract provided for two pictures per year, at a salary starting at $105,000 per picture. The films would be budgeted between $750,000 and $800,000. As added incentive, the team would receive 5 percent of the net profits if the picture came in under $800,000; 10 percent if the final costs were under $750,000; and an additional 5 percent if the net profits exceeded $2.25 million, or three times the cost of the picture. The studio was so anxious to renew the contract that it made a considerable concession: Abbott and Costello could appear in one independent production per year. In 1947, that outside film was *The Noose Hangs High*.

THE SCRIPT

Noose is a remake of a Universal picture called *For Love of Money* (1939). Julian Blaustein, Daniel Taradash, and Bernard Fein wrote the original story, and Arthur Horman and Charles Grayson collaborated on the screenplay. For the remake, Howard Harris and John Grant retailored the film to accommodate Bud, Lou, and Leon Errol.

THE CAST

Cathy Downs (1924–1978) started out as a model and made a few films at Fox before being signed for *Noose*. Later, she played Joe Palooka's girlfriend in the short-lived TV series, then turned up in sci-fi classics like *The Amazing Colossal Man* (1957) and *Missile to the Moon* (1959).

Joseph Calleia (1897–1975) was originally a well-known opera singer before settling in Hollywood in the 1930s. Adept at both sinister and comedic roles, he appeared in classics such as *Algiers* (1938), *My Little Chickadee* (1940), and *Gilda* (1946).

Leon Errol (1881–1951) was a vaudeville and Broadway headliner for nearly forty years. Before entering show business, he briefly practiced medicine in his native Australia. Errol broke into films in 1930 and livened up numerous shorts and features—most notably as Lord Epping in the *Mexican Spitfire* series with Lupe Velez.

THE PRODUCTION

Noose was originally intended for production at Universal as far back as 1945. But since Bud and Lou's new contract allowed one independent feature per year, the newly formed Abbott and Costello Productions purchased the story from the studio and made the film at Eagle-Lion Studios. Budgeted for twenty-four days and $652,833, it eventually came in one day and $41,900 under. The boys were permitted to borrow Charles Barton to direct, and the team's longtime executive producer at Universal, Milton Feld, agreed to produce. (Several crewmembers from Universal were also hired, including cinematographer Charles Van Enger.) Just before production was to begin, however, in August 1947, Feld died. It was decided that Barton would both direct and produce, as he had done on a few minor features at Universal. Feld's widow, Shirley, and Lou's mother, Helene (Lolly) Cristillo, were named Associate Producers. In an inside joke, the horse Lou bets on in the film is named Lolly C. Another delay pushed production back when Lou suffered a fall in his home, straining the ligaments in his leg. He was required to stay off his feet for several weeks, but Lou certainly didn't mind staying home.

Special Art Effects:
  Jack R. Rabin
Costume Supervision:
  France Ehren
Make-Up: Em Westmore,
  Russell Drake
Hair Styling:
  Joan St. Oegger,
  Gwen Holden
Sound: Leon S. Becker,
  Robert Pritchard

Ted Higgins . . Bud Abbott
Tommy Hinchcliffe
  . . . . Lou Costello
Carol. . . . . . . Cathy Downs
Nick Craig . . Joseph Calleia
J. C. MacBride
  . . . . Leon Errol
Chuck . . . . . Mike Mazurki
Joe . . . . Jack Overman
Doctor. . . . . Fritz Feld
Elevator Girl . Vera Martin
Spud. . . . . Joe Kirk
Mack . . . . Matt Willis
Secretary . . . . Joan Myles
Stewart . . . . .Ben Weldon
Messengers
  . . . . Jimmy Dodd
                   Ben Hall
Maid . . . . Ellen Corby
Miss Van Buren
  . . . . Isabel Randolph
Upson . . . Harry Brown
Dentist . . Murray Leonard
Dentist's Assistant
  . . . . Sandra Spence
Bit Woman . . . Elvia Allman
Woman on Street
  . . . . Lois Austin
Man with Coat
  . . . . Herb Vigran
Traffic Cop. . James Flavin
Workman . . . . . Lyle Latell
Jewelry Proprietor
  . . . . Paul Maxey
Manager . . . Russell Hicks
Race Track Announcer
  . . . . Oscar Otis

It gave him a chance to get acquainted with his new daughter, Christine, born a few weeks earlier on August 16. Production didn't get under way until November, which conflicted with the team's next feature at Universal. That film was pushed back until after the new year.

A reporter for *Collier's* was on hand when Bud, Lou and Charles Barton had a story conference on *Noose*:

"You boys got any bright ideas?" Barton inquired. This is the same as asking an ex GI if he has any gripes against the Army.

"We've never done 'Mustard' in a movie," Abbott said. [Apparently Bud had forgotten about *One Night in the Tropics*.]

Barton's raised eyebrows were the go-ahead signal. They raced through a telescoped version of the sketch, pitching cues with triphammer rapidity.

"Sounds good," Barton commented. "We can work in a scene at a hot dog stand while you're chasing the dame. What else?"

"We killed them at the Roxy with 'Hole in the Wall,' " Costello said.

Like a trained bear hearing his music, Abbott went into the act. "Isn't this a magnificent building?"

Costello (reverently): "It sure is. Wouldn't I be a dirty, despicable man if I made a hole in that beautiful wall?"

Abbott (sternly): "Why did you do it?"

Costello (blankly): "Do what? I was just saying . . ."

Abbott (severely): "You just admitted you made a hole in the wall."

This piles up until Abbott has Costello ready to surrender to the police for vandalism.

Without drawing a deep breath, they plunged into 'Burned Toast.' (Costello, a bashful oaf, is introduced to a beautiful girl in a restaurant. In the confusion, he stuffs a piece of bread he is eating in his pocket. The girl kisses him with such ardor that the bread turns to toast.) Abbott brought out a bill and they were off and running on "Ten Dollars You're Not Here," another old chestnut from burlesque. (Abbott bets Costello ten bucks he can prove the other fellow is not where he thinks he is. Through circumlocution too devious to relate, Abbott wins the ten. A stranger approaches. Costello, falling all over himself with anticipation, tries to pull the same dodge on him. The fall guy gives the wrong answers and picks up the marbles, leaving Costello covered with frustration.) The four sketches took six minutes, by the clock.

"We can do the 'Telegram Elimination Gag,' Abbott proposed.

Barton threw up his hands. "Let me kick these around for a while." Costello left for the hospital to see his wife and baby, and Abbott departed to sample the waters served in the bar he owns in the San Fernando Valley.

"They can toss these old routines at you all day long," Barton said, "and come up with stuff adaptable to any situation. You've got to hang the gags on the thread of the story, or the picture will become a series of vaudeville acts."

Of course, Bobby Barber sojourned to Eagle-Lion to provide his unique services. Charles Barton recalled, "Arthur Krim, the president of Eagle-Lion Studios, had seen the bill for the pies—$3,500. He couldn't get over the amount of money being spent, but he understood they were necessary. Lou believed throwing pies and other pranks cleared the air and relieved tension. Lou was like a little kid on the set. I told Mr. Krim, 'You're just lucky you haven't been hit by a pie yet.' But some of his staff complained that the stage was too dirty from firecrackers and pie crust all over the floor. Krim wanted to know what Bobby Barber's role was. He called Bobby up to his office and asked Bobby what he was doing. Bobby said, 'Well, I'm here with Lou. I stand in for Lou and do what I can for him.' Krim said, 'That's not enough. I want you to get a broom and a dustpan and clean up the stage.' So Bobby fetched himself a broom and a dustpan and brushed all the garbage into a box. He put the box on a dolly and strolled up to Krim's office. The girl wouldn't let him in. He said, 'I'm sorry, but I have to see Mr. Krim *now*.' He walked straight past the secretary into Krim's office and

dumped all the stuff onto the floor and said, 'I just wanted you to see how hard I've been working.' A studio official today would have killed him. But not Krim. He took it all to heart."

Howard Koch, who later produced *The Manchurian Candidate* (1962) and *The Odd Couple* (1968), was Barton's assistant director on the picture. When the team's perpetual card game interfered with production, it was his job to coax them back on the set. "If they were unduly reluctant, I'd remind them that they were the producers, which worked when nothing else did. They didn't mind spending money on cards, but the idea that their production money was going down the drain got them moving."

Charles Barton recalled, "Howard was so nervous worrying when Lou was going to get him with a pie. Lou finally got him at the end of the picture. Howard said, 'I only wish he'd have gotten me on the very first day!' "

BUD AND LOU'S SCENES

Despite the contentions of film critics, the team's burlesque routines had been weeded out of their more recent films. Evidently the shock to the boys' systems was so great that that when they got carte blanche on *The Noose Hangs High,* they decided to indulge themselves. They play these routines with the great affection they must have had for them.

Virtually all of the gags had appeared in earlier films. Even the funny dentist scene, with the always dependable Murray Leonard in Coke-bottle glasses, reprised some of the gags from the barber shop in *Abbott and Costello in Hollywood*. Ted brags to the nurse, "I want to have a tooth pulled. I don't want anesthetic, and I don't care how much it hurts." The nurse is impressed. "Oh, my, what a brave man you are. Which tooth is it?" Ted pulls Tommy over. "Show her the tooth," Ted says. "I'm Dr. Richards," says the dentist. "I'm painless." "Well *I'm* not," cracks Tommy. (Curiously, the dentist scene originally appeared later in the script, when the boys were tracking down the money.) A routine from *Rio Rita,* "You're Not Here," was also dusted off and performed with Mike Mazurki.

Still, John Grant tried to freshen things up. He wrote a new version of the "Pack/Unpack" sketch previously used in *Hit the Ice*. Instead of packing a grip, Lou would alternately dress or undress, depending on Bud's verbal cues. Bud and Lou saw it in the script for the first time on the day it was to be shot. According to Barton, they were discontent with the revision, and began performing the original version. Barton yelled "Cut!" and asked the team what they were doing. Lou explained that they'd done it their way a thousand times and it never failed. Barton said, "That's just the trouble—we need a fresh approach to it." Lou said, "Come on, Charlie. We're not going to sit here and learn this whole new routine. We'll do the old

TOP LEFT: Rehearsing the "Dentist Scene" with Murray Leonard. TOP: A deleted sequence has Tommy consult a Chinese laundry man, played by Benny Rubin. In stereo-typical Chinese, Tommy asks, "You gettee lettee from mailee manee, chop, chop, withee muchee greenee backee thisee mornee?" The laundry man is incensed. In flaw-less English he replies, "Don't talk like a jerk. I received no such epistle containing anything of monetary value whatso-ever."

161

one." Barton pulled up a chair and sat down. "Okay, Lou. You want to do the old 'Pack and Unpack'? Go ahead." Bud and Lou began the routine, with Lou hastily packing a valise while Bud debates whether they should run away or stay put. About halfway through the routine, Barton's stony countenance caught Lou's eye. "Aren't you gonna say 'cut?'" Lou asked. "I'm waiting for something funny," was Barton's reply. Lou bristled. "Come on, Bud!" He grabbed Bud by the arm and the two of them walked off the set and out of the studio. Legend has it they stayed home for three days without speaking a word to Barton. On the fourth day, Bud and Lou returned to the studio, with the new routine memorized. No one ever mentioned the incident again, and even Barton was at a loss to explain it. We don't doubt that Charles Barton had trouble shooting the routine, but there are two inconsistencies with this tale. The first is the fact that the original "Pack/Unpack" utilizes a suitcase. Since the boys were being held captive in Nick's office, not their apartment, the suitcase would be totally incongruous— even to Bud and Lou. The second—that the team stayed home for three days—seems improbable considering that not only was the production financed with Abbott and Costello money, but it ultimately finished *ahead* of schedule.

The "Mudder and Fodder" routine was a sentimental favorite of the boys, since it was the first bit they performed on the Kate Smith program in 1938. It was a natural for the picture's horseracing sequences. In this instance, Lou performs the bit with Leon Errol during a riotous billiard game.

Another scene was first performed in *Keep 'Em Flying*. At the Television Club, Tommy telephones Nick, but he is not in his office. Nick's secretary gives Tommy a number where he can be reached. Tommy dials the number, and the phone in the next booth rings. A waiter answers, and Tommy asks to speak to Craig. Nick and Tommy proceed to have a loud argument, each unaware that the other is in the adjacent booth!

The bulk of the team's routines—including "Mustard," "Hole in the Wall," "You're 40, She's 10," and "What Are You Doing at the Depot?"—are performed in one long session at the nightclub, as the boys deliberately run up the tab. These, as we have noted, are part of a classic burlesque straight man lecture called, "Handful of Nickels." The sequence runs about five and a half minutes. Their timing, and the effortless way these separate routines are weaved together, are marvelous.

DELETIONS AND ADDITIONS

Nick sends the boys to pick up $50,000 from a Mr. Stewart in the Liberty Building. In a deleted exchange, Ted wonders where the building is:

Tommy: It's opposite the yimka.
Ted: (checking envelope) That's "Y.M.C.A."
Tommy: That's right. Y.M.C.A.—yimka.
Ted: "Y" is the first letter.
Tommy: I don't know; why is the first letter?
Ted: "Y" *is* the first letter.
Tommy: All right, I'm askin' you—why is the first letter.
Ted: I told you—"Y" is the first letter.
Tommy: Look, there's gotta be a first letter.
Ted: Yes.
Tommy: The letter?
Ted: "Y."
Tommy: Who's askin' who? I'm asking you—
Ted: You're asking me so I'm telling you—"Y" is the first letter.
Tommy: I'm asking you what's the first letter!
Ted: "Y."
Tommy: Because I gotta find out!

Later, Ted suggests that Tommy do something to get them arrested. If they're in jail, he reasons, Nick and his goons can't hurt them. In one attempt, Ted instructs Tommy to insult a woman passerby. In the script, a dignified woman approaches, Tommy blurts out, "Hello, kid." She stops, and, in a deep, gravelly voice cracks, "Hiya, toots! What are you doing tonight?" Tommy reacts and runs away in disgust. Ted asks what happened, and Tommy cracks, "She was one of the boys." An obvious transvestite gag, it was no doubt cut by the Breen Office. It was reshot without the offending dialogue. Tommy says, "Hiya, Toots," and the woman grabs him by the lapels. "Toots? Don't you dare call me 'Toots.' I quit the mob ten years ago, see? And I'm trying to go straight, see? And if you guys don't leave me alone, I'll get One-Eyed Pitsy after you. And you know what *that* means! Now get goin'! Take a powder!" She composes herself and walks away. Ted and Tommy's exchange remains, with Tommy's quip, "She's one of the boys," still appropriate. Next, Ted tells Tommy to shove a policeman. The cop goes flying and lands violently about eight feet away. Suddenly, a car speeds by between the cop and the boys. The officer reacts and thanks them for saving his life!

REVIEWS

Variety: " 'The Noose Hangs High' gives Abbott & Costello full oportunity to display their fine slapstick art. The pair of buffoons deliver in great style. It's a funfest from start to finish, chockful of strong laughs for the A&C fans. Routines, despite their age, have a freshness that wallops the risibilities in the artful hands of the comics. All of the gags are good, with several that reach the acme of hilarious nonsense. Such a one is the on-and-off pants routine, a display of apt timing and fine comedy talent. Another is the oldie, 'you can't be here,' played to top results."

The New York Times: "['Noose'] is, perhaps, no better, and certainly not any worse, than any previous A&C exercise you may recall offhand. It has some laughable moments and it has others, all too numerous, which make one wish that the boys would take a vacation until a natural script comes their way. Under the proper circumstances they can be vastly amusing indeed. The trouble with A&C is that when they hit on a funny bit of business, such as a disrobing routine, they run it into boredom. That's what happens, too, when Costello tries to explain to Leon Errol that a horse that eats its 'fodder' must be a horse without a 'papa,' and, naturally, the little fellow has a hard time figuring out how a 'mudder' can also be a 'father.' A little of this can go a long way."

Hollywood Reporter: "Whether one is familiar with the skits is not the question, for when Abbott and Costello play them, even the most ancient blackouts become fine slapstick art. 'The Noose Hangs High' includes a couple of immortals—the 'you're not there' bit and a superbly timed sequence in which Costello dresses and undresses to the accompaniment of Abbott's running chatter. Charles Barton's production is shrewdly devised to show the comedians at their best and, of course, his experience in directing the team shows throughout."

POSTSCRIPT

After completing *Noose,* Bud and Lou returned to Universal to begin work on their next film. Meanwhile, negotiations began to bring the act to the London Palladium. According to *Daily Variety,* the team was booked for two weeks at the Palladium beginning January 19, 1948 at a flat $15,000 per week. "That figure," the tradepaper reported ". . . is the top coin the Palladium will pay for an act."

But with Universal behind on the starting date of the team's next feature, Bud and Lou had to cancel this tour. The team eventually made the trip in 1950.

ABBOTT AND COSTELLO MEET FRANKENSTEIN

Earliest Draft:
February 14, 1947

Production Start:
February 5, 1948

Production End:
March 20, 1948

Copyright Date:
September 8, 1948

Released:
August 20, 1948

Running Time:
83 minutes

Reissued: March 23, 1956
(with *Abbott and
Costello Meet the Killer,
Boris Karloff*)

Directed By:
Charles T. Barton

Produced By:
Robert Arthur

Original Screenplay By:
Robert Lees, Frederic I.
Rinaldo, and John Grant

Music By: Frank Skinner

Director of Photography:
Charles Van Enger

Art Direction:
Bernard Herzbrun,
Hilyard Brown

Film Editor: Frank Gross

Sound: Leslie I. Carey,
Robert Pritchard

Set Decorations:
Russell A. Gausman,
Oliver Emert

Orchestrations:
David Tamkin

Gowns: Grace Houston

Hair Stylist: Carmen Dirigo

Make-Up: Bud Westmore

Special Photography:
David S. Horsley ASC;
Jerome Ash ASC

Assistant Director:
Joseph E. Kenny

SYNOPSIS

Chick and Wilbur, railroad baggage clerks in LaMirada, Florida, receive two huge crates addressed to MacDougal's House of Horrors. MacDougal confides to Wilbur's beautiful girl-friend, Sandra Mornay, that the crates contain the remains of the Frankenstein Monster and Dracula. When Wilbur mishandles the crates, MacDougal demands that the boys deliver them to his museum for inspection by an insurance agent. Chick and Wilbur open the crates, but find them empty. Wilbur knows that the monsters are alive and have in fact escaped, but Chick refuses to believe him. While MacDougal has the boys arrested, the Monster and Dracula rendezvous with Sandra at a castle on an isolated island. Sandra is a gifted doctor who has mastered Dr. Frankenstein's notebooks. She plans to install a harmless, pliable brain in the Monster. That brain presently belongs to Wilbur. Meanwhile, Lawrence Talbot has tracked the monsters from Europe in hopes of destroying them. An investigator from MacDougal's insurance company, Joan Raymond, is also on the trail of the exhibits and pretends to be enamored with Wilbur.

Wilbur, Joan, and Chick arrive at the castle to escort Sandra to a masquerade ball. While they wait, Talbot telephones and tells Wilbur to search the castle for Dracula and the Monster. Chick, anxious to debunk the supernatural, leads the way. Once again, however, only Wilbur glimpses the monsters. Dracula (now disguised as Dr. Lejos) Wilbur, Sandra, Chick, Joan, and Sandra's gullible assistant, Dr. Stevens, attend the ball. Wilbur and Joan are captured by Dracula and Sandra, who is now a vampire herself, and taken back to the island for the operation. Chick and Talbot return to the castle, but just as he rescues Wilbur, the full moon rises, and Talbot turns into the Wolf Man. Dracula fights off the Wolf Man, while the semi-restored Monster pursues Wilbur and Chick. The Wolf Man and Dracula both plunge to their deaths off a balcony while the Monster chases Chick and Wilbur to the pier. Joan and Dr. Stevens set the dock afire and destroy the Monster. Chick and Wilbur begin rowing to shore when they are surprised by the Invisible Man.

BACKGROUND

The brainstorm of resurrecting Frankenstein's Monster is credited to producer Robert Arthur. It wasn't an idea without precedent, however. The Monster had made a brief gag appearance in Olsen and Johnson's *Hellzapoppin'* (1941), and supposedly had a cameo that was cut from O&J's *Ghost Catchers* (1944). Bud and Lou themselves had considered teaming up with the Monster, Dracula, and the Wolf Man for a Broadway show. They reportedly discussed the logistics of the make-up with Universal's make-up wizard, Jack Pierce, in 1942. Some exhibitors had successfully teamed Bud and Lou with Universal's goons in 1943, when *It Ain't Hay* played on double bills with *Frankenstein Meets The Wolf Man*.

"You know, nobody was writing stories for Abbott and Costello," Arthur recalled. "It was up to us to come up with ideas. At that time, Ed Muhl and I used to sit around and wonder, 'What do we do next?' Ed was the fellow that realized what Abbott and Costello meant to the studio. One night I thought, 'Who could they meet? Suppose they met Frankenstein.' And Ed said, 'Is there any story in it?' I said, 'I just thought of it a minute ago—give me a chance.' I came back a few days later and told him the idea. A guy has the Frankenstein Monster, and the Monster's getting too smart. They need a pliable brain to put in the Monster's head, so they pick out Costello's. Ed Muhl gave me the go ahead. He said, 'But as long as you're doing that, why does it have to be some legitimate character that has the Monster? Why can't it be Dracula? And instead of having some leading man warn Bud and Lou, we added the Wolf Man . . . just kicking it around in Ed Muhl's office at night. Before we brought in the writers, we knew we wanted to make a picture with the Monster, the Wolf Man, and Dracula."

Even this aggregation was not novel. The Monster, Dracula, and the Wolf Man had appeared together in both *House of Frankenstein* (1944) and *House of Dracula* (1945). Early press releases stated that Marjorie Main, as well as the Mummy and Count Alucard, the son of Dracula, were also considered for the film.

Chick Young	Bud Abbott
Wilbur Gray	Lou Costello
Lawrence Talbot	Lon Chaney, Jr.
Dracula	Bela Lugosi
Monster	Glenn Strange
Sandra Mornay	Lenore Aubert
Joan Raymond	Jane Randolph
Mr. MacDougal	Frank Ferguson
Dr. Stevens	Charles Bradstreet
Mr. Harris	Howard Negley
Man	Joe Kirk
Man in Armor	Clarence Straight
Man	George Barton
Man	Charles Sklover
Sergeant	Paul Stader
Man	Joe Walls

THE SCRIPT

For the record, the concept did not crystalize quite so instantly. While Lees and Rinaldo were busy writing *The Wistful Widow of Wagon Gap,* Arthur gave first crack at the project to screenwriter Oscar Brodney, who worked for two weeks in January 1947, on a treatment that is not in the studio archives. Arthur next enlisted Bertram Milhauser, a veteran of the studio's Sherlock Holmes series, to deliver a treatment in February 1947.

Milhauser's forty-seven-page treatment, titled *Abbott and Costello Meet Frankenstein,* was submitted on February 12, 1947, and does not revolve around filching Costello's brain. Instead, the sinister Dr. Fell steals Dr. Frankenstein's formula for reanimating the Monster, Dracula, and the Wolf Man from the Baroness von Frankenstein. The dormant monsters are on exhibit in a New York museum where Fell is curator. The Baroness alerts her granddaughter, Jan Newcome, who, along with FBI agent Dan Barlowe, waits for Fell to arrive by ocean liner. But Fell is tipped off by a cablegram and hides the formula, which is on microfilm, in a matchbook. Pretending to be a government agent, he dupes two stewards, Abbott and Costello, to carry the matchbook off the ship and rendezvous with him later at the museum. Much of the story involves A&C inadvertently losing the matchbook, then tracking it down as it is innocently passed from person to person in the city. Of course, Barlowe's search of Fell and his luggage proves fruitless. But Jane has another idea. She asks Fell to escort her to a costume ball at the Waldorf Astoria, and he consents. Eventually, Jane maroons Fell in a elevator while she and Dan head for the museum to search for the stolen formula.

Naturally, the ever-gullible Abbott and Costello rescue Fell, and the three of them catch up with Jane and Dan at the museum. Fell subdues Jane and Dan, and begins examining the formula in his office. The oblivious Abbott and Costello, meanwhile, raid the museum's kitchen and concoct a meal of baked beans, salt, and vinegar. At the same time, Fell reads that salt and vinegar will revive the Monster, and baked beans will reanimate the Wolf Man! As for Dracula, one need only remove the stake in his chest. Bud and Lou decide to eat in the room with the exhibits. When the table they sit at wobbles, Costello looks for something to steady it and notices a skeleton with a stake in its ribs. He plucks the stake out and uses it to fix the table. As the boys eat, some food miraculously (and ludicrously) finds its way onto the faces of the Monster and the Wolf Man. Soon, all three monsters are chasing the boys, Fell, and Jane around the museum. At the last minute, the Baroness arrives with a remedy. Lou

165

sprays the three monsters with an atomizer and they shrink to four inches tall! Jane frees Barlowe, who arrests Fell, and the Baroness permits Bud and Lou to exhibit the tiny creatures on Broadway. But, she warns them, you must never, ever let them come in contact with olives! On opening night, Lou eats a deli sandwich backstage. On his plate are three olives. . . .

Milhauser had, in fact, recycled the plot of his screenplay *Sherlock Holmes in Washington* (1941), which revolved around Holmes' pursuit of secret microfilm hidden in a matchbook. Needless to say, Milhauser's inane scenario was tossed out, and Lees and Rinaldo started on the project. Robert Lees explained, "One of my major theories is that comedy is rooted in fear. So when you get Abbott and Costello meeting not only Frankenstein but Dracula and the Wolf Man—you can't miss. The minute the studio told Fred and I the basic idea, we said, 'This is the greatest idea for a comedy that ever was!' But that's all they gave us. We came up with the rest." Lees said that they didn't screen the studio's previous Frankenstein films. "After all, I had practically grown up on the Bram Stoker story and Mary Shelley's 'Frankenstein' so it was all second nature to me."

Their first treatment, dated April 21, although not built around the pursuit of Costello's brain, is quite close to the film we know today. Dracula, as Dr. Lejos, enlists Dr. Stevens to help him revive the Monster. Larry Talbot arrives to team up with baggage handlers Bud and Lou to stop him. This early scenario does not include Sandra, and Jane is merely a camp counselor who gets swept up in the action. Lees and Rinaldo's second pass at the story, delivered in June, brings the story in line with the finished film. It also amends the title to "The Brain of Frankenstein."

"You know it has a very complicated plot for an Abbott and Costello picture," Lees recalled. "We had two women—one was a heroine and one was a villain. And nobody could figure out why these two beautiful girls were after Costello. Another thing I like is that whole business about the costume ball and the confusion that resulted over the wolf costume. The romantic scene between Lenore and Lou in the woods—that's all Fred's. It was exceedingly good. Even when I read it today, I get hysterical. Some of the best lines in the picture, like 'I'll bite'—'No, I will,' or when Chaney tells Costello the full moon turns him into a wolf and Costello says, 'You and twenty million other guys,' . . . that's all Fred's stuff. He was so good with verbal jokes. I would say I did about two-thirds of the story and Fred did two-thirds of the dialogue."

But not everyone was enamored with the script.

"Lou *hated* the script," Robert Arthur recalled. "In fact, he came charging in the office one day and said, 'My daughter could write a better script than this. You're not serious about making it, are you?' Now at that time we had a deal on account of the tax situation. Bud and Lou could buy 10 percent interest in the picture. Lou said, 'I'm not gonna put my money in this piece of junk.' I said, 'Lou, I'll make you a deal. I'll buy your percentage and give you a profit on your 10 percent.' He said, 'You got a deal.' Now, he couldn't make that deal without the consent of the IRS, who said, 'We can't stop him from making the deal, but any profit you give him goes to Internal Revenue.' So my idea of buying 10 percent fell apart."

Robert Lees explained, "You have to remember that Abbott and Costello were stand-up comics from burlesque. They loved 'Who's On First?' They had done it for so long they knew where every laugh was. And they had an audience when they did their radio show. But on a soundstage the only reaction they could get was from the crew. So they were nervous about new material and *Abbott and Costello Meet Frankenstein* was all new. I think the "Moving Candle" is the only stock routine in it. I credit Bob Arthur for that, because he knew when he had a good story and a good script and he did what he could to protect it. That's the first Abbott and Costello picture Fred and I could look at and say, 'That's the script.' "

THE CAST

Lon Chaney, Jr. (1906–1973) waited until after his famous father's death to break into films. (Chaney Sr. was vehemently opposed to Lon Jr. becoming an actor.) He wallowed in B- and

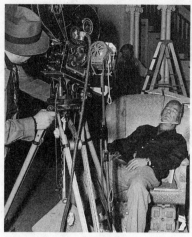

TOP LEFT: Celebrating Lou's birthday on the set.
TOP CENTER: Shooting one of Lon Chaney's transformation scenes.
ABOVE: Glenn Strange and Bud Jr.

C-grade westerns until he triumphed as Lennie in a West Coast production of *Of Mice and Men,* and reprised the role in the 1939 film version. Universal signed him to link the Chaney name with a new generation of horror films, and after his success in *The Wolf Man* (1941), he portrayed virtually every monster in the studio stable. "All of the best monsters were played for sympathy," he once said. "That goes for my father, Boris Karloff, myself, and all the others. They won the audience's sympathy. The Wolf Man didn't want to do all those things. He was forced into them." With the horror cycle foundering in the mid-1940s, Chaney was cast as heavies opposite Olsen and Johnson (*Ghost Catchers*), Abbott and Costello (*Here Come the Co-Eds*), and Bob Hope (*My Favorite Brunette*). After *Abbott and Costello Meet Frankenstein,* except for roles in *High Noon* (1952) and *The Defiant Ones* (1958), Chaney fell into another rut of B- and C-grade films. Happily, he saw his films enjoy a revival on television before he passed away in 1973.

Bela Lugosi (1882–1956), after his great success in the 1930s in *Dracula, Murders in the Rue Morgue, White Zombie,* and *The Black Cat,* had suffered through dozens of inferior horror films by the 1940s. Finally, after completing a personal appearance tour with an act that was part Dracula lore and part magic tricks (and represented by Eddie Sherman), Lugosi was signed for *Meet Frankenstein* on January 28, 1948. (A memo dated September 9, 1947, penciled in Ian Keith for the role. Ironically, Keith was scheduled to play Dracula in the 1931 original.) Bela was relieved that Universal had not asked him to do anything unbecoming the Count's dignity. "There is no burlesque for me," he told *The New York Times.* "All I have to do is frighten the boys, a perfectly appropriate activity. My trademark will be unblemished." The film would be Bela's last blaze of glory. In 1956, after courageously recovering from morphine addiction and appearing in countless grade Z productions, Bela Lugosi died at the age of seventy-four.

Lenore Aubert (b. 1918?) fled her native Yugoslavia after the Nazi invasion, and modeled and acted in Paris and Lisbon before arriving in New York. Before long, she was in Hollywood, cast in foreign intrigues (*They Got Me Covered, Action in Arabia, Passport to Adventure*) or costume dramas (*The Wife of Monte Cristo, Bluebeard's Eighth Wife, Barbary Pirate*). Lenore wasn't the original choice for Sandra. That September 9 studio memo suggests Patricia Morison for the role. Lenore was finally signed on January 22, 1948. She worked with the boys again in *Abbott and Costello Meet the Killer, Boris Karloff* (1949) and retired from the screen soon after.

Jane Randolph (b. 1919) had appeared in *Cat People* (1942), *The Curse of the Cat People* (1944), *The Falcon's Brother* (1942) and *The Falcon Strikes Back* (1943), as well as some good crime dramas at Eagle-Lion in 1947. Jane inherited her assignment in *Meet Frankenstein.* Dorothy Hart was originally considered for the role, then Ella Raines. Raines asked to be released because she felt she couldn't compete with the monsters. Jane retired from the screen after making the film and now lives in Europe.

167

Glenn Strange (1899–1973) was called on to play the Frankenstein Monster for the third and final time. Boris Karloff retired from the role after *Son of Frankenstein* (1939) and wouldn't even *see Abbott and Costello Meet Frankenstein*, much less appear in it. "I'm too fond of the Monster," he said. "I'm too grateful for all he did for me and wouldn't want to watch anyone make sport of him." But Karloff had nothing but respect for his successors in the role, which included Chaney, Lugosi, and Strange. "Anybody who can take that make-up every morning deserves respect," he told *The New York Times* in 1948. Strange, a former cowboy and rodeo performer, started as a stuntman at MGM in 1927. "One day at Universal, Lou asked, 'Did you ever jump a white horse off a building into a big redwood tank at Metro?'" Strange recalled. "I said yes, I did. And he said, 'How about that! I helped build that tank. I was a laborer over there then!'" Glenn portrayed heavies in scores of B westerns until he tested for the role of the Monster in *House of Frankenstein* (1944). Karloff, also cast in the film, coached him. "I'd never have been the Monster I was if it hadn't been for Boris Karloff," Strange said. "He showed me how to make the Monster's moves properly, and how to do the walk that makes him so frightening." *Meet Frankenstein* was Glenn's only performance as the Monster that included dialogue. (He was also supposed to be the voice of the Invisible Man in the film's end gag.) Between stints as the Monster, Strange returned to westerns and appeared with the boys in *The Wistful Widow of Wagon Gap* and *Comin' Round the Mountain* (1951). He was probably best known for his roles on TV as the Lone Ranger's nemesis, Butch Cavendish, and as Sam the bartender on *Gunsmoke*.

THE PRODUCTION

The production was originally budgeted at $759,524. It was, in fact, the studio's second least expensive production in 1948; *Feudin', Fussin', and A-Fightin'* cost only $454,000. *Meet Frankenstein* was scheduled for thirty-two days, but ran seven days and $32,746 over budget. The most expensive items were, of course, Bud and Lou's salaries ($105,000), the writers' salaries ($48,916), and the cost of building the various castle sets ($21,500). Other items of interest:

·Make one heavy and one light shipping crate for Dracula—$173.
·Make one heavy and one light shipping crate for Monster—$153.
·Make one wooden coffin, two balsa wood Dracula coffins—$710.
·Upholster three Dracula coffins—$105.
·Make one battery belt for moving candle gag—$5.
·Make and paint bat—$627.
·Rig bat to fly—$150.
·Make one 75' rubber chain—$200.
·Rig secret door to revolve—$260.
·Rigging Wolf Man dummy and bat for fall into water tank—$170.

The new head of the studio's make-up department, Bud Westmore, was instructed to find a way to expedite the arduous make-up process. Chaney's Wolf Man make-up usually took up to four hours to apply, while Strange's Monster appliances required six hours. After experimenting for two weeks, Westmore created sponge rubber masks for both that could be applied in only an hour. Westmore estimated that the new method reduced the make-up cost for each character from approximately $10,000 to $2,000.

Robert Arthur recalled, "Now I'll tell you about Bill Goetz, the new head of production at Universal. It wasn't just a snooty thing. About a week before we were ready to shoot, I asked him if he had read our script. He said no. I said, 'Well, do you have any comments about it?' And he made the most brilliant executive decision I ever heard. He said, 'Look, Bob. These guys are not funny to me. I never willingly went to see one of their pictures. So any suggestion that I make would only hurt you. So I leave it in your hands. God bless you and God help you.'"

Charles Barton recalled, "None of the front office bigwigs ever even visited our set. They wouldn't even tell us after the picture was finished if it was good or bad. They just wanted to get the picture out as soon as possible so it could make several million for them."

Early on, Barton found Bud and Lou obstinate. "Bud and Lou had quite a chip on their shoulders about doing it, and they'd fight me like hell," Barton said. "But I stood my ground with them and so did Bob Arthur." Eventually, Barton managed to get the team to cooperate. "We had a great relationship," he recalled. "You hear a lot of things about little Lou, and he was a terror. But for some reason, with me, and I don't know why the hell it was, we got along even better than brothers. Things that I'd like him to do in a picture he would at least try—something he wouldn't do with many directors—and that showed he had confidence in me."

About three weeks into production, concern surfaced over the title, which was still "The Brain of Frankenstein." A memo from John Joseph states:

> There was a great deal of discussion at the sales meeting concerning the title, "Brain of Frankenstein," for the Abbott and Costello comedy currently in work. A good many members of the sales department feared that the picture might be confused with one of our horror jobs. I advised Mr. Goetz of this reaction and he immediately ordered a title test. The title tested was "Abbott and Costello Meet Frankenstein" . . . People found [it] indicated something that was funny, that had laughs, that was scary, that was spooky. I suggest that we start using this title immediately inasmuch as it is clear and available.

Meanwhile, Bud, Lou, and Bobby Barber were up to their usual pranks off-camera. One day, Barton was blocking out the sequence in the castle's hidden chamber with Bobby standing in for Lou in the pillory. After lining up the shot and setting up the lights, the company broke for lunch—and left Bobby behind, locked in. Glenn Strange called *Meet Frankenstein* "one of the most enjoyable pictures I ever worked on. We [shot it] in about seven weeks. We should have done it in about five, but if you know Abbott and Costello, they play about a quarter of the time and then work the rest of the time." The March 1 *Valley Times* Handshaker in Hollywood column reported:

> On the first day's shooting of Abbott and Costello's *Brain of Frankenstein,* the director got an egg on his noggin from above. Bobby Barber had come in early and ascended the rafters. Lou calls Bobby's antics "a wonderful tonic." Bobby, 52, is a professional stooge. His function in Hollywood is to keep Bud and Lou happy. I watched fifteen minutes of his madness. Abbott built a fire under his chair . . . Bobby fell backwards out of another chair whose back had been loosened . . . He pretended to smash the still-man's camera. . . . He stooged for jokes. Lou: "What comes after 75?" Bobby: "76." Lou: "That's the spirit!"
>
> Bobby loads himself with seltzer bottles, Fourth of July buzz bombs, exploding cigars, trick card decks, and crazy costumes for his forced-draft humor. He may appear in old-fashioned golf knickers and use an electric razor to shave his fuzzy socks. Or dash through a scene in his shorts screaming, 'Fellows, be quiet! I can't sleep!'—ruining the take. Or smash his employers in the face with pies. He used up $300 worth of pies and other props on another recent Abbott-Costello picture.
>
> Bobby says no victim has ever punched him in the nose. His salary is reportedly $25 a day. When I left, somebody was pasting a strip of adhesive tape across his head and somebody else was about to pour a soft drink on him. I felt a little sorry for Bobby.

Sometimes, Lon Chaney joined the seltzer and pie fights, while Glenn Strange was declared off-limits due to the handicap of his make-up. Bela Lugosi generally steered clear of the mayhem. As Strange recalled, "[Bela] was a very hard person to get acquainted with. A very sincere person. He didn't want any playing on the set . . . and, of course, we played a lot."

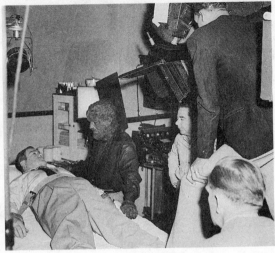

ABOVE: Court Jester
Bobby Barber gets it from
Lou, Bela, and Bud.
ABOVE RIGHT: Setting up
for Wilbur's reaction to
the Wolfman.

Bud and Lou were careful not to offend Bela. "Bud and Lou had great respect for these people," Barton explained. "They were professionals, and Bud and Lou knew it."

Lou was also up to his old habit of taking home studio props. Robert Arthur recalled that one morning an antique clock was missing from the mantel in Dracula's castle. Without it, all of the previous day's scenes would have to be reshot. "We both knew he had the clock, so finally I said, 'Lou, tell you what I'll do. I'll make you a deal. Anybody who will bring back the clock so we can get this scene finished can have it after we've finished shooting.' Lou looked at me with a gleeful grin of victory and said, 'Will ya put that in writing?'"

Bud and Lou's fun became infectious. One day, Lenore Aubert, wrapped in a mink, put a leash on Strange and, accompanied by Bud, Lou, and Lon in full make-up, took the Monster out for a stroll on the lot just in time for the studio tour tram. According to the pressbook, the monsters were barred from the studio commissary because the diners had little stomach for the loathsome creatures. One day, however, Strange lunched on the back lot with Ann Blyth, who was in full body make-up for her role in *Mr. Peabody and The Mermaid*. An unwary tourist turned the corner, shrieked, and walloped Strange with her purse—leaving him with his lunch on his face and costume.

Filming was not without its hazards for Glenn, either. In the scene where the Monster hurls Dr. Mornay through the lab window, the window frame failed to break, sending the stuntwoman swinging back into Strange, who was knocked flat on the floor, fracturing an ankle. Barton recalled that Lon Chaney heard about the mishap the next day. "He said I'll put the make-up on. I'll do it. He had done it before [in *Ghost of Frankenstein* (1942)], and that was a hell of a job to put that make-up on and everything. No quarrels . . . just as happy as he could be to do it." So in the finished film, it is Chaney as the Monster who tosses Sandra through the lab window. This time stuntwoman Helen Thurston had to be taken to the hospital when some of the candy glass splintered in her eyes. Strange returned two days later in a metal cast to chase the boys through the castle.

Of course, Bud and Lou had brought their children to the studio many times in the past. But going to the *Meet Frankenstein* set was a special treat. Bud Abbott, Jr., recalled, "We were there a couple of times. We were really small then. We didn't see Lon Chaney that particular day, but we saw the Monster and Dracula. It was the scene where Dad and Lou were walking down the stairway in the basement of the castle. That was all one set—the revolving door, the secret room, and the dock. It was really incredible! But the thing was, in those days, they shot in black-and-white! You wonder why didn't they shoot it in color! It was just fantastic in color." Vickie Abbott recalled, "Glenn Strange had trouble getting through the revolving door because he was so tall. His head kept hitting the top of the panel, ruining his headpiece!"

Paddy Costello recalled, "Glenn Strange was so sweet—'Frankenstein' was always walking around with a smile. I always got a big kick out of that—seeing the monsters between scenes, sitting in a chair reading a newspaper or chewing gum, or laughing and smoking like regular people. And then how all of that reality was suspended so this fantasy could come to life. I remember the day our mother brought Chris to the set. She was about a year old, and Glenn Strange wanted to hold her. He was the nicest, sweetest gentleman, and very, very friendly. [laughs] But Chris took one look at him and she went *crazy!* They had to take her off the set."

Bud Jr. recalled his meeting with the Monster. "They took a picture of us sitting on Frankenstein's lap, and the only thing I can remember was my sister—she's three years younger than I am, she's a little squirt—she looked up into that Frankenstein face and says, 'I have to go to the bathroom!' " Vickie explains, "We thought they were going to take pictures of us with Dad and Lou. Then they told us it was going to be with the monsters! I was so terrified by Glenn Strange that I ran to the ladies' room. It took my mom fifteen minutes to talk me out! I finally met Mr. Strange, who turned out to be a very kind, gentle man, and Bela Lugosi."

Bud Jr. was also impressed by the laboratory. "It was a pretty awsome-looking set, but when they got ready to shoot, they lit up everything, and the lightning and the electricity was just incredible! It just froze you when it went off. Those aren't sound effects you hear—that's the actual cracking and crackling of the electricity! Dad used to tell me that the greatest geniuses in the world are in special effects."

Another component contributing greatly to the effectiveness of the film is composer Frank Skinner's (1898–1968) thrilling score. Skinner's scores for *The House of Seven Gables* (1940), *Back Street* (1941), *Arabian Nights* (1942), and *The Amazing Mrs. Holliday* (1943) had garnered Academy Award nominations. Skinner had also scored *Son of Frankenstein* (1939), *Destry Rides Again* (1939), *Hellzapoppin'* (1941), and *Saboteur* (1942). His work on *Meet Frankenstein,* if not his best, certainly is his most ubiquitous: Universal reprised it for each succeeding *Abbott and Costello Meet . . .* film.

BUD AND LOU'S SCENES

Appropriately enough, the company began shooting the House of Horrors sequence on Friday, February 13. "The 'Moving Candle' scene from *Hold That Ghost* got very big laughs," Robert Lees explained. "That was something they did in burlesque. So we used it again in *Meet Frankenstein,* but we put it on the coffin." Norman Abbott, dialogue director on the film, explained John Grant's invaluable contributions to the film. "John Grant would help Charlie Barton block the scenes. I remember John was so sweet with Charlie, he never took Charlie's job over. They were great friends. He'd say to Charlie, 'Well, this is the way I wrote it. Let me show you what I think. See if you like it, Charlie.' He was very gracious. If Lou was reluctant to try something, John would do it first. I remember the scene in the House of Horrors where Bela Lugosi came out of the coffin. On the day we rehearsejd it, John Grant impersonated Lou with Bud, and everybody fell down laughing, because here was John—6'2" with gray hair—playing Lou Costello! Lou rolled around practically on the floor. Then of course Lou'd come around and he would do it. John was instrumental in getting that scene done."

Charles Barton remembers another instance of coaxing Lou into doing a memorable scene. "Do you remember that pantomime scene where Lou sat in the Monster's lap, and he got his hands mixed up with the Monster's? Well, Lou didn't want to do that. I had worked with John Grant on that bit and when Lou read it he said, 'What the hell is this?' I said, 'Well, if you just listen and try it, you'll find out that it is *beautiful.*' At first Lou didn't understand it, but he finally became very enthusiastic. He just loved it. Well, we began shooting the scene and right in the middle of it, Glenn Strange started to laugh. And by God he couldn't stop! So Lou got mad at him. I'll never forget that. Lou said, 'Dammit, Glenn, you're just trying

171

to make it worse for me!' Glenn said, 'No, of course not. I don't know what it is about you, but even on the back of your head I can see what's going on!' " The scene was originally shot on February 20, and then later reshot on March 4, indicating a commitment on Lou's part to get the scene just right.

In this sequence, Wilbur runs out to grab Chick and bring him through the revolving panel to show him the Monster. Listen closely and you'll hear Costello in his excitement call Chick "Abbott." There are other "mistakes" in the film. For horror fans the most glaring is Dracula's reflection in Sandra's bedroom mirror. (*Son of Dracula* [1943] makes the same gaffe.) Another is the fact that Larry Talbot was "cured" of lycanthropy in *House of Dracula!*

The sequence in the bayou, where Wilbur mistakes the Wolf Man for Chick in a costume, was essentially one of the boys' stock routines. Bud usually offered to don either a bear, lion, or gorilla suit so that Lou could appear to be brave in front of some other characters. Naturally, a real bear or lion or gorilla wanders into the scene in place of Bud, leaving the unwitting Costello to tussle audaciously with the genuine article.

The final chase sequence is one that is entrenched in the mind of every adult who, as a child, alternately laughed and screamed at the team's close calls with the monsters. As Robert Lees explained, "All these gags were thought out and written for that chase. Like when they pile everything against the door and the door opens the wrong way. Or the whole tug of war with Costello on the gurney. These were visual gags that Fred and I were very proud of." In the scene where Bud and Lou lock the Monster in one of the bedrooms, there was another minor mishap. "They had marks for Lou and Bud to be standing on," Strange recalled. "They stood so close that there was only enough room for my fist to come through between them. Well, I'm beating on this door and they said to [Abbott and Costello], 'Whatever you do, stay on your marks, okay?' Well, Lou isn't going to stand on anybody's mark. And through I came and hit him right there [pointing to the nose]. They kept the scene in . . . you can see it in the film." Barton was so pleased he never did a second take, according to the assistant director's report.

DELETIONS AND ADDITIONS

Several little bits of business were added that do not appear in the script. In the baggage room, MacDougal is frustrated by Wilbur's ineptitude and barks orders at him. In an added exchange, Wilbur asks, "How long you been here?" MacDougal shouts, "Five minutes!" Wilbur replies, "What are you beefin' about—I been here for five years. You don't see me goin' around like that yellin'."

MacDougal demands that the boys deliver the mistreated crates to his House of Horrors. Wilbur advises him, "Well then it's going to cost you overtime, because I'm a union man and I work only sixteen hours a day." MacDougal snarls, "A union man only works eight hours a day." Wilbur cracks, "I belong to *two* unions!"

Wilbur is terrified by one of the exhibits in the House of Horrors. Chick admonishes, "Oh, come on. It's only a dummy." "Dummy nothing," Wilbur whimpers, "it was smart enough to scare *me.*"

As the boys arrive on the island to pick up Sandra for the masquerade ball, Chick complains that Wilbur now has two dates and he hasn't any. Wilbur retorts that on their double date the previous week, Chick took the good-looking girl. "Mine had so much bridgework," he says, "everytime I kissed her I had to pay a toll." Lou shamelessly and confidently delivers the antediluvian joke.

MacDougal assaults Wilbur at the masquerade ball and Chick dares him to try it in front of a witness. This routine, we have seen, pops up in a few of the team's films. In *Meet Frankenstein,* Chick's witness wears a knight's helmet, and the face plate inopportunely blocks his view of the action. In a deleted bit, Chick corrals a photographer, but his flashbulb suddenly goes dead when MacDougal thrashes Wilbur for a third time.

In the scene where Dracula telepathically summons Wilbur back into the cave, Wilbur was supposed to try to run away but be inexorably drawn backwards by the Count's unseen force. The effect would be achieved with a treadmill buried in the ground. Budget limitations may have killed the gag, which in Costello's hands could have been hilarious. Robert Lees recalled, "I was just absolutely furious, because I thought that it would have been one of the funniest pieces of business, Costello trying to fight this invisible force. It was like a gag that Buster Keaton had done—he throws a line and catches a fish and skids out on his rear end. Either they felt it was too hard to do, or too expensive."

REVIEWS

"We had a *sensational* preview at the Academy Theater in Inglewood," Robert Arthur recalled. "And Lou's mother came over and gave me a big hug and said, 'I haven't laughed this hard in years.' And Lou got furious. He had just taken a position early on, and he wasn't going back on it. But he worked very hard on the picture."

Robert Lees recalls, "The scene with Lou on the operating table caught between Dracula and the Wolf Man brought down the house and we knew we had a hit. For the end gag we had the Invisible Man, and Bob Arthur turned to us and said, 'That's your next picture.'"

On May 19, John Joseph reported to Universal president Nate Blumberg,

By the time this reaches you I am sure that Bill Goetz will have reported on the sneak preview last night of "Abbott and Costello Meet Frankenstein." If he hasn't told you that the picture is a big hit, he is guilty of underselling one of our attractions because "Abbott and Costello Meet Frankenstein" played like a million dollars last night at the Academy in Inglewood.

I think it's the best sneak we have ever had on an Abbott & Costello picture. As you know yourself, from having gone to some of the A&C sneaks, the first preview of this type of comedy is sometimes very spotty. We purposely leave in all of the footage shot to see what plays or what doesn't play.

In this one every scene played and paid off one hundred per cent and I have never seen that happen before with the boys. The Academy audience was in a high state of laughing excitement from the main title until the end of the picture; it never let down once.

If anybody is in doubt about the Frankenstein angle of the title such doubt should be immediately buried deep in the ground. You should have heard the shriek of approval that went up when the title flashed on the screen. Around here we always thought the idea of Abbott and Costello plus the three monsters was terribly funny. I'm glad to report that the public agrees with us.

Variety: "'Abbott and Costello Meet Frankenstein' is a happy combination both for chills and laughs. The comedy team battles it out with the studio's roster of bogeymen in a rambunctious fracas that is funny and, at the same time, spine-tingling . . . Abbott and Costello work with less of their standard routines than usual, but keep the fun at high level. Bela Lugosi, Glenn Strange and Lon Chaney bulwark the chills and thrills. . . . The Robert Arthur production is neatly tied together by Charles T. Barton's direction. Latter realizes on all the fun possible and misses no bets in sharpening blood-curdling sequences."

Chicago Sun Times: "[We] have no idea why the studio decided to toss their favorite comedians to the mercy of the monsters. The boys, Bud and Lou, bear up as bravely as possible under the circumstances, but to tell the truth, the collection of ghouls assembled by the studio has taken the life right out of them. . . . The film emerges a good deal more 'Frankenstein' than 'Abbott and Costello'—and, let's face it, a considerable bore."

Hollywood Reporter: "The idea of teaming Abbott and Costello with the stable of monsters that cavort at U-I is one of those brainstorms that could be nothing less than hilarious in its completion. Happily, 'Abbott and Costello Meet Frankenstein' is just that—a crazy, giddy

173

show that combines chills and laughs in one zany sequence after the other. . . . Robert Arthur's production spells out showmanship right down the line, and Charles T. Barton's direction keeps things moving at a lively, vigorous pace. Arthur and Barton both know the Abbott and Costello fans and their handling of the comedy is geared to the best slapstick traditions."

Los Angeles Examiner: "Technically, funnymen Bud and Lou are the stars of the picture, and I'll not quarrel with any of their devoted fans to whom their mere presence in a movie is sufficient unto the day and the humor thereof. In all fairness, however, I must say I think the real stars of this fantastic venture in movie-making are Producer Robert Arthur, Director Charles T. Barton, and whoever was responsible for the original and hilarious idea. . . .

"Granted the idea was a natural, the concoction nevertheless might have gone very sour indeed were it not for the subtle production values given it by Producer Arthur; the sound judgement of Director Barton in playing the horror stuff straight, thereby making the outrageous nonsense twice as funny; and the restrained performances of Lon Chaney, Bela Lugosi and Glenn Strange. Their temptation to go overboard, farcically, must have been well nigh unbearable, but praise be, the fort held, and the end result—a smash comedy—more than justifies the collective forbearance.

"No such constraint was placed upon Abbott and Costello, and thus we have another repetition of their familiar routine of shoving, mugging, and yapping at each other. Their stylized antics, however, actually are a welcome contrast, particularly when the tension generated by the machinations of the three horror boys (such manly little lads!) gets a bit thick. For the nerves, that is."

In New York, a record heat-wave combined with a strike by air conditioning engineers made the Criterion Theater a hot box, according to manager Charles Moss. This may have accounted for the irritability of the New York critics.

The New York Times: "Most of the comic invention in 'Abbott and Costello Meet Frankenstein' is embraced in the idea and the title. The notion of having these two clowns run afoul of the famous screen monster is a good laugh in itself. But take this gentle warning: get the most of that while you can, because the picture does not contain many more."

New York Sun: "Having seen 'Abbott and Costello Meet Frankenstein' we feel that we have seen everything the movies have to offer in horror and horrible pictures. It is possible that Abbott and Costello fans will regard this Universal-International offering as the greatest comedy ever made, but there surely will be some moviegoers willing to disagree. . . . It was a grand idea, but it was too bad that it could not have been attended to by persons capable of satire rather than pie-throwing comedy only."

The *Hollywood Reporter* berated the New York critics: "The New York critics bore us stiff sometimes. One of those sometimes is when they get around to reviewing Abbott and Costello cinemas. The chief critical complaint is that if you've seen one of those flickers, you've seen 'em all. Well, if you've read one review on an Abbott and Costello comedy, you've read 'em all."

However, some critics were able to appreciate the film:

New York Daily Mirror: "This is definitely one of Abbott and Costello's funnier efforts simply because they have cut down on the 'Who's-on-first-base?' [sic] type of comedy and confined themselves chiefly to situation humor. The spook stuff, blended with their familiar zany antics is the best laugh material they have exhibited in a long while. . . . While junior will be sure to enjoy this, you may find yourself on the receiving end of a chill and chuckle too."

New York Star: "Nobody excels Costello at strangulated, speechless terror. Nobody can top Abbott at failing to see the cause for it. Nobody can beat Frankenstein, Dracula, The Monster, and Dr. Mornay at engendering it separately and together behind Abbott's back, but always in Costello's full view. Not until almost the end of the movie does Abbott, previously blinded by his idiotic common sense, believe the little Costello. . . . Yet it's heart-warming to see all our favorite monsters once more, each inexorably expressing his individuality, all at the same time. It's kind of like a class reunion. They look a little older now, and a little tired. . . . Still, everybody connected with this nostalgic travesty of horror movies deserves credit at least for playing it straight. All together, though stumbling now and then, repeating their specialties rather too often, and failing to realize the full extent of the wild hilarity implicit in their situation, they have made 'Abbott and Costello Meet Frankenstein' a broad, friendly comedy, good to see. It's real American folklore; look at it that way."

Most of the critics seemed more frightened by the matinee audiences they rubbed elbows with:

Los Angeles Times: "[The title] was followed—at least at the Ritz matinee yesterday—by a bedlam which had soon communicated itself from shadows to spectators, most of them in their teens or younger. They shrieked with that infusion of terror and glee which only a motion picture of this sort can inspire. Having already attained my majority, I didn't shriek. But I wouldn't have missed the show—the one going on around me, anyhow—for anything. As a matter of fact, the film has been put together with enormous ingenuity. Its comic inventiveness seldom falters, yet it never seriously violated the tradition of the three celebrated creatures who are its antagonists."

Dayton Journal: "One thing we can say . . . is that all the monsters aren't on the screen. Pint-sized ones surrounded us at yesterday's matinee, and their blood curdling shrieks, their maniacal guffaws, their shouted instructions and their frenzied, weird bodily contortions as the hapless heroes stumbled from horror to horror, will haunt us long after the final film fades from our nightmares."

An exhibitor in Albany, Oregon, wrote to *Box Office:* "While we did excellent business, the broken seats, crying kids and screams from the women hardly made this one worth it. The most walkouts of any picture we ever played. This hurt our business as well as Abbott and Costello's reputation for comedy."

The film's horror sequences were deemed too intense for audiences in some countries. At first, the local censor board in British Columbia rejected the film completely, and Universal's appeal was denied. Only after many of the Wolf Man's scenes were deleted was the film approved. The Australian board was more severe: virtually *every* scene involving a monster was excised, leaving the film an abbreviated, confused mess.

POSTSCRIPT

Columnist Erskine Johnson reported on August 13: "*Abbott and Costello Meet Frankenstein* is the hottest box office draw U-I has had in three years, outdoing *The Egg and I* and *Naked City* by a comfortable margin." The film grossed $3.2 million worldwide in 1948, to become the studio's third biggest hit of the year. On the strength of it Bud and Lou were catapulted back into the Motion Picture Herald's Top Ten box office attractions, placing third in 1948. Of course, the success of *Meet Frankenstein* led to a series of Abbott and Costello horror vehicles. Lon Chaney once blamed Abbott and Costello for the demise of classic horror films. "I used to enjoy horror films when there was thought and sympathy involved. Then they became comedies. Abbott and Costello ruined the horror films; they made buffoons out of the monsters." That may have been true in the team's weaker horror comedies, but the truth is, *Meet Frankenstein* treated the monsters with more reverence than *House of Dracula* did.

Abbott and Costello, meanwhile, were subpoenaed to testify in Chicago before a Federal Grand Jury investigating the income tax returns of their poker pal, Mike "The Greek" Potson. According to the assistant U.S. attorney, Bud and Lou had paid Potson off in checks totaling $85,000 between 1940 and 1943. The *Chicago Daily News* reported: "On arrival here, Costello said, 'I lost $15,000 to $20,000. That's only $10 a week.' He did not explain his arithmetic."

MEXICAN HAYRIDE

Earliest Draft:
  August 23, 1946

Production Start:
  June 11, 1948

Production End:
  August 12, 1948

Copyright Date:
  December 6, 1948

Released:
  December 27, 1948

Running Time:
  77 minutes

Directed By:
  Charles T. Barton

Produced By:
  Robert Arthur

Screenplay By:
  Oscar Brodney and
  John Grant

Based on the Musical Play
  By: Herbert and
  Dorothy Fields and
  Cole Porter

Music Arranged and
  Conducted By:
  Walter Scharf

Director of Photography:
  Charles Van Enger

Art Direction:
  Bernard Herbrun and
  John F. DeCuir

Set Decorations:
  Russell A. Gausman
  and John Austin

Costumes: Yvonne Wood

Dance Director:
  Eugene Loring

Film Editor: Frank Gross

Make-Up: Bud Westmore

Hair Stylist: Carmen Dirigo

Special Photography By:
  David S. Horsley ASC

Sound: Leslie I. Carey and
  Robert Pritchard

SYNOPSIS

Joe Bascom catches up with con man Harry Lambert at a Mexico City bullring. Lambert swindled Bascom and his friends with a phoney oil stock deal back in Iowa. Lambert is now promoting Joe's ex-girlfriend, Mary, as Montana, a great toreador. Montana will launch the Amigo Americana Week festivities by tossing her hat into the crowd, and the lucky recipient will be named good-will ambassador. Lambert has arranged for Montana to select Gus Adamson, another confidence man from the States. Through the resulting publicity, Lambert, Adamson, and Dagmar hope to sell shares in a fictitious silver mine to unwary tourists. Montana, however, spots Bascom in the crowd and in anger throws her hat at him, accidentally making him the honoree. Lambert and Dagmar conspire to continue with their plan and use Bascom in the silver mine scam. Bascom, also a fugitive, takes an alias, Humphrey Fish.

As the Amigo Americana, Humphrey addresses a gathering of Mexican and American notables with a speech that extolls the phoney silver mine, and several wealthy financiers purchase stock. The U.S. consul attache, David Winthrop, learns Humphrey's true identity and has two detectives arrest Harry and Joe. Joe manages to escape, but the detectives take Harry in custody. When their car gets a flat on a country road, Joe, disguised as a Mexican woman, helps Harry escape. They both race to Mexico City to be the first to find Dagmar and the money. Although the detectives have staked out the bullfight arena, Harry and Joe slip in disguised as Mexicans. Joe flees into the ring and is chased by a bull. Dagmar, who has hidden the money in her hat, tosses it to Joe in the ring. Harry and Joe fight over the hat while being chased by the bull. Joe finally recovers the money and returns it to Winthrop. The boys are cleared for selling the silver mine stock, but not the oil well in Iowa. Dagmar, however, turns in another bankroll, bilked from Adamson, to settle that charge as well. Harry, Joe, and Dagmar are now free to return to the States.

BACKGROUND

After the success of *Meet Frankenstein*, Abbott and Costello sought to renegotiate their contract with the studio. According to *The New York Times,* Bud and Lou demanded an additional $25,000 per picture or they wouldn't report on *Mexican Hayride.* Universal suspended the team for a week. "In the course of the battle," the *Times* reported, "Costello announced that salary was only a secondary issue, and that their main demand was for better supporting casts in their pictures. 'But,' [Costello] added, 'if the studio is determined to kill us off with bad support, at least they can give us some more money while we last.'

"Costello objected vehemently to the supporting cast scheduled for 'Mexican Hayride,'
which consists of John Hubbard, Luba Malina and Patricia Alphin," the *Times* continued.
Reportedly, Lou wanted Tony Martin, Carmen Miranda and Lucille Ball for the cast. (Bud's
reservations, however, were over the script; he was quoted as saying, "It stinks.") "After a
week's negotiation," the *Times* continued, "he and Bud surrendered, having caused only two
days' delay in the start of production. Officials of the studio insisted that Universal-International
had not given an inch and that the comedians would receive no concessions. According to
Abbott, however, the settlement was a compromise, but he declined to specify what he and
his partner had wrung from the U-I management."

One concession the studio made had nothing to do with the picture. Abbott and Costello
demanded the 16mm rights to their films, and they won. As for *Mexican Hayride,* the only
upgrade we can determine was that Patricia Alphin, originally cast as Montana, was replaced
by Virginia Grey after working three days on the production. Alphin had previously been
replaced by Audrey Young on *Wistful Widow* when she suffered an attack of appendicitis.

THE SCRIPT

Originally a Broadway musical produced by Mike Todd in 1944, *Mexican Hayride* ran for sixteen
months and featured Bobby Clark, June Havoc, and Luba Malina. (Bud and Lou had appeared
on Broadway with Clark in *The Streets of Paris* in 1939.) Universal purchased the screen rights
to *Hayride* specifically for Abbott and Costello in February 1946 for $50,000. Screenwriter
Oscar Brodney delivered his first draft on September 18, 1946. Eighteen months later, Brodney
and John Grant resumed work on the screenplay, with incidental contributions by Sid Fields
and Monte Brice.

The Breen Office cautioned the studio over Dagmar and Humphrey's seduction scene.
"Care will be needed to avoid any sex-suggestive action in this scene on the couch. At no
time should the couple be in a horizontal position. Dagmar's line, 'Let's turn on the generator,'
and Humphrey's line, 'My battery must be overcharged,' are unacceptable and must be
changed."

THE CAST

Virginia Grey (b. 1917) was born in Hollywood, where her father, Ray, was a director, and
her mother, Florence, was one of the first woman film editors. One day at the age of nine,
Virginia was visiting her mother at Universal when she was spotted and tested for the role
of Little Eva in *Uncle Tom's Cabin* (1927). Virginia returned to the screen in the late 1930s as
a contract player at MGM. Her other releases in 1948 were *So This Is New York, Unknown Island,*
and *Jungle Jim.*

Luba Malina, making her film debut, was just about the only aspect carried over from the
original Broadway show.

John Hubbard (b. 1914) had appeared in several Hal Roach comedies, notably *Turnabout*
in 1940. *Hayride* was his first major film after being discharged from the Army. Hubbard later
appeared in two short-lived TV shows, *The Mickey Rooney Show* (1954–55) and *Don't Call Me
Charlie* (1962–63).

Pat Costello (1903–1990) had been Lou's stunt double on the team's earlier features. After
the war, Pat joined the writing staff of the team's radio show, then produced the Abbott and
Costello television series in the 1950s. Pat recalled that Lou insisted that he try acting in films.
Pat kept replying that he was a musician, not an actor. Still, he took the role, but recalled
he was so nervous that he could barely form words.

Fritz Feld (b. 1900), by his own count, has appeared in 422 pictures. He has been a stage
director, screenwriter, and dialogue director. "Working with Abbott and Costello was one of
the biggest thrills of my life," he recalled. "Each time I worked with a big star I got a big
thrill out of it. I worked with Chaplin. I had great admiration for Abbott and Costello. My

Harry Lambert
. . . . Bud Abbott
Joe Bascom/Humphrey
  Fish . . . . . . Lou Costello
Montana . . . . Virginia Grey
Dagmar . . . . . . Luba Malina
David Winthrop
. . . . John Hubbard
Senor Martinez
. . . . . . Pedro de Cordoba
Prof. Ganzmeyer
. . . . Fritz Feld
Ed Mason . . . Tom Powers
Tim Williams . Pat Costello
Gus Adamson
. . . . Frank Fenton
Mariachi Leader
. . . . Chris Pin Martin
Reporter . . . . Sidney Fields
Trio . . Flores Brothers Trio
Indian Woman
. . . . . Argentina Brunetti
Girls . . . . Mary Brewer
        Marjorie L. Carver
              Lucille Casey
                 Toni Castle
          Lorraine Crawford
Mr. Clark . . . . . Eddie Kane
Proprietor . . . Pedro Regas
Mr. Lewis . . Charles Miller
Businessman
. . . . Harry Brown
Second Businessman
. . . . Joe Kirk
Ticket Seller
. . . . Julian Rivero
Artist . . . . Joe Dominguez
Artist's Model
. . . . . . Suzanne Ridgway

177

wife, Virginia Christine, who was Mrs. Olsen, the coffee lady, did two of their TV shows. She came home delighted, because they were so nice." After Lou's death in 1959, Feld nearly teamed with Bud Abbott. "I talked to Bud. I wanted to revive the whole thing with me as a fast-talking Frenchman, and he as the straight man. The idea was great, but it didn't work out."

THE PRODUCTION

Hayride was originally planned for production in 1947. Brodney's first draft dated September 18, 1946 was broken down in two budget estimates—one for black-and-white, and one for Technicolor. The black-and-white version would take some sixty days and cost $1,758,750. The Technicolor version would require seventy days and $2,195,250. Certainly Universal wasn't about to spend such an astronomical sum on *any* production, particularly one for Abbott and Costello. Production was postponed, at least until a realistic budget could be worked out. (One other consideration may have been the fact that an MGM release in 1947, *Fiesta Brava,* similarly featured Esther Williams as a lady bullfighter. In fact, Universal bought footage from this film for use in Virginia Grey's bullfighting sequences.)

Eventually, after rewrites, Robert Arthur pruned the production down to thirty-four days, plus eight days of second unit shooting. A two-acre bull ring was built on the studio's enormous process stage, and a second unit shot long-shots of Costello's comic bullfight with doubles at the famous old Juarez Bull Ring across from the Rio Grande in El Paso. Arthur's budget was now $898,462—one of the highest for an Abbott and Costello feature. It was not Universal's most expensive production of 1948, however; *You Gotta Stay Happy,* with Jimmy Stewart and Joan Fontaine, came in at $1,673,000.

A few weeks before the start of production, producer Robert Arthur had lunch with Lou. Arthur realized that he needed Bud and Lou's complete cooperation to bring *Hayride* in on time and on budget. Everything hinged on the team working a nine-to-six day. Arthur recapped his conversation with Lou in a memo to Ed Muhl:

> [A] matter was raised by Costello which is beyond my control and which I feel should be called to your attention. The following statement by Costello introduced the point at issue: "I intend to make the picture and want to make it as good as possible; but when you're going to finish it, I don't know."
>
> Pointing out to Costello that the picture is budgeted on a maximum 36-day schedule, I inquired as to exactly what he meant. Costello informed me that he was dissatisfied with the results of his negotiations with the studio for a new deal; and therefore felt under no obligation to adhere to anything approaching a nine-to-six working arrangement. Commenting that he intended to get back to the way he worked prior to "The Wistful Widow of Wagon Gap," he stated, "about a quarter to four, you better figure on my leaving, because at four sharp, even if you're in the middle of a set-up, I'm going."
>
> I pointed out to Costello that a four o'clock day would vastly increase the cost of the picture and stated that in my opinion the film should not be made under any such arrangement. He merely reiterated that he would be ready to start the picture June 5 or 8; that he would do the best he can to make it good; but that he intended to quit at four.
>
> Subsequently, I spoke to Bud Abbott on the telephone and reported Costello's viewpoint to him. Abbott replied that he, too, was dissatisfied with their studio situation and also felt that they were no longer bound in good faith to work any harder or longer than they did prior to "The Wistful Widow"—namely, four o'clock.
>
> Although both conversations were on a most friendly basis, I was unable to effect any change in the boys' attitude.

The team had been without Eddie Sherman's services since Lou fired him during *Wistful Widow.* One thing could be said for Eddie—he knew how to negotiate with the studio bosses.

FAR LEFT: Lou's make-up test showing his "tattoos." LEFT: Lou, Bud, and Charles Barton (glasses) run through the scene where Humphrey, using a magician's props, changes water into wine.

Had he been in the loop, the team might have had a better shot at gaining concessions. In any case, having Eddie to run interference certainly would have made Robert Arthur's job easier.

With Bud and Lou intransigent, a third assistant director was assigned to the picture for the sole purpose of documenting Abbott and Costello's behavior on the set. Hindrances, as well as compliances, were duly noted in a virtual minute-by-minute log kept by Charles Bennett. It was the only time the studio so monitored the boys, probably for leverage in any future negotiations with them. After a week observing the production, Bennett summarized,

> After one week of shooting on the picture in no case have I seen what could be called deliberate stalling on the part of Abbott or Costello. As you know, Costello bears the brunt of the work and I must say that he has been very cooperative at all times. While it is true that he is sometimes slow to get ready in make-up and wardrobe in the mornings, he has never been late reporting for his first call. Once he has been made-up and dressed, he is generally prompt in coming on the set when called and in the past two days has remained on the set almost all of the time. The delays that have been caused by his discussing the way a scene should be shot so far have been for the betterment of the picture as a whole.
>
> Late in the afternoon it becomes obvious that he is beginning to tire as his efforts toward comedy become more apparent and while he asks to leave early, I don't believe that much would be accomplished by forcing him to stay until 6 pm. The man is just plain tired out.
>
> The above remarks will also apply to Abbott as he also has been very cooperative so far. Both of them seem to be putting forth a great effort to make it a good picture.

During the first four weeks, Bud and Lou never worked to six pm, and usually left the set between five and five-thirty. Arthur met with the team to discuss the fact that the picture was now running badly behind schedule. In a memo to Morrie Davis, Arthur reported:

> I requested that they cooperate toward eliminating lengthy delays during the day and pointed out that the shooting time allocated to the picture was predicated on a nine-to-six shooting day. Neither would commit himself to working until six but did agree to stay later than in the past where necessary to complete a sequence.
>
> Being Saturday, Costello insisted that they would have to leave by noon [for their children's radio program]. I pointed out that if they would stay until one o'clock, we

could complete the sequence shooting and not have to return to stage 16 at a loss of several hours. . . . Costello refused to stay and he and Abbott left at 12:10.

In this discussion, I pointed out to Costello that he was hardly being consistent after our talk of the previous day. . . .

The following day Lou worked to six twenty-five, while Bud was dismissed at five-thirty. The next few nights, however, Lou and Bud left between four-thirty and five. Arthur confronted the team again:

I informed Costello that I was fed up with pleading with him to stay. I advised him that he was of legal age, had a contract, and certain contractual obligations, and that if he didn't know what those obligations were, he had better consult a lawyer and find out. Costello answered that since we now were getting technical, he had better hang around.

In view of his attitude, Barton shot with Costello only and finished with him at 3:05. After Costello was dismissed, Barton completed the day with Abbott and others of the company.

During the above discussion, Costello reiterated a remark made several times previously. He would try to help us get a good picture, but how long it was going to take us he wouldn't even try to guess. He also stated that he thoroughly disliked Mr. Spitz and Mr. Blumberg and felt that being difficult was a good way to show it.

In the middle of July, the picture lost more time when Bud wrenched his shoulder and missed four days of work. The company was able to shoot around him, but Lou continued to leave around four o'clock. Arthur had another discussion with him:

Today, Costello flatly refused to stay after 4 pm, stating that he was tired. I reminded him again that on numerous occasions he had told me that they had worked on "The Noose Hangs High" until 6:30 and 7:00 night after night. Costello answered that "The Noose" was a picture he wanted to make so he never got tired—and that he probably would never tire on his next outside picture ["Africa Screams"] either.

Toward the end of the month, the production fell further behind when Lou caught a cold, and worked for only half a day on three occasions. Arthur again tried to reason with him:

This morning I pointed out to Costello that virtually all the remaining picture to be shot required him and that every hour lost due to his absence pushed us further behind schedule and was extremely costly.

Costello flippantly suggested that he was open to a deal. For a bonus of $5,000, he would stay late, even nights, and we could then finish the picture sooner than otherwise. I asked what change $5,000 could make in his frequently used plea of weariness, and Costello answered that $5,000 would give him a brand new source of energy. . . . I told him I would not subject the front office to the indignity of even considering such a proposal.

Lou still managed to have some fun on the set. On July 8, 1948, assistant director Charles Bennett reported, "Throughout the day, Costello was playing with a water pistol which at times caused a little delay, but the day ended as the best we have had since the start of the picture as far as page count is concerned." Director of photography Charles Van Enger recalled, "He was squirting everybody with this water pistol. So at lunchtime I went out and bought half a dozen water pistols and handed them out to people on the set. I said, 'When I give you the signal, let him have it.' So after he did his scene, I gave the cue, and we all ran up and let him have it—he was soaking wet! He laughed and laughed."

Robert Arthur recalled a time he was summoned to location. He recalled, "They were shooting out at Calabassas, and I got a call from Joe Kenny that I'd better come out there. We had made the biggest mistake in the world. Automobile telephones had just come in, and we had one in one of the limousines on the set. Lou was using it to place bets on the horses. Nobody could find him because he'd drive up on a hill so the telephone would get better reception. So I went out there and just switched limousines. I told Lou, 'You just couldn't resist the telephone.' He accepted it; no fights.

"A couple of days later, assistant director Joe Kenny called and said Bud wanted to see me. So I went out to Calabassas again, expecting another crisis. Bud had some cracked crab flown in from Philadelphia, and he was inviting me to lunch. Bud, Lou, and I went into Bud's trailer, and Bud's man, Smallwood, fixed lunch. It was all very pleasant, and the conversation went as follows. Bud started to tell us about some woman who had phoned him to use his house for a charity event. He said, 'It was the damndest thing, I couldn't get her off the phone! Every time I started to hang up, she'd say something. She's going to call me back.' And Lou started to laugh. Bud said, 'I don't think it's funny.' And Lou said, 'I couldn't get rid of her either, so I gave her your number and told her you had a bigger house!' Bud said, 'I wish you wouldn't do that. I fact, I'm going to change my phone number.' And Lou said, 'If you're going to change your number, don't bother to give it to me. Then I won't give it out to anybody.' Bud said, 'Okay, that's what I'm going to do.'

"With that, Lou gets up and walks out. A few minutes later, Joe Kenny came in and said, 'What happened? Costello's gone home.' I said, 'Oh, for God's sake. Is there anything we can shoot with Bud?' Then Bud says, 'If he's going home, I'm going.' And he went home, too. There we were, sitting out at Calabassas at one-fifteen with no stars. So I got in the car and drove to Bud's house. I said this is all very silly, and he said, 'I know it is, but I just can't be made a fool of and be out there working when Lou is not there.' So I said, 'If Lou comes back to work, will you come back?' He said 'Of course I will.' So now I go to Lou's house, and he admitted he felt a little silly. But he asked if it was worthwhile to go back out there so late in the day. I said yes, if we can get back by three o'clock. So he said okay. Big crisis. So I got back in the car and I called Bud's house and said Lou's on his way back. They both went back to the set, and everything was fine after that."

Norman Abbott, dialogue director on the film, recalled that Bobby Barber was up to his usual antics. "I remember one day in Calabassas, Bobby Barber was asleep in a chair and Frankie Van and Harry Raven tied Bobby's legs to the chair, shoveled horseshit in front of it, and yelled, 'Bobby on the set right away!' Of course when he got up he fell right into the horseshit. [laughs] Another time, these planes were flying overhead and ruining the shots. So Lou told Bobby, 'Take this red flag, go up on that hill, and wave the flag when you see a plane coming.' So he climbed the hill. You had to use binoculars to see him. But there he was, on top of the hill, waving at planes. It was hysterical."

On August 12, much to Robert Arthur's relief, principal photography on *Mexican Hayride* was finally completed. The production ran some eighteen days over schedule and $133,756 over budget. The final cost was $1,032,218—making it the second most expensive Abbott and Costello film at Universal. But the film became Universal-International's third biggest grosser of 1949, taking in $2.2 million.

BUD AND LOU'S SCENES

There's an inside joke when Joe first catches up with con man Harry Lambert at the bullfight. Joe (Lou) says, "Who told me there was oil in my back yard? Who got me to sell phoney stock to my friends? Who ran away with the money? Who got Mary mad at me? And if you're tired of hearing Who, I got a What for you—on second base!"

Lou's brother Pat plays a detective on the trail of Joe Bascom. Their uncanny resemblance is the subject of a brief routine:

Pat: This guy adds up to Joe Bascom. Joe Bascom is short and dumpy.
Lou: Like you?
Pat: Like me. And he's got a roly-poly face.

Lou: Like you?

Pat: Like me! And he's got short, stumpy legs.

Lou: Like you?

Pat: YEAH, LIKE ME!

Lou: Officer, arrest that man!

One of the early bright spots is provided by Sid Fields as a reporter interviewing Costello. This routine was added to replace one of the show's original production numbers, "Girls, Girls, Girls." In typical style, Sid doesn't give Lou a chance to answer any of his rapid-fire questions: "How do you feel about this tremendous responsibility that's invested in you as the Amigo Americana? You're pretty sure of yourself, aren't you? Wouldn't you say the inter-American relationship as exemplified by your lackadaisical efforts to promote good will could possibly accomplish anything [sic]? Why do you attempt to use polysyllabic conversation when your intelligence quotient is obviously minus nil? You don't mind if I get a word in or two?" "No," Lou replies sarcastically, "you go ahead. I'm getting hoarse." Finally, Sid reprimands Lou, "Remember, in the future, when a reporter comes in and asks you for an interview, *don't talk so much!*"

In another classic bit, Bud notices the initials "J. B." on Lou's clothing. Since Lou is now supposed to be Humphrey Fish and not Joe Bascom, Bud worries that the monograms will give him away. So Bud systematically tears off layer after layer of Lou's clothing until Costello is left standing in his underwear! In the film the sequence ends before Bud can tear the undershirt off Lou, revealing "J. Bascom" tatooed on his chest! Later, in another cut scene, Joe has camouflaged the tattoo by drawing a line through it and lettering in "Humphrey Fish."

A more familiar Abbott and Costello turn is the "Silver Ore" routine. Bud admires some native jewelry. "Just think," he says, "when it came out of the ground, it was nothing but crude hunks of silver ore." "Silver or what?" Lou wants to know. "Silver ore! That's the way they find silver," Bud explains. "It's been lying in the ground for thousands of years. When they dig it up, they smelt it." Lou reacts. "If it's a thousand years old, *no wonder* they smelt it." Bud continues, "Then after it's melted down, it's made into these ornaments by a smith." Lou asks, "Couldn't they be made by a Jones?" "Certainly," affirms Bud, "but Jones would have to be a smith." Incredibly, this scene required thirty-one takes. Many were ruined by noise from a low-flying airplane. But in other instances, Bud himself got mixed up by the routine!

The bullfight was assembled from location footage shot earlier in the production, then matched using a mechanical bull's head and bulls brought onto the studio's process stage. The script includes a lot of technical cues for various shots (e.g., traveling matte, process, optical printer, step print, mechanical bull, etc.). Lou's bits of business and David Horsley's special effects combine to keep the sequence consistently amusing. For the final scene in the sequence, stuntman Irving Gregg was butted in the rear by a mechanical bull's head and flown into the stands on wires.

DELETIONS AND ADDITIONS

Universal utilized none of the music from the original Broadway show, and although Walter Scharf and Jack Brooks were given the musical chores, lots of stock music was taken from other U-I features, particularly Leith Steven's score for *Feudin', Fussin' and A-Fightin'* (1948). Virginia Grey and John Hubbard performed Cole Porter's "I Love You," during the banquet sequence, only to have it cut from the film. Robert Arthur explained, "We tried to use some of the numbers from the show. There was some awfully good music that came out of *Mexican Hayride*. But you knew at the preview the audience was there to laugh at Abbott and Costello. They didn't want the music."

The film's running gag—Joe breaking into a dance every time he hears the samba—was not in the final shooting script. It was added during production.

Lou and the crew duel with water pistols during the banquet scene.

REVIEWS

The New York Times: " 'Mexican Hayride' is an obvious and weary little farce, bearing slight (if any) resemblance to the stage musical on which it is 'based.' Lou is a sorry substitution for Bobby Clark in the leading role. He goes through his stumbling encounters like a man thoroughly bored with his work. It's too bad that the bull doesn't hoist him any farther than it does with that final butt."

Los Angeles Daily News: "The film was taken—quite freely taken—from the musical play by Herbert and Dorothy Fields and Cole Porter. . . . What remains is a vehicle which may be stopped at any point to give the two comics a chance to be Abbott and Costello. You get three minutes of story, then you get five minutes of vaudeville routine, then back to the story, and so on. Things get quite jumpy and fidgety before long. . . . Costello has a genuinely funny sequence in a bullring and makes truly violent love to actress Luba Malina, a lady who sings one number well and looks remarkably attractive for the years she must be carrying. Funniest thing in the film, we thought, was tubby little Costello involuntarily going into a samba every time somebody played the appropriate music. . . . Fritz Feld stole the sequence in which he played a speech expert. . . ."

New York Star: "Arrayed against the hardy Abbott and Costello comedy formula in 'Mexican Hayride' is ruthless economy of production budget, imagination, and time. Beset by forces so unsympathetic to their art, Abbott and Costello can only survive, they can't win. On the stage, the plot of 'Mexican Hayride' was properly covered over by musical comedy extravaganza. It was the diffident excuse to change lavish scenes. Stripped of its kindly trappings by the movie, it moves into the foreground a rickety but dogged little vehicle."

New York Sun: "The team still indulges in verbal sparring, using some of the most dreadful and most aged puns in the English language. The comics have forgotten none of their vaudeville routines. They dash through the scenes with bounce and verve, right in the old variety tradition. That at least keeps the show going. But it is a dull show for grown-ups. It is the little ones, the below-10 year olds, who will laugh the loudest at 'Mexican Hayride.' "

Film Bulletin: "It doesn't have the juvenile appeal of some of its predecessors; there's a lot of amatory scrimmaging and some of the gags weren't meant for the kiddies. But when Lou gets going with his frenetic slapstickery, his fans will love it and even the more sophisticated may find themselves having a good time . . . Lou is a riot. In a variety of disguises, he's an old crone selling super-hot tortillas, a frustrated trombonist, a dashing toreador. His samba is marvelously ungraceful, he throws the bull—and vice versa."

POSTSCRIPT

That fall, the boys went to Nassour Studios to make "Don't Bring 'Em Back Alive," a.k.a. *Africa Screams,* as one of their outside pictures. Universal permitted the team to use most of their regular crew, including director Charles Barton.

AFRICA SCREAMS

Earliest Draft:
October 1948 (?)

Production Start:
November 10, 1948

Production End:
December 22, 1948

Copyright Date:
May 27, 1949

Released: May 4, 1949

Running Time:
79 minutes

Reissued: April 15, 1953
(with the Marx
Brothers' *Love Happy*)

Directed By:
Charles T. Barton

Produced By:
Edward Nassour

Original Screenplay By:
Earl Baldwin

Associate Producer:
David S. Garber

Music: Walter Schuman

Director of Photography:
Charles Van Enger

Film Editor: Frank Gross

Art Direction: Lou Creber

Set Decorations:
Ray Robinson

Special Effects: Carl Lee

Production Manager:
Joe C. Gilpin

SYNOPSIS

Diana Emerson, looking for a copy of the book *Dark Safari* by famed explorer Cuddleford, inquires in the book department of Klopper's Department store. When Diana declares that she will pay up to $2,500 for a map in the book, Buzz passes Stanley off as a great explorer who accompanied Cuddleford on his expedition. Stanley claims he can reproduce the map, and Diana asks the boys to meet her at her house that night. Diana's henchmen include Harry, her whiny butler; Boots Wilson and Grappler McCoy, two behemoths; and a pitifully nearsighted gunman named Gunner. When Buzz overhears Diana offer Clyde Beatty $20,000 to lead the expedition, he realizes that the map is worth far more than he imagined.

Once in Africa, Buzz learns the true goal of the safari—to locate a Ubangi tribe with an immense fortune in uncut diamonds. Buzz plans to negotiate a better deal with Diana, but discovers to his dismay that the only map Stanley can draw leads to Klopper's Department store! The boys attempt to bluff their way through and continue on the expedition. The group finally stumbles upon the Ubangi tribe, and the chief offers the diamonds to Diana in exchange for Stanley, who he thinks will make a sumptuous meal. While the cannibals chase after Stanley, Buzz gets hold of the diamonds and buries them for safekeeping. The tribe is finally frightened off Stanley's trail by the orangutan gargantua. Meanwhile, a gorilla Stanley rescued earlier has dug up the diamonds. When the scene shifts back to the States, we discover that Stanley now owns his own department store in partnership with the grateful gorilla, and Buzz is employed as an elevator operator.

BACKGROUND

Africa Screams may have had its roots in August, 1947, when Lou, on the way home from a story conference for *The Noose Hangs High,* spotted a dog chasing a cat down an alley. According to a reporter from *Collier's* who was with him, Lou mused, "Hey, how about a jungle picture called 'Bring 'Em Back Dead,' with Frank Buck? Have we got animal jokes!"

With the team now producing one independent feature per year, the boys sought a deal with an outside studio. Norman Abbott recalled, "Bud and Lou were friends with David Garber, who was a studio manager at Universal. He went to work for the Nassour Brothers and made a deal with Bud and Lou to do *Africa Screams* there." Bud and Lou were to get straight salary *plus* 60 percent of the film's profits. Garber also arranged for the loan out of many of the team's regular crew from Universal, including cinematographer Charles Van Enger and assistant director Joe Kenny.

The Nassours, Edward and William, had produced industrial films for years. In fact in 1947 they produced a short, *10,000 Kids and a Cop,* that helped publicize the Lou Costello Jr. Youth Center. *Africa Screams* would be the brothers' first major production. (Their other releases were *Mrs. Mike* [1949] with Dick Powell, and *Tripoli* [1950], with Maureen O'Hara.) Edward was the producer, and William, board chairman of the Hollywood State Bank, the financier. Nassour Studios, spread over a five acre lot at the corner of Sunset Boulevard and Van Ness Avenue, is now the home of the Fox television affiliate in Los Angeles.

Dialogue Director:
  Norman Abbott

Assistant Director:
  Joe Kenny

Buzz Johnson
  . . . . Bud Abbott
Stanley Livington
  . . . . Lou Costello
Diana Emerson
  . . . . Hillary Brooke
Grappler McCoy
  . . . . Max Baer
Boots Wilson
  . . . . Buddy Baer
Clyde Beatty . . . . . Himself
Frank Buck . . . . . . Himself
Gunner . . Shemp Howard
Harry . . . . Joe Besser
Bobo . . . . Burton Wenland
Gorilla . . . Charles Gemorra

THE SCRIPT

The title of the film is a takeoff on the 1930 documentary, *Africa Speaks* (1930). Earl Baldwin, who had written the first draft of the team's MGM feature *Lost in a Harem*, developed the screenplay, and Norman Abbott suggested that two young writers on the team's ABC radio program, Leonard Stern and Martin Ragaway, be brought in to punch up the script. "Norman was our good friend and strongest advocate," Leonard Stern recalled. "Lou thought our gags were terribly funny, and we were adopted as the bright young people needed to infuse something new into their movies. John Grant was there, as a sort of paternal figure. He represented the history of Abbott and Costello and a lot of burlesque, and we were impressed with John. He was sort of incongruous with his background. He was a tall, elegant man. We didn't see John much, but we knew of his presence."

The Breen Office was concerned with the producers' plan to use stock footage from an earlier Clyde Beatty picture. The film was notorious for a brutal fight sequence between two lions. David Garber assured Breen that this particular sequence would not be used in *Africa Screams*. Breen then had another serious concern. He wrote to Garber, "While the basic story seems acceptable under the provisions of the Production Code, the present version contains one very important problem which will have to be rectified before a picture based on this material could be approved by us. We refer to those instances in your story in which the comedy is based upon, or bordering upon, the idea that the animals are falling in love with Stanley. Such a suggestion, *in any form,* would cause serious, unfavorable reactions generally, as well as being a Code violation. We direct your attention to. . . . Page 75, where Leota [the female gorilla] falls for Stanley. This element reappears several times during the story, notably on the next page, pages 113, 131, 132 and, importantly, in the tag."

The solution was simple: the female gorilla was changed to a male gorilla. In his book, *Movies Are Better Than Ever,* Andrew Dowdy cited the incident, and noted, "Presumably, the alteration cleaned up the context of the gag, but writers along the Strip were quick to spread the word that this year gay gorillas were in with censors."

THE CAST

Hillary Brooke (b. 1914) had been a model in New York before migrating to Hollywood in the late 1930s. After small roles in films such as *The Philadelphia Story* (1940) and *Dr. Jekyll and*

185

Mr. Hyde (1941), Hillary appeared in *Jane Eyre* (1944) and *Ministry of Fear* (1944). One of her most memorable performances was in the Sherlock Holmes mystery *The Woman in Green* (1945), one of three Holmes films she did. Hillary soon edged into comedies, playing opposite Bob Hope and Bing Crosby in *Road to Utopia* (1945); Hope in *Monsieur Beaucaire* (1946); and Red Skelton in *The Fuller Brush Man* (1948). "I was a tall blonde," Hillary explained, "and comedians love to work with tall blondes."

Nothing, however, prepared Hillary for *Africa Screams* with Bud and Lou. "My agent was Ed Henry, with the Eddie Sherman Agency. After the first day, I called him up and said, 'I can't do it, Ed. I can't keep up with them. I'm a nervous wreck. I never get a cue!' Ed said, 'Stay with it, Hillary, you're going to have a wonderful time.' And of course he was absolutely right. I loved working with Abbott and Costello. Lou and I had a very unusual, wonderful friendship. We both really *liked* one another. I think he was without a doubt the most spontaneous ad-libber in the business. What it did was, it made you *aware*—you had to *listen*. Because you never knew what they were going to do. He was one of the funniest men I ever worked with. He taught me more about comedy than anyone I ever worked with. I was not a comedienne by any means, but he taught me timing and how to handle a joke. It was so instinctive with him. And I must say that Bud was one of the greatest straight men that ever existed, and he never got credit for it. His timing was impeccable. The secret was, you just had to know how to work with them. Once you mastered that, it was a ball! It was the type of experience where you couldn't wait to get back on the set the following morning and you never wanted to leave at night. You would laugh so much, your cheeks would ache! I believe that every actor and actress should be allowed to do at least one Abbott and Costello film. It's a shame they're both gone now." The secret, Hillary discovered, was to wait for Lou to stop talking, then get her lines in as best she could. When Hillary worked with Bud and Lou again in *Abbott and Costello Meet Captain Kidd,* she was able to pass her experience along to none other than Charles Laughton. Today she is fondly remembered as the leading lady on the Abbott and Costello TV series.

Max Baer (1909–1959) made his film debut opposite Myrna Loy and Otto Kruger in 1933's *The Prizefighter and the Lady*. In 1934, Baer KO'd Primo Carnera to become the World Heavyweight Champion, then lost the title in 1935 to Jimmy Braddock. After retiring from the ring in 1940, Baer appeared in several films, including a whimsical western, *Skipalong Rosenbloom* (1951) with Hillary Brooke. Max also turned up in an episode of Bud and Lou's TV series. His son, Max Baer, Jr., played Jethro on TV's *The Beverly Hillbillies*.

Buddy Baer (b. 1915), Max's "little" brother, was twice heavyweight boxing champion of Ireland, knocking out Jack Doyle in 1935 and Michael Patrick Barry in 1936, and nearly became the world heavyweight champion. *Africa Screams* marked his film debut, and he later appeared with Bud and Lou as the Giant in *Jack and the Beanstalk*.

Clyde Beatty (1903–1965) was a popular circus star, famous for his daring lion-taming act. He had been hospitalized over thirty times due to mishaps during his performances. Beatty must have shared some great stories with Bud, who had been born, as the saying goes, under a circus tent.

Frank Buck (1888–1950), a noted explorer, had produced and starred in several adventure films in the 1930s, including *Bring 'Em Back Alive* (1932), *Wild Cargo* (1934), and *Fang and Claw* (1935). After filming *Africa Screams,* Buck planned his first post-war safari to Africa to capture a rare white rhinoceros.

Shemp Howard (1900–1955) rejoined the Three Stooges in 1946 after the serious illness of his brother, Curly Howard. Shemp had been a contract player at Universal in the 1940s and livened up several comedies including *The Bank Dick, Hellzapoppin', and Crazy House*. A favorite of Abbott and Costello's, Shemp appeared in *Buck Privates, In the Navy, Hold That Ghost,* and *It Ain't Hay* with the team.

Joe Besser (1907–1988) was another favorite of Bud and Lou's, and a big fan of the team. "They were the greatest comedy team," Joe told Chris Costello in 1977. "The only regret I

TOP: As usual, Lou breaks up Hillary Brooke, Joe Besser, and other cast members. TOP CENTER: At Nassour Studio's Stage 4. TOP LEFT: One of the dozens of pies finds its final resting place with Shemp Howard and Bobby Barber.

have today is that I was not in burlesque. I had offers, but I was doing so well in vaudeville, I said why do I want to go into burlesque? I never realized the training it gave you. Every week, new jokes and new scenes were thrown at you, and you learned them. It was the greatest schooling in show business. That's the background Bud and Lou had." Besser first met Lou in the mid-1920s, when Joe played the Lyric Theater in Paterson. "Lou used to come backstage and spend time with me. This was before he was in show business. He liked my work and I liked him right off the bat. Then the years passed by, and I didn't see him again until I played the Oriental Theater in Chicago. Somebody said, 'Hey, Joe, there's a comedian over at the burlesque show who looks just like you. His name is Lou Costello.' I went to see him, and it was such a happy reunion. That's how we used to run into each other—on and off through the years. We didn't become very close until I moved out to Hollywood." Joe had appeared in vaudeville and on Broadway before making his film debut in the 1938 short, *Cuckoorancho.* Ultimately he appeared in over sixty shorts and features, including *Hey, Rookie* (1944) for director Charles Barton.

In 1951, Besser joined Hillary Brooke in the cast of the Abbott and Costello television show as the malevolent brat, Stinky. Besser was even more prolific on television, appearing on over 250 programs, cartoons, and commercials. In 1955, after Shemp's death, Joe, who was then under contract to Columbia, became the third Stooge for sixteen shorts. He was later replaced by Joe DeRita. Besser was particularly proud to be on hand when the Stooges received their star on the Hollywood Walk of Fame in 1983.

The July 28, 1948 issue of *Variety* carried a blurb that mentioned Spike Jones and his zany band would be included in *Africa Screams.*

THE PRODUCTION

Production on *Africa Screams* was pared down to just sixteen days, with a budget probably below $500,000. The major expense (aside from Bud and Lou's salary) was re-creating the Ubangi River on Stage 4. Two hundred thousand gallons of water—mixed with condensed milk for photographic purposes—filled the enormous soundstage to a depth of three feet. An eleven-foot synthetic crocodile, worked by hydraulics and nicknamed Ernest, was created for the production.

Despite the lush tropical setting and notable cast, *Africa Screams* may be best remembered as the picture on which the team's legendary pie fights and practical jokes reached their zenith. Bobby Barber stopped off every morning and picked up a dozen or more pies. According to Charles Barton, the "pie budget" on *Africa* exceeded $3,500! No doubt the fact that the boys had surrounded themselves with friends and family contributed to the lunacy. Norman Abbott and Blake Edwards served as dialogue directors, while Bud's niece Betty worked as script supervisor. Betty has been the script supervisor on Blake Edwards' films for many years.

Writer Martin Ragaway recalled visiting the set several times. "It was a big, big thrill for Len and me to be on the set. After all, this was the movies! There seemed to be a friendly feud between the Abbotts and the Costellos. Different people on the set had been enlisted on different sides. Somebody would blow a whistle and suddenly, on this jungle set, people began throwing pies at one another. There was a pie war! They weren't big pies. They were just big enough to get a grip on—great for throwing. I remember saying to myself, well, this is how pictures are made. Apparently they had to have something to relieve the tension, and this was it. About three or four years later, I happened to stop in this little bakery in the Valley, and there in the bakery was this large picture of Lou Costello, autographed 'To my baker.' I said to the owner, 'Do you bake for Mr. Costello?' And he said, 'Oh, yes. In fact he loves our stuff so much, he takes it to the studio with him. Do you know Mr. Costello?' I said, 'No, no.' [laughs] I didn't have the heart to tell him how his pies were being used!"

Hillary Brooke appreciated the practical jokes and the pie fights. "I'm a laugher. I love comedy and I love funny people. Anytime there was a practical joke going, that was for me. Of course they loved to get Max and Buddy, who were two of the nicest, dearest men. My husband, Ray Klune, was on the other side in the business as the general manager at MGM. He thought these antics were dreadful. But it's very important when you're dealing in comedy to keep up that peak of energy. It was all very necessary for Lou."

Hillary continued, "Shemp was terrified of water. In one scene, he's supposed to be sitting on top of all the luggage on one of the rafts. [Look closely at the scene and you can actually see Shemp fidget.] As soon as we finished the scene, we broke for lunch. We left him sitting there on top of the raft because we knew he hated water. When we finally got him down, he ran to the bathroom!

"One thing they didn't dare do was throw pies at me because of my costumes. But they were all waiting for me after the very last shot! [laughs] And I knew it. So when I finished the shot, I turned around and ran, and they chased me. My dressing room was outside the set, and I ran into my dressing room and closed the door. Lou came out of the stage with a pie in his hand, followed by the whole crew. They were all waiting for Hillary to get it. Well, there were two small windows in the back of the dressing room. I crawled out one window and circled back behind the whole crowd of people. And when Lou finally opened the door, there was no one inside. They didn't know where I had gone. And I called out, 'Lou, I'm here!' He turned around and it was the first time I ever saw Lou speechless. They couldn't believe I'd gotten out of that little window. But I was determined to get out. Then of course they turned around and chased me around the lot. They finally got some on my shoulder."

Not everyone was amused. Producer Eddie Nassour, who had a lot of his own money tied up in the picture, was particularly annoyed. He ordered his staff to keep an eye on the production and report any monkeyshines directly to him. Eddie would have a fit each new day the production ran over. "It went on and on and on," Hillary said. "Of course we were playing and having fun. Meanwhile the budget was getting bigger and bigger. Finally Lou put pictures of Eddie Nassour all around the set. They had one picture of him before we started shooting, and then they made another one up with a thin face and his mouth turned down. [laughs] They said, 'This is the way he looks after four weeks on the picture!' We started calling the picture 'Nassour Screams.'"

Mel Bassett worked for Nassour for thirty-five years. "Eddie was basically a nice guy. But his brother used to egg him on a bit, and Donald Crisp instigated a lot of the friction between Lou and Eddie. Donald controlled the financing and was very tight with the buck. Eddie would tell him, 'Just one more day, Don. Just one.'"

According to Charles Van Enger, however, Nassour reached the breaking point. "Eddie Nassour had the studio painted and charged it to our production. Lou refused to pay it. They had a hell of a fight. Eddie came down to the set with a gun, looking to kill Lou. Really! I took the gun away from him." (Eddie Nassour died in 1962, an apparent suicide.)

BUD AND LOU'S SCENES

Lou's character, Stanley, is deathly afraid of animals. In one scene, Buzz picks up a lion cub.

"Now don't get excited," Buzz says to the petrified Stanley. "This little cat was raised on milk." "So was I," cracks Stanley, "but I eat meat now!"

Joe Besser is another naturally funny comedian. His "sissy" character is one of the funniest things in the film. Besser also re-created one gag he made famous in the Broadway show *Sons O' Fun* with Olsen and Johnson. As Buzz berates Stanley for getting them into this mess, Harry flits in and out of the tent to fill a little cup with water. He does this enough times to finally annoy Buzz. "Where you going with that water?" Buzz snaps. Harry whines, "It's not for me, my tent is on f-i-r-e!!"

After Stanley inadvertently rescues a gorilla from a trap, the boys sit down to have lunch with Frank Buck. The grateful gorilla peers out through the jungle to watch Stanley, who becomes so frightened that he cannot eat or form words. Meanwhile, Buzz and Frank Buck enjoy their repast, totally unaware of the danger. Costello once again proves that he is the master at expressing sputtering fear.

Bud and Lou reprised their lion skin sketch, which had appeared in another form in *The Naughty Nineties*. Buzz tries to bolster Stanley's image as a fearless hunter by putting on a lion skin and letting Stanley "tame" him in front of Diana and her henchmen. Of course, Stanley mistakes a real lion for his partner, and fearlessly bullies the lion into a cage and locks himself in. Stanley is impressed by the authenticity of Buzz's performance. "Hey, Buzz, I gotta tell you, you walked into this cage like a real lion. You even hopped around like a real lion. You wanna know something else? You even *smell* like a real lion," he whispers. (This sequence is achieved quite effectively with better-than-average rear screen projection and mattes created by the special effects department at Universal.) Buzz finally appears outside the cage and urges Stanley to escape. Stanley begins to chuckle over their ruse. "Hey, Buzz—did we fool them! I wish you could have seen their faces when they saw you in here. Now go away before you queer it. They don't know you're inside the lion skin!" In a marvelously delayed take, Stanley suddenly realizes his predicament, and his laughs seemlessly turn to sobs.

Stanley manages to escape and run into the jungle, where he overhears Buzz lamenting the loss of his little pal. In an improved version of a scene first played in *Abbott and Costello in Hollywood*, Buzz chastises himself for mistreating Stanley, and Stanley joins in:

Buzz (sobbing): Oh Stanley, it's all my fault. Don't blame anyone else but me. How was I to know that a real lion would go into the cage?
Stanley sits down and tries to comfort Buzz, who's too upset to notice him.
Buzz (oblivious): Aw, stop it. I just lost the best friend I ever had. Oh, if he were only here! A kid who never did a bit of harm to anyone—
Stanley: He was a nice boy.
Buzz: But I never appreciated it until now.
Stanley: No, you didn't. You was mean to him all the time.
Buzz (sobbing more): Now it's too late; he's gone. Oh, the way I used to send him into things! I wouldn't send my worst enemy out to do the things I taught him to do. The way I used to cheat him—
Stanley (also sobbing now): You used to slap that poor kid all over the place.
Buzz:—I used to cheat him—
Stanley: That kid never did nothin' to nobody.
Buzz: Oh, if he were only here. I feel like jumping off a cliff. But no—I haven't got the nerve. If he was only here to tell me what to do. *(To Heaven:)* Stanley, what should I do?! *(Suddenly:)* I know what I'll do. It's that lion, the one that got him! I'll spend the rest of my days right here in this forest. I'll get that lion if it's the last thing I do. *(Mounting excitement:)* I'll spend the rest of my life right here in this forest! I—
Stanley: You don't have to—
Buzz (sharply): Don't tell me what to do. *(finally notices Stanley)* Stanley! *(Earnestly)* Stanley, it's really you. You're all there? The lion didn't hurt you? It's really you, Stanley?
Stanley: Whaddaya think I am, a mirage or somethin'?

Buzz: You're no mirage?

Stanley: No!

Buzz: You're real?

Stanley: Sure!

Buzz (instantly): You double crosser! *(He slaps him, knocking him off the log.)*

Bud's performance here is outstanding. This soliloquy is a long way from the verbal blitz of "Mustard" and the like, yet Bud's performance is just as convincing. He acts so distraught and incoherent that it's totally plausible he wouldn't notice Lou for the longest time. It's also funny to watch Lou chime in and help Bud berate himself. The scene further underscores the essence of the Abbott and Costello on-screen relationship, which is that of a parent/guardian and child. Just like a parent, Bud is upset when he thinks Lou, the child, is hurt, but also furious with him for making him worry.

REVIEWS

Los Angeles Daily News: "[A] movie considerably better than the stuff they've been turning out in recent years. Costello seems to have remembered he is a pantomimist of some talent and the story points are offered more subtly than is usual by this team. . . . However, the two comedians still hammer home their gag sequences with the force of a 10-pound double jack. The picture is really one long sequence of what might be called the "delayed action" gag, and this facet of the thing does get tiresome. By delayed action gag is meant the type wherein it takes Costello five minutes to realize that it is a real, live lion he is sitting with. . . . The audience . . . laughed so hard it was difficult to hear the dialogue, which must mean the picture satisfies Abbott and Costello fans."

Cue: "In addition to Abbott and Costello—who amble amiably through long-familiar comedy routines—this low-grade burlesque of a looney safari in Africa has little to boast of, other than a novel supporting cast. . . . If you've been making a point of avoiding these Abbott and Costello comedies, you'd do well to continue the practice. If you haven't, you know what to expect."

Los Angeles Examiner: "Far and away the funniest picture the boys have made in years. . . . The two star comedians could not show to better advantage. Costello has a frantic scene with a lion that clocks as one of the longest sustained laughs ever filmed, and Bud gets his inning in a sequence in which he pretends to be a crazed diamond hunter. . . . Charles Barton had a hodge podge of ideas to work with, but he ties them all together in one whale of a job of fast-paced direction."

Hollywood Reporter: "Charles Barton, an old hand at pacing the Abbott and Costello antics, accomplishes his usual light-hearted directorial job. He keeps the action humming and the laughs constant. . . . Costello milks the laughs for all they're worth and really does a terrific job in that scene with the king of beasts. . . . Joe Besser's mincey comedy style is a show in itself. Abbott and Costello do themselves no harm by sharing the laugh spotlight."

The New York Times: "Abbott and Costello are remarkable fellows, indeed. With each picture they seem to become more silly and less funny. . . . [R]oly-poly Lou runs through his familiar routines. He is pathetically scared and frustrated and blusteringly brave, but only occasionally amusing, for every gag is put through the wringer at least twice."

POSTSCRIPT

In November 1950, Bud and Lou filed suit against the Nassours, alleging that some of the costs claimed by the producers were fictitious. These overcharges were estimated at $250,000. The Nassours denied that they had added excessive and unreasonable charges to the film and asserted that any excess in the cost of the picture was attributable to Costello's own conduct. The suit was eventually settled, to no one's satisfaction.

ABBOTT AND COSTELLO MEET THE KILLER, BORIS KARLOFF

SYNOPSIS

Famed criminal attorney Amos Strickland checks into the Lost Caverns Resort Hotel, where Freddie Phillips, an inept bellboy, later discovers the lawyer murdered in his room. The house detective, Casey Edwards, begins an investigation to clear Freddie, but Inspector Wellman and his assistant, Sergeant Stone, order Freddie held. Strickland was about to publish his memoirs, which would compromise seven of his former clients—Swami Talpur, Angela Gordon, T. Hanley Brooks, Mrs. Hargreave, Mike Relia, Mrs. Grimsby, and Lawrence Crandall. All of them have come to the resort, and all are under suspicion. At a meeting, they decide that their pasts must remain secret and that Freddie must be made the fall guy. Angela attempts to charm Freddie into signing a confession, and Swami Talpur tries to hypnotize him into committing suicide, but both fail.

Casey, Wellman, and Freddie plot to let the other suspects know that Freddie found a blood-stained handkerchief at the scene of the murder. The real killer, they reason, will go to any lengths to get it. After Freddie is nearly killed in a steam cabinet, he rigs several booby traps in his room. A mysterious voice instructs Freddie to bring the handkerchief to the resort's Lost Cavern, where Freddie nearly falls into a bottomless pit. A masked figure offers to save him in exchange for the handkerchief, but when Freddie inadvertently reveals that it is in his room, the cloaked figure leaves him in danger of being drowned. Wellman and Stone rescue Freddie and race back to the hotel. As the remaining suspects gather, Stone returns with a pair of mud-stained shoes belonging to Melton, the hotel manager, proving that he was the masked figure in the caverns. He and Gregory Milford, Strickland's secretary, had entered into a scheme to blackmail Strickland's former clients. Trapped, Melton pulls a gun and attempts to make his escape through a window when one of Freddie's booby traps knocks him out.

BACKGROUND

Robert Arthur explained, "Lou always wanted to do a good detective film. But I could never get a real good script for him."

Earliest Draft:
August 30, 1946

Production Start:
February 10, 1949

Production End:
March 26, 1949

Copyright Date:
September 8, 1949

Released:
August 22, 1949

Running Time:
82 minutes

Reissued: March 23, 1956
(with *Abbott and Costello Meet Frankenstein*)

Directed By:
Charles T. Barton

Produced By:
Robert Arthur

Screenplay By:
Hugh Wedlock, Jr.,
Howard Snyder, and
John Grant

Original Story By:
Hugh Wedlock, Jr.
and Howard Snyder

Director of Photography:
Charles Van Enger

Art Direction:
Bernard Herzbrun and
Richard H. Riedel

Set Decorations:
Russell A. Gausman
and Oliver Emert

Music:
Milton Schwarzwald

Film Editor:
Edward Curtiss

Sound: Leslie I. Carey and
Robert Pritchard

THE SCRIPT

The original treatment submitted by Hugh Wedock, Jr., and Howard Snyder was conceived as a potential vehicle for Bob Hope. Titled "Easy Does It," it was the story of radio and screen star "Easy" Davis, who is so overworked that he is on the verge of a nervous breakdown. He plans an extended vacation, but Amos Strickland, the lawyer for his radio show's sponsor, insists that Easy continue his weekly broadcasts. Easy's agent suggests broadcasting the show from a wonderful spa called Arrowhead Springs. That way, Easy can get his rest and keep the sponsors happy. But when Easy discovers Strickland murdered in his suite at the hotel, Easy becomes the prime suspect. The rest is very close to *Meet the Killer*.

After Universal bought the story in 1946, Wedock and Snyder began reworking it for Abbott and Costello, with the title revised to "Abbott and Costello Meet the Killers." Oscar Brodney also contributed to the screenplay, without credit. Curiously, Boris Karloff's character in the final shooting script (dated December 12, 1948), was originally a woman named Madame Switzer. Karloff was signed on February 5, 1949, to give the picture a name co-star and further capitalize on his association with the Frankenstein monster.

The Breen Office was naturally quite concerned with the black humor of the script. "With regards to the considerable amount of business concerning the corpses, you will be aware of the potential censor board problems. It has been our experience that the political censor boards are quite sensitive to any gruesomeness involving the bodies of dead people, and we fear that unless this business is handled with the greatest of restraint, and as much as possible by suggestion, it may be subject to wholesale deletions. We believe it will be well worth your while to give this matter very careful consideration."

The warning proved prophetic. Local boards in Australia and New Zealand removed virtually every scene that contained a corpse—including the card game—and trimmed the cavern sequence "to decrease tension"! But even more remarkable than this was the fact that the film was *banned* in Denmark because of the card-playing scene with the corpses. Imagine, an Abbott and Costello film being banned in Denmark.

THE CAST

Boris Karloff (1887–1969) appeared in sixteen films in 1931, but only one of them is remembered today: *Frankenstein*. Although he fought against being typecast, he admitted, "The monster was the best friend I ever had." He went on to appear in dozens of horror films, including *The Mummy* (1932), *The Bride of Frankenstein* (1935), *The Black Room* (1935), *The Raven* (1935), *Son of Frankenstein* (1939), *Black Friday* (1940), *House of Frankenstein* (1944), and *The Body Snatcher* (1945). Between films, Karloff returned to the stage, most memorably in *Arsenic and Old Lace* in 1941, as well as *The Linden Tree* in 1948. Karloff also appeared in *The Secret Life of Walter Mitty, Dick Tracy Meets Gruesome,* and as an Indian chief in both *Unconquered* (1947) and *Tap Roots* (1948). In 1949 he found himself in a dreadful play, *The Shop at Sly Corner,* when he was offered a role in *Meet the Killer*. In a later interview, Karloff said of the film, "Bud and Lou are wonderful chaps to work with, but we've all got to work, don't we. So the less said about this film, the better." The following year, he returned to Broadway to portray Captain Hook in *Peter Pan*. The show was a big hit, and ran for 321 consecutive performances.

Lenore Aubert (b. 1918) returned for her second picture with the boys. In an interview in 1987, Lenore explained, "Lou—he was so funny—he wanted me again. He told them, 'We like Lenore, we want her in the next film, too.' But the studio said, 'What are you trying to do here? Turn this into a *trio?*'"

Alan Mowbray (1896–1969) frequently turned up in thrillers or sophisticated comedies. He had appeared in *My Man Godfrey* (1936) and *Topper* (1937), as well as *Terror by Night* (1946) and *My Darling Clementine* (1946). He twice portrayed George Washington—first in *Alexander Hamilton* (1931) and again in *Where Do We Go From Here?* (1945).

Roland Winters (1904–1990) had recently begun playing Charlie Chan in a series of features

192

at Monogram. In 1965, Winters was featured on the Smothers Brothers sitcom as Dick's boss, Mr. Costello.

THE PRODUCTION

Universal-International had spent far too much on *Mexican Hayride* to make much of a profit, so *Meet the Killer* was scaled back appropriately. Robert Arthur's initial budget was only $685,800, of which Bud and Lou were paid $113,750 (plus their usual incentive deal for a share of the profits). Boris Karloff received $20,000 for his nominal role, while Alan Mowbray, the real killer, was paid $5,000.

When Harold Swisher, motion picture editor for United Press, visited the set, he found the mood as somber as the film itself:

> Our reporter found Costello sitting quietly by himself. Lou's round face was long, for a change. He was unsmiling as he talked about the Lou Costello Jr. Youth Foundation, and the $80,000 he and Bud must raise to pay off the mortgage. If they don't come through, the building and three-acre property will be sold.
>
> The comedians are trying to arrange a title match in Los Angeles between lightweight champion Ike Williams and challenger Enrique Bolanos. Prospects are bright that the bout will come off in May, but there's still a possibility that it will fall through.
>
> "And if it does," said Lou, "we can say goodbye to the Foundation. Should the mortgage be foreclosed, 10,000 needy kids will be the losers."
>
> Abbott and Costello have $260,000 of their own money in the project to date. But they can't wipe out the mortgage from their own pockets. If the debt is met, they are willing to continue paying the costs of operations from their personal funds.
>
> "Bud and I just bit off more than we could chew," Costello said. "The community chest hasn't given us a nickel. We asked the race track people to help us out with one of their charity days, but so far they haven't. No one in Hollywood or Los Angeles has given us a hand. I get more support from my home town, Paterson, New Jersey, than from this city where the project is located."
>
> In his dressing room, straight man Bud Abbott was going over the script of their next radio show. He and Lou have been on the air steadily for 11 years. They have four more years at U-I, for two pictures a year. Right now they're talking over a new contract. It will carry a bigger salary and an increased percentage of the profits of their movies, which have always been among the studio's top money-makers. Said Abbott:
>
> "I hear the rumor is out again that Lou and I are breaking up. Please help us deny it. We have been together 13 years—day and night. We do everything but sleep together. Sure, we have squabbles. What partners don't? But they're never serious. We'll continue as a team for many years to come."

Universal was also concerned about the future of the Youth Center—and if the failure might seriously affect Lou's popularity and value to the studio. A month before shooting began, the studio's executive committee briefly considered absorbing some of the debt. Ultimately, however, it was decided that Costello's box office popularity would remain intact no matter what happened to the Youth Center. They didn't consider what effect it would have on Lou's health. Lou, meanwhile, spent many lunch hours (from which he was late getting back to the set) in conferences and on the telephone, soliciting help. His anguish over the Youth Center clearly began to affect his health, and by the time he was shooting the cavern sequence, Lou had to take frequent breaks in his dressing room. Soon after wrapping the film, Costello suffered a serious relapse of rheumatic fever that left him bedridden for several months. In an interview in the *Los Angeles Evening Herald* with Patricia Clary, Lou discussed the circumstances of his illness:

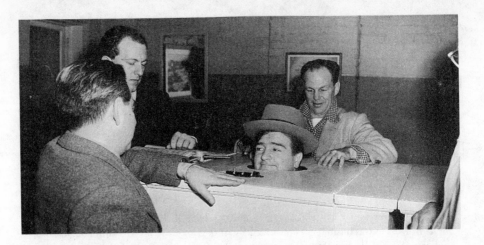

Charles Barton, Norman Abbott, Lou, and Frankie Van discuss the "Steam Cabinet" scene.

Costello had a nervous breakdown while he was making "Abbott and Costello Meet the Killer."

"I didn't have time for it," he said, "I told the director, Charlie Barton, 'You're directing a dead man.'" After the picture he really got sick. "I lost 50 pounds in five days. I've been flat on my back for four months."

Considering his faltering health, one mishap during the production might well have proved fatal. Costello was knocked out by carbon dioxide gas during the scene in the steam cabinet. Instead of using real steam, the special effects department immersed dry ice in water, releasing clouds of white CO_2 vapor. Although not poisonous, the gas built up and cut off the oxygen supply in the cabinet. After working in the cabinet for fifteen minutes, Lou complained of a headache, and a few minutes later he passed out. He was quickly revived with no ill effects reported.

Meanwhile another cast member was facing his own personal problems. During production, Mikel Conrad, who played Sergeant Stone, ironically was the object of a police manhunt on an assault warrant.

The production ran fourteen days over schedule and $52,000 over budget, with the largest overages in talent, electrical, miniature and process photography. According to a studio summary, the schedule ran over due to inclusion of two days' worth of added scenes and due to personality problems and illness of Abbott and Costello. When all the effects were in, the bottom line was $744,245.

Meet the Killer received more than the usual amount of publicity afforded an Abbott and Costello production. *Life* magazine reported that theater owners had voted Bud and Lou the country's top popcorn salesmen; Karloff politely plugged the film on two TV shows—Milton Berle's *Texaco Star Theater* and a TV production of *Arsenic and Old Lace;* and Lou, Anne, and their daughters were the subject of a picture spread in the May issue of *Woman's Home Companion.*

Yet the returns on *Meet the Killer* were disappointing. Executives worried that perhaps the title was at fault. Originally titled "Meet the Killers," the 's' was dropped to avoid a lawsuit by Mrs. Mark Hellinger, whose husband had produced *The Killers,* one of the studio's finest films, in 1946. Universal considered modifying the title to *Meet Boris Karloff* or *Meet the Menace, Boris Karloff,* until president Nate Blumberg himself intervened. The studio determined that what had actually hurt business were the almost simultaneous bookings and playdates of *Africa Screams.* "It would seem that this one really turns the most avid A&C fans away from the fold," a Universal memo explained. "Dating-wise, we hit up against this picture right along and are usually two or three weeks behind it. On a number of occasions, we even held back our date in order to get some clearance."

But while gross receipts were down (*Meet the Killer* was the studio's eighth biggest grosser of 1949, taking in $1,850,000), the film turned out to be one of the studio's more profitable releases, since the budget had been held under $750,000.

BUD AND LOU'S SCENES

Meet the Killer really doesn't contain many Abbott and Costello routines, per se. In fact, the boys may be considered to be split up in the film; Lou plays many of his scenes without Bud.

One gag that wasn't in the shooting script is a variation on the "Changing Room" scene from *Hold That Ghost*. Milford's body turns up in Freddie's bed, and Freddie runs out of the room to drag Casey in. By then, of course, the body is gone. Casey, naturally, thinks Freddie's nuts. But when Freddie goes into the bathroom, Milford's body is lying in the tub. Casey is summoned again, but the body disappears a second time, then even a third time.

In another funny sequence, Casey and Wellman fear that Angela, who poisoned her husband with an arsenic cocktail, is about to do Freddie in. Armed with an array of antidotes, they burst into Freddie's suite as he is about to drink a glass of champagne with her. Without explanation, Casey drags Freddie into the bathroom and begins pouring virtually every concoction known to man down Freddie's throat. In the original script, this action was to be played entirely off camera, with Freddie's gurgling and protests being heard while Wellman interrogates Angela. In the film, however, Casey dashes in and out of the room to get another potion from Sergeant Stone. These round-trips are the funniest part of the scene. When Freddie finally stumbles back into the scene, he is several shades lighter. When he is finally able to speak, Freddie bleats that he didn't even drink the champagne!

Lou has a good scene when Karloff tries to hypnotize him into committing suicide. The Swami patiently coaxes Freddie to hang himself, then shoot himself—but Freddie bungles each attempt. The Swami tries a different tactic. "Maybe you'd prefer to select your own method," he says. "How do you wish to die?" Freddie drones, "Of-old-age." After Freddie fails to jump out of his window, the exasperated Swami declares, "You're going to commit suicide if it's the last thing you do!" Freddie then manages to avoid stabbing himself with a knife. "Amazing," sneers the Swami, "even under hypnosis, the will of an idiot to cling to life."

The film's climactic cavern sequence doesn't evoke the chills and laughs that the monsters had in *Meet Frankenstein*. A bottomless pit is, after all, just a bottomless pit, and it pales in comparison with the specialized terrors offered by Dracula, Frankenstein, and the Wolf Man. This is unfortunate, because the special effects and scenic artists really did quite a masterful job creating their illusions, which must have been impressive on a large screen.

DELETIONS AND ADDITIONS

In a deleted scene that is more typically Abbott and Costello, Casey talks Freddie into apologizing to Strickland and offers to rehearse him. "We'll pretend I'm Mr. Strickland. Now, you come up to me and apologize." Freddie begins, "Mr. Strickland, I apologize." Casey roars, "What?! Get out of here, you clumsy fool!" Casey slaps him, shakes him up violently, and sends Freddie sprawling. Casey now changes character. "Well," he asks, "how'd you make out?" Freddie replies, "He turned me down. You should have seen what he did to me." Casey is sympathetic. "That's too bad," he says, "I guess he's still angry with you. But don't give up. Ask him again. Maybe next time he won't be so harsh." Freddie tries again. "Mr. Strickland, I'm sorry for what I did. Can you ever forgive me?" Casey erupts again, "What?! Are you back again? Get out of here before I have you thrown out!" He slaps him, roughs him up, and sends him sprawling once more. Freddie gets up a little more slowly and painfully. Casey anxiously inquires, "Well, what did he say this time?" Freddie sighs, "It's no use, Casey. I ain't gettin' no place with this guy." Casey reasons, "Wait a minute. You can't expect a man like Mr.

Strickland to forget so easily. Try him again, but this time be a little more humble." Freddie agrees to try it once more. He drops to his knees and begins kissing Casey's hand. He pleads, "Mr. Strickland, I didn't mean to sprinkle ink on your shirt, break your glasses, and punch you in the nose." "You didn't punch me in the nose," Casey corrects him. Freddie stands up. "No, but I will if I don't get my job back!"

In another deleted exchange, Casey tries to pursuade Inspector Wellman that Freddie is innocent. "I've known him all my life, and believe me, he hasn't got the brains to commit a murder," he says.

> **Freddie:** Thanks, Casey.
> **Casey:** I know he's a suspect, but just look at him. It took nerve to commit this murder, and this pathetic imbecile hasn't got the backbone of a jellyfish.
> **Freddie:** You said it.
> **Casey:** He is absolutely spineless—
> **Freddie:** He knows me like a book.
> **Casey:**—and he's yellow and chicken-livered! No, Inspector. This cowardly moron could never have done it.
> **Freddie:** Thanks, Casey. I knew you'd go to bat for me.

A major deletion occurs as Freddie is enjoying a shave and a manicure as a guest of the state. Strickland's former clients are gathered around the hotel pool. The Swami (identified in the script as Mme. Switzer), explains, "Each one of us has a past we want to leave buried." Mrs. Hargreave adds, "So any one of us might have killed Strickland to prevent him from publishing his memoirs." Angela, Mr. Brooks, Mrs. Grimsby, Mrs. Hargreave, and the Swami bicker over their respective pasts. Angela was accused of poisoning her husband with a champagne cocktail. Mr. Brooks' wife fell out of a window one week after he took out an insurance policy on her. Three wealthy women committed suicide and left their fortunes to the Swami. "Well," Brooks reasons, "we won't get anywhere baiting each other. We've been lucky so far. As long as the police think that bellboy killed Strickland, the rest of us are safe from the investigation." Mrs. Hargreave and Mrs. Grimsby, however, wish there was a way to pin it on Freddie permanently. The Swami suggests, "It would be extremely provident if suspect number one were to sign a confession and then—disappear." Angela picks up the lead. "That bellboy's not too bright. I think I can convince him to—shall we say?—cooperate." She stands up and shows off her figure. Mr. Brooks muses, "I'm sure you'll be most convincing, Angela. After all, you can catch more flies with honey." "Or cocktails," adds the Swami ominously. The film picks up here, with Angela telephoning Freddie in his suite.

REVIEWS

Variety: "Picture will be relished by the comics' following and is okay for the family trade. Long running time of 84 minutes, however, could be trimmed to give the film a swifter impact. Lengthy title, too, presents a problem to exhibitors with short marquees. The plot is just one of those things. But the dialogue is buttered so well with the bon mots and pratfalls which have made the comedians an American institution that their fans will likely overlook the inanities of the 'story.' "

Hollywood Reporter: "This latest item has more plot than the others, and consequently holds the spectator's attention in the interludes between the comedy sequences. As for the laugh routines, the boys are in exceptional form. Costello has a wonderful time with a chase in an underground cavern with a bottomless pit, and no end of fun with the bodies that are disposed of by the killers. Robert Arthur's production is frankly geared for laughs, and he keeps them going in fast succession. Charles T. Barton has a way of getting the best out of Abbott and Costello, and his direction, in this instance, is no less resourceful."

Motion Picture Herald: "Abbott and Costello have often been funnier, much funnier, but they

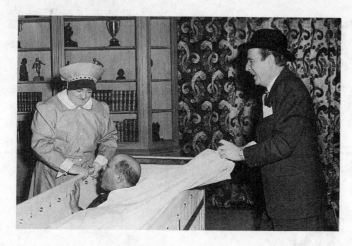
Bobby surprises Bud and
Lou during a take.

have never been more fantastic than they are in the current opus. It is to be expected that
the events and sequences in an A and C production are incredible, this being one method of
stretching the comedy line. But in this new Abbott and Costello film, some of the sequences
are so farfetched and fantastic that even the most faithful followers of this comedy team are
apt to find the film draggy. . . . Through all this, and until the fadeout, Abbott and Costello
do their best at being funny. Boris Karloff is also thrown into the film, but his role is brief
and unimportant. This is unfortunate, since something very humorous could have been made
out of the Karloff part."

The New York Times: "[M]ost of the humor—if that's what you'd call it—is derived from
the slapstick display of the two comedians juggling a couple of very stiff corpses in a
hotel. . . . 'This ain't funny,' says the fat comedian at one point—and, believe us, he is right.
Meanwhile, poor, dreary Mr. Karloff wanders into and out of a few scenes. . . . But, outside
of a few hypnotic passes and a couple of sinister looks, he brings little more to this picture
than the dark implications of his name."

New York Post: "For this long-time Lou Costello fan, there are always a couple of bright
moments in an Abbott and Costello screen vehicle. In 'A&C Meet the Killer,' alleged comedy,
you can count the laughs—probably without topping number ten. The new farce is a grim
thing, wherein everybody starts off alive and then, one by one, becomes a stiff."

POSTSCRIPT

On the strength of *Mexican Hayride, Africa Screams,* and *Abbott and Costello Meet the Killer,* Bud
and Lou placed third on the Motion Picture Herald's Poll of the Top Ten box office attractions
of 1949. (Bob Hope and Bing Crosby placed first and second.) It was the second year in a
row that the team had cracked the top ten.

Once again, however, as the team's popularity crested, Lou found himself bedridden with
a serious relapse of rheumatic fever. He was cheered by the news that the Ike Williams–
Enrique Bolanos fight finally did come off on July 25, and nearly $86,000 from the gate was
donated to save the Youth Center. However, Lou's illness prevented the team from making
any personal appearances in 1949. The irony was that Lou's rheumatic fever, which had
originally inspired the project in 1943, now kept him from sustaining it. In October, Lou
surrendered to the inevitable, and suggested the Center be taken over by the City of Los
Angeles. Still in operation today, it continues to bear the name, "Lou Costello Jr. Youth
Center" and serves another generation of poor kids in East Los Angeles.

Bud and Betty Abbott celebrated the official adoption of their second child, Victoria, in
October 1949. Vickie, who was then seven years old, had already been living with the Abbotts
for about two years.

ABBOTT AND COSTELLO IN THE FOREIGN LEGION

Earliest Draft:
  December 27, 1948

Production Start:
  April 28, 1950

Production End:
  May 29, 1950

Copyright Date:
  August 11, 1950

Released: July 24, 1950

Running Time:
  80 minutes

Directed By:
  Charles Lamont

Produced By:
  Robert Arthur

Screenplay By:
  John Grant,
  Martin Ragaway,
  Leonard Stern

Original Story By:
  D.D. Beauchamp

Director of Photography:
  George Robinson ASC

Art Direction:
  Bernard Herzbrun
  and Eric Orbom

Set Decorations:
  Russell A. Gausman
  and Ray Jeffers

Sound: Leslie I. Carey and
  Robert Pritchard

Musical Direction:
  Joseph Gershenson

Film Editor: Frank Gross

Technical Advisor:
  Mahmud Shaikhaly

Hair Stylist:
  Joan St. Oegger

SYNOPSIS

Wrestling promoters Bud Jones and Lou Hotchkiss are dismayed when their star, Abdullah, refuses to follow their script, which indicates he is to lose, and he returns to his native Algeria. Because they borrowed $5,000 from the syndicate to import him, Bud and Lou follow to bring him back. Abdullah's cousin, Sheik Hamud El Khalid, and a traitorous Foreign Legionnaire, Sergeant Axmann, have been organizing raids on a railroad construction crew, with the intention of extorting money from the railroad. The villains assume that Bud and Lou are spies for the railroad and order them killed. Lou further infuriates Hamud by inadvertently outbidding him on the purchase of six beautiful slave girls, including Nicole, a spy from French Intelligence who intends to gain entry to Hamud's camp. The boys seek refuge at the headquarters of the Foreign Legion, where the devious Axmann dupes them into enlisting.

Hamud's forces seem to anticipate the Legion's every move, and the Commandant suspects a leak within his troops. Although Lou has great difficulty in boot camp, the Commandant, on orders from a higher authority, grants the boys a pass to go into town. They rendezvous with Nicole, who instructs them to search Axmann's quarters. Axmann catches them in the act, but Bud and Lou are temporarily spared when reinforcements must be rushed to Fort Apar. That night at the Legionnaire's desert camp, Bud and Lou wander off to search for a camel when Hamud's men ambush the troops and slay everyone but Axmann. Bud and Lou wander through the blazing desert, until they are captured and brought to Hamud's camp, where Axmann arrives with Nicole as his prisoner. Hamud decrees that the boys shall die at the hands of his wrestlers, one of whom is Abdullah. He fakes a fight with Lou that leads to a riot, and in the melee, Bud, Lou, Nicole, and Abdullah escape in Axmann's Jeep. They head for Fort Apar, lure Hamud's forces into the fort, and blow it up. Bud and Lou are decorated for distinguished service, and discharged from the Legion.

BACKGROUND

Foreign Legion was to begin shooting in December 1949. But Lou had no sooner recovered from rheumatic fever when his doctors diagnosed a gangrenous gall bladder and operated on him in November 1949. "I shook hands with the Lord twice," Lou said about his illnesses that year. "I don't want to hold hands no more." Lou needed a few more months to recover, and the studio suspended the team's salary. By January, Lou reported he was fully recovered and ready to begin working on the film, but the studio postponed *Foreign Legion* until April. "I think these guys out here have been telling the bosses I'm dying," Lou told the United Press. "I ain't sick; I'll prove it if I have to swing 'em around like I was weight-lifting. I can't figure out any other reason why they don't insist that they put us back to work—us, the country's third greatest box office attraction." The layoff, Lou said, hurts Universal more than it does him. "We keep the place in the black. We're the biggest money-makers at the studio according to the polls, and have been for ten years. I don't know where our pictures play, but they sure do business. I always wanted to make good pictures. I never got 'em, but I always wanted 'em."

Before beginning the film, however, a few things had to be rectified. Lou explained, "I signed a new contract when I was sick. I was out of my head; I must have been. I gave away the radio rights we've always had and our rights to an outside picture. They're going to have to give those back. I didn't know what I was doing." Fortunately, Eddie Sherman had visited Lou during his convalesence, and the two men reconciled their differences. Eddie was put back to work doing what he did best—renegotiating the team's contracts.

By now, director Charles Barton had moved on to the Donald O'Connor vehicles *The Milkman* (1950), which was written by Martin Ragaway and Leonard Stern, and *Double Crossbones* (1951), a pirate spoof scripted by Oscar Brodney and John Grant. Barton had great affection for Bud and Lou, but he had had enough of the card games, the hangers-on, and the delays. Who could blame him after his last two films at Universal with the team. But Barton had served them well on eight films, including two of the team's best, *The Time of Their Lives* and *Abbott and Costello Meet Frankenstein,* and remained friends with them. Robert Arthur recalled, "Both of them loved Charlie Barton, and they tried not to give Charlie any miseries. But there were problems that would come up."

Veteran director Edward Sedgwick was initially selected to helm *Foreign Legion*. Sedgwick (1892–1953) directed a string of Buster Keaton films in the late 1920s and early 1930s, including *The Cameraman* (1928), and the innocuous comedies of Joe E. Brown. But after directing Laurel and Hardy in the disappointing *Air Raid Wardens* (1943), Sedgwick found sporadic work in the 1940s. Considering Abbott and Costello's recent history, however, Robert Arthur needed a director known for his dispatch.

One director on the lot had earned a reputation for shooting so quickly and efficiently that he had become the bane of the studio's still photographers. Charles Lamont usually finished shooting one scene and was on to his next setup so fast that the photographers never had time to take their stills. His movies invariably finished ahead of schedule and under budget. Lamont directed *Bagdad* for Robert Arthur in 1949, and the producer recruited him to pick up where Barton had left off in the Abbott and Costello series. Seven years earlier, Lamont directed Bud and Lou in one of their funniest outings, *Hit the Ice*. Since then, he had helmed the Yvonne DeCarlo pictures *Salome, Where She Danced* (1945), *Frontier Gal* (1945), and *Slave Girl* (1947)—all in Technicolor—and the first two Ma and Pa Kettle films. "I refused to do a second Abbott and Costello film after *Hit the Ice* was completed," Lamont explained. "I didn't want to be labeled an 'Abbott and Costello director.' I liked working with Bud and Lou and I wanted to do other things. Universal finally offered me a seven-year contract and a big salary and I forgot my ambitions. Abbott and Costello *were* my future."

THE SCRIPT

In December 1948, D. D. Beauchamp pitched an original idea to place Bud and Lou in the Foreign Legion, and his treatment was completed in January 1949. Martin Ragaway and Leonard Stern were then assigned to write the screenplay based on Beauchamp's story. Stern

Make-Up: Bud Westmore
Special Photography:
  David S. Horsley ASC

Bud Jones ... Bud Abbott
Lou Hotchkiss
.... Lou Costello
Nicole..... Patricia Medina
Axmann ....Water Slezak
Hamud El Khalid
...... Douglas Dumbrille
Hassam.... Leon Belasco
Frankie .. Marc Lawrence
Abdullah
........Wee Willie Davis
Abou Ben... Tor Johnson
Bertram .. Sam Menacker
Commandant
.... Fred Nurney
Ibn............ Paul Fierro
Ibrim........ Henry Corden
Ali Ami.... Jack Raymond
Thugs ....Jack Shutta
            Harry Wilson
            Ernesto Morelli
            Jack Davidson
            Chuck Hamilton
Josef ...... Dan Seymour
Lieutenants
.... Alberto Morin
            John Cliff
Saleem .... Guy Beach
Corporal ...... Peter Ortiz
Arab Proprietor
.... Ted Hecht
Referee
...... Mahmud Shaikaly
Flashy Arab Girl
.....Charmienne Harker
Newsboy .. David Gorcey

remembered, "Bud and Lou had an avuncular, if not paternal, feeling toward us. We were in our early twenties then. If memory serves me, we did familiarize ourselves with their earlier pictures. But we did not try to duplicate *Buck Privates*. We were story oriented, so we always tried to find a story that would give legitimate drama or support to the outrageous comedy. We just followed one of those classic formulas—the fish out of water, suddenly in danger. If you look through most of Hitchcock's work, it's the innocent who's swept up in the intrigue."

The Breen Office expressed concern over two facets of the production. Foremost was the costuming of the harem girls. "We wish to emphasize once again, with all the force at our command, the necessity of guarding most carefully the problem of costumes in this picture. As we review this material, it seems to us that there are many occasions for difficulties with inadequate costumes for the women in the harems and the like to crop up during the course of the filming of the picture. We recommend this problem to your most careful supervision. . . ."

Breen's other caveat was over a bit of mayhem in the wrestling scenes. "Furthermore, we direct your attention to a problem which has developed in this latest edition of the story [draft dated November 16, 1949]. We refer to the business on pages 98 and 99, in which various characters jab their fingers in each other's eyes. We consider this type of thing to be extremely dangerous to put on the screen, having in mind that it is the kind of business which is likely to incite imitation among the many youthful members of your audience. Consequently, we feel that this eye-jabbing routine is definitely inacceptable under the Code, and could not be approved in a finished picture. Some other device will have to be invented as a substitute." An alternate shtick—a slap across the bridge of the nose—was developed. Meanwhile, the eye-poke remained an unchallenged staple of the Three Stooges for years.

THE CAST

Patricia Medina (b. 1920) was born in England and appeared in British films before coming to Hollywood in the mid-1940s. In the late 1940s and early 1950s she frequently found herself in costume adventures. The titles say it all: *The Foxes of Harrow, The Three Musketeers, The Fighting O'Flynn, Fortunes of Captain Blood, The Lady and the Bandit, The Magic Carpet, Lady in the Iron Mask, Siren of Bagdad, Sangaree, Botany Bay, The Black Knight*. At the time of *Foreign Legion*, Patricia was married to British actor Richard Green. They were divorced in 1952, and she has been married to actor Joseph Cotten since 1960. In 1949 she played a French spy in *Francis* with Donald O'Connor. That picture, directed by Arthur Lubin, was produced by Robert Arthur. When he needed a French spy for *Foreign Legion,* he thought of Patricia.

"When Robert Arthur asked me to do the picture, I was such a fan of theirs I thought it was going to be a simply marvelous experience," she recalled. "And it was. But I remember everyone at the studio saying to me, 'Ohhh, you don't know what's going to happen to you!' I asked what they meant. 'Wait till Costello pulls some of his gags on you! Watch the chair you're sitting in. It'll probably go up in smoke.' But nothing like that ever did happen. They must have sensed that I was frightened, so they played it just the other way. He was a perfect gentleman, and so helpful to somebody who hadn't done very much acting. He'd ad-lib out of habit—he just couldn't help it. He certainly didn't do it to throw you, and if he did throw you, he was terribly apologetic and sweet. The only thing was, it was very difficult to look him in the eye without breaking up—he had that angelic face. He was a naughty little Peter Pan; he never grew up. And although he was a child, you can't be that great a performer without being a *true* sophisticate. He was that. Many children are most sophisticated, and Lou was a very sophisticated child. I thought he was the greatest comedian I had ever seen. There's that earplug routine [from *Abbott and Costello in Hollywood*] in *That's Entertainment, Part 2*—it's the best thing in the picture."

Walter Slezak (1902–1983) had worked with director Charles Lamont on *Salome, Where She Danced* (1945) and menaced Danny Kaye in *The Inspector General* (1949) before being signed

Bud and Lou celebrate their 15th Anniversary as a team with Patricia Medina.

to *Foreign Legion.* In 1955 he won both the Tony and the New York Critics awards for his role in the Broadway musical *Fanny.*

Douglas Dumbrille (1890–1974) had appeared with Bud and Lou in their other desert opus, *Lost in a Harem,* in 1944. In the 1950s, Dumbrille was seen in *Son of Paleface* (1952), *Julius Caesar* (1953), and *The Ten Commandments* (1956), as well as the television series *The Life of Riley.*

THE PRODUCTION

Robert Arthur's budget for *Foreign Legion* was the lowest of any of the Abbott and Costello pictures he produced—$735,750.

It had been ten months since Bud and Lou had been in front of the cameras, but Lou seemed ready to pick up where he had left off. On April 28, he and Bud reported to Stage 9 for their first day on the picture with firecrackers. Lamont shot the entire enlistment sequence in the Legion office and finished with Bud and Lou at four-ten. The director had set a good precedent, and by the following week the studio records noted that Bud and Lou were being "much more cooperative than usual." One reason could have been that Lou's condition precluded the usual off-screen antics. Bobby Barber had to tone it down, according to a release, since "Costello, who almost died last winter during his illness, will not be permitted by his physicians to carry on active horseplay on the set of this film . . . so Bobby must be funny by himself to keep the two famous comics in the proper mood for their clowning."

Lou's stunt double was now Russ Coles, yet Lou preferred to wrestle Wee Willie Davis in the harem scenes. As a result, Lou suffered a wrenched arm socket and a stretched tendon in the scene. His arm was taped by the studio nurse, and he was photographed only on the right side of his body for the rest of the day. (In a deleted scene, Bud scraped his wrist crashing through a breakaway door in the barracks when Lou fires a machine gun.) Lou also wasn't watching his diet very carefully. "Within a half-hour yesterday," a press release reports, "Costello consumed two Cokes, three cups of coffee, a popsicle, a nut candy bar, and two Arab apples. But Arab apples aren't what they sound. They are raw onions. Costello swears they give him strength for his wrestling bouts with Wee Willie Davis."

Lamont breezed through the rest of the production and wrapped on May 29, five days

The film's big hit was the scene with the fish that recovers an older Arab's dentures. The fish, equipped with the choppers, torments Lou in an inspired variation of the "Oyster Stew" routine.

ahead of schedule and $56,063 *under* budget. Universal was anxious to finish post-production on the film since Bud and Lou were scheduled to leave for Europe and wouldn't be available for dubbing work. The studio also wanted to get the picture out as quickly as possible, since the boys were still a profitable commodity. "Every effort is being made to move this picture along as quickly as possible," a memo declares. "At the present time we have moved the preview date ahead two days, and we hope to be able to pick up another two or three days. In order to expedite the completion of this picture an additional feature editor has been added for one week to work on the last part of the picture."

Meanwhile, the publicity department was busy touting *Foreign Legion* as the team's twenty-fifth film, marking Bud and Lou's tenth anniversary in Hollywood. Fortunately, the wire services and columnists picked up on the angle, because the advertising budget for the film was a paltry $25,000. Of the twenty-nine pictures Universal released in 1950, only two had lower ad budgets. In contrast, the studio spent $300,000 promoting *Francis;* $135,000 on *Winchester 73;* and $90,000 on *Ma & Pa Kettle Go To Town.*

BUD AND LOU'S SCENES

The wrestling sequence is quite funny—and still timely today. Bud literally reads the match from a script! He enlists Lou to help demonstrate the action to the wrestlers, and the little guy is thoroughly thrashed. Bud, of course, is never satisfied. "Lou, will you please fall faster," he says impatiently, "you're slowing up the tempo of the whole script! And I'm not at all happy with that fall." Lou struggling to his feet, whimpers, "That makes two of us."

The scene where the Commandant grants the boys a furlough contains a brief bit of the old Abbott and Costello by-play:

Commandant: You men be at 82 Rue Lafayette at eight o'clock.

Bud and Lou: Us!?

Commandant: Oui.

Lou: Oh, the three of us are goin'?

Commandant: No, just you two.

Bud and Lou: Us?

Commandant: Oui.

Lou: Yes, that's what I said, the three of us are—why don't you make up your mind?! Are you goin' or aren't you goin'!?

Commandant: *(snapping)* Get out! Get out!

Later in the film, the boys wander aimlessly in the desert, with Lou particularly prone to mirages. In one, a skeleton speaks to him. In an odd quirk of fate, the voice of the skeleton was provided by Candy Candido. In 1960, Candido would briefly team up with Bud and reprise some of the classic routines in a nightclub act.

The film's final chase includes some good gags. After Abdullah helps the boys escape by creating a riot, Bud and Lou are pounced upon by a dozen Arabs, who pile on top of them. Hamud and Axmann begin pulling Arabs off the pile and come to two Legionnaires, lying face down. Hamud pulls the figures to their feet and turns their faces to him. They are two Arabs wearing Bud and Lou's clothes—somehow they've exchanged costumes! They steal Axmann's Jeep and tear around the camp. In a brief instant they drive into Hamud's harem, where dozens of towels marked "Hers" hang around one large towel marked "His." They barrel through another tent, which peels away to reveal an Arab sleeping on the hood of the Jeep. It's Bobby Barber. Lou makes a sharp turn that sends Bobby flying head first into the sand and an ostrich egg. The chase also borrows a little from *Ride 'Em Cowboy,* as dozens of Arabs on horseback pursue the Jeep. Later, when Lou literally holds the doors of the fort, a battering ram bursts through *a la Meet Frankenstein.* Bud accidentally trips the detonator, demolishing the fort, and, it appears, Lou. This allows Abbott to do "Bud's Lament" one more time, even though the team had used it recently in *Africa Screams.*

DELETIONS AND ADDITIONS

Perhaps the funniest gag in the mirage sequence is the newspaper boy, played by East Side Kid David Gorcey. "Can I help it if they gave me a bad corner?" he complains. The bit was added during production.

In the boot camp sequence, Bud scrambles under the barbed wire while Lou simply walks along on the outside. In the script, he was supposed to have the obvious difficulties crawling under the barbed wire, including losing his pants.

REVIEWS

At the first preview of *Foreign Legion* on June 27, 50 percent of the audience rated the picture Excellent or Very Good, and 35 percent rated it Fair or Poor. *Meet Frankenstein,* by comparison, was rated Excellent or Very Good by 62 percent of its preview audience, and Fair or Poor by only 20 percent.

Hollywood Reporter: " 'Abbott and Costello in the Foreign Legion' may not be the most outstanding of the duo's enterprises, but it is many shades better than the average slapstick comedy. The boys have plenty of good gags to work with, and the Robert Arthur production smartly gives them much to do. Charles Lamont knows his way through an Abbott and Costello script blindfolded, so there is no need to dwell at length on the quality of his direction. It's geared for the maximum laugh response, and most of the time, that is exactly what happens. The A. & C. fans will like their favorites in this frolic with its shots of Arabian horsemen, dancing girls, harems and the like."

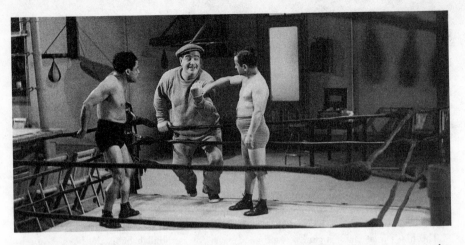

In this deleted scene in the opening sequence at the gym, Lou has recruited two midget wrestlers to grapple in a small ring. "What's the idea of teaching midgets to wrestle?" Bud asks. "They're for those small television sets!" Lou explains.

The New York Times: "It may be assumed that after turning out so many exercises in what was construed as comedy, that the team of Abbott and Costello would become weary. And, in . . . their twenty-fifth excursion before the cameras . . . it may be reported that the boys, the script, and the remainder of the cast are definitely tired. Plodding is the word for the pace of this number. . . . The laughs, oddly enough, are rarely abdominal. There are a few chuckles as the pair . . . belabor each other, wander into harems, blow up a fort, and tear around the desert in a jeep. Lou Costello grimaces, grunts, squeals and gets the lion's share of sight gags and this season's puns. Example: Mr. Costello on being informed that he is to receive a citation inquires, "What do I want with a horse?" . . . Make no mistake about it, however. This corn is not green. It is strictly parched."

Los Angeles Times: "The French Foreign Legion may not seem very funny to some people, but to comedians it appears irresistible. Laurel and Hardy once made a very funny comedy [*The Flying Deuces* (1939)] with that background, and now Abbott and Costello in 'Foreign Legion' are finding just as many laugh chances when they, too, join the rugged men of the desert outposts. . . . The truly sidesplitting gags arrive when the boys get lost in the desert, seek water, and see mirages, with Lou finally refusing to believe Bud when he does find an oasis. They fish and find an alligator [sic] which has appropriated an Arab's false teeth, and have other zany adventures."

POSTSCRIPT

On June 23, Bud, Lou, and a large entourage sailed for Europe on the *Queen Mary* for a two-month combination tour and vacation. They arrived in Glasgow, Scotland, where they played the Empire Theatre, then it was on to London, where the team headlined at the Palladium for four weeks, at $18,000 a week. According to a press release, "The hundreds of thousands of servicemen who spent part of the war in England unintentionally did Bud and Lou a big favor. They introduced American baseball to the English and it became so popular that it's now one of the Briton's top sports. All of which helps the zany comics . . . because their 'Who's On First?' routine is one of the team's chief comedy assets, and the pair are planning to tour the British Isles in July. In fact, Abbott and Costello were working on an English routine in which cricket would be substituted for baseball in order that the British fans would understand them."

Following the English tour, the boys invaded the Continent, doing a month of shows at U.S. Army camps in Germany, Italy, and France. At the end of August, they sailed back to New York, reinvigorated by the enthusiastic crowds that turned out to see them. Bud and Lou vowed to return to Europe again in the near future.

ABBOTT AND COSTELLO MEET THE INVISIBLE MAN

SYNOPSIS

Bud Alexander and Lou Francis no sooner graduate from a private detective training school when their first case bursts in. Middleweight boxer Tommy Nelson, accused of murdering his manager, has escaped from jail. He persuades Bud and Lou to accompany him to the home of his fiancée, Helen Gray. Helen's uncle, Dr. Philip Gray, is working on a serum for invisibility and a re-agent to counteract it. Tommy wants Dr. Gray to inject him with the serum that will make him invisible and enable him to prove his innocence. As the police arrive, Tommy injects himself with the serum. While Detective Roberts questions Helen and Dr. Gray, Bud and Lou attempt to capture Tommy themselves. Bud locks Lou in a room with Tommy, who becomes invisible before Lou's eyes and escapes.

Back at their agency, Tommy and Helen persuade Bud and Lou to work with them to clear Tommy's name. Tommy explains that he was ordered to throw a fight with Rocky Hanlon, but that he knocked Rocky out instead. Tommy's manager was then beaten to death by goons employed by promoter Morgan, with the blame placed on Tommy. Tommy has Lou pose as a fighter and Bud act as his manager. They work out in Stillwell's gym, where Rocky goads Lou into a fight. When the invisible Tommy knocks Hanlon out, everyone thinks Lou did it, and a real bout is arranged between Hanlon and Lou. Morgan enlists the voluptuous Boots Marsen to persuade Lou to take a dive. But with the invisible Tommy at his side in the ring Lou flattens Rocky. Morgan decides to give Lou and Bud the same treatment he gave Tommy and his manager. Tommy, Bud, and Lou thwart the gangsters, although Tommy is nearly killed by a knife. At the hospital, a blood transfusion with Lou as the donor saves Tommy's life, but some of Tommy's blood, full of the serum, backs up into Lou's veins, making him invisible. Lou expects to become the world's greatest detective, but the serum wears off after a few minutes. When he becomes visible, Lou finds that his legs are on backwards!

BACKGROUND

Producer Robert Arthur left Universal for Warner Bros. on completion of *Foreign Legion*. He had his problems with the boys, but for the most part, he enjoyed working with them. "We were never terribly close personally. But I had a wonderful relationship with them because of the way we started—being honest with each other. Of course they took great delight in

Earliest Draft:
February 17, 1948

Production Start:
October 3, 1950

Production End:
November 6, 1950

Copyright Date:
April 18, 1951

Released: March 19, 1951

Running Time:
82 minutes

Directed By:
Charles Lamont

Produced By:
Howard Christie

Screenplay By:
Robert Lees,
Frederic I. Rinaldo,
and John Grant

Original Story By:
Hugh Wedlock, Jr.
and Howard Snyder

Suggested By:
H. G. Wells' "The
Invisible Man"

Director of Photography:
George Robinson ASC

Art Direction:
Bernard Herzbrun
and Richard Riedel

Musical Direction:
Joseph Gershenson

Song "Good Old DDT"
By: Frederick Herbert,
Milton Rosen and
Joseph Gershenson

Film Editor: Virgil Vogel

Set Decorations:
Russell A. Gausman
and John Austin

Sound: Leslie I. Carey and
Robert Pritchard

Hair Stylist:
  Joan St. Oegger

Make-Up: Bud Westmore

Special Photography:
  David S. Horsley ASC

Bud Alexander
  .... Bud Abbott

Lou Francis . Lou Costello

Helen Gray... Nancy Guild

Tommy Nelson
  .... Arthur Franz

Boots Marsden
  .... Adele Jergens

Morgan
  .... Sheldon Leonard

Detective Roberts
  .... William Frawley

Dr. Philip Gray
  .... Gavin Muir

Radio Announcer
  .... Sam Balter

Rocky Hanlon .. John Day

Torpedo
  .... George J. Lewis

Referee ..... Frankie Van

Sneaky .... Bobby Barber

Lou's Handler
  .... Carl Sklover

Rocky's Handler
  .... Charles Perry

Dr. Turner ... Paul Maxey

Milt .... Ed Gargan

Stillwell ... Herbert Vigran

Fight Announcer
  .... Milt Bronson

Ice Cream Vendor
  .... Donald Kerr

teasing me. This is what happens when you're a square and I was not the type of fellow to play cards with them, which is what happened to Alex Gottlieb. You can't be that familiar with your stars, you see. I've never been one to go to anybody's home. In the thirty-odd years that I was in the picture business, the only thing I ever used publicity for was to keep me *out* of the papers. But Lou was always more serious with me. I was never a part of the pies. You'd have a pie-throwing routine on the set, then he'd come over and sit in my office and seriously discuss the problems of the country, the way people were living, and not just the Youth Center he built, but the whole problem of poverty. It affected him deeply. Then, of course, he'd go back to clowning with Bobby Barber. I think that maybe was an outlet for him." Arthur later returned to Universal in 1954, and went on to produce some of the studio's biggest hits, including *Man of a Thousand Faces* (1957); *Operation Petticoat* (1959); *Lover Come Back* (1962); *Father Goose* (1964); *Shenandoah* (1965); and *Sweet Charity* (1969).

Arthur suggested that Howard "Red" Christie succeed him as the team's producer. Christie had been an assistant director on many of their films. Lou and Bud consented, and they agreed to give Howard their full cooperation. "If he fails it'll be his fault, not ours," Lou told Arthur. Christie immediately inherited three projects Arthur already had in development for the team: *Abbott and Costello Meet the Invisible Man,* "The Real McCoy" (*Comin' Round the Mountain*), and "The Sourdoughs" (*Lost in Alaska*).

THE SCRIPT

After they completed "Easy Does It" (a.k.a. *Abbott and Costello Meet the Killer*) Hugh Wedlock and Howard Snyder wrote a straight sequel to *The Invisible Man's Revenge* (1944) titled "The Invisible Man Strikes Back" early in 1948. Arthur considered using it as the basis for an Abbott and Costello vehicle until another writing team, Russell Rouse and Clarence Green, developed an original screenplay called "Abbott and Costello Meet the Invisible Man" that fall. It appears that Abbott and Costello were scheduled to make this film after *Africa Screams*. But Arthur brought in Robert Lees and Fred Rinaldo to rework the screenplay. Lees and Rinaldo had written *The Invisible Woman* in 1941. Robert Lees explained, "We had the Invisible Man from the gag ending on *Meet Frankenstein*. The concept of him being the third man in the ring was developed before the story began. The whole story was built to that. We put in some of the gags from *The Invisible Woman,* and it turned out to be a good Abbott and Costello picture."

THE CAST

Nancy Guild (b. 1925) returned to the screen after a two-year absence. Previously she had appeared in *Somewhere in the Night* (1946), along with Sheldon Leonard; *The Brasher Doubloon* (1947), a Philip Marlowe mystery; *Give My Regards to Broadway* (1948); and Orson Welles' *Black Magic* (1949). She retired from the screen in the early 1950s after marrying Broadway producer Ernest Martin.

Arthur Franz (b. 1920) is barely in the picture, yet *The New York Times* said, "Franz is as good as Claude Rains ever was as the invisible man (no comment, please, on that critical observation)." In 1949 Franz had appeared in *Sands of Iwo Jima* with John Wayne. He recalled, "I have no idea how I was cast in *Abbott and Costello Meet the Invisible Man* because I was in Australia doing *Streetcar Named Desire* in the part Marlon Brando played in New York. We played ten months, and when I finished my run, I flew back and started work on the picture.

"They all treated me with great, great respect. I was there every day, and spoke my lines off-camera. The only problem I can remember there ever being on the set was not my problem with them, but poor Charlie Lamont's problem with them—they would lock themselves in their trailer to play gin rummy, and they would not come out because one or the other was *always* in the hole. One of the funniest lines came out of those daily conflicts. Charlie would beat on the door to get them to come out, and Lou would scream back, 'Hey—you rehearse

it too much it loses all its spontanuity!' [laughs] He was taking two words, spontaneity and continuity, and running them both together. It was a Costello original.

"I did not attend the preview. I only took part in one big party that they both threw after the shooting was over, and I think it was at Bud's house out in Encino. It was a party for them to, before all of their friends, present a check to the IRS that bought them their freedom for another year. It was a real wing-ding, and it was a *huge* check."

Two veterans of previous Abbott and Costello films, William Frawley and Sheldon Leonard, rounded out the cast. Jesse White had originally been cast in the role of Detective Roberts. Frawley had been in the team's first picture, *One Night in the Tropics,* almost exactly ten years earlier. In the fall of 1951, some months after the release of *Meet the Invisible Man,* Frawley began his role as Fred Mertz on *I Love Lucy.* Sheldon Leonard had appeared in *Hit the Ice* (1943) with the boys. Director Lamont called Leonard his "favorite heavy," and cast him in both pictures. Leonard recalled being a victim of one of Bobby Barber's pranks. "As we started rehearsing a scene, this short little mustached guy cut in, 'That's not the way to do it, Mr. Leonard.' Then he would direct me how to play the scene. Well I didn't pay him any attention and I started the scene again. Again he interrupted. 'No, no, Mr. Leonard! That's not the way we discussed it!' He just kept harassing me until I said, 'Get him away from me before I kill him!' Everybody burst into laughter; Abbott and Costello had set him on me."

THE PRODUCTION

The picture was scheduled for thirty-four days, plus sixteen days of trick unit photography. The budget was a mere $697,000, with Bud and Lou now receiving $150,000 for their services. In addition to a 10 percent share of the profits, Lou's company, Cosman Productions, purchased a 30 percent interest in *Meet the Invisible Man.* Nearly $50,000 was budgeted for the myriad special effects, although several were stock effects lifted from *The Invisible Man Returns* (1940), with Vincent Price. In fact, several props were made or painted to match those in the earlier film, including a suitcase and a guinea pig.

A week into filming, Lamont was creeping ahead of schedule. The studio's executive committee meeting notes reported, "Abbott and Costello seem to be quite serious about getting a good picture as quickly as possible. They are cooperating very well."

United Press Hollywood correspondent Patricia Clary paid a visit to the set, and to Bud and Lou's sanctum, the trailer:

> Abbott and Costello have stocked the thirty-foot dressing room with enough assorted laugh-making gadgets to supply all the clowns in a three-ring circus. You'd think you'd stepped into the branch office of the state insane asylum.
>
> First thing you see in the A & C abode is a stuffed moose with neon antlers. "We used him in one of our early pictures," Costello explained. "We've kept him around

TOP LEFT: Make-up man Russell Drake sprays Lou to look as if he's perspiring. TOP CENTER: The world premier for *Abbott and Costello Meet the Invisible Man* was a gala benefit for the Los Angeles *Examiner*'s Fund for Wounded Veterans of the Korean War. The spectacular stage show included Bud and Lou, Martin and Lewis, Danny Thomas, Lena Horne, Jerry Colona, Allan Jones, Janis Paige, the Weire Brothers, and Nat Young's Orchestra. TOP: Danny Thomas, Dean Martin, Jerry Lewis, and Bud at the benefit.

ever since for good luck. One of the electricians rigged up an electric eye gadget in the doorway. The neon antlers light up whenever anybody comes in."

Julius Caesar sits in a chair near the door. Costello picked up the waxworks figure in Rome earlier this year. When he's called away to make a scene, he sticks his cigar in Caesar's mouth. It's lined with tin. Caesar is also wired for electricity. Anybody who shakes hands with him—as Abbott and Costello urge everybody to do—gets a shock.

A rusty iron cowcatcher is propped against one wall. The boys got it off a locomotive used in one of their past films. "We keep it around in case a cow should ever wander into the joint," Costello explained. There's a reason for everything.

Other mementoes from past Universal-International pictures starring the two comics are a replica of the Sing Sing electric chair; a stuffed swordfish wearing a Westmore toupee and false whiskers; a church organ; and a chair with rubber legs.

For most of the film, Arthur Franz read his lines off-camera. For a few scenes, however, he was wrapped uncomfortably in thirty yards of gauze. A flat flask filled with ice water was strapped to his waist underneath his suit and equipped with a long siphon that reached to his mouth.

When Lamont wrapped on November 6, he finished four days early and $70,000 under budget. Even the trick unit shaved four days off its schedule. The studio committee duly noted, "Abbott and Costello and Mr. Lamont are mainly responsible for this good showing."

BUD AND LOU'S SCENES

The film seems to have a special significance for Bud and Lou, since they use their real first and middle names for the names of their characters. Also, Lou must have been thrilled to do a boxing scene, since he had once fought as a club fighter around Paterson. Jack Dempsey was originally scheduled to portray the fight referee; Frankie Van, who ran the studio gym and appeared in bit parts in several of the team's films, took the part.

There are several imaginative sight gags and camera tricks that help make *Invisible Man* the best of the team's films of the 1950s. David S. Horsley's special effects in many ways managed to outdo those in the original 1933 film. Bud and Lou work very convincingly with the effects, with Lou particularly outstanding in the boxing sequence. Costello's gift for pantomime was rarely more apparent or used to greater effect than in the marvelous sequence when Tommy supposedly holds him up in the ring under his arms. Incredibly, the majority of the shots that comprise the fight sequence were done in only one take—suggesting great preparedness on the part of Costello and Lamont. The director also covered the sequence flawlessly with just two cameras.

DELETIONS AND ADDITIONS

Lamont kept this film even closer to the script than he had *Foreign Legion*. One addition for Bud and Lou was the team's classic money-changing routine. Tommy's transformation back to visibility was also greatly expanded during shooting, with an excellent series of effects as his entire vascular structure becomes visible in stages. Also added was the film's final gag of Lou running away backwards. For the closing gag in the script, he simply notices that his legs are on backwards and says, "I never expected The End to be like this!"

REVIEWS

Variety: "Abbott and Costello, whose fun-making routines had become decidedly weary in some of their more recent films, partially redeem themselves. . . . Team's stock doubletakes and bewhiskered gags are still fulsome, but the hackneyed quips achieve a new gloss in this entry.

It's geared for healthy grosses. . . . In light of New York's current basketball expose and other alleged sports-dumping, exhibitors will find the film a piece of exploitable merchandise. Charles Lamont directed at a breezy pace that milked the script's levity dry."

Motion Picture Daily: "A rainy Monday night audience at the Ritz Theater in Los Angeles promptly forgot about the 'unusual' California weather outdoors when this brightly-conceived and alertly-executed A&C comedy [began]. Laughter that got rolling within the first minute rippled steadily along the first hour and then broke into crashing waves when Costello entered a boxing ring to meet the title challenger with the Invisible Man alongside to deliver the knockout punch. Foyer comment in the theater tended to suggest that this may be their best all-around comedy in years."

The New York Times: "The boys try hard and, on the whole, they appear to have recaptured a good deal of their old spunk, but their efforts are not always rewarding over the picture's eighty-two minutes running time. . . . [T]hings reach a high degree of helter-skelter fun when Nelson suddenly deserts the ring. For sheer slapstick tomfoolery this fight is one of the funniest things Abbott and Costello have had to offer in a long, long while. . . . If you don't expect too much this latest Abbott and Costello excursion into nonsense won't let you down too hard."

POSTSCRIPT

This film was to be the start of a prospective series of A&C films with sports as backgrounds. Reportedly, the team's next project would be "Two Bums with the Yankees," a baseball farce wherein Lou runs into a scientist who has invented an atomic ring which bestows incredible powers. The ring gives Lou such terrific speed that no catcher can throw him out on the base paths. As the team's star pitcher, Costello's remarkable fastball blasts holes in the backstop, shatters brick walls, and petrifies hitters. He even threatens to break Ruth's record of sixty home runs. But at the peak of his fame, Lou loses the ring in the middle of a particularly crucial game, and he is reduced to being a "bum" once again.

While this film never came about, Bud and Lou did begin the most prolific period of their careers with *Invisible Man.* For many years, their contract with Universal prohibited television appearances by the team. (Costello made two solo appearances on Milton Berle's *Texaco Star Theater* in 1948 and 1949.) CBS had first crack at signing Bud and Lou, but Eddie Sherman wasn't satisfied with the network's offer. In the fall of 1950, NBC introduced *The Colgate Comedy Hour,* a big-budget variety hour alternately hosted by Eddie Cantor, Bob Hope, Martin and Lewis, Donald O'Connor, Jimmy Durante, and Fred Allen. Allen disliked the format and departed that December. Sherman approached NBC president Pat Weaver, who leapt at the chance to add Abbott and Costello to the line-up. Their first appearance was on the January 7, 1951, program, for which they were paid $22,500. Bud and Lou appeared on the show another nineteen times through 1955. Virtually every Abbott and Costello routine was performed as it was meant to be—in front of a live audience. The spark it gave Bud and Lou was palpable. As Bud Jr. observed, "They loved live work. That's where they came from, the stage. They did pretty well in front of a movie camera, but when they had the chance to be on live from coast to coast, they loved it." The boys were instantly hooked by television, and after their initial Colgate show, began planning their own half-hour series. In addition to making six films between 1951 and 1953, Bud and Lou hosted the *Comedy Hour* fourteen times; shot fifty-two episodes of their classic TV series; and made another tour of Europe! It was in many ways an Abbott and Costello renaissance, and the boys approached their work with renewed vigor and enthusiasm.

COMIN' ROUND THE MOUNTAIN

Earliest Draft:
  May 18, 1950

Production Start:
  January 15, 1951

Production End:
  February 12, 1951

Copyright Date:
  May 28, 1951

Released: June 18, 1951

Running Time:
  77 minutes

Directed By:
  Charles Lamont

Produced By:
  Howard Christie

Screenplay By:
  Robert Lees and
  Frederic I. Rinaldo

Additional Dialogue By:
  John Grant

Director of Photography:
  George Robinson ASC

Art Direction:
  Bernard Herzbrun
  and Richard Riedel

Set Decorations:
  Russell A. Gausman
  and Joe Kish

Sound: Leslie I. Carey and
  Robert Pritchard

Musical Direction:
  Joseph Gershenson

Film Editor:
  Edward Curtiss

Gowns: Rosemary Odell

Hair Stylist:
  Joan St. Oegger

Make-Up: Bud Westmore

Special Photography:
  David S. Horsley ASC

Assistant Directors: Fred
  Frank and Les Warner

Al Stewart . . . Bud Abbott

Wilbert . . . . . . Lou Costello

Dorothy McCoy
  . . . . Dorothy Shay

Clark Winfield
  . . . . Kirby Grant

Kalem McCoy
  . . . . Joe Sawyer

SYNOPSIS

Al Stewart, a theatrical agent, has finally come up with a hit nightclub act in Dorothy McCoy, the Manhattan Hillbilly. But Al has also managed to get his worst client, The Great Wilbert, an escape artist, booked into the same club. When Wilbert is unable to escape from his shackles and locks, he yells for help, and Dorothy recognizes his cry as the McCoy clan yell. A photograph and a concertina in Wilbert's dressing room identify him as the grandson of "Squeeze Box" McCoy, leader of a feuding Kentucky clan. Granny McCoy will reveal the whereabouts of a fortune in gold only to kin of "Squeeze Box." Wilbert, Al, and Dorothy head for the mountains, where Dorothy recounts that the McCoys have been feuding with the Winfields for over sixty years. Dorothy, Al, and Wilbert meet up with the McCoy clan— Granny, Kalem, Uncle Clem, Luke, and Kalem's sister, Matt, on the way to the fair.

Wilbert, who knows nothing about guns, is chosen to represent the McCoys against Devil Dan Winfield in the turkey shoot, and the feud starts anew. Granny McCoy insists that Wilbert be married before she reveals the secret of the treasure. But Dorothy refuses the honor, explaining that she prefers Clark Winfield. Granny suggests Wilbert obtain a love potion from Aunt Huddy the witch to use on Dorothy. The potion, however, gets mixed up with other jugs in the cabin, and while Dorothy falls for Wilbur, he falls for Matt, who in turn falls for Al. When the potion finally wears off, Dorothy marries Clark just as the irate Winfield clan arrives. A random bullet strikes the love potion jug, and Devil Dan conveniently gets a taste of the potion and adopts Wilbert with great affection. When the map is found in Wilbert's concertina, it reveals that the treasure is hidden in the Lost Springs Mine in Winfield territory. Devil Dan blithely helps the boys gain entrance to the mine, which turns out to be above a vault at Fort Knox. Al and Wilbert break into the vault, and are arrested by armed guards.

BACKGROUND

In 1947, *The Egg and I* was one of Universal's biggest hits, and the studio attempted to spin-off two popular characters from the film, Ma and Pa Kettle, into a series of low-budget comedies. Not coincidentally, the first two Kettle films were directed by Charles Lamont. This series proved to be nearly as much a windfall for Universal-International as the Abbott and Costello films. Presumably the success in merging A&C with the studio's horror cycle is responsible for the studio's attempt to blend the team with the then-popular hillbilly genre. If Bud and Lou couldn't meet the Kettles themselves (Charles Barton was shooting *Ma and Pa Kettle at the Fair* [1951] simultaneously on the lot), Lees, Rinaldo, and Grant could come up with a close approximation.

THE SCRIPT

Actor Robert Easton, who played Luke McCoy, recalled having several conversations with John Grant about the script. "John was on the set just about every day, and he was a very,

very nice man and very, very talkative. Bud and Lou would confer with him if they needed a gag. I didn't get to know Lees and Rinaldo as well. I asked John if he'd been influenced by the Paul Webb cartoons in *Esquire*. The script is *very* derivative of Webb's rural characters; it's really quite remarkable. [In fact, the studio publicity department considered having Webb illustrate the movie ads and posters.] He said, 'Whenever I'm going to write something for Bud and Lou, I screen everything that I can see that's ever been done on the subject. Then I get ideas that I can switch and parody.' For example, he said the turkey shoot came from the film *Sergeant York* (1941) with Gary Cooper. Then he said he screened all the films about the Hatfield-McCoy feud, including *Roseanna McCoy* (1949). Of course, the feud involved the two families being on opposite sides in the Civil War, and it went on for generation after generation. Another thing John told me that was interesting was that he would in fact make a list of props and think, well, how can we use them? If they were going to do a scene in a barn, he thought of every kind of prop that could be in the barn and what Abbott and Costello could do with them. It was very interesting to think backwards, from the prop to the gag."

This indeed may have been Grant's procedure, but the fact is that Robert Arthur had assigned Robert Lees and Fred Rinaldo to "The Real McCoy" as *Foreign Legion* was being shot in the spring of 1950. Lees and Rinaldo's earliest treatment, dated May 18, 1950, includes all of the key sequences of the film, ostensibly before John made his contributions of "Additional Dialogue." As Lees explained, the comedy situations were obvious. "We knew we had to have a mountain feud, we knew we had to have love potions, which meant we had to have a witch."

THE CAST

Dorothy Shay was actually billed as the Park Avenue Hillbillie, and entertained cafe society with her rustic songs. She had a hit song in 1947 with "Feudin' and Fightin' " (from the Broadway musical *Laffing Room Only*). Dorothy sings five songs in *Mountain,* including her hit, "Agnes Clung" (by Shay and Hessie Smith). It was the most music an Abbott and Costello film had contained since *Abbott and Costello in Hollywood* (1945).

Kirby Grant (1911–1985), had previously appeared with Bud and Lou in *In Society* (1944). He has even less to do in this film. In the late 1940s and early 1950s, Grant portrayed a Canadian Mountie in several films, then went into television as "Sky King" (1953–54).

Ida Moore (1883–1964) had appeared in several rural films, including *The Egg and I, Ma and Pa Kettle,* and *Roseanna McCoy.* She has the film's funniest running gag. Whenever somebody calls her "old woman," she blasts their corncob pipe with a pistol shot.

Shaye Cogan (b. 1932?) was discovered by Bud and Lou singing at the Copacabana in New York. She became a vocalist with Vaughn Monroe's orchestra for a brief time. Shaye was cast as the Princess in the team's very next film, *Jack and the Beanstalk.*

Joe Sawyer (1901–1982) was in *Hit the Ice* and *The Naughty Nineties* with Bud and Lou, and later appeared in an episode of their TV series. Sawyer was in *Sergeant York,* and later appeared in *It Came From Outer Space* (1953). From 1954 to 1959, Sawyer portrayed Sergeant Biff O'Hara on television in *Rin Tin Tin.*

Glenn Strange (1899–1973) had previously menaced the boys as the Monster in *Abbott and Costello Meet Frankenstein.* Here, however, Glenn has more to do and is quite effective as Devil Dan Winfield.

Margaret Hamilton (1902–1985) is best remembered as the Wicked Witch of the West in *The Wizard of Oz* (1939). She was reluctant to accept a seemingly similar role in *Comin' Round the Mountain.* "I just did not want to become typecast for those kinds of parts," she explained. "The studio convinced me that wasn't the case, so I accepted the role. Of course, I went through the usual anxieties attendant to a Lou Costello picture. The first thing I heard was to be careful of the rest rooms, because Lou wired the toilets to give you a shock. Of course nothing like that actually happened at all. It was all part of the legend being created about the man. What I remember most was his overabundance of energy, always tearing around the

Devil Dan Winfield
.... Glenn Strange
Granny McCoy
.... Ida Moore
Clora McCoy
.... Shaye Cogan
Uncle Clem McCoy
.... Guy Wilkerson
Luke McCoy . Bob Easton
Jasper Winfield
.... Virgil "Slats" Taylor
Aunt Huddy
..... Margaret Hamilton
Judge... Russell Simpson
Zeke.....O. Z. Whitehead
Zeb...... Norman Leavitt
Gangsters
.... Peter Mamakos
Jack Kruschen
Barry Brooks
Man .... Joe Kirk
Old Mountain Man
.... William Fawcett
Second Mountaineer
.... Harold Goodwin
Captain
.... Robert R.
Stephenson
Square Dance Caller
... Sherman E. Sanders
Bit Woman . . Shirlee Allard
Bit Woman... James Clay

211

set like somebody with an itch that couldn't be scratched. He was a fun and dear man to work with."

Robert Easton (b. 1931) had just finished working on *The Red Badge of Courage* (1951) for John Huston. "In fact, some of the same people, like Glenn Strange, were in the picture. One day, I was on the Universal lot and Howard Christie saw me and called me into his office. He was preparing *Comin' Round the Mountain* and he asked me to read for him. Of course, I fell in love with the part and really enjoyed it. There's one line in there that I loved: 'I'm teched. I got kicked in the head by a mule.' And I suggested to Charles Lamont that we make that a running gag as I met new people, as if it was my claim to fame. Charlie was very open to that; he had a wonderful sense of comedy."

Easton, who is today Hollywood's foremost dialect coach, remembers being thrilled to work with Bud and Lou. "I was very excited because I had seen a lot of their films and found them very, very funny. Working with them, my perception was that they were totally different people. Bud was a very quiet, very pleasant man who kind of kept to himself and was *extremely* professional at all times. And of course I would not be the first to say what an *incredibly* gifted straight man he was. People who know comedy always say that no matter how brilliant the comic is, if you haven't got a straight man who really knows how to pace things, you're in big trouble. Bud knew exactly how much rope to give Costello and when to pull it back in. I think a lot of people didn't properly appreciate what a genius Bud Abbott was. I had the feeling that Lou was a very complex person—very kind, generous, philanthropic, charitable. But basic comedy the world over has quite an element of hostility in it; it has a lot to do with people losing their dignity and suffering tiny physical and psychological hurts. I think Lou really understood all of that, and found this character of being a 'baaad boy'—a mischievous kid—and that enabled him to do all these things that would be insane behavior for an adult but totally acceptable for a child. He could make it work because he was still the naughty child."

Vic Parks (b. 1907) was reunited with Bud and Lou on *Comin' Round the Mountain*. Parks first met the boys in 1937 in the vaudeville unit "Hollywood Bandwagon." "I was an acrobatic dancer, and I had just played the London Palladium for eight months. When I came back to New York my agents, Leddy and Smith, said, 'We have a unit called 'Hollywood Bandwagon' that's going to go out on the road, and there's a couple of comedians out of burlesque and Atlantic City; you might be able to do bits with them.' I thought that would be fun. There were no real names in the show—just good talent. Nobody had heard of Abbott and Costello yet. Monday morning I went to rehearsal and Bud and Lou walked in. Lou walked up to me and said, 'Hey, Abbott, this guy looks like me!' And I said, 'Yeah, you do look like me.' Everybody in the show thought we were brothers. We played all the best houses, like Loew's State in New York, the Michigan Theater in Detroit, the Oriental Theater in Chicago. They had never played houses like that before, but I had. That's where the 'Drill Scene' was put together. I was the guy who used to hit him in the head with the rifle, and sometimes instead of doing six minutes, we'd do twenty—the audience just laughed and fell over each other. They also did the baseball routine in that show. Then when this show broke up, Eddie Sherman saw Abbott and Costello and had a fight with Leddy and Smith over them."

Bud and Lou eventually moved on to the Kate Smith show and then their first film, *One Night in the Tropics* (1940). After finishing the film, the boys went on a vaudeville tour and ran into Parks in Chicago, where he was also working in vaudeville. Lou asked Vic to join them in Hollywood as his stunt double, but Parks' own career was going too well for him to give it up. Finally, in 1951, Lou offered the job to Parks again, and although he owned a Ford dealership at the time, Vic accepted. For the next five years he doubled for Costello in the team's films, television series, and *The Colgate Comedy Hour* appearances. Vic still has the matching derby he wore for many of his scenes as Lou Costello. By strange coincidence, he seemed destined to work with Lou: Vic was born exactly one year to the day after Lou.

212

THE PRODUCTION

Comin' Round the Mountain was budgeted at $640,120, on a twenty-four-day shooting schedule, eleven days of which were exteriors. Bud and Lou received $150,000 for their services, plus 10 percent of the profits. Lou's company, Cosman Productions, purchased an additional 30 percent interest in the picture. Lamont shot the film almost entirely in sequence, beginning with the nightclub scenes. Despite weather delays, the picture still finished about $2,000 *under* budget. According to a report to the executive committee, "Abbott and Costello have been cooperating very well except for one flurry when Costello insisted on the hiring of a certain bit player [Joe Kirk] to replace one already hired for the Spieler bit."

Robert Easton observed Bud and Lou's working methods with great interest: "If the scene was working very well, then they would pretty much stick to the script. If it wasn't working terribly well, then they'd start improvising or send for John Grant or discuss it with Charlie Lamont. They didn't over-rehearse. Bud and Lou both felt that they wanted to get it on film while it was still spontaneous. The essence of comedy is spontaneity. They also preferred to do the scene in the master shot; they didn't like to break up a routine into close-ups and reaction shots."

Some of the horseplay with Bobby Barber also fascinated Easton. "As often happens with somebody whose professional image is somebody who is not very sophisticated and a very child-like character, the other side of him likes to be well-dressed and sophisticated. Quite often when Lou was kidding around with Bobby they would do a kind of role reversal. When Lou was working with Bud, Abbott would be the straight man who would boss him around, correct him, or hit him. When Lou would kid around with Bobby, Lou would be the sophisticated one and Bobby was the buffoon. Costello would set up stuff for him, hit him— do all the stuff that the straight man normally does. But I never felt, as some people did, that it was sadistic. I thought that since Bobby was a comedian, Lou was letting him do what he wanted to do—get laughs."

BUD AND LOU'S SCENES

Comin' Round the Mountain remains one of the team's weaker efforts, despite the standout sequence with Margaret Hamilton. One of the problems is the preponderance of Dorothy Shay's musical numbers, which are difficult to endure. Charles Lamont recalled, "The picture didn't turn out as funny as I hoped it would. Lou objected to playing second fiddle to Dorothy Shay. When she was doing one of her songs, he'd stand behind her and make faces and try to steal the scene from her. So I had a helluva time trying to cut that picture."

The boys had a quick inside joke at the county fair that refers back to one of their most popular routines. Wilbert buys Matt a unique hot dog that has mustard injected inside. When she bites into it, the mustard sprays into Wilbert's face. When Bud comes into the scene, Lou cracks, "Now you know why I don't like mustard!"

A typical Grant exchange was added as Al and Wilbert prepare to go to bed. Wilbert wonders why his kinfolk live in such a crude cabin. "Probably your forefathers lived here," Al explains. "Beg your pardon," asks Wilbert. Al repeats himself. "I say, probably your forefathers lived here." "My four fathers?" exclaims Wilbert. "Sure," affirms Al. "I didn't have four fathers," Wilbert protests. "Sure you did," declares Al. "Well, if I did," cracks Wilbert, "only one came home nights!"

Grant also wisely added the team's classic "You're Forty, She's Ten" dialogue, first used in *Buck Privates*. It fits the Ozark locale perfectly since it concerns Lou falling in love with a very young girl.

The spooky scene with Aunt Huddy the witch is scored with stock music from *Abbott and Costello Meet Frankenstein*. Aunt Huddy is incensed that the boys doubt her powers. She quickly produces a hunk of clay and molds it into a figure that resembles Wilbert. He asks Al what

With Hollywood's perennial witch, Margaret Hamilton.

Huddy is doing. "It's an effigy," Al explains. "I don't know what letter it starts with," Wilbert says, "but that's beginning to look like *me!*" Huddy threatens to jab the effigy unless the boys pay her $5 for the potion. "Not until we get the potion," Al declares. "She can't stick us for five bucks." Huddy jabs the pin into Wilbert's effigy. Wilbert immediately grabs his arm and yells, "She can too," he says. "Pay her the money." Al still refuses, so Huddy then jabs the effigy of Wilbert in the posterior. He lets out a howl. Al scoffs, "Aw, that's all in your mind." Wilbert, hands on his rear, whimpers, "You got a poor sense of direction. Please pay her the money." Al finally complies, and as Huddy is busy preparing the potion, Wilbert sculpts a figurine of her. The two of them then engage in a bizarre, hilarious duel, alternately jabbing each other's effigies with pins. It is easily the funniest sequence in the film, and one of the best the boys ever did.

At the end of the sequence, Wilbert climbs on the witch's broom and rockets out of the cabin. Vic Parks recalled, "This broom was flown with three piano wires by about fifteen guys. What worried me was if one of those wires snagged, it would cut my head off. We worked on this for half a day, and it's a split second of film. One time, as they started to pull it, it jerked, and I lost my balance and nearly fell off. I managed to hang on by my arms but I wrenched my back and had to go to the studio hospital."

Bud Abbott, Jr., visited the set on February 10, when the scene with Margaret Hamilton was shot. Although Hamilton's make-up briefly impressed him, Bud Jr. was a little bored. "I had brought a squirt gun with me. There were these huge studio lights, maybe three feet across. I was fascinated by them. It was a big soundstage, and I was in the back, away from where they were shooting. I could hear them say, 'Okay, quiet on the set. Action!' Everybody would get quiet, and I'd squirt these bulbs with my squirt gun. Because when the water hit the bulb, it went *shhhhhhhhhh!* It would vaporize immediately! [laughs] It was great! So I heard, 'Quiet on the set, camera, action,' and I squirted this son of a gun and it blew up! I mean pow!, it shattered! There were screams from the people on the set. Well, I *ran*. I ran out the back door of the stage, ran down about two more stages to these rest rooms, and I hid. I thought, 'They're gonna kill me!' Because they were all cursing—'Son of a bitch! What the hell's going on!?' When I got my nerve back I sort of mosied back to the stage and they kind of ignored me. I thought, 'Wow, I got away with it.' Then my dad called me over and said, 'You know something, it's very dangerous to squirt those bulbs.' I don't know how he knew. And he said, 'It's okay what you did. But don't do it again because you might get hurt.' "

DELETIONS AND ADDITIONS

Wilbert goes through most of the film thinking that Matt is a boy. In a deleted scene at the fair, Wilbert asks Matt why "he" isn't dancing like the rest of the boys. "I ain't the dancin' type," Matt replies. "I'm the marryin' type." Wilbert asks, "Find the lucky girl yet?" Matt is shocked. "Girl! What'd I want a girl fer? Some day I'm gonna wear a dress and high heeled shoes and walk like a lady." Wilbert, of course, does a take upon hearing this. "If you do, people are gonna talk about you."

In a cut gag in the bedroom sequence, Wilbert tries to sleep among the hillbillies despite the fact that Luke's snores blow Uncle Clem's beard into his face. The scene probably wasn't nearly as funny as the version in *Lost in a Harem* (1944) because the hillbillies are rather benign compared to the menacing Arabs of *Harem*.

Following the scene with Uncle Clem's beard, Zeb arrives to join the rest of the cast in the bed. When he climbs in, Wilbert is pushed out. The final film ends the sequence here, deleting an elaborate gag that followed. Wilbert now decides to pull rank and take the cot from Al, who reluctantly climbs up on a shelf to sleep. Meanwhile, the driving rain outside the cabin has begun to seep inside. Eventually, the water has risen almost level with the shelf Al is sleeping on. Several ducks swim about nonchalantly, while Wilbert sleeps blissfully on his floating cot. Four small spurts of water appear on the surface of the water near Wilbert. The camera pans down under the water to follow the spurts to their source—the brass bed containing the McCoys! They sleep peacefully as streams of bubbles issue from their mouths. The next morning, virtually every trace of the high water is gone. Al, on his shelf, and the McCoys, in their bed, are still asleep. But we discover that Wilbert's cot teeters precariously on a rafter. When he awakes, he obliviously tosses his feet over the side, drops through the air and crashes on the sleeping McCoys below.

REVIEWS

The studio's advertising budgets for *Abbott and Costello Meet the Invisible Man* and *Comin' Round the Mountain* were $25,000 each. Only one Universal-International feature in 1951 had a smaller ad budget—*Undercover Girl* at $20,000. Meanwhile the studio spent $160,000 to promote *Frances Goes to the Races* (directed by Arthur Lubin), and $150,000 on *Ma and Pa Kettle Back on the Farm*.

Variety: "This comedy venture by Abbott and Costello is below par for the course, lacking the raucous hilarity expected of the comics. . . . Abbott and Costello manage to wring out several neat laughs but badly missed are their standard routines that could have been counted

From the deleted flood sequence: after the water recedes, Wilbert finds himself marooned on a rafter in the cabin.

to assist any material, no matter how thin. Miss Shay undoubtedly will rate further screen assignments. Her personality comes over strongly, and her singing...peps up the footage.... Charles Lamont's direction of the Howard Christie production gives it okay pacing and some chuckles despite the poor material written by Robert Lees and Frederic I. Rinaldo.

Los Angeles Daily News: "About the only thing different with this version of A. and C. is the locale. It is laid in the mountain country.... However the fat one and the thin one are aided considerably by the presence in this picture of Dorothy Shay, a personable young lady who whimsically bills herself as the Park Avenue Hillbillie. (Get that spelling!) Miss Shay blasts her way through four or five songs in the picture, and these are planted to give relief from the tired comedics of Costello and the bored and boric straightmanship of Abbott."

New York Journal-American: "I have nothing against Abbott and Costello. For the first hundred or so times I laughed, too. Then I got tired. Now I seem to have developed a violent allergy, and if I have to see many more of them I'm afraid I'll have to start crying.... I think I'm being fair and restrained when I assert that this is the worst Abbott and Costello to date.'

Film Daily: "Hieing themselves to the Kentucky hills this time, and with the Park Avenue Hillbillie, Dorothy Shay, as guide, Abbott and Costello deliver up a roundly good entrant for the summer laugh running. There's lots of fun for all as they meet up with a comic assortment of folks in the course of their search for a hidden treasure. Yarn has plenty invention in the comedy line and the gags run full range from mild to out-right uproarious quality. Show was cleverly directed by Charles Lamont for the yaks and they come easily. A&C are in top form, the best they've been in some time. Dorothy Shay has looks, sings with a fine flair for the hillbilly ballad and also makes with the romance."

POSTSCRIPT

Between 1948 and 1951, Abbott and Costello made eight films. Yet, during the same period, *fifteen* of the team's earlier films were re-released. Not only did this saturation eat into the profits, but it also confused the team's fans. Lou Hart, manager of the Schine theater chain in the northeast, wrote to Universal, claiming moviegoers could no longer tell the new movies apart from the old ones. He suggested that every ad carry a line proclaiming "brand-new," or "just finished." The studio took Hart's advice in the advertising for many of the team's subsequent releases.

This was the last Abbott and Costello film screenwriters Robert Lees and Fred Rinaldo worked on. They were blacklisted in the early 1950s. "Bob Arthur was executive secretary of the Motion Picture Alliance for the Preservation of American Ideals," Lees recalled. "This was the extreme right-wing motion picture group; this was the one that was friendly to the House Un-American Activities Committee. We had a very amicable relationship, and we thought that Bob Arthur was a damn good producer; he understood what we wanted to do, but politically we were 180 degrees apart. And in front of the Committee he said that he had to watch that we didn't put anything subversive into the Abbott and Costello pictures! [laughs] Talk about the Breen Office! What subversive line could Abbott say? Was 'Who's On First' supposed to be Stalin? I don't know. [Laughs]. When *Comin' Round the Mountain* was released, I was working as a maitre d' in Tucson, Arizona. Then Paramount released *Jumping Jacks* with Martin and Lewis. That was an interesting story. We had written a service comedy when we were at Paramount (1941–43), but they couldn't cast it! They even considered bringing in Cantinflas from Mexico! Anyway, it wound up on a shelf for ten years until Martin and Lewis came along. So we had two pictures out. It was particularly tough on Fred and me because just at the time we were blacklisted television was coming in. We had written a picture for Desi Arnaz [*Holiday in Havana* (1949)] and we had a great relationship with him. We would have moved so fast with our credits into televsion and *I Love Lucy*, so it was very ironic. But overall, life has been very good to me and at this late date I have no complaints."

Lees and Rinaldo found steady work writing for television in the late 1950s and early 1960s, and are now comfortably retired.

JACK AND THE BEANSTALK

SYNOPSIS

Jack and Dinkle are dispatched by Polly at the Cosman Employment Agency to the home of Eloise Larkin, who needs a sitter for her obnoxious kid brother, Donald, and their infant sister. Jack tries to read the fairy tale "Jack and the Beanstalk" to Donald, but Jack falls asleep and dreams himself into the fairyland of the story. The Giant has stolen all the country's food as well as the crown jewels, so to regain the jewels, the Princess must marry Prince Arthur, whom she has never seen. On his way to town to sell his last possession of value, the family cow, Jack meets Prince Arthur, who is also kidnapped by the Giant. Mr. Dinklepuss, the fast-talking butcher, trades five magic beans for Jack's cow. Word comes that the Princess has been kidnapped by the Giant, and soon after, the cow as well.

Jack plants the magic beans and overnight the beanstalk grows into the sky. Jack declares that he is going to kill the Giant, rescue the Princess, and retrieve Nellie, the hen that lays the golden eggs. Intrigued by Nellie, Dinklepuss joins Jack on his climb. At the top of the beanstalk, the boys are quickly captured by the Giant, who hauls them off to his castle where the Prince and Princess are now imprisoned. Jack and Dink conspire with the Giant's house-keeper, Polly, to escape. After a furious chase through the castle, the prisoners escape by catapulting over the castle wall. Jack quickly follows the others down the beanstalk, where the King and the villagers celebrate their arrival. Jack chops down the beanstalk, sending the Giant to his death. He is about to be decorated by the King when he wakes up from his dream in Donald's room and Eloise and Arthur return from their date.

BACKGROUND

Rather than deal with another studio, Abbott and Costello decided that they should produce the independent films that were permitted under their Universal contract. The team also insisted that these productions be made in color; if Universal wasn't going to give them a color film, they'd do it themselves. Early in 1951, Lou formed Exclusive Productions and Bud formed Woodley Productions to produce these films. Lou's company would own the first film, *Jack and the Beanstalk,* with Bud working on salary, and Bud's company would own the next production, *Abbott and Costello Meet Captain Kidd,* with Lou working on salary. Alex Gottlieb, who had produced the team's first ten hits at Universal, was recruited once again. "I got a phone call one day from Eddie Sherman," he recalled. "I had left Warner Bros. and was making independent pictures. Eddie said he had just made a deal with Warners to finance two independent Abbott and Costello films. Bud will make a picture for Lou, and Lou will make a picture for Bud. Lou wanted to be the boss on the first picture. He picked the writer,

Earliest Draft:
June 1, 1951

Production Start:
July 9, 1951

Production End:
August 2, 1951

Copyright Date:
April 7, 1952

Released: April 9, 1952

Running Time:
78 minutes

Reissued: 1960 by RKO

Directed By:
Jean Yarbrough

Produced By:
Alex Gottlieb

Executive Producer:
Pat Costello

Screenplay By: Nat Curtis

From a Story By:
Pat Costello

Additional Comedy By:
Felix Adler

Words and Music By:
Bob Russell and
Lester Lee

Choreography By:
Johnny Conrad

Music Supervisor:
Raoul Kraushaar

Musical Score Composed
and Conducted By:
Heinz Roemheld

Choral Direction By:
Norman Luboff

Director of Photography:
George Robinson ASC

Film Editor:
Otho Lovering ACE

Sound: William Randall,
Joel Moss

Art Director:
McClure Capps

Production Supervisor:
Clarence Eurist

Set Decorator:
Fred McClean

Costumes: Jack Mosser,
  Lloyd Lambert

Make-Up: Abe Haberman

Special Effects: Carl Lee

Dialogue Director:
  Milt Bronson

Photographic Effects:
  J. R. Glass

Assistant Director:
  Alfred Westen

Photographed in
  SuperCineColor

Color Consultants:
  Wilton R. Holm,
  Clifford D. Shank

Dinklepuss . . . Bud Abbott

Jack . . . . Lou Costello

Sergeant Riley/The Giant
  . . . . Buddy Baer

Polly . . . . Dorothy Ford

Mother . . . Barbara Brown

Donald . . . . . David Stollery

The King . . William Farnum

Eloise/The
  Princess . . Shaye Cogan

Arthur/The Prince
  . . . . James Alexander

Johnny Conrad and
  Dancers

and he cast the picture. He wanted Shaye Cogan and James Alexander. I said 'Lou, they can't sing.' He said, 'I own this picture.' I said, 'Lou, anything you want, I'll give you.' I also put a clause in the contract that I didn't have to play cards with them. That was fine with Lou, because he didn't want to spend too much money on the picture. He wanted to make the picture for $400,000. He said, 'Watch every penny, Alex. I know you can do it.' "

Meanwhile, ratings for the team's first two appearances on *The Colgate Comedy Hour* had been excellent, and NBC wanted to sign the team for two more seasons. Lou was anxious to begin their own half-hour television series, and Eddie Sherman persuaded NBC to finance filming of the first 26 episodes of *The Abbott and Costello Show* with an option to buy. The *Hollywood Reporter* reported the deal on May 8, 1951: "Abbott and Costello yesterday signed a five-year exclusive TV deal with NBC guaranteeing them $15,000,000 for the period starting in September. The comedians are free to do their regular feature picture work and make personal appearances. . . . Under the contract, termed the most fabulous deal in TV to date, Abbott and Costello will do 22 half-hour shows on film and four to eight live one-hour shows in the first year. During the last four years they will do 44 TV shows annually, half on film and half live. Contracts were signed by A&C's TCA Corp., which will produce the half-hour shows on film at Hal Roach studios."

Gottlieb and director Jean Yarbrough were already involved in pre-production on *Jack and the Beanstalk* when the NBC deal was signed, and they were immediately recruited to produce and direct the team's television series. Hillary Brooke, Sid Fields, Gordon Jones, and Joe Besser were signed for the cast, and Eddie Forman wrote the first six episodes, which were filmed at the end of May 1951. Two months later, production began on *Jack and the Beanstalk*.

THE SCRIPT

The Abbott and Costello films had always been popular with children, so it seemed logical to gear at least one film for matinee audiences. According to the pressbook, Costello got the idea for the movie while reading "Jack and the Beanstalk" to his four-year-old daughter, Christine. "I was only part way through the book when I started to look at the pretty pictures and thought what a wonderful movie this would make. Then I remembered that some of the biggest box-office smashes have been fantasies—*The Wizard of Oz* and the Disney films."

Lou hired a screenwriter named Nat Curtis to do the screenplay. Alex Gottlieb recalled, "Lou gave me his script and said this is what we're going to shoot. I said, 'Lou, it needs a lot of work if we're going to make a real good picture.' He said, 'I love the script, I don't want to change it.' He was the boss." Lou explained to *The New York Times*, "I just got tired of hearing people all the time say we're using the same routines over and over again—even if they do get laughs. I said, 'Abbott, let's see if we can make a picture without using one thing anybody can say is an old burlesque gag or something we've done before. It's now or never.' "

THE CAST

Buddy Baer (b. 1915) had appeared in *Africa Screams* with the team. The ex-boxer had recently completed his role as Ursus in *Quo Vadis* (1951). Lou visited him on location at Cincetta in Italy during the team's European tour in 1950.

Shaye Cogan (b. 1932?) made her debut in *Comin' Round the Mountain*, yet preferred to think of this as her first film. Shaye later married a record company executive and appeared in Alan Freed's *Mr. Rock and Roll* (1957).

James Alexander (1902–1961) had starred as Curly, the singing cowboy, with the road company of *Oklahoma!* He later appeared in two episodes of the team's TV series, including, appropriately enough, *The Western Story*.

Dorothy Ford (b. 1923) had appeared with Bud and Lou briefly in *Here Come the Co-Eds*

FAR LEFT: Bud and his longtime stunt double, Joe La Cava. LEFT: Lou caught between stunt double Vic Parks and unidentified stand-in.

(1945). In *Beanstalk,* she performs a comic dance with Lou that is reminiscent of his waltz with Joan Davis in *Hold That Ghost.* Dorothy had performed a comic jitterbug with Mickey Rooney in *Love Laughs at Andy Hardy* (1947).

David Stollery later appeared on TV's *Mickey Mouse Club* as Marty in "The Adventures of Spin and Marty" (1955–57).

THE PRODUCTION

Except for the opening and closing sequences, *Beanstalk* was shot in Super CineColor, a new three-strip color process. Jean Yarbrough shot the picture in twenty-two days—two days less than scheduled—and a considerable amount of money was saved by using sets from *Joan of Arc* (1948) that were still standing at Hal Roach studios. The cost of producing *Beanstalk* was just $417,742—quite frugal considering the fact that color film stock is approximately twice as expensive as black-and-white. With Bud and Lou each receiving $115,000, and other expenses, the final cost was reported as $682,580.

Bud was interviewed about the team's working arrangements. "I see no reason why we shouldn't just make pictures for ourselves," he said. "It should work out very well. The system has worked out fine so far. When we make pictures at U-I, we set a time limit for working, say four o'clock in the afternoon. When it gets to that time we say, 'Okay, that's enough for today,' and we go home. But I've been working like a dog on Lou's picture, and I know he'll do the same for mine."

Joe Glaston, Jr., the son of Bud and Lou's longtime press agent, remembered visiting the set as a two-year old. "I became buddies with Buddy Baer, the Giant; he really liked kids. At one point there's a scene where they hit him in the gut with a battering ram. I just went bananas when I saw them do that to him. I cried and I ruined the take. They had a meeting to discuss whether the scene was too violent, and they decided that it was only because I knew Buddy Baer off the set that I was so appalled that they had hit him. They figured that the kids in the audience are going to see him as the evil Giant and they won't give a damn—they'll probably cheer. So they left the scene in."

Vickie Abbott recalled that her dad grew his trademark mustache for the film. "I remember coming to breakfast one morning when he started growing the mustache. I said, 'Dad, what is that?' He said, 'It's a mustache, Vickie. I've got to have it for the movie.' I said, 'Well, I hope you're not going to keep it, are you?' He said, 'I don't know. I think it kind of makes me look debonair.' A lot of people remember him with the mustache; it gave him a whole new look."

Chris Costello recalled that the cow found a home at the Costello ranch, and the golden

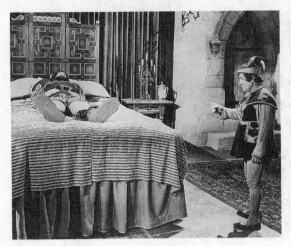

ABOVE: In a deleted scene, Jack attempts to steal the keys to the dungeon from the sleeping Giant. The Giant, dreaming he is bowling, grabs Jack by the head and "bowls" him several times across the room!

ABOVE RIGHT: The recording session for *Jack and the Beanstalk*.

egg found a nest in Lou's den. "Patrick the harp became a fixture in our upstairs sitting room, and I remember being terrified of it." [laughs]

BUD AND LOU'S SCENES

Because the film adheres to the original story quite faithfully, Bud and Lou have little chance to use their tried-and-true routines. But trying to film the story without lapsing into the routines proved a difficult task. Seemingly innocent words or phrases automatically triggered a routine, a gag, or a line. It was tough, for example, for them not to use their classic "Cow's Udder" byplay, first seen in *Ride 'Em Cowboy*. In another scene, Lou unconsciously ad-libbed, "I got brains I haven't even used yet." Bud, hearing his cue, replied, "Well don't let them go to your head." In another, Lou climbed into bed with the Giant for some standard monkey business. "We cut both of them out," Lou says. "Altogether we cut out $50,000 worth of shooting." The boys did include at least one inside joke: the Cosman Employment Agency is named after another of Lou's production companies.

Without the routines, Lou relied on playing to the camera more than ever, giving one of his least restrained performances in years. He is particularly charming in his song number, "I Fear Nothing." Bud, meanwhile, has several funny moments as the avaricious butcher and proves that he would have made a fine comic villain if given the opportunity.

DELETIONS AND ADDITIONS

James Alexander had two songs cut from the production. The first was a version of the "Lord's Prayer," sung to Donald before the baby-sitters arrive. A second number, "Darlene," was mercilessly (or mercifully) reduced to just three repetitions of the title. In the late 1970s, when *Beanstalk* was first syndicated to television in color, the distributor used a first-cut preview print that included three extra minutes of footage, including the complete version of "Darlene," and an extra verse of "The Dreamer's Cloth."

The film ends with Jack reprising his song, "I Fear Nothing," and dancing out the door of Eloise's house. The script had quite a different ending. After Donald crowns Jack with a water pitcher, Polly and Sergeant Riley drive up to the house as Eloise and Arthur return from their rehearsal. Eloise and Arthur wear their stage costumes as the Princess and Prince. Polly wants to check up on Jack. All four of them enter, and Dink explains that everything is fine. Jack, however, dazed from the water pitcher, hears Sergeant Riley's booming voice and thinks he's the Giant. He creeps into the living room brandishing a letter opener and exclaims, "I'll save you, Princess!" Riley dodges Jack and is about to thrash him when Polly intervenes. She clobbers Riley, and Jack ends up in her arms, his head nestled in her waistline. "My hero," he sighs. Fade out.

REVIEWS

Hollywood Reporter: "The Abbott and Costello comedy talents are well fitted for the zany concept of the classic fairy tale, resulting in a lot of fun.... Jean Yarbrough's direction [sets] a lively pace that makes the fairy tale part of the picture seem all too short.... Costello is genuinely funny as Jack, with Abbott getting laughs as a larcenous butcher. The capers of both should add to the team's following."

Los Angeles Daily News: "The film lacks much of the old Abbott and Costello comedy punch and appears to have suffered somewhat from meager production efforts. Actually, our chief criticism of the vehicle is the casting of Costello as Jack.... If Abbott and Costello wanted to do something with 'Jack and the Beanstalk,' they should have figured out some way to capitalize on the appeal of the story without gross miscasting. They could have worked themselves into the story and still preserved much of its delightfulness. Perhaps Lou could have been cast as the Prince. At least the comic possibilities in that direction would be more apropros.... The best performer in the movie was Buddy Baer as the giant. We somehow felt that he was one guy who wasn't miscast."

The New York Times: "There's always room for improvement, and 'Jack and the Beanstalk' ... proves the accuracy of the maxim. Abbott and Costello were in a rut before they decided to tackle the legend.... They have not refined their particular brand of slapstick to any great degree, and the marked improvement can be traced mainly to their choice of a story. While the pair have turned out a film that falls far short of distinguished slapstick comedy, they deserve a plaudit or two for leaving behind the dreary routine of inane stories and meaningless antics. Stay with it, boys, you're gaining."

Los Angeles Examiner: "The mishaps of Costello as the sad-sack Jack are sufficiently ingenuous to appeal to the juvenile mind, and the village where Jack meanders around being stupid has a story-book quality that springs right out of the book's pages. The role of the butcher who trades Jack out of his valuable possesion, his cow, for five magic beans, has been expanded so Bud Abbott can be in the act all the way up the beanstalk and back. The team's antics aren't as frenetic as customary in their regular slapstick pictures, but Abbott is in his familiar groove, taking advantage of his partner at every turn. For the uncritical and the Abbott and Costello fans, 'Jack and the Beanstalk' should be fun, but our personal opinion is that the realm of fantasy still belongs to Walt Disney."

POSTSCRIPT

The World Premiere of *Jack and the Beanstalk* was held at Paterson's Fabian Theater on April 5, 1952. That weekend, Bud and Lou hosted *The Colgate Comedy Hour* with Charles Laughton as their guest (they had recently completed filming *Abbott and Costello Meet Captain Kidd*), then appeared at the Warner Theater for the film's New York premiere. The team followed with a two-week promotional tour for *Beanstalk,* stopping in Philadelphia, New Haven, Boston, Pittsburgh, Harrisburg, Reading, Washington, D.C., Cincinnati, Cleveland, Detroit, Toronto, Buffalo, and Rochester. Warners released some 400 prints in time for Easter vacation. Universal watched how *Beanstalk* was received with great interest, particularly with the added support of a personal appearance tour by the team. The studio requested reports from local theater managers. Despite the team's live appearances, *Beanstalk* did disappointing business. One reason was the script. But Alex Gottlieb theorized, "It didn't work because Lou was the wrong fellow for it. He was too old; he couldn't be a little boy." Even so, *Jack and the Beanstalk* made back its cost in its first two days in release, and turned out to be Warner's biggest grosser in England that year. Bud and Lou also released a *Jack and the Beanstalk* record, with songs and spoken dialogue, on the Decca label on June 9, 1952.

LOST IN ALASKA

Earliest Draft:
    May 19, 1950

Production Start:
    December 3, 1951

Production End:
    December 31, 1951

Copyright Date:
    June 24, 1952

Released: July 28, 1952

Running Time:
    76 minutes

Directed By:
    Jean Yarbrough

Produced By:
    Howard Christie

Screenplay By:
    Martin Ragaway
    and Leonard Stern

Original Story:
    Elwood Ullman

Director of Photography:
    George Robinson ASC

Art Direction:
    Bernard Herzbrun
    and Robert Boyle

Set Decorations:
    Russell A. Gausman
    and Ray Jeffers

Sound: Leslie I. Carey
    and Harold Lewis

Musical Direction:
    Joseph Gershenson

Film Editor:
    Leonard Weiner

Musical Numbers Staged
    By: Harold Belfer

Costumes: Kara

Hair Stylist:
    Joan St. Oegger

Make-Up: Abe Haberman

Tom Watson
    .... Bud Abbott

George Bell . Lou Costello

Rosette ..... Mitzi Green

Nugget Joe McDermott
    .... Tom Ewell

SYNOPSIS

Two firemen, George and Tom, rescue Nugget Joe McDermott from drowning off a pier in 1890s San Francisco. Joe has a $2 million fortune in gold in Alaska, but he wants to die because Rosette, a dance hall girl, no longer loves him. Tom and George keep watch on him until Joe receives a letter informing him that Rosette still loves him. He plans to return to Alaska, and Tom and George join him for the voyage. On arriving in Skagway, Tom and George discover that Joe is a marked man. He once was a sheriff and hanged many people whose friends are now out for revenge.

Jake Stillman, who runs the casino where Rosette works, demands that Rosette marry Joe. Jake then plans to kill Joe, marry Rosette, and gain possession of the fortune. Rosette reveals the plot to the boys, who foil the scheme by sending Joe and Rosette away from Skagway to hide the gold. George and Tom try to hold off Jake and his henchmen. After a series of adventures on the frozen tundra, where the boys thwart the gang, the gold is finally lost when the sled sinks into a crevice in the ice. With nothing to fight over, Stillman, Joe, and Rosette become friends again and plan a wedding celebration.

BACKGROUND

One day in 1951, Eddie Sherman happened to stroll by the Castle Films store on Vine Street. A sign in the window advertised, "Abbott and Costello in 'Oysters and Muscles.'" Sherman recalled, "I walked in and asked, 'What is this?' The guy told me he was selling a four-minute film of Bud and Lou's 'Oyster' routine. I said, 'What do you get for it?' He said $17.50. I said, 'Do you sell a lot of them?' He said he couldn't keep it in stock, and that it was distributed all over the country. I asked if he had any others. 'Oh yeah,' he said. 'We've got five other Abbott and Costello routines.'

"Now, not because of any genius on my part, but when we wrote our last contract with Universal I put a clause in that said they could never release any portions of the Abbott and Costello pictures. I was trying to protect the team. I didn't want them to take any clips of Lou by himself and sell them. So I got hold of an attorney and he read the contract, went down to Castle Films, and got the whole story.

"Also during that time we found out that the reissues of their pictures were doing tremendous business. Some friends of mine who were exhibitors told me that some of the pictures had done bigger business in reissue than they had in their original run! When I went to Europe in 1949 a lot of the theater managers said, 'The biggest thing over here are the reissues of Abbott and Costello.' But there was nothing we could do, because our participation in them ended after seven years."

And so, on November 9, 1951, a month before starting on *Alaska,* Bud and Lou filed a $5,000,000 damage suit in Federal Court against Universal and Realart Pictures, claiming that the studio "schemed to cheat and defraud and deprive them of their rights and to destroy their interests in films" in which they had a participation. A&C charged that since 1940 Universal had supplied them with false accountings and deliberately created a complicated accounting system to confuse and bewilder them. The complaint contended that Universal, without the team's consent, chopped up some of their features into shorts and received in excess of $1,250,000 from their distribution, yet made no accounting of the profits. The suit charged that the shorts were sold for showing in the home and "cheap places of entertainment and low repute," in saloons, nickelodeons, and for use in slot machines. The team contended that their artistic reputation had suffered and would continue to suffer because of Universal's alleged slander on their stature and position and by alleged misrepresentation of their acting abilities. It also charged that Universal entered into a secret agreement with Realart in 1947 to resissue their feature films without the team's consent. Realart paid Universal $3,250,000 plus 35 percent of the gross. An accounting to July 1950, showing sales on the reissues at $1,450,000 was actually $600,000 short. It was also discovered that the team was improperly charged for interest, amortization, and expenses of a penthouse apartment maintained for social purposes by a Universal executive.

These were the unpleasant accusations in the air as Bud and Lou reported for work at Universal.

THE SCRIPT

Robert Arthur had an idea to place Bud and Lou in the Klondike as early as March 1949. In the spring of 1950, Arthur assigned comedy veteran Elwood Ullman to develop a treatment, called "The Sourdoughs," then assigned the scripting chores to Leonard Stern and Martin Ragaway.

Stern explained, "We alternated between Abbott and Costello and Ma and Pa Kettle. There's a distinct advantage in tailoring something. It's quite different today, where you write a script and you have no idea who's going to get it. . . . Robert Arthur was very much a story person. We had endless story conferences with Robert. He was a very dear man and very aware of the writer's responsibilities and creative needs.

"Marty and I were looking for locations Bud and Lou hadn't been, always searching for something different physically. I think the thing that keyed us was the fact that we'd have to work with a dog team; we'd be in igloos; ice; people they hadn't encountered before. Then we had a theme that I fell in love with: what if the person they're trying to protect is the most hated person in the world. That became the enchanting notion, and we were committed to working it out. To this day I try to do revisions on the same theme.

"We also developed the roulette routine, and I remember how proud we were of that, and I never felt it was shot as well as it could have been. What generally happened was, the writer was noticeably absent from the set. In our case we were always working on another movie. So we would go to dailies and the scene would be an accomplished fact. There was very little you could do about it. Also, physical comedy is very difficult to interpret unless there are meetings. Sometimes it was just a misinterpretation of what was intentioned. Then suddenly you realized, 'My God, there could be another vision to this joke!' But very often that was the only way it could be done. I think that's what led writers to become either producers or directors—so they could protect their material.

"I had an interesting retrospective conversation with Lou when I was directing the *Steve Allen Show.* Bud and Lou had split and Lou had become a semi-regular on our show. He literally sat down and apologized in many ways for not giving all of his comic attention to the things we wrote for them. He and Bud had a history of angst and anger that they suppressed, and it suddenly started to manifest itself in those years. So Lou felt, in 1958, that he had done a disservice to the material. He felt it was more inventive than the things they

223

With Tom Ewell during one of Lou's specialties—the laugh that melts into tears.

had done in the past and he should have recognized that. It was quite fascinating. He had mellowed and become quite cognizant of his strengths and weaknesses."

On the other side of the coin, director Jean Yarbrough thought the script was poor, but agreed to direct the film as a favor to Lou. Also noticeably absent were the contributions of John Grant. About this time, Lou was swept up in the anti-Communist hysteria of Joseph McCarthy. He was thoroughly convinced that there was a Communist conspiracy to infiltrate the film industry, and he demanded that his employees sign a petition swearing that they had no part in any Communist work or organization. John Grant was one who wouldn't sign, for whatever reason, and Lou fired him. Grant was never blacklisted, however, and continued to work. In fact, he contributed some very funny gags to Martin and Lewis' new service comedy, *Sailor Beware* (1951), which was released as *Alaska* was put into production. Lou realized his mistake, and Grant rejoined the fold with the team's next picture, *Abbott and Costello Meet Captain Kidd*.

THE CAST

Tom Ewell (b. 1909) had come from Broadway, where he established himself as a fine character comedian, to make his film debut in *Adam's Rib* (1949). When *Alaska* was released later in 1952, Ewell was starring on Broadway in *The Seven Year Itch*. He recreated his role in the 1955 film version with Marilyn Monroe. Tom recalled how he was cast in *Alaska:* "I was under contract to Universal and I was doing a picture called *Up Front* (1951), based on Bill Mauldin's cartoon characters, Willie and Joe. Lou came out of a screening room, where he was watching his rushes, and he went in and looked at my rushes. He came to me and said, 'Look, Tom, I just think you're wonderful. Would you be in our next picture?' I had seen them in New York in *Streets of Paris* and I just fell over in the aisle. I said 'Certainly! I'd be happy to be in it.'

"Well, when I first showed up to pick up my script and to talk to the director, Lou said, 'Look, Tom, I have great respect for you. I've seen your work, and I think that you're a marvelous actor and a marvelous comedian. I know you're from the theater and that you study your lines. But Bud and I don't work that way. We never even read our scripts. We'll have them bound in leather, and some day when I'm old I'll sit down and read them. We don't even call each other by the names of the characters. We call each other Bud or Lou. Because we have a way of working that we find works for us. That way is this. A dialogue director will come in before a scene and read the scene to us. Now, mind you, we've never read the script; we don't know what the hell the damn thing is about. He reads the scene to us once or twice and we think about it—but we don't rehearse. We go out and play the scene. We come from burlesque and vaudeville. That's the way we work. We take an idea and work it over. I know that's going to be difficult for you, because you don't work that way. But we can't change. I'm sure when you get used to it you'll like it. But just feel free anytime to say anything you want to in the scene. Everyone has that freedom. I know you'll study the script. But just remember that when we take off in a scene, you're welcome to come in and get on the boat and ride along with us.'

"So the night before I did the picture, I worried about this. I had Judy Holliday over for dinner and I told Judy about it. I said, 'What am I gonna do? I'm scared to death.' And she said, 'Honey, it's just rape, that's what it is. Just lay down and enjoy it.' So I went to the studio the next day. At the end of the third day, Lou called me over and said, 'Tom, you've been in the scenes now for three days and you haven't said anything yet.' And I said, 'Well, to tell you the truth, Lou, I haven't thought of anything to say.' I just stood around for three days and then of course I got into it and played right along with them."

Mitzi Green (1920–1969), a former child star, returned to the screen, after a fifteen-year absence, at the age of thirty-one. (Denise Darcel was originally scheduled for the role.) Mitzi made seventeen pictures in the early 1930s, including *Tom Sawyer, Huckleberry Finn, Girl Crazy,* and *Little Orphan Annie,* and appeared on Broadway in *Babes in Arms* and *Billion Dollar Baby.* She followed *Alaska* with *Bloodhounds of Broadway* (1952), and had a short-lived sit-com in 1955 in which she played a stuntwoman. Mitzi was married to director Joseph Pevney (also at Universal) for twenty-seven years.

Bruce Cabot (1904–1972) is probably best known for rescuing Fay Wray in *King Kong* (1933). He had recently appeared in *Sorrowful Jones* (1949) and *Fancy Pants* (1950) with Bob Hope and Lucille Ball, and the offbeat western *Best of the Badmen* (1951).

THE PRODUCTION

Alaska was budgeted for $672,230 on a twenty-four-day shooting schedule. The studio's process stage was turned into Arctic tundra by 1,000 bags of untoasted cornflakes and one ton of gypsum. Fully half of the shooting time was spent on this set. The most interesting item on the budget, however, cost just $61.80. It was an order for six derbies for Lou from the Hutchinson Hat Manufacturing Co.

From all accounts, Bud and Lou didn't let their pending lawsuit interfere with their work. Studio memos describe the boys as being "cooperative." Make-up man Abe Haberman recalled, "There was this scene where I needed to freeze Bud and Lou. Two dummies were made that looked just like Bud and Lou that were actually frozen—then I had to simulate that on the real Bud and Lou. I used an egg sealer with epsom salts for the overall effect of snow. We were shooting on a very hot soundstage, and here were Bud and Lou, troupers that they were, dressed up in these heavy snow parkas—not one complaint from either of them. That's why I say they were both troupers."

Tom Ewell remembers the production as a wonderful experience. While Tom didn't like the script, he enjoyed the experience of working with Bud and Lou. "My overall impression was that Lou was a mischief-loving imp inside of a man's body. He was one of the nicest people I ever met. He loved to laugh and he loved for everyone else to laugh. Most comedians just want the other people to laugh, but he really enjoyed the joke. He had a wonderful sense of humor. They also had three or four people in kind of a retinue; everybody in those days had retinues. But the people he had were all practical jokers, and they'd keep the set in an uproar of laughter by playing pranks on people and visitors. But they were never mean. That's the one thing about Lou. You see, comedy can be very cruel at times. I know comedians that can be cruel and take cracks at people. Lou's comedy was a sweet comedy; there was never anybody hurt in it. He got his laughs in a very wonderful, nice way, and I think that's one of the things that I can honestly say I admired about him. He never did anything to poke fun at anyone. Now, he'd poke fun at people on the set between scenes; he'd do anything for a laugh then. But that was to keep things up. The set was in a constant uproar and the grips loved him, of course, because there was always something going on."

Yarbrough wrapped *Alaska* on schedule on December 31 and only $5,000 over budget. This was ascribed to unforeseen problems with the snow sets.

BUD AND LOU'S SCENES

The overall plodding pace of *Alaska* certainly undermines two potentially classic Abbott and Costello routines. After George and Tom rescue Nugget Joe, they bring him back to their rooming house and put him to bed. Tom suggests that they take turns watching Joe, in case he tries to commit suicide again. "We'll have to sleep in two-hour shifts," Tom says, pointing to the alarm clock. "It's almost eleven now. Wake me up at one." George starts to protest, but Tom climbs into bed. George shrugs resignedly and sits down at the table. The hands on the clock sweep off two hours, and George wakes Tom up, announcing, "It's one o'clock." Tom gets out of bed and George climbs in. Tom instantly sets the clock ahead to three o'clock, and rouses George out of bed. "Boy, I sure needed that. The first two hours is the best," George declares, seemingly revived. Tom gets into bed, and sleeps undisturbed for another two hours. George faithfully wakes him at five o'clock, and they switch places. Once more, Tom automatically sets the clock ahead, and after only a few seconds, pulls George out of bed. "Gee, time flies. I feel like a new man," he says. This business is repeated a few more times. It is a routine perfectly fit to the Abbott and Costello mold, yet it just misses the mark because of its pacing.

Tom and George learn that they are suspects in Joe's apparent death. When they relate this to Joe, he finds it ironic and hysterically funny. Tom and George are swept up in the laughter, until Tom realizes that they could be hanged as murderers. Tom Ewell was particularly impressed by another Costello specialty in this scene. "I remember one thing that he did that amazed me. He was really a brilliant actor. He had one moment that I'll never forget. I've never seen anybody else do it. He could start to laugh, then something would happen, and he'd go right from laughter to tears. It was a wonderful moment, and I've never known anybody in the world who could do it."

The second block scene is the roulette game in the Alaskan saloon. The boys, in need of a lawyer, find one named Higgins losing at the roulette table. As they consult with Higgins, the croupier insists that George place a bet or move away from the table. George exchanges a dollar for one chip and makes a perfunctory bet on number one while continuing to question Higgins. Tom steps away from the table. When the wheel stops turning, the ball falls into the number one slot, and the croupier piles thirty-five chips on George's number one. George is too preoccupied asking a series of questions to notice. "Number three—are you in love with Rosette?" Higgins denies that he is. The croupier asks for his next bet, and George, speaking to Higgins, says, "Number four—have you ever had any relatives hung by Nugget Joe McDermott?" The croupier moves George's stack onto number four, and once again, George inadvertently wins. This continues, with the oblivious George proceeding to win thousands of dollars. Finally, he loses it all on his last inadvertent bet. Tom returns and nonchalantly asks George how he did at the table. George asks the croupier, "How'd I do?" "You lost," the croupier responds with a nervous smile. "So I lost a buck," George shrugs. (This routine was later reprised on the Abbott and Costello television series, and Stern and Ragaway exhumed it in the 1960s in an episode of *Get Smart*, which they produced.)

Lost in the frozen wastes of the process stage (with one of the least convincing landscape paintings behind them), Tom and George try to catch some fish. Sitting back to back, they have each dug a hole in the ice and dropped their lines in. The lines hook each other, and George yanks at his and pulls Tom into the water, under the ice, and up through his hole. Soaking wet, Tom slaps George and kicks him into the hole. Vic Parks doubled for Lou in the scene. Paddy Costello was visiting the set that day. "I remember all of a sudden they got real nervous when Vic didn't come up." Parks had lost his bearings under the studio "ice,"

The studio's process stage, transformed into the Alaskan frontier by tons of cornflakes.

which had only the two small holes to the surface. He finally scrambled up, out of breath and chilled. "It was extremely cold in California that month," Parks recalled, "and I was down in this water in a scuba suit that leaked. Oh, it was cold!"

DELETIONS AND ADDITIONS

A few minor sight gags were omitted from the film. When George and Tom round up their sled dogs, they spot a greyhound with a bus painted on its side. Later, when the boys are nearly frozen, George opens his mouth to speak and an ice cube drops out. And still another gag was cut showing the boys tunneling like two gophers to escape from the igloo.

The script's original ending is funnier than the film's. After George gives the boomerang a final fling in Alaska, the scene was to fade out. We then pick up George and Tom back at the San Francisco pier where the story began. The boomerang suddenly comes flying in over San Francisco Bay and knocks George into the water! In the film, however, he flings the boomerang and we cut to a shot of it in the sky. Yarbrough then used a shot of Lou (after the totem pole gag) being clipped by the boomerang. To make it look like a different shot,

227

film editor Leonard Weiner flopped the film and optically enlarged it to get closer in on Lou. The giveaway is that Lou's costume is totally dry when he falls; when he released the boomerang, he was soaking wet.

REVIEWS

Universal held up release of *Lost in Alaska* from July to August 1952 because of the release of *Jack and the Beanstalk* that April.

Variety: "Abbott and Costello fail to do right by their fans in 'Lost in Alaska.' Film is a slipshod 76 minutes of footage marked by more tedious stretches than humor. Film starts with a poor story by Elwood Ullman and an indifferent script by Ragaway and Stern. Dialogue is weak and only a few situations are able to get laughs, mostly because of the basic physical comedy involved. Tipoff on the material is fact that the best laugh comes from such an old device as having a whale steak spout back at Costello. . . . Production values have a penurious look, although extra glossing would not have helped put this one over."

Motion Picture Daily: "The picture churns up a lot of comic energy and rates very well with predecessors in the series. It will easily please the team's fans. What really matters is that by the time the film runs its course a lot of zany comedy has passed on the screen."

Hollywood Reporter: "A feeble bit of film fare, 'Lost in Alaska' is one of the weakest and unfunniest of the Abbott and Costello comedies, one that only the most fanatic A&C devotees will find at all amusing. . . . The Howard Christie production is obviously tossed off on a very limited budget, with practically no story and nothing in the way of backgrounds. . . . Brightest intervals are a couple of songs banged over by Mitzi Green in lusty and pleasing style. Tom Ewell also furnishes a few chuckles by playing the slapstick straight, using a deadpan technique that serves as a refreshing contrast to the frenzied caperings of the comedy stars. . . . Abbott and Costello have proved themselves very funny comedians many times in the past. But the best of comics need some sort of a story as a prop for their gags. 'Lost in Alaska' offers them nothing in the way of plot support."

POSTSCRIPT

The team's suit against the studio dragged on for several months until Eddie Sherman finally got a call from Nate Blumberg. Sherman continued, "Blumberg said, 'I'd like to meet with you, away from my lawyers and away from your lawyers.' I said I'd be happy to, and we sat down together. He said, 'Eddie, the *Wall Street Journal* is carrying this story; it's hurting us. What will you take to settle it?' I said, 'I want 50 percent of all the profits you made on the Castle Shorts, with a stipulation that you can never do it again. The ones already in distribution we'll let go through. But we want an accounting for 50 percent.' He said, 'You've got it. Fine.' I said, 'Wait a minute. I haven't come to the main point. Our profit participation in every picture ends after seven years. I want it now in perpetuity.' His eyes opened wide and he screamed, 'Oh, Jesus!' I said, 'That's the deal. Everything in perpetuity, no matter what medium it goes through. That includes sales to television, and it includes all the money you have taken in on the reissues. All retroactive.' Finally he said, 'Okay, Eddie. That's the way we'll settle it.' "

Universal settled with Abbott and Costello for more than $2 million. As part of the agreement Bud and Lou would drop the suit and issue an apology. Prepared by the studio, it said, in part: "The comedians acknowledge, 'The suit was initially filed on the basis of an incomplete audit by our representatives. Subsequently, on completion of the audit, we found the facts to be contrary to our contentions.' " Meanwhile, on the same day they dropped the suit, October 29, 1952, the team signed the Eleven Picture Participation Contract, giving the team and its heirs a percentage of the profits of its earlier films, from *One Night in the Tropics* through *In Society*. It was also one of the studio's concessions. Two weeks later, Bud and Lou signed another contract, extending their tenure at Universal through 1955.

ABBOTT AND COSTELLO MEET CAPTAIN KIDD

SYNOPSIS

On their way to work at the Death's Head Tavern on Tortuga, Oliver and Rocky are stopped by Lady Jane and asked to deliver a love note to Bruce Martingale, a singer at the tavern. Meanwhile, the ruthless Captain Kidd dines with female pirate Captain Bonney. She argues that the Captain raided ships in her territory, and she wants the booty that rightfully belongs to her. He informs her that the treasure is hidden on Skull Island, and only he has the map to it. They decide that Bonney will sail to the island on Kidd's ship, and her own vessel will follow ready to attack if Kidd tries to doublecross her. Oliver nervously waits on the two pirates and serves them dinner. In a scramble, Oliver's love note and Captain Kidd's map are switched. Rocky discovers that Oliver now has the map and bargains with Captain Kidd for a piece of the treasure. Kidd consents, but plans to kill the boys once he regains the map.

The pirate ship sets sail with Kidd, Bonney, Oliver and Rocky, and Bruce, who's been shanghaied. The Captain's attempts to do away with Rocky and Oliver are foiled several times as the map and the love letter continue to be mixed up. Captain Bonney, meanwhile, thinks Oliver inspired the gushing love note and is intrigued. On their way to Skull Island, Kidd's men raid an English ship and kidnap Lady Jane. On the desert island, Oliver and Rocky dig up the treasure and Kidd reveals that he plans to doublecross Bonney. She signals her ship, and her men open fire on Captain Kidd's crew. Oliver and Rocky help her recover the treasure, join her crew, and take Captain Kidd as their prisoner.

BACKGROUND

Bud Abbott was a big fan of costume adventure films, which were popular in Hollywood at the time. He and Gottlieb came up with the idea for a spoof of swashbucklers for Bud's first independent production. Alex Gottlieb recalled, "It was their idea to get Charles Laughton. I said, 'You'll never get him.' They said, 'You'll get him for us. You go to Boston and talk to him.' So I went to Boston, saw the play he was in, and went backstage. I said, 'Tell me. Why would you, an Oscar-winner and everything, why would you want to be in a picture with Abbott and Costello?' He said, 'You want to know why, honestly? I don't know how to do a double-take. I think I can learn from Lou.' Can you imagine? He said, 'This is a very funny man. You don't realize how talented Lou Costello is.' "

Earliest Draft:
January 8, 1952

Production Start:
February 27, 1952

Production End:
March 25, 1952

Copyright Date:
December 12, 1952

Released:
December 27, 1952

Running Time:
70 minutes

Reissued: 1960 by RKO

Directed By:
Charles Lamont

Produced By:
Alex Gottlieb

Screenplay By:
Howard Dimsdale
and John Grant

Director of Photography:
Stanley Cortez ASC

Art Director: Daniel Hall

Film Editor:
Edward Mann ACE

Sound: Ben Winkler,
"Mac" Dalgleish

Set Decorator:
Al Orenbach

Production Supervisor:
Maurie M. Suess

Dialogue Director:
Milt Bronson

Special Effects:
Lee Zavitz

Script Supervisor:
Don McDougall

Musical Score By:
Raoul Kraushaar

Songs By: Bob Russell
and Lester Lee

THE SCRIPT

Gottlieb hired Howard Dimsdale to write the screenplay. Dimsdale recalled, "Alex said, 'We got Laughton for Captain Kidd, can you come up with something?'" We were all working very closely together.... Bud had a lot of confidence in Alex and I think that gave him a certain sense of security. Bud was very pleasant and very affable, but he had some problems with Internal Revenue at the time, which seemed to preoccupy his time. But once we agreed on a story, I'm not sure if I even wrote an outline; I think I started with the screenplay. Then John Grant came in right after the script was finished and put in special material. I knew from the beginning that he would come on afterwards to do a rewrite, but I don't know that I ever met him; I may have, but I don't recall it." Dimsdale unfortunately never got a chance to visit the set during production. "While I was finishing the script, I was blacklisted. I didn't show up much in studios thereafter." His own assessment of the picture: "They didn't set out to do a work of art and neither did I. We set out to make the best Abbott and Costello we could, but it was a genre picture and it had certain limitations on both sides. Within those limitations we did the best job we could. I think they did as good as could be expected. It was not outstanding nor a failure."

THE CAST

Charles Laughton (1899–1962) had won an Oscar for *The Private Life of Henry VIII* (1933) and turned in a series of great performances in *The Barretts of Wimpole Street* (1934), *Ruggles of Red Gap* (1935), *Les Misérables* (1935), *Mutiny on the Bounty* (1935), *Rembrandt* (1936), *The Hunchback of Notre Dame* (1939), and *The Suspect* (1944). He had created the role of Captain Kidd in a 1945 movie directed by Rowland V. Lee. Laughton was not totally unfamiliar with Abbott and Costello. He was a guest on their radio show on New Year's Eve 1942, when the boys received awards as the nation's Number One Box Office Stars. On radio, however, due to the constraints of time, Bud and Lou stayed much closer to the script. Laughton was totally unprepared for work with Abbott and Costello on a movie set.

Hillary Brooke (b. 1914) had recently completed filming the first season of the Abbott and Costello television series when she was tapped for *Captain Kidd*. Hillary loved the experience of working with Bud and Lou. "You were just part of a gang, part of a group, and you loved them for it. You know you didn't feel 'in' unless they played tricks on you. They played jokes on everybody, including Laughton." But, Hillary confided, she was a little concerned about working with two incredible scene-stealers. "I wondered how I could outdo Lou and Charles Laughton. So I said well I think I'll just pad my brassiere in this picture. [laughs] I want a silk shirt with long sleeves and I'll stand on the poop deck with the wind blowing." [laughs] Hillary joined the cast of TV's *My Little Margie,* while continuing in films like *Never Wave at a WAC* (1952), *The Lady Wants a Mink* (1953), *Invaders From Mars* (1953), *Heat Wave* (1954), and *The Man Who Knew Too Much* (1956). In 1960 she married Raymond Klune, MGM's general manager. Klune passed away in 1988.

Leif Erickson (1911–1986) had appeared with Bud and Lou ten years earlier in *Pardon My Sarong.* Erickson appeared with Martin and Lewis in *Sailor Beware* in 1951 and was reunited with Hillary Brooke on *Invaders from Mars* (1953). In the late 1960s, Erickson starred in *High Chapparal* on television.

Bob Shirley was somewhat of a singing prodigy in his hometown of Indianapolis. He went on to sing on radio, nightclubs, movies and was featured on the Broadway stage in Olsen & Johnson's *Pardon Our French.*

Fran Warren made her film debut in *Captain Kidd.* She started as a dancer with the Gae Foster Girls at the Roxy Theater in New York and was featured vocalist with the Art Mooney and Charlie Barnett bands. She had the lead in the Broadway musicals, *As the Girls Go,* and *Finian's Rainbow.*

TOP LEFT: Charles Lamont (standing) and dialogue director Milt Bronson stand by as Bud and Lou work out their dialogue. TOP: With one of their biggest fans, Charles Laughton.

THE PRODUCTION

Captain Kidd was only slightly more expensive than *Beanstalk* to produce, despite the fact that co-star Charles Laughton was paid $50,000 for his services and more than $30,000 was spent on set construction. The pirate ship, which took up the largest stage at the Motion Picture Center Studios, cost $21,000 to build. In all, the budget reached $701,668, which included Bud and Lou's fee of $125,000 apiece. As producer, of course, Bud also received a percentage of the profits. Alex Gottlieb, at Bud's insistence, hired Charles Lamont to direct. If Lamont could bring their Universal films in on time and under budget, he could do the same here. And he did.

The boys were visited a couple of times by *Los Angeles Daily News* columnist Howard McClay. McClay was particularly impressed by art director Danny Hall's pirate ship:

Ninety feet long and bristling with cannon, it takes up just about all of one stage. And when you stand off a ways and squint at it, you'll swear it's in the middle of the ocean. Unlike most studio-built craft, it employs the rocking chair principle, and when they want the thing to list and roll, someone just pushes it. In fact, it is so carefully balanced that Abbott's young son can rock the thing with ease. Abbott is mighty proud of his ship and the only thing that worries him now is the possibility of Costello making a Navy film and building a full-sized battleship somewhere in Hollywood. (Don't laugh. With these two guys the sky is the limit.)

McClay then spoke to Bud and Lou:

"I'm knocking my brains out," exploded Abbott. "This producer business is a pain in the neck, but I'll go on sticking out my neck."

"For the first time in my life, I'm having three days off right after the start of a picture," exclaimed Lou. "Bud thought producing would be fun. He's learning. I've been through it with 'Jack and the Beanstalk.' What headaches. Oh, oh, oh—what headaches!"

"If Lou thinks he's going to have an easy time of it in 'Captain Kidd,' he doesn't know anything yet," said Bud. "We had some musical numbers to shoot, so he could take a few days off. But he'll be down to his last pants before he's through with this picture."

"I told Bud I didn't like the name Oliver he gave me in 'Captain Kidd,'" said Lou.

231

"I've had it before [in *Here Come the Co-Eds*]. I thought a minute and said, 'Call me Pudd'n'. It makes the audience immediately think of 'head'. We've got a final gag about that when I win the girl, which I do, played by Hillary Brooke."

"This is the real beginning of our careers," emphasized Bud. "You can't carry the ball alone all the time. Getting a star like Laughton is a great step forward. And, imagine it, he wanted to play in our picture. I'd never have had the nerve to ask him."

"Here's this Laughton—a big shot," exclaimed Lou excitedly, "goes around the country reading from the Bible, and playing sold-out houses, turning 'em away, and he's willing to toss in his chips with a couple of comics like us."

Both of them said, "Laughton told us that whenever he feels depressed, he looks over the papers to see where one of our pictures is playing; then he goes to it, and comes out feeling like a new man. What a compliment!"

Charles Laughton's first day on the production was Monday, March 3. It was also the first day on the pirate ship set. Morgan brings Rocky and Oliver aboard the ship, and Captain Kidd asks the boys if they've brought the treasure map with them. (Their first meeting in the film, in the Tortuga tavern, wasn't shot until March 19.) Make-up man Abe Haberman recalled, "Charles Laughton once confided to me that he was very nervous working with Lou. Then Lou confided to me that *he* was nervous working with Laughton, because he respected him! The first day of shooting, both men were extremely nervous around each other. I don't recall Bud being nervous, but I can sure tell you that Lou was. However, after the first take, everything relaxed and it was just beautiful."

Hillary Brooke also offered Laughton some advice. "I told Charles, 'You have to learn to work with Lou; he can't learn to work with you.' Lou just had a certain way of working, and you just had to adapt. Now, that didn't mean that you were not a good actor; it didn't mean that you didn't know timing. It was just his way of working. Then, after a few days, when you get into the swing of the fun, and Lou's timing, it's so many laughs and really such a delightful, wonderful thing to do, you'll never want the picture to end."

According to everyone we spoke with, Laughton quickly relaxed and had a ball. Abe Haberman: "You should have seen Laughton! He *refused* to go home! He would hang around the set after his shots were completed for the day, running around in the long johns he wore in the film. Off camera, between scenes, Laughton would sit with Bud and Lou. He would never go off to his personal trailer, like some actors might. No way. He pulled up his chair alongside of Bud and Lou and they would talk and talk and talk."

Director Charles Lamont remembered, "What I remember most about that film was that Charles Laughton played Captain Kidd and was absolutely marvelous. You know, he wouldn't let a stuntman do his pratfalls for him. The first day he was on the set, Laughton saw Sailor Vincent dressed in a costume identical to his. 'Oh, no!' he yelled. 'I want to do my own pratfalls! That's why I'm making this picture. I want to be a buffoon!' I said 'Okay, it's your rear end!' "

Abe Haberman added, "There's a scene where Laughton gets hit with a shovel—of course it was a rubber shovel—and he loved it! I think for the first time he was allowed to be a kid and sincerely enjoy himself while working."

Cinematographer Stanley Cortez recalled, "The idea of Charles Laughton playing Captain Kidd opposite Abbott and Costello in itself is a very funny concept. I had known Charles Laughton from a picture called *The Man on the Eiffel Tower* (1950). I know that Charles had a very good sense of humor, and he played right along with them, which doesn't happen very often. Working with Abbott and Costello was just a wonderful experience. It was laugh after laugh after laugh—they were two wonderful, funny guys. The two of them were always kidding around, playing all kinds of pranks off the set like two big kids. When the picture was over, Bud gave me a $20 gold piece money clip, inscribed, 'To Stanley, from your pal, Bud.' Now, that doesn't happen very often. But it shows you the kind of guy that Bud was. They were two very nice people to work with and we miss people like that today."

BUD AND LOU'S SCENES

John Grant added a few standard Abbott and Costello gags, including the "Handcuff Scene" first used in *Who Done It?* (1942). Captain Kidd magnanimously offers to demonstrate how shackles should be worn. Once Oliver realizes the Captain is helpless, he proceeds to taunt him. This sequence was shot during Laughton's first two days on the production. At least one take, according to the production notes, was ruined by Laughton laughing at Costello.

Hillary recalled marvelling at Lou's sense of comedy in the scene where he brings Fran Warren a tray of food. "They hadn't rehearsed it. In the scene Fran is very depressed and very dejected because she misses her boyfriend. Lou brought in a tray of food, and she was standing looking out the window. She said she wasn't hungry, and he said won't you please, please eat something. She said no, just put it somewhere. So he went over to one of the dressers, opened the drawer, and put the tray of food in the drawer and closed the drawer! [laughs]—which I thought was absolutely sensational. We almost spoiled the take because we started to laugh; we didn't expect it. This suddenly just came to him in the scene. When she said 'Put it somewhere,' he had that kind of a mind—he was so quick—and it was marvelous to watch him work, because he was so creative."

Bud and Lou have a rare pantomime scene together when they dig for the buried treasure. They inadvertently stand on each other's shovels; Lou absentmindedly piles dirt from his hole into Bud's, etc. Expertly timed and played, it is one of the funniest scenes in the picture.

The final chase, with Oliver dressed as Captain Kidd, and Captain Kidd stripped to his long underwear, is fascinating. Here are two stars, either side of fifty years old, from vastly different backgrounds, cavorting about quite convincingly as if they were either side of five years old. Their refreshing abandon never fails to bring a smile to our faces.

DELETIONS AND ADDITIONS

A long shipboard chase was scripted but never shot, with Oliver climbing up into the rigging for a high and dizzy routine. Captain Kidd fires a cannon at Oliver, and Oliver nonchalantly catches the cannon ball as if it were a basketball and throws it back! It clunks Captain Kidd on the head. Bonney ultimately saves Oliver declaring, "I was willing to give up half the treasure, but I won't give him up!"

Columnist Howard McClay reported a scene that was ad-libbed during the production: "Director Lamont had lined up a shot in which Bud and Lou were supposed to dig a hole on a desert island. Laughton, who stood menacingly over them, suddenly got an idea. He suggested that a skull be buried where Bud and Lou were digging and that Costello unearth the skull with his shovel. At this point, Lou was to recite that memorable speech from Hamlet (Act V, Scene 1), 'Alas, poor Yorick! I knew him, Horatio, etc.' They shot the scene just that way and there was no stopping Lou after that. Laughton later came up with the opinion that Shakespeare penned several characterizations which could be handled with great effect by Bud and Lou. 'Abbott and Costello are not merely the broad-type comic,' Laughton said. 'They can't simply be described as slapstick comedians. They really have great skill—the skill of the funnyman who knows how to win the audience's heart.'"

For the final shot in the film, where Captain Kidd hangs upside down, the script indicates he is to yell, "Hey, Abbott!" But in the finished film, one of his earlier screams for "Morgan" was dubbed in. If you watch carefully, you'll notice that they cut to him in the middle of saying "Abbott."

REVIEWS

Variety: "There's not much rhyme or reason to the plot, other than to permit the comics to cross quips and cutlasses with Laughton's Captain Kidd while Charles Lamont's direction keeps pace with the cut-ups.... Kiddie fans will find that there is too much music to suit their tastes, but the physical funmaking of A&C will be much to their liking. Mixed in are a number

233

Hillary helps with the cake for the wrap party.

of very amusing routines, such as a wave that splashes Costello, that prove to be stout laughgetters. Laughton hams delightfully, thoroughly enjoying himself in abandoning longhair dramatics for low comedy. Hillary Brooke is a mighty fetching Captain Bonney...."

Los Angeles Examiner: "The zany stars of the film, along with Charles Laughton, are at their hilarious best in this SuperCineColor film which represents Abbott's first venture as an independent movie maker. Of course the atmosphere of this picture is somewhat different from what we have come to expect from Abbott and Costello, since it turns out to be a musical comedy version of an adventure plot featuring piracy on the high seas. However, this becomes an asset rather than a detriment to their whimsical abilities, and amazingly enough, they both show up rather well in competition with that veteran Thespian, Charles Laughton, who portrays Captain Kidd."

Los Angeles Times: "Charles Laughton is here, debuting in slapstick, and adds prodigiously to the fun and may be said to almost steal the picture. As the doughty pirate he even does a pratt fall or two, and his mugging is very funny.... It's a good take-off on pirate screen yarns, anyway, and Laughton, besides his slapsticking, adds some amusing satirical touches. 'I hope the London newspapers get this right,' says Capt. Kidd after one incident, 'They haven't been doing very well by me lately.' Also, when Costello finds a skull while treasure digging and begins the 'Alas, poor Yorick' routine, Laughton reminds him, 'That's not the right play!' Costello, of course, does his usual silly stunts as Abbott's stooge and makes a hit, especially in the last scenes when he blunders into outwitting Capt. Kidd."

POSTSCRIPT

Bud and Lou were very optimistic about their future in independent productions. "We'll do our next picture after 'Captain Kidd' for Universal," continued Bud. "Then Lou will make another film. Next we'll do a second for U-I, and I'll do one independently. Then one more for U-I and that winds up our contract. After that we'll probably go on working independently." Projects announced but never realized included "Who's On First?" with Joe DiMaggio for Exclusive Productions, and "Well-Oiled" for Woodley Productions.

Not long after completing *Captain Kidd,* Bud and Lou hosted the April 6, 1952 *Colgate Comedy Hour* and brought Charles Laughton along with them. Laughton allowed himself to break up on live television with the boys, and it's obvious that they all had great affection for each other. Laughton appeared with the team again in a two-minute theatrical commercial for Christmas Seals in December 1952.

ABBOTT AND COSTELLO GO TO MARS

SYNOPSIS

Orville, the eldest orphan at the Hideaway Orphans Home, accidentally stows away in a truck headed to a top secret experimental laboratory. After questioning, Orville is turned over to Lester to help load supplies into an experimental rocket ship. When Orville accidentally pushes the ignition, the rocket blasts off with he and Lester aboard. After terrifying the residents of New York they rocket to Louisiana and set down in the woods near New Orleans. The Mardi Gras is in progress, and when they see the celebrants in grotesque masks and costumes, Lester and Orville think that they have landed on Mars.

Meanwhile, Mugsy and Harry the Horse, escapees from a nearby penitentiary, come upon the rocket, discard their convict uniforms for space suits and head for New Orleans to pull a bank job. Lester and Orville, similarly dressed, are blamed for the robbery and quickly return to their ship. Mugsy and Harry force Lester to take off, and the ship ultimately lands on Venus. Orville is captured by female guards and brought before Queen Allura, where he learns that Venus is inhabited only by women. Allura takes a fancy to Orville and says he can be her consort if he remains true to her. Orville has Harry and Mugsy thrown in jail, but Mugsy dispatches one girl to flirt with Orville to prove to the Queen that Orville cannot be trusted. Furious, the Queen orders all four men to leave Venus. The rocket returns to earth for a hero's welcome. Allura watches the celebration from Venus and sends her regards to Orville. A flying saucer hovers high above Manhattan and drops a huge egg on his head.

BACKGROUND

It had been a busy year thus far for Bud and Lou. They had appeared on *The Colgate Comedy Hour* three times; shot the first thirteen episodes of the second season of their television series; completed *Abbott and Costello Meet Captain Kidd;* and did an extensive two-week tour with the opening of *Jack and the Beanstalk*.

THE SCRIPT

Several people, it seems, had the idea of launching Abbott and Costello into space. The first may have been in the summer of 1943, when Charlie Chaplin and his bride, Oona O'Neill, visited Lou during his convalescence. During the course of the conversation, Charlie said that he had an idea for an Abbott and Costello comedy with the tentative title *Abbott and Costello on Mars*. Years later, the May 21, 1950 *New York Times* reported that Robert Heinlein, the

Earliest Draft:
  December 5, 1951

Production Start:
  August 1, 1952

Production End:
  August 28, 1952

Copyright Date:
  March 10, 1953

Released: April 6, 1953

Running Time:
  77 minutes

Directed By:
  Charles Lamont

Produced By:
  Howard Christie

Screenplay By:
  D. D. Beauchamp
  and John Grant

Original Story By:
  Howard Christie and
  D. D. Beauchamp

Director of Photography:
  Clifford Stine ASC

Art Direction:
  Alexander Golitzen
  and Robert Boyle

Set Decorations:
  Russell A. Gausman
  and Julia Heron

Sound: Leslie I. Carey and
  Robert Pritchard

Musical Direction:
  Joseph Gershenson

Film Editor:
  Russell Schoengarth
  ACE

Costumes: Leah Rhodes

Hair Stylist:
  Joan St. Oegger

Make-Up: Bud Westmore

Special Photography:
  David S. Horsley ASC

Assistant Director:
  William Holland

physicist who wrote *Destination Moon,* then in production, and Ben Babb, chief of publicity for the picture, had collaborated on a finished script "Abbott and Costello Move to the Moon." According to the *Times,* "this one is about a serious scientist (like Dr. Heinlein himself) who is imported to Hollywood to write a technical story on a trip to the moon, and then finds his work 'goes Hollywood' to fit two comedians. The scientists' ingenuity finds a Machiavellian way of evening the score—by having A&C take off, not in what they think is a sham rocket, but the real thing."

While this story was obviously a publicity gimmick, the film *Destination Moon* probably did more to launch *Abbott and Costello Go to Mars* than anything else. The landmark film instantly created a new genre in Hollywood, and producer Howard Christie and screenwriter D. D. Beauchamp quickly blocked out a story to send Bud and Lou into space. Meanwhile, Universal logged receipt of at least three unsolicited story treatments, including one titled "Strictly from Venus," that attempted to do the same thing.

Of course the preponderance of scantily clad Venusian handmaidens made the Breen Office anxious, and it repeatedly warned the studio about undue exposure of the girls. "Inasmuch as so much footage of this proposed production will be given over to the beautiful women of Venus, it might be well to submit to this office costume stills for prior approval." Breen also forced a modification in the Venusian balloons segment. Originally the balloons were supposed to inflate and burst when Orville thinks about women. The symbolism was too much for Breen, and so the balloons merely burst without inflating.

THE CAST

Mari Blanchard (1927–1970), at age 21, was the world's highest-paid bathing suit model. She was signed to a long-term contract at Universal, and had just completed playing a spy in *Back at the Front* (1952) with Tom Ewell. In 1954 she appeared in *Destry* with Audie Murphy.

Robert Paige (1910–1987) must have had a feeling of déjà vu: he had appeared with Bud and Lou in *Pardon My Sarong* (1942), which marooned the boys on a tropical island with beautiful native girls. But Paige actually has less to do in *Mars* than he did in *Sarong*. Paige began to appear on television frequently in the early 1950s, hosting game shows and then as a newscaster in Los Angeles.

Horace McMahon (1906–1971) had recently turned in a memorable performance in *Detective Story* (1951). In 1957 McMahon and Martha Hyer appeared in Jerry Lewis' first solo effort, *The Delicate Delinquent.* He is probably best remembered as the older cop in television's *Naked City* (1959–62).

Martha Hyer (b. 1924) later appeared in two sci-fi classics, *Riders to the Stars* (1954) and *First Men in the Moon* (1964). In 1959 she was nominated for an Oscar as Best Supporting Actress in *Some Came Running.* She is the widow of producer Hal Wallis.

Jack Kruschen (b. 1922) had briefly appeared in *Comin' Round the Mountain*'s opening nightclub sequence. In 1960 Kruschen was nominated for an Oscar for Best Supporting Actor in Billy Wilder's *The Apartment.* Curiously, he appeared in two other classic films about Mars—*The War of the Worlds* (1953) and *The Angry Red Planet* (1960.)

THE PRODUCTION

The budget for *Abbott and Costello Go to Mars* must have made the studio bosses wince. At $762,446, it was nearly $100,000 more than *Lost in Alaska* had cost. Certainly it was justified considering the unique sets and props to be built and the large costuming order. The sets for the spaceship and the Queen's Palace cost $15,000 and $12,000, respectively. (Universal was able to recycle some of the props, however. The Venusian cars were later modified and used in the classic *This Island Earth* [1955].) Another budget luxury was dispatching a second unit crew to New York to shoot background footage for the spaceship's wild barnstorming scenes.

Lester and Orville's spaceship cabin was cradled in a giant wheel mounted on rollers. It

could spin 360 degrees in various directions to give the effect of flight. At one point, some occupants (they are not specified) became too seasick to deliver their lines, and the studio nurse was summoned. Lou's double, Vic Parks, needed more than the nurse while working on the spaceship set. "I went to the hospital three times in one day. They put me in boots, and they bolted the boots to the floor. And they turned the set upside down. Well, all this furniture and stuff in the cabin is falling toward *me!* And I'm bolted to the floor, trying to duck this stuff."

Bud Abbott, Jr., also remembers the spaceship set a little too well. "They had stored the spaceship out on the back lot. At that time, Universal was a really neat place. You could just walk off the set and wander around on all these back lot sets. Every now and then I could bring a friend with me. We saw the spaceship and we said, 'Great! Let's climb up in it!' If you remember the movie, there was a hatch in the center of the floor. We get up inside and we're playing around and we closed the hatch—only there was no handle on the inside! [laughs] Here we are, stuck in this spaceship, tucked away in a storage bin, and all we see are these round portholes. We can see someone walk by every ten minutes and we start knocking. We were petrified, just petrified. [laughs] We were really stuck for about forty-five minutes to an hour. Luckily a laborer walked by when we were beating on the windows and screaming. He looked up like, 'What the hell is that noise?' and saw us. Thank God. I might still be there, you know."

Make-up man Abe Haberman remembers, "I liked working on all the Abbott and Costello films, although I did like *Go to Mars* 'cause we worked with all those Miss Universe gals! The last two days before the film wrapped, there was this scene where the lead gal, Jackie Lockwood, was supposed to kiss Lou and then become 102 years old. The head of the make-up department said, 'Yeah, we can do it. But it'll take two weeks and $2,500.' Well, having worked before with one of the greatest make-up artists, Jack Pierce, who was with Universal for a long time, I said, 'Wait a minute. Let me try something. Get me a lady about fifty years old, the same size as Jackie.' They did. They brought this woman in and we used this old technique, the

ABOVE: The intricate spaceship cabin set, which could be rotated 360°.
ABOVE LEFT: Lou needs help removing his costume as Bud looks on with amusement.

237

Lou in the doorway of the rocket.

cotton-and-spirit gum method of aging. In fact, Jack Pierce used to use this method on the Mummy films at Universal. Well, it took me three hours using this special Egyptian cotton and spirit gum for the wrinkles. It worked, and they used it in the film."

BUD AND LOU'S SCENES

Go to Mars has been unfairly lambasted as the team's worst film. That, of course, is debatable. Critics harp on the point that even the title is wrong, since the boys actually go to Venus. They fail to get the joke, which is, if Abbott and Costello set out for Mars, being Abbott and Costello, they'd end up on Venus.

There are a few funny gags in the spaceship's flight sequence, including its passage through the Lincoln Tunnel and under the Brooklyn Bridge. Today, of course, we are jaded by the advances in the technology of movie special effects. The flight of this spaceship seems positively prehistoric by comparison, but that is part of its charm.

Arguably the film's funniest scene occurs when the boys and the gangsters escape Earth's gravity and become weightless. The entire sequence, including dialogue, is played in slow motion (evidentally a post-production inspiration). The distorted voices, inane dialogue and lethargic movements combine to make the scene hysterically funny. Some years later Woody Allen used a similar device in *Broadway Danny Rose* (1984). Allen and Mia Farrow are chased into a warehouse containing the Macy's Thanksgiving Day floats. Gunfire pierces the helium balloons and releases the gas. The two of them carry on a frantic, squeaky conversation as the helium affects their voices.

John Grant wrote a variation of the "Tree of Truth" routine from *Pardon My Sarong* for a sequence in the Queen's palace. Allura admits, "I must say, it's rather nice to have a man around the house again. I've been lonely for so long. If only I could trust you. But with so many girls, I fear the temptation would be too great." Orville asks her to trust him, and his first opportunity comes when the Queen is summoned away. Before she leaves, she hands him three silver balloons. "These are Venusian balloons," she explains, "developed in our laboratory of cybernetics. They possess extra-sensory perception. Your slightest thought of a woman will be transmitted to the balloon, causing it to break. If I return and find one balloon broken, I will know that you have trifled. And I will cast you from the planet and you will

238

drift in space forever!" Mugsy dispatches a beautiful girl to flirt with Orville. The first balloon pops. Lester grabs the remaining two out of Orville's hand. "I'll hold the balloons," he declares. "That way, nothing will happen." But when Lester looks at the girl, a second balloon pops. Orville snatches the last balloon from Lester. "Gimme the balloon back before the Queen hurtles me through space!" he whimpers. But Lester has an idea. He has Orville put on a glove to break the contact. Orville now chuckles with glee when it works, and he exclaims, "I'm gonna kiss her!" Before he does, he inadvertently switches the balloon into his bare hand. The last balloon pops resoundingly just as the Queen returns.

DELETIONS AND ADDITIONS

One make-up gag was planned for the film but abandoned after some test footage was shot. When the spaceship blasts off from New Orleans, the passengers' faces become distorted in a parody of similar scenes in science fiction films of the period. Orville's face was to be the most severely affected, swelling up like a balloon and going through other contortions. A rubber mask of Lou's face was to be built for the effect.

Once on the throne of Venus, Orville says that he is hungry and would like a steak. In the film, the Queen immediately replies, "The preparation of food that way is outmoded. Food pills are much easier." This cuts out a sequence where Orville and Lester eat an entire five-course meal consisting of pills. Lester, of course, is fully satiated but Orville is still hungry. He grabs a handful of "steak" pills and gulps them down. He hiccups and asks, "Anyone for bicarbonate?"

REVIEWS

Variety: "In addition to the comics filling in their laugh chores expertly, the Howard Christie production tosses in a lot of pulchritude to give the picture sight values. . . . So much in the looker department is unusual for an A&C comedic romp. . . . Charles Lamont's direction keeps the picture moving at all times, while leaving A&C with free reins to hit their laughs hard. Technical effects help the fun . . . McMahon and Kruschen are broad comedy types, while Paige, Joe Kirk, James Flavin and the others are capable supporters."

Motion Picture Herald: "Perhaps the story is ludicrous at times. Sometimes the actions of the supporting players are stilted by the facetiousness of the dialogue. But all this does not deter the comedy stars from accomplishing their task and presenting a pleasant little farce. Without a doubt, Abbott and Costello are masters of the techniques of the double-take, the pie in the face and the innumerable methods the old vaudevillian used to keep his audience roaring. As usual, Abbott is the perfect straight man and Costello the perfect buffoon."

Los Angeles Examiner: "All in all, this Abbott and Costello bit is a touch above the regular mill-run, so help yourself to a piece of corn."

Hollywood Reporter: "[T]his piece is on a par with the usual A. & C. product, replete with pratfalls, slapstick, and outrageous gags of the type that delight the duo's fans and bring reluctant guffaws from others who have to laugh at the screwball antics despite them-selves. . . . The two romp through their roles with their customary ebullience, and McMahon as a physics-spouting convict and Kruschen as his partner both contribute laughs. . . . Special effects are only fair, the entire film giving the impression of having been made in a hurry."

POSTSCRIPT

When the film opened in April 1953, Bud and Lou planned to show excerpts on *The Colgate Comedy Hour,* then re-create the Venusian palace on stage in a sketch with Mari Blanchard. Mari, however, became ill during a personal appearance tour she made with Anita Ekberg, and the sketch was cancelled. The *Comedy Hour* sketches were built around Abbott and Costello going to the film's premiere instead.

ABBOTT AND COSTELLO MEET DR. JEKYLL & MR. HYDE

Earliest Draft:
August 28, 1952

Production Start:
January 26, 1953

Production End:
February 20, 1953

Copyright Date:
June 26, 1953

Released:
August 10, 1953

Running Time:
76 minutes

Directed By:
Charles Lamont

Produced By:
Howard Christie

Screenplay By: Lee Loeb
and John Grant

Based on Stories By:
Sidney Fields and
Grant Garrett

Director of Photography:
George Robinson ASC

Art Direction:
Bernard Herzbrun
and Eric Orbom

Set Decorations:
Russell A. Gausman
and John Austin

Sound: Leslie I. Carey and
Robert Pritchard

Musical Direction:
Joseph Gershenson

Film Editor:
Russell Schoengarth
ACE

Dance Director:
Kenny Williams

Costumes:
Rosemary Odell

Hair Stylist:
Joan St. Oegger

Make-Up: Bud Westmore

SYNOPSIS

Slim and Tubby, two American police officers studying London police methods, and Bruce Adams, a newspaper reporter, become involved in a brawl at Hyde Park instigated by Vicky Edwards and other militant suffragettes. Bruce and Vicky are jailed, and Slim and Tubby are bounced off the force. Vicky's guardian, Dr. Henry Jekyll, arranges for her bail. Dr. Jekyll conducts strange experiments in a laboratory in his home. A hypodermic injection changes Dr. Jekyll into Mr. Hyde, a monstrous creature who has panicked London. He jealously notices that Vicky and Bruce are becoming fond of each other. The monster tries to kill Bruce at a musical hall where he watches Vicky perform. Tubby and Slim spot the monster and a chase ensues, joined by Bruce. Tubby traps Mr. Hyde in a cell in a wax museum, but when he returns with the Inspector and Slim, the creature has become Dr. Jekyll again. Nobody believes that he is the monster.

Dr. Jekyll asks Tubby and Slim to escort him home, where Tubby drinks a potion that temporarily turns him into an oversized mouse. When the serum wears off, the boys rush to Scotland Yard to inform the Inspector, who still refuses to believe them. Meanwhile, Vicky announces that she and Bruce are to be married. The jealous Dr. Jekyll once again becomes Mr. Hyde and tries to kill Vicky. Bruce returns in time to save her, but Mr. Hyde escapes. In the confusion, Tubby falls against the syringe and gets enough of the serum to become a monster. A chase follows, with Bruce leading one group after the real Mr. Hyde, and Slim another after Tubby. The chase ends back in Dr. Jekyll's home, where Mr. Hyde falls to his death from an upstairs window. Meanwhile, Slim brings Tubby into custody, and Tubby doesn't change back to his normal self until he has bitten half a dozen bobbies and the Inspector. They turn into monsters and chase Slim and Tubby.

BACKGROUND

On December 5, 1952, a month before *Jekyll and Hyde* began shooting, the team's classic television series began running in syndication across the country. These episodes had actually been filmed in the spring of 1951, but it took Lou nearly eighteen months to find a distribution deal to his liking. The show became an immediate hit, and coupled with the team's continuing appearances on *The Colgate Comedy Hour*, Abbott and Costello's popularity surged once again. Quick to capitalize, Realart reissued *In Society, Keep 'Em Flying,* and *Buck Privates,* while United Artists dusted off *Africa Screams.* Add to this three new releases—*Abbott and Costello Meet Captain*

Kidd, Abbott and Costello Go to Mars, and *Abbott and Costello Meet Dr. Jekyll and Mr. Hyde*—and you will note that seven A&C films were on the market in 1953!

THE SCRIPT

Robert Arthur received an unsolicited treatment titled *Abbott and Costello Meet Dr. Jekyll and Mr. Hyde* on December 9, 1949. It bears no resemblance to the finished film except for the title, but did contain an amusing end gag: Costello turns into . . . Abbott!

On August 28, 1952, Howard Christie purchased a four-page outline by longtime Abbott and Costello pal Sid Fields. Fields was working on the team's television series and *Colgate* shows as both a writer and performer. His treatment, called "Flowers at Midnight," also bears little resemblance to the film.

Christie liked the idea of *Jekyll and Hyde* better than another script that had been kicking around since mid-1952, "Abbott and Costello in the South Seas," and screenwriter Grant Garrett was put to work developing Fields' treatment. Gradually, the story evolved into the film as we know it. Lee Loeb wrote the final screenplay, with additions from John Grant. Production on "Abbott and Costello in the South Seas" was pushed back six months, while another script, "Fireman Save My Child" (also in development since 1952), was prepared for production.

The Breen Office cautioned, "It is required that the actual injection of the hypodermic syringe be masked from the audience. We presume there will be nothing offensive in Tubby's reaction to the fact that he has sat on the hypodermic syringe."

Although the film was approved for release in the United States, it received an "X" rating in England because of the scenes with Mr. Hyde; no one under sixteen was permitted to attend without an accompanying adult!

THE CAST

Boris Karloff (1887–1969) was not the studio's first choice for Dr. Jekyll; Basil Rathbone was. Charles Lamont suggested Karloff after Rathbone turned the role down. Karloff had appeared in *Abbott and Costello Meet the Killer, Boris Karloff* in 1949. After completing *Meet Dr. Jekyll and Mr. Hyde,* Karloff began filming a syndicated television series called *Colonel March,* in which he played a Scotland Yard inspector.

Helen Westcott (b. 1928) was a former child actress who returned to films as an adult in the late 1940s. In addition to *Meet Dr. Jekyll and Mr. Hyde,* Helen appeared in *The Charge at Feather River* and *Cow Country* in 1953.

Craig Stevens (b. 1918) is probably best remembered as private eye "Peter Gunn" on the long-running television series. He is married to actress Alexis Smith, and was a neighbor of Lou's in Sherman Oaks.

Reginald Denny (1891–1967) was the quintessential stiff-upper-lip Englishman. He had appeared in *Rebecca* (1940), *The Secret Life of Walter Mitty* (1947), and *Mr. Blandings Builds His Dream House* (1948). He more or less retired after 1950 to devote his time to his aircraft company.

THE PRODUCTION

Generally, the studio preferred not to exceed $650,000 on the budgets for the Abbott and Costello films during this period. *Meet Dr. Jekyll and Mr. Hyde* was budgeted more generously at $734,805, including an allotment for stereophonic sound. Lamont was given twenty-three days to shoot the picture and still managed to bring it in $10,000 under budget.

It might be instructive to reiterate director Charles Lamont's working methods here. "Things were left entirely to John Grant and myself. John was always on the set with me, and together we came up with a finished script. Neither Bud nor Lou ever bothered about okaying a script.

Special Photography:
  David S. Horsley ASC

Assistant Director:
  William Holland

Slim	Bud Abbott
Tubby	Lou Costello
Dr. Jekyll & Mr. Hyde	Boris Karloff
Vicky Edwards	Helen Westcott
Bruce Adams	Craig Stevens
Inspector	Reginald Denny
Batley	John Dierkes
Can-Can Dancers	Patti McKaye
	Betty Tyler
	Lucille Lamarr
Javanese Dancer	Carmen De Lavallade
Javanese Actor	Henry Corden
Militant Woman	Marjorie Bennett
Mrs. Penprase	Isabelle Dwan
Rough Character	Harry Cording
Mr. Penprase	James Fairfax
Bartender	Arthur Gould-Porter
First Drunk	John Rogers
Second Drunk	Clyde Cook
Victim	Herbert Deans
Woman on Bike	Judith Brian
Man on Bike	Gil Perkins
Nursemaid	Hilda Plowright
Jailer	Keith Hitchcock
Suffragette	Betty Fairfax
Chimney Sweep	Donald Kerr

Once in a while they'd suggest a gag or an ad-lib. I'd let them do it, because it was easier than arguing with them. I'd say, 'Yeah, that's great, we'll leave it in.' Then when I was cutting the picture, anything I didn't want, I cut out. If they asked, 'Where's that scene of so-and-so?,' I'd say, 'I had to cut it for time.' [laughs] The alibi is easy, you see."

The rooftop chases certainly took their toll on the stuntmen. Lou's double, Vic Parks, pulled a leg muscle, and Karloff's double, Eddie Parker, broke his ankle. Parks not only doubled for Lou in the chase sequences, but even did the bulk of the transformation scenes. "Lou would do the first part of the transformation, in close-up, then I did the rest. It took about two and a half hours to get that make-up on. I turned into a mouse, too. They had stills of me in the make-up and they asked me if I wanted them. I said, 'What for? Nobody would believe it was me.'"

BUD AND LOU'S SCENES

There's very little of the classic Abbott and Costello wordplay in this or in the team's next picture, *Abbott and Costello Meet the Keystone Kops.* It was an interesting period for Bud and Lou. After completing *Meet Dr. Jekyll and Mr. Hyde,* the boys went on to film episodes for the second season of their television series. These episodes introduced a new format that was also devoid of the team's signature routines. Bud and Lou felt they needed to give the routines a rest, since they'd been on prominent if not simultaneous display in both the first season of the television series and on various episodes of *The Colgate Comedy Hour.* Unfortunately, however, this meant more of a reliance on pure slapstick than ever before. Bud and Lou whack each other over the head, and Bud probably takes more pratfalls in these two films than in all of the team's previous pictures combined.

While *Meet Dr. Jekyll and Mr. Hyde* includes the kind of sight gags and scare takes that made *Meet Frankenstein* and *Meet the Invisible Man* successful, there are none of the satiric wisecracks to balance them. Although John Grant is credited with the screenplay, none of his writing style is evident. One scene that had great potential for inside jokes is squandered: Lou's encounter with the Frankenstein monster—a curious homage to a film he supposedly despised—is little more than obvious and obligatory double-takes. (The film also borrows liberally from Frank Skinner's marvelous score for *Meet Frankenstein,* and the music does far more to convey terror than the silly make-up.) Even though Lou is turned into a mouse and into a monster, it is pointless to discuss his characterizations since he didn't perform in the make-up—Vic Parks did.

DELETIONS AND ADDITIONS

The script indicated that other wax figures were to react to Tubby's encounter with the Frankenstein monster in the wax museum sequence. The wax figures of Dracula and George Washington cover their eyes, and Buffalo Bill reaches for his gun.

The film's climax was to be more violent. Mr. Hyde attempts to jump out of the window with Vicky, killing both of them. She manages to clutch at the side of the window in a death grip. Mr. Hyde lurches forward and almost carries her with him to the pavement below. Vicky teeters on the sill and is about to fall when Bruce finally breaks down the door and saves her. They look down and see Mr. Hyde crumpled on the street below. Slowly he begins to transform back into Dr. Jekyll.

REVIEWS

According to studio memos, the picture had the best sneak preview of any Abbott and Costello since *Meet Frankenstein,* and the film became a surprise hit.

Film Daily: "Pulls all the comedy stops. If the audience reaction at a sneak preview of the film can be taken as a criterion, then Universal-International has another big treat for the

ABOVE: Lou waits patiently to be rigged for the clothesline gag. ABOVE LEFT: Vic Parks offers Bud a light.

Abbott and Costello fans. There were heard throughout the theater uninhibited laughter and squeals of delight that did not let up throughout the unfurling of the film."

Los Angeles Mirror: "Robert Louis Stevenson doesn't get any screen credit, although he invented the quick-change, virtuous-become-vile dual character whom A&C meet in their latest movie pranks. . . . Boris Karloff plays Dr. Jekyll and Mr. Hyde and puts into his acting all the time-tested Karloffisms of leer and sibilance, streamlined and hoked up enough to be in tempo with the A&C pratfalls, muggings and gags. . . . The spectator is best served if he forgets all about Stevenson and settles down to absorb the typical A&C tomfoolery."

Los Angeles Times: "[I]f Robert Louis Stevenson is turning over in his grave, it's probably only so he can get into a more comfortable position for a belly laugh. 'Abbott and Costello Meet Dr. Jekyll and Mr. Hyde' is a real giggle-getter, despite many of its ancient gags, for it has some that even old Maestro Mack Sennett himself may wish he had thought of. Gags include the very funny one when Dr. Jekyll's transmigration cocktail turns fat little Lou into a mouse, and the screamingly comic one when a Jekyll injection wishes a Monster make-up on him. These are climaxed by the still more rib-tickling situation when four policemen, having been bitten by Lou, all draw monster make-ups."

POSTSCRIPT

A few months after completing *Meet Dr. Jekyll and Mr. Hyde,* Bud and Lou went to the real London as part of a second tour of Europe. In performances at the London Palladium they continued to avoid the old dialogue routines in favor of two of their strongest pantomime sketches. First was the "Haunted House" scene, which included the "Moving Candle" routine. For the second sketch, Lou attempted to follow the instructions of a radio masseur and give Bud a rubdown, but when the announcer digressed to a commercial about auto body repair, Bud was literally sanded, pounded, and daubed with black and green paint. The London reviewers loved it. The *Daily Mirror* exclaimed, "Funny? It was a riot—a lesson for all in glorious clowning and superb slapstick. The Palladium has had nothing funnier in months." The London *Star* thought, "Those maestros of knock-out nonsense, Abbot [sic] and Costello, are actually funnier on the stage than they are on the screen." The *Daily Mail* reported, "These Hollywood comedians return to London with two sketches so robustly and riotously in the tradition of British pantomime as to leave us wondering why the Americans should consider it such an alien art." It was the *News Chronicle,* however, that understood Abbott and Costello's true gift: "These two energetic clowns, in short, trot out jokes and gags and riddle-me-rees which we must all remember from our earliest childhood, and perform antics which we certainly saw in our first pantomime. But the laughter they occasion in every part of the house proves that they have a talent for making such old things new again."

ABBOTT AND COSTELLO MEET THE KEYSTONE KOPS

Earliest Draft:
  October 2, 1953

Production Start:
  June 7, 1954

Production End:
  July 9, 1954

Copyright Date:
  December 1, 1954

Released:
  January 31, 1955

Running Time:
  78 minutes

Directed By:
  Charles Lamont

Produced By:
  Howard Christie

Screenplay By:
  John Grant

Original Story By:
  Lee Loeb

Director of Photography:
  Reggie Lanning

Art Direction:
  Alexander Golitzen
  and Bill Newberry

Set Decorations:
  Russell A. Gausman
  and Julia Heron

Sound: Leslie I. Carey and
  William Hedgcock

Film Editor:
  Edward Curtiss ACE

Costumes:
  Jay A. Morley, Jr.

Hair Stylist:
  Joan St. Oegger

Make-Up: Bud Westmore

Assistant Director:
  William Holland

Music Supervision:
  Joseph Gershenson

Harry Pierce . Bud Abbott

Willie Piper . . Lou Costello

Gorman/Toumanoff
  . . . . Fred Clark

SYNOPSIS

In 1912 New York, at the height of the nickelodeon craze, Harry Pierce convinces his friend, Willie Piper, to invest $5,000 in a motion picture studio. A fast-talking con man named Joe Gorman sells Willie a deed to the old Edison Studio and quickly skips town with his girlfriend, Leota Van Cleef. They head for Hollywood, where Gorman poses as famed European director Sergei Toumanoff and plans to make a star of Leota. Harry and Willie, meanwhile, pursue Gorman across the country. Hopping off a freight train outside Los Angeles, the boys stumble into a western being filmed by Toumanoff. The director is furious, but Mr. Snavely, the head of Amalgamated Pictures, is impressed by their stunt work and hires them.

Toumanoff plans to get rid of Harry and Willie before they can discover his true identity. He arranges for Willie to double for Leota in an airplane sequence, and has his henchman, Hinds, rig the airplane to crash. After a wild flight, Harry and Willie miraculously escape. Reviewing the uproarious footage in a screening room, Mr. Snavely thinks Harry and Willie will make a great comedy team, and assigns Toumanoff to direct them. On the eve of their first picture they catch Gorman and Leota robbing the studio safe of $75,000, and the chase is on. Thinking they are real policemen, Harry and Willie enlist the aid of the studio's Keystone Kops. The Kops follow, believing that the boys are part of their team. The wild chase continues through city streets, down a country lane, through a hay field, until the villains are finally apprehended at the airport, but the money is blown away by the plane's prop-wash.

BACKGROUND

After returning from Europe, Abbott and Costello were scheduled to make their fourteenth appearance on *The Colgate Comedy Hour* on November 1. The day before, after the team finished a rehearsal for the show, Lou headed to the airport to keep a speaking date in Phoenix with Senator Joseph McCarthy. Lou collapsed from exhaustion while boarding the plane. An ambulance brought him home, and his doctors ordered him to rest. The *Los Angeles Times* reported, "One of the first persons to call Bud Abbott upon learning of Lou's troubles was Jerry Lewis. Jerry and his partner, Dean Martin, offered to help in any way they could to keep the show going. So tomorrow Martin and Lewis take time out to do a few skits to help their fellow comics. A grand gesture, indeed." This raised a few eyebrows in Hollywood, since the two teams were rumored to be feuding for some time. The feud stemmed from Lou's personal contract with Dean in 1946, which called for a percentage of Martin's earnings. When Dean balked at the terms, Lou sued him. They settled out of court for $20,000. Any feud was over as of November 1, however. Bud would introduce kinescopes from some of the team's previous appearances, then turn the second half of the show over to Dean and Jerry.

For Lou, it was his sixth critical illness in ten years. He'd had three bouts with rheumatic fever; one gangrenous gall bladder; and one near-drowning from internal fluids. Confined to bed for three weeks, he wouldn't be permitted to work until the spring of 1954 on doctor's orders. The pace had simply caught up with him. Between 1951 and 1953, Abbott and Costello made thirteen appearances on the *Comedy Hour;* filmed fifty-two episodes of their television series; made six movies; and toured Europe!

The team was scheduled to start on another film, "Fireman Save My Child," with Spike Jones on November 3. (Interestingly, the picture was originally budgeted to be made in 3-D). Charles Lamont and Howard Christie had already taken a small cast and crew—including Vic Parks—to San Francisco for location shots. Christie scrambled to replace Abbott and Costello and salvage the footage. He found contract players Hugh O'Brian and Buddy Hackett, and began shooting on November 20. Charles Lamont backed out of the film and was replaced by Leslie Goodwins. "My agent [Eddie Sherman] saw the test I shot with Hackett and O'Brian and he was horrified," Lamont explained. "He said, 'You'll be cutting your own throat if you do that picture.' So I didn't do it."

Meanwhile, Lou's doctors decreed he couldn't return to work until March. Lou told the Associated Press he had received "more fan mail than I've gotten in all the years I've been in Hollywood. It's been terrific. A lot of get-well-soon letters, but a lot of just plain fan letters. That's from the TV series, I guess." By Christmas 1953, one doctor said he was well enough to return to work tomorrow. To be safe, however, he started slowly. In February, he and Bud made a brief guest appearance on the *Comedy Hour,* then returned to host the program in March, April and May of 1954.

In the interim, the team signed a new contract with Universal that guaranteed them $200,000 plus 50 percent of the profits of their next two films, *Meet the Keystone Kops* and *Meet the Mummy.*

THE SCRIPT

Charles Lamont recalled that *Meet the Keystone Kops* was his idea. The director had cut his teeth on the Keystone comedies. "I felt that the Keystone Kops were the funniest comedies ever made," he explained. "Stupid, but very, very funny. Really unique. I called up Mack Sennett and I said I'm going to do a picture about the pictures you made. We were good friends. I asked him how much he wanted for the use of the name, 'Keystone Kops.' He said $500. I said fine. Then I asked how much he wanted to do a bit part in the picture as himself. He said 'Another $500.' "

Originally, however, Universal didn't have much faith in the Keystone Kops name. According to a studio memo, "A lot of objections have been voiced regarding the title, 'Abbott and Costello Meet the Keystone Kops,' and I think there is great justification. The people who remember the Keystone Kops are not going to the movies today, and I think we should carefully consider a change of title." After the picture was shot, it was temporarily retitled "Abbott and Costello in the Stunt Men." Finally, on October 12, 1954, the title reverted back to *Abbott and Costello Meet the Keystone Kops.* The picture was timely for two reasons: television stations across the country were rerunning the Keystone Komedies, and Mack Sennett's biography, *The King of Comedy,* was due to be published in November 1954.

THE CAST

Fred Clark (1914–1968) had a prolific career in films as a character comedian and was a regular on the *Burns and Allen Show.* Clark's casting may have been in honor of his performance

Leota Van Cleef
.... Lynn Bari
Snavely ..... Frank Wilcox
Hinds
..... Maxie Rosenbloom
Mack Sennett.... Himself
Cameraman
........Herold Goodwin
Comic...... Heinie Conklin
Prop Man .... Hank Mann
Wagon Driver
.... Roscoe Atles
Jason .... Paul Dubov
The Hunter .. Joe Besser
Piano Player... Harry Tyler
Second Brakeman
.... Henry Kulky
Policeman..... Joe Devlin
First Tramp
.... William Haade
Burglar .... Jack Daly
First Officer . Byron Keith
Pilot ...Houseley Stevens
Studio Cop
.... Murray Leonard
Projectionist
.... Donald Kerr
Cashier in
   Theater
.... Carole Costello

245

in *Sunset Boulevard* (1950). Clark's other films of the period include *The Caddy* (1953), *How to Marry a Millionaire* (1953), *Here Come the Girls* (1953), *Living It Up* (1954) and *Daddy Long Legs* (1954).

Lynn Bari (1913–1988) had appeared memorably in two musicals with the Glenn Miller Orchestra, *Sun Valley Serenade* (1941) and *Orchestra Wives* (1942), as well as *The Magnificent Dope* (1942) and *The Bridge of San Luis Rey*. Lynn had just worked on *Francis Joins The WACS* (1954).

Maxie Rosenbloom (1903–1976), a former boxer, was nicknamed "Slapsie Maxie" by none other than Damon Runyon for his unique style of punching. He turned up in *Nothing Sacred* (1937), *The Amazing Dr. Clitterhouse* (1938), and *Each Dawn I Die* (1939). In 1951, Abbott and Costello's headwriter in television, Eddie Forman, wrote an irreverent western spoof called *Skipalong Rosenbloom* for Slapsie. Also in the cast was Hillary Brooke. Slapsie appeared in Martin and Lewis' last film together, *Hollywood or Bust*, in 1956.

Heinie Conklin (1880–1959), Hank Mann (1887–1971), and Herold Goodwin were original Keystone Kops.

THE PRODUCTION

Although *Meet the Keystone Kops* was budgeted at $743,520, it was on a thirty-one-day shooting schedule. *Meet Dr. Jekyll and Mr. Hyde* had approximately the same budget on a twenty-four-day schedule. Some of the locations utilized for the film included a railroad tunnel opposite the Corrigan Ranch; a Eucalyptus Grove was in West Los Angeles (at Wilshire and San Vincente); and the Universal lot itself, which doubled for Amalgamated Studios.

Christie discussed working with Bud and Lou in a studio press release. "It was fun working on *Buck Privates* and it's been fun on all of them ever since. Of course, there are times when I don't know whether to laugh or pull my hair. For example, when you go to the rushes and see a scene you know darn well wasn't there the last time you worked with the writers. It's just that Bud and Lou have invented another routine on the spot. It used to make me nervous, but now I count on the spontaneous material being good, so we just go to work and fit it into the story.

"You either like the boys or you don't," he continued. "There's no in between. Their comedy is slapstick—falls and chases and such. So was that of the Keystone Kops. They were the first slapstick comedians. Combine the two and what have you got? Slapstick to top all slapstick."

Some of that slapstick was nearly fatal. Second unit director Tom Shaw took stuntmen Vic Parks, Carey Loftin, and several others out to Bracket Airport in Laverne, California, for the bi-plane sequences. Hank Coffin piloted a 1930 Gypsy Moth (an anachronism, by the way) while Parks doubled for Lou. Vic recalled, "I had been out on the wings and on the fuselage of that thing all day long. We even jumped over a car. But I refused to do the last scene of the day. I felt I had pressed my luck. So this guy Bob Herron, who was doubling the machine gunner, said, 'Let me do it for you.' They dressed him up like me and they started shooting air-to-air shots with a helicopter. The plane got caught in the downdraft and lost altitude. The wheels clipped the top of a hill, then the wing caught a guywire on an electric pole that spun the plane into the pole. The plane was totalled. The gasoline tank sits right over the passenger's head. Hank and Bob were cut up, and Bob had gasoline all over him. They took them to the hospital in Pomona, and they were released. The next day they had a sign on the set for me: 'Parks Knows When to Quit.' "

Vic Parks recalls the film's harrowing train sequences. "Carey Loftin doubled Bud. He and I are walking into the train tunnel as the train comes around a curve behind us. I'm skipping along with the suitcases. Now, Lamont is shooting from inside the tunnel looking out. I've got to get past the camera before I can jump off the track, because if I jump off any earlier, the camera will see me. When I got past the camera in the tunnel I jumped—just as the train came by and clipped one of my suitcases and almost knocked it out of my hand! Then,

ABOVE LEFT: Vic Parks is on the left. ABOVE: Filming the motorcycle chase on the process stage.

after the train goes through, a guy sticks his head into the entrance to the tunnel and shouts, 'Was that alright?' [laughs] We had to do the whole thing over again. Then we had to shoot the train coming out of the other side of the tunnel. I suggested to Lamont, 'Hey, let me be on the cow catcher.' He said, 'No, I want you running out of the tunnel ahead of the train.' So Carey and I come running out with the train behind us. This time when I jumped off the track, the train actually knocked one suitcase out of my hand—that's how close it came. Now Charlie Lamont says, 'Okay, back up the train; we'll do a take this time.' Lou said, 'Are you kidding!? I don't want you to do it again, it's too dangerous!' But I said, 'Yeah, I'll do it again.' Then there's another scene where I'm supposed to have my foot caught in the track as another train is coming. Do you know that train was ten or twelve feet behind me when I jumped!" Parks' footage in this scene wasn't used in the final film, however. The scene was achieved with Lou through a process shot.

BUD AND LOU'S SCENES

This is the team's second period picture in a row; Lou even wears the same coat he wore in *Meet Dr. Jekyll and Mr. Hyde.*

Grant reworked the "Oyster" and "Frog" routines with a squirrel that burrows into Willie's loaf of bread. There's also a mistaken-identity routine. The boys suspect Toumanoff is Gorman, and Harry, disguised as a burglar, plans to search his house for evidence. In the event Toumanoff catches Harry, Willie is dressed as a cop. The plan is complicated by a real burglar and a real policeman who happen to resemble Harry and Willie. But as in the previous film, the script relies more on slaps and falls than snappy dialogue. Bud continues to get thrashed more than usual or warranted for his character. To an even greater extent than in *Meet Dr. Jekyll and Mr. Hyde,* the real stars of this film are Universal's stuntmen, particularly Vic Parks and Carey Loftin.

There are a few amusing inside jokes. Lou's daughter Carole can be seen briefly as a theater cashier. When Willie buys a ticket from her, she says, "You're silly," and he replies, "So's your old man." Later, Harry and Willie visit the studio Gorman sold them. The weary old guard explains that they're not the first suckers to "buy" the historic landmark. He reveals a series of studio signs from previous victims, including one that reads "Grant Productions."

The bi-plane sequence includes a couple of funny pokes at Hollywood egos and foibles. Toumanoff explains to stuntmen Willie and Harry that in this scene, Leota is supposed to be flying to Washington for a peace treaty with the Indians. "But Mr. Toumanoff," Harry objects, "there were no airplanes when we were fighting Indians." Toumanoff snaps, "Can I help it if I'm ahead of my time?" Toumanoff orders Willie to fly the plane into the setting sun. "Mr. Toumanoff," interrupts Willie, "Washington is in the east, and the sun sets in the west." The director shouts, "In *my* pictures, the sun sets where *I* vant it to set!" In no time the boys have taken off in the plane, leaving the stunned pilot behind. Leota gasps, "Good gracious, Piper will be killed!" Snavely gushes, "*Killed?* Oh, I hope Toumanoff gets it on film!"

DELETIONS AND ADDITIONS
Additions and deletions were so minimal as to not be worth mentioning.

REVIEWS
The advertising budget for *Keystone Kops* was just $20,000. Only *Abbott and Costello Meet the Mummy* had a smaller ad budget at $18,000.

Variety: "When Bud Abbott and Lou Costello finally meet up with Mack Sennett's Keystone Kops in this program comedy, a wild and amusing chase finale results. Until the old and more contemporary funsters get together, however, it's dull filmfare that will tax the loyalty of the more avid A&C fan. . . . Howard Christie's production has a number of nostalgic values that are better than the antics the stars are put through in the John Grant script from a story by Lee Loeb. Charles Lamont's direction seems slow, until the finish, and the laughs are extremely spotty."

Hollywood Reporter: "Somebody had a good basic idea when they decided to mix up Bud Abbott and Lou Costello, the popular comedy team, with the early-day Sennett custard pie farces. But the results failed to get many laughs at the preview. Lee Loeb's story and John Grant's screenplay take too long to make its points and the director, Charles Lamont, doesn't succeed in routining his sight gags so that they build. . . . The funniest sequence in the show is at the opening when Lou, blubbering over a silent showing of 'Uncle Tom's Cabin,' keeps getting thrown in and out of a nickelodeon as a result of Bud's conniving. Here the boys are being themselves and there is much laughter and no spectator confusion."

POSTSCRIPT
Universal had fallen behind on its quota of Abbott and Costello releases due to Lou's illness. The executive committee looked forward to getting back in step as quickly as possible. Christie, like Alex Gottlieb, compiled a list of characters for Abbott and Costello to meet in the future, ranging from Paul Bunyan to Cleopatra. On March 25, 1954, Christie suggested than an abandoned script, "Willie and Joe in the Navy," could be converted to an Abbott and Costello picture, "Abbott and Costello in the Frogmen." Ed Muhl, however, read the screenplay and thought better of the idea. Another property would have to be found.

ABBOTT AND COSTELLO MEET THE MUMMY

SYNOPSIS

Pete and Freddie, Americans stranded in Cairo, overhear archeologist Dr. Gustav Zoomer reveal that he has unearthed the mummy of Klaris, guardian of the Tomb of Princess Ara and a sacred medallion that pinpoints its legendary treasure. The news is also overheard by members of two dangerous groups: the age-old Followers of Klaris, led by Semu and his aids Hetsut, Iben, and Habib; and Madame Rontru and her henchmen, Charlie and Josef. Pete and Freddie show up at the doctor's home to apply for a job, accompanying the mummy back to the United States. But shortly before they arrive, the doctor is killed by Iben and Hetsut, who steal the mummy. In their haste, however, they leave behind the medallion. The next night, in an effort to trap the killers, Pete and Freddie return to Dr. Zoomer's home. But Iben and Hetsut, as well as Rontru, Charlie, and Josef, turn up to search for the medallion. The boys manage to find it and escape.

When Pete and Freddie attempt to pawn the medallion, Rontru offers them $100. Pete suddenly realizes its value and sets the price at $5,000. Rontru agrees to meet them with the money at a Cairo cafe. When a waiter explains that the medallion is cursed, Pete hides it in Freddie's hamburger, and Freddie eats it. Rontru drags the boys to a doctor's office and puts Freddie under a fluoroscope, but, to Rontru's dismay, the directions to the tomb are in hieroglyphics. At this point, Semu arrives posing as an archeologist, and offers to guide Rontru's party to the tomb. Meanwhile, in the tomb's sacred temple, Semu's followers have restored Klaris to life. Later, Freddie stumbles into the tomb and overhears Semu's plot to kill their party. Rontru captures Semu, and then enters the tomb with Charlie disguised as Klaris to dupe his followers. Pete also disguises himself as Klaris. Then he and Freddie rescue Semu and also enter the temple. Rontru plans to dynamite a wall that leads to the treasure, but to everyone's confusion, all three mummies convene in the temple. In the melee, the dynamite explodes, destroying Klaris and revealing the treasure. To preserve the legend of Klaris, the boys convince Semu to turn the temple into a nightclub.

BACKGROUND

Some time after completing *Abbott and Costello Meet the Keystone Kops,* Lou suffered yet another relapse of rheumatic fever, and missed a few appearances on *The Colgate Comedy Hour* until he returned in March 1955. Their last appearance on the program was in May, when *Mummy* opened.

THE SCRIPT

The surprising success of *Abbott and Costello Meet Dr. Jekyll and Mr. Hyde* may have rekindled interest in Abbott and Costello horror spoofs. The one copyrighted monster overlooked until

Earliest Draft:
July 1, 1954

Production Start:
October 28, 1954

Production End:
November 24, 1954

Copyright Date:
March 3, 1955

Released: May 23, 1955

Running Time:
79 minutes

Directed By:
Charles Lamont

Produced By:
Howard Christie

Screenplay By:
John Grant

Original Story By:
Lee Loeb

Director of Photography:
George Robinson ASC

Art Direction:
Alexander Golitzen
and Bill Newberry

Set Decorations:
Russell A. Gausman
and James M. Walters

Sound: Leslie I. Carey

Film Editor: Russell
Schoengarth ACE

Gowns: Rosemary Odell

Hair Stylist:
Joan St. Oegger

Make-Up: Bud Westmore

Special Photography:
Clifford Stine ASC

Assistant Director:
Phil Bowles

Music Supervision:
Joseph Gershenson

Script Supervisor:
Betty Abbott

Dialogue Director:
Milt Bronson

Peter Patterson
.... Bud Abbott

now was the Mummy. After Karloff created the role in 1932, the studio churned out four more pictures in the early 1940s: *The Mummy's Hand* (1940); *The Mummy's Tomb* (1942); *The Mummy's Ghost* (1944); and *The Mummy's Curse* (1944). (These last three starred Lon Chaney, Jr.) It's hard to believe that an Abbott and Costello "Mummy" script hadn't been kicking around before June 21, 1954, when Lee Loeb was given the assignment, but it's true. Loeb's original treatment was titled "Abbott and Costello in the Mummy." In an alternate ending to the script, Iben orders Abbott and Costello killed after Klaris and the temple are destroyed. But Lou, who has sneaked away, reappears disguised as Princess Ara and saves everyone.

THE CAST

Marie Windsor (b. 1922) was a former Miss Utah who trained for the stage under Maria Ouspenskaya. She had appeared in the noir classics, *The Narrow Margin* and *The Sniper* (1952), but always loved doing comedy. "It was very flattering to be accepted by these two fixtures in the world of comedy," Marie explained. She watched Bud and Lou's method of working with interest: "Lou and Bud would take the guts of the scene and improvise on top of it; they were masters at that. But it isn't terribly unusual because I know a lot of actors who get a lot more out of their scenes by working that way." Marie also recalled, "Lou was especially sweet and helpful to me about timing. He'd give me little tips." She also noticed that the team didn't screen their rushes. "My impression was that they just did it and went about their business. I think they looked upon their scenes like they did on the stage, where you did it and that was it and the audience had it and you let 'em keep it." Marie followed *Meet the Mummy* with *The Killing* (1956) and *The Story of Mankind* (1957) (as Napoleon's Josephine).

Michael Ansara (b. 1922) had recently appeared as Judas in *The Robe* (1953); as Pindarus in *Julius Caesar* (1953); and in *Sign of the Pagan* (1954). "I was nervous, I was new, and I didn't know what to expect," Ansara recalled. "I sort of expected the ad-libbing because I knew the way stand-up comics worked. If you're attuned to it, it doesn't catch you by surprise. I don't recall them changing the script much, but I do know that while the scene was going on, anything could happen. Their type of comedy was spontaneous; that's what made them so funny. I don't think I realized then how much fun that picture was. I remembered it as sort of a nothing movie, just another Abbott and Costello picture that was all them and nobody else. But when I saw it again a few years ago, it surprised me. I thought it was kind of funny and cute. I enjoyed it." In 1956, Ansara portrayed Cochise in the television series *Broken Arrow* (1956–58).

Richard Deacon (1921–1984) was making one of his earliest film appearances. "I came into the business in 1952, so that was one of my first pictures. I was on it because of the director, Charlie Lamont, who I adored. H. B. Warner was supposed to play my part originally, but he was too ill. He was probably eighty himself, and here I was, thirty-three years old, playing this H. B. Warner part. It was a learning experience for me. Bud and Lou were both gentlemen every time we worked together. They were very helpful. In one scene they had to cover me with canvas. I remember Lou heard me tell one of the prop men that I was claustrophobic. And Lou asked me, 'Will it bother you if we cover you lightly, then take it right off of you?' I said no, it wouldn't. So Lou told Charlie about it and said let's get it done fast and get him out of there.

"There was another incident. Bobby Barber came over to me and asked me to sign a pro-McCarthy petition. From my standpoint, I knew that Lou was thinking of America, which is fine. But I happen to think that McCarthy was the most evil thing that ever happened. So I refused. He said, 'If this gets back to Bud and Lou, you'll never work on this lot again.' I said, 'Be my guest. If that's what I have to do to stay in the business, then I don't want any part of it.' But it was never mentioned to me by Bud or Lou, and, of course, I worked at Universal again and again." From 1957–1963 Deacon was a regular on *Leave It to Beaver* as Lumpy's father, Fred Rutherford. In 1961 he began his most memorable role as producer Mel Cooley on the classic *Dick Van Dyke Show* (1961–1966).

Eddie Parker (1900–1960) was stunt double for all of Universal's horror stars. He had appeared in bit parts in earlier Abbott and Costello films and doubled for Karloff in *Meet Dr. Jekyll and Mr. Hyde*.

THE PRODUCTION

Christie budgeted twenty-five days and $738,250 for *Meet the Mummy*. Ultimately Lamont finished a day early and $12,000 under budget.

Los Angeles Examiner columnist Neil Rau visited the set on the day Carole Costello shot her scene as a café flower girl:

I expect to find the proud papa as tense as a bow string, but Carole apparently is a chip off the old block and is so relaxed that Lou doesn't seem to be showing any strain at all.

Since her real identity is known on the set, it appears to be a real test for the aspiring actress because all eyes are upon her. But an outsider who didn't know would never guess that a father and daughter are playing their first movie scene together.

Balanced adroitly on her arm is a tray containing Egyptian-style delicatessen items, and Lou, according to the script, is so impressed with her grace that he impulsively gets up and makes a half-bow in her direction.

And still according to script, Carole returns the compliment with a curtsy, dumping all the gooey edibles, and tray as well, into her father's lap. The action then calls for Carole to grab a pitcher of water and dab a napkin into it to help remove the tell-tale marks. But this is an Abbott and Costello movie and she naturally spills the aqua pura all over her old man.

It is hard to tell whether Director Lamont or Lou is more enthusiastic about Carole's one-take performance, but Lou is the first with words. "Gee," he sings her praises, "you did it right the first time. Come here, chickie, give me a hug." Carole embraces her father and there is a round of applause from the crew. She has proven herself a real trouper.

Carole's scene in the finished film is altogether different. Lou tries to deposit the cursed medallion in her flowers, but she makes him a gift of the flowers and, in doing so, returns the medallion.

Vic Parks recalled some of his stuntwork in the film. "I did a lot of crazy stuff in that picture. One was where I drop ten feet through a cut-out in the floor. That was the hardest thing for me to do, drop down into this tunnel, because I couldn't see where I was going to land. When you can see, you can anticipate and break your fall. Then in the finale, I'm supposed to run through this huge glass wall. Beyond the glass wall was a solid wall. I went so fast through the candy glass and hit that wall, I was dazed, I could hear Charlie Lamont yelling, 'Get out of there! Get out of there!' "

Henry Mancini scored portions of the film, including the opening title and Apache dance sequence by the Mazzone-Abbott (no relation) dancers. Mancini's first film score work ever was on portions of *Lost in Alaska*.

The advertising budget for *Meet the Mummy* was just $18,000—the lowest of any feature produced by Universal that year. The studio actually spent only $13,450 of that allotment. Meanwhile, *Francis in The Navy* received a $40,000 ad budget, while *To Hell and Back* topped the list at a whopping $450,000.

BUD AND LOU'S SCENES

Although the the boys' characters were named Pete and Freddie in the script and in the film's credits, Bud and Lou used their own names throughout the picture. Several times, in fact,

1784-14

Marie Winsdor holds the cursed medallion.

Lou uses his trademark "Hey, Abbott!" yell. The only other time they used their real names was in their very first picture, *One Night in the Tropics*.

Mummy trimmed some of the pointless slapstick and reworked a few of the boys' best routines very effectively. Much of the old Abbott and Costello was back. Early on, Lou plays hide and seek with Dr. Zoomer's body. Iben and Hetsut keep moving it around: first it's in a closet, then the bathroom, then an armoire, and finally the office. As we have seen, Bud and Lou did this surefire scene (which itself is a variation of *Hold That Ghost*'s "Changing Room") in *Ride 'Em Cowboy* and *Abbott and Costello Meet the Killer*.

Charlie and Josef think the boys are ruthless killers when they overhear this conversation outside Dr. Zoomer's home: Bud: "How many times did you shoot Dr. Zoomer?" Lou: "Five. I shot the body three times and I shot the head twice." Of course, they're talking about photographs. A similar mix-up occurred in *Hit the Ice* with Sheldon Leonard.

The "Transcription Room" scene from *Who Done It?* no doubt inspired the two sequences where Lou plays with Dr. Zoomer's tape recorder. In the first, Lou thinks the Doctor is alive and carries on a conversation with the machine. In the second, he makes a recording of himself as a tough guy that successfully fools both the police and Rontru's henchmen. Costello's versatility here is quite funny. After he barks orders in a loud, gruff voice, he instantly switches back to his usual meek, quivering tones.

Bud tries to foist the cursed medallion on Lou, and vice versa, in a switch on the old Mickey Finn routine first used in *Pardon My Sarong*. Bud ultimately drops the medallion in the ketchup. Lou pours the ketchup—and inadvertently the medallion—on his hamburger and eats it. Costello's expressions here, with accompanying sound effects, are priceless. Abbott and Costello first performed the routine seven months earlier on a *Colgate Comedy Hour*.

In a sequence reminiscent of the "Dice" game in *Here Come the Co-Eds*, Rontru examines Lou with a fluoroscope. The screen reveals random letters from the medallion in Lou's stomach. Charlie and Josef shake Lou up in an effort to rearrange the letters, but they spell out "Help." In a second attempt to reassemble the medallion, Rontru has Bud and Charlie twirl Lou like a jump rope. When they let go, Lou shoots up through the ceiling. Vic Parks remembers that stunt. "I was shot fifteen feet straight up by compressed air. They had two guys up in the

252

ceiling to catch me so I could dangle my legs. I said, 'I want some mattresses around because if these guys don't catch me, I could fall down and break an arm or my neck.' They said 'Well, this is the last scene of the evening; can you get by without them?' I said, 'No way, man.' Believe it or not, the first time they shot me up there, they used sixty-five pounds of pressure. That doesn't sound like much, but they tested me with five, ten, and twelve pounds. I remember shooting up, crashing through the ceiling, and the guys missed me. I fell down on a big mattress. We had at least 200 people watching this scene, and I remember hearing somebody say, 'Oh, that poor man.' Lamont ran over and said, 'Are you hurt?' Well, I learned a long time ago never to say you're not hurt. I said, 'I don't know; I haven't moved yet.' So, we did it again, and this time they caught me. Charlie Lamont yelled to me, 'Dangle your feet! Dangle your feet!' So I dangled my feet. When we were done with the shot, they pulled me up through the hole. I walked back down to the stage to take a bow, and not a person was there!" [laughs]

DELETIONS AND ADDITIONS

One of the funniest verbal routines in the film was added during production. Rontru orders the boys to dig a ditch. Lou has several tools and tells Abbott to take his pick. Bud grabs a shovel. "Wait a minute," Lou says, "I told you to take your pick." "That's what I did," replies Bud. "The shovel is my pick." Lou can't follow this, so they start over. Once again, Bud selects the shovel. "The shovel is my pick; my pick is the shovel," he explains. "How can a shovel be a pick!?" Lou demands. Bud has him repeat after him: "The shovel is your pick and your pick is the shovel and the pick is my pick." Bud beams, "Now you've got it!" Lou whimpers. "Now I got it? I don't even know what I'm talking about!"

A second Peggy King song, "Sing You Sinners," was cut.

REVIEWS

Director Charles Lamont was pleased with the film. "It was one of the best ones that I ever made with them," he said. "It was a very funny picture."

Variety: "Abbott and Costello pick up the entertainment pace in 'Meet The Mummy' and make it one of their best comedies in some time. . . . Producer Howard Christie and director Charles Lamont mix up laughs and chills, plus some suspense, to keep the footage rolling at a good clip for its 79 minutes. Bats, cobras, mummies that still live after thousands of years in wrappings and other dusty accoutrements of musty ruins are gimmicks seen frequently and used for scary comedy in the John Grant screenplay, based on a story by Lee Loeb. . . . Footage rolls along with several very funny A&C routines to keep the laughs coming."

Hollywood Reporter: "This is a considerable improvement over the last Abbott and Costello picture. For one thing, the rest of the cast (particularly the heavies) do not try to be funny. This gives the boys something to play against. There is one really good Abbott and Costello routine in which the two comics, having been stuck with a death charm, try to slip it into each other's hamburgers. Here they exhibit the timing and the interplay of comic suspense that reminds you that Bud and Lou really are capable actors.

"Here and there through the picture, both comics sound some echo of their great days, but their material is pedestrianly hokey. . . . This is the 40th [sic] picture made by Abbott and Costello in their 15th year at Universal. It probably is presumptuous to give advice to anyone who can last that long. Nevertheless, as one of their fans, I wish they would get stories that would let them be as good as they can be. I can remember when they made a navy picture you could believe, for a moment, it was a real navy. And when they became involved in a haunted house party, you could believe it was a real house party. Farce is always doubly potent when played against a semblance of reality. Furthermore, I believe Costello should recall that all the great clowns, from Chaplin to Jacques Tati, were at their best not when enacting a series of absurd funny-paper gags, but when impersonating a state of mind. Lou, in his characterization of a naively simple guy who masked his dumbness with futile rages, was once as good as the rest of them. But he has traded his birthright for a mess of pratfalls. With a sound story, both he and Bud could probably be great again."

POSTSCRIPT

It was fortunate that Lamont finished a day early because Macy's wanted Bud and Lou for its number one float in the 1954 Thanksgiving Day parade. The parade's theme was "Joy of Children Everywhere," and Macy's felt nobody embodied that better than Bud and Lou. After wrapping the picture on Wednesday, November 24, Abbott and Costello arrived in New York the following morning in plenty of time to lead the parade.

Meanwhile, no one realized it yet, but Bud and Lou had made their last film at Universal. The executive committee realized that the team's contract was up after *Mummy*. Howard Christie suggested that "Abbott and Costello in the South Seas" be the team's next project. But, according to Charles Lamont, "Bud and Lou cut their own nose. Universal wanted them to sign a new contract and Lou said no. I thought for sure the guys would resign. But they dropped it there. They wanted more money than the studio thought they were worth."

The announcement that Abbott and Costello were leaving Universal didn't reach the papers until May 31, 1955, but the team had a few things in the fire. "Their next picture," Eddie Sherman was quoted as saying, "may be for one of their own companies, or on a releasing deal with Universal or some other studio." Reportedly the team planned a series of comedies to be shot in foreign capitals (something Universal never allowed them). For one film to be set in Paris, Lou is mistaken for the director of the Paris ballet.

While Eddie Sherman shopped for a new studio contract, Bud and Lou toured Australia in June 1955.

During production Mamie Van Doren helped announce the naming of "Abbott and Costello Street" on the studio back lot.

254

DANCE WITH ME, HENRY

SYNOPSIS

Lou Henry, owner and operator of Kiddyland, is in trouble with Miss Mayberry of the welfare board, who doesn't think his home is a fitting environment for two adopted strays, Duffer and Shelly. One reason is Lou's friend and partner at Kiddyland, Bud Flick, a gambler who owes $10,000 to Big Frank. Big Frank offers to forget the debt if Bud takes $200,000 from a bank robbery to Chicago for laundering. One of Frank's men, Mushie, will meet Bud at Kiddyland that night with the money and a plane ticket. Lou, however, tips off District Attorney Proctor. When Mushie spots the DA, he hides the loot at the amusement park, then kills Proctor and frames Lou. Lou's arrest is the last straw for Miss Mayberry, who takes Shelly and Duffer away.

Bud pays Mushie a visit and reveals that he knows Mushie killed the DA. Mushie threatens to kill Bud, but Big Frank and Dutch arrive and shoot Mushie. They accuse Bud of stashing the $200,000 somewhere in Kiddyland. They take Bud to their hideout. Meanwhile Lou is released in hopes that he'll lead the police to Bud. Dutch kidnaps Lou and brings him to the hideout. To save Lou, Bud lies and tells Frank he knows where the money is stashed. As the police follow, Big Frank and his men take Bud and Lou to Kiddyland. In the park's recording booth, Bud tricks Big Frank into confessing while the recording machine is on. Lou tries to escape with the record, leading to a chase around the park. Bootsy and Duffer, playing in the park, run to the orphanage for help and return with thirty kids to foil the gangsters. Big Frank is captured by the police, Bud and Lou donate the reward money to the orphanage, and Duffer and Shelly are returned to Lou.

BACKGROUND

Dance With Me, Henry began production a full year after the team's last film with Universal, *Meet the Mummy*, was released. The boys had many false leads in the interim, including an announcement, in July 1955, that they were planning to film *Don Quixote* in Mexico. Bud would play the title role, with Lou portraying his faithful servant, Sancho Panza. The film would be made in color and Cinemascope.

Whatever future projects the team had lined up, they most assuredly couldn't be in the same Abbott and Costello mold. On November 19, 1955, their head writer and unsung third member of the team, John Grant, died. He was sixty-four. He left his wife, Dorothy, a brother, and three sisters. He was buried at Forest Lawn.

Earliest Draft:
December 1955 (?)

Production Start:
May 23, 1956

Production End:
June 22, 1956

Copyright Date:
December 9, 1956

Released:
December 14, 1956

Running Time:
80 minutes

Directed By:
Charles Barton

Produced By:
Bob Goldstein

Screenplay By:
Devery Freeman

Original Story:
William Kozlenko,
Leslie Kardos

Director of Photography:
George Robinson

Assistant Director:
Herb Mendelson

Musical Direction:
Paul Dunlap

Film Editor:
Robert Golden ACE

Art Direction:
Leslie Thomas

Set Decorations:
Morris Hoffman

Property Master:
Max Frankel

Make-Up: Abe Haberman

Wardrobe: Albert Deano

Hair Stylist: Anna Malin

Orchestrations By:
Frank Comstock

Script Supervisor:
Eleanor Donahoe

Special Effects:
Herman Townsky

Music Editor:
   Robert N. Tracy

Sound Effects Editor:
   Verna Fields

Sound: Early Snyder

Lou Henry . . Lou Costello

Bud Flick . . . . Bud Abbott

Shelly . . . . Gigi Perreau

Duffer . . . . . Rusty Hamer

Miss Mayberry
   . . . . Mary Wickes

Big Frank . . Ted DeCorsia

Ernie . . . . . . Ron Hargrave

Bootsy . . Sherry Alberoni

Father Mullahy
   . . . . Frank Wilcox

Mushie . . Richard Reeves

Dutch . . . . . Paul Sorenson

Proctor . . . Robert Shayne

Knucks . . . . John Cliff

Muckey . . . . Phil Garris

Drake . . . . Walter Reed

Garvey . . . . Eddie Mary

Savoldi . . David McMahon

McKay . . . . Gil Rankin

Porter . . . . . . Rod Williams

THE SCRIPT

Devery Freeman was hired to write the screenplay based on a treatment by William Kozlenko and Leslie Kardos. Freeman had written five Red Skelton vehicles, including *The Fuller Brush Man* (1948). "I always liked Abbott and Costello and I thought it would be fun to do a picture with them," Freeman explained. "I was invited to do it by either Bob Goldstein or Charlie Barton. Charlie loved my work. My memories are warm and nice of the whole experience."

Dance was part of an image change for Abbott and Costello. "Slapstick is outdated for us," Lou told the Associated Press. "No matter what we do, it looks like something we've done before. We tried to be different with our last picture. But it was still slapstick. The critics murdered us. We've agreed: let someone else do slapstick. We've had it."

"*Dance With Me, Henry* was different, but nobody ever said it was to be different," Freeman explained. "It was different because it was in my nature and style to do comedy that way. Basically, most of the time, I will start with a totally serious subject. From all angles, that creates the best comedy. Every comedian has to be able to be a serious actor before he can be a comedian. This picture started from the heart, and that's what Lou felt. For some reason they were very sentimental about it, particularly Costello, while they were doing it. He was so delighted because he had something that he thought really had heart in it. He repeatedly referred to it as his first serious role. [laughs] But it was a comedy."

THE CAST

Gigi Perreau (b. 1941) made her film debut at the age of two in *Madame Curie* (1943), and appeared most memorably in *Shadow on the Wall* (1950). *Dance With Me, Henry* was one of her first roles as a young adult. She also appeared in *The Man in the Gray Flannel Suit* in 1956.

Rusty Hamer (1947–1990) was appearing as Danny Thomas' son on the comedian's long-running television series, *Make Room for Daddy* (1953–1964), when filming began.

Mary Wickes (b. 1916) had previously appeared in *Who Done It?* (1942) with Bud and Lou. According to the pressbook, the team frequently sought her services again only to find that she was booked on other projects. In 1956, Mary was also a regular on *Make Room for Daddy*.

Robert Shayne (b. 1910) is most affectionately remembered as Inspector Henderson on TV's *Superman* from 1951–1957. He appeared in other films during the same period, including *Invaders From Mars* (1953) and *The Indestructible Man* with Lon Chaney, Jr. (1956). "To be perfectly frank, I was slightly in awe of Bud and Lou when I came onto the set the first day," Shayne recalled. "There was no reason I should have been, because I was quite secure in my own career by that time, but nevertheless they awed me. They were very professional in their work. Bud and Lou were famous for playing rummy, and they finally seduced me into playing with them. I won a couple of times, but most of the time I lost. I enjoyed working with them very much, and I was fascinated by their repartee and their quick humor. Then we would go to lunch and they would keep me in stitches all during the lunch hour exchanging the banter between them."

THE PRODUCTION

Dance With Me, Henry was filmed at RKO-Pathe Studios in Culver City. The film was budgeted for twenty-three days and approximately $450,000, and Charles Barton brought it in on time and budget. No doubt the single largest expense (aside from Bud and Lou's salaries) was the construction of Kiddyland on the studio back lot. This included a Ferris wheel, miniature trains, ponies, and merry-go-rounds.

Los Angeles Examiner columnist Neil Rau recorded a visit to the set:

With practically everyone in Hollywood from Marilyn Monroe to Lassie going in for that new Actor's Studio approach to acting, I'm not one whit surprised when I arrive

on Stage 8 at Pathe Studios and am told Abbott and Costello are doing a switch in their new film.

ABOVE LEFT: From the deleted dream sequence. ABOVE: On the 20th Anniversary of their association, Eddie Sherman visits Bud and Lou on the set of what would be the team's final film.

At first glance there doesn't seem to be any change. But they do their Kiddyland carnival scene and I begin to wonder. It looks like serious emoting to me, with kids and human interest stuff, so I ask Lou if it's true and he and Bud are doing a Marlon Brando.

"It's nothing fancy like that," grins Lou. "We're just acting for a change. Before we played only slapstick, but now we're playing two real, warm-hearted characters and putting in less of the pure corn."

"It is something new!" Bud contradicts. "We're even sticking to the script." Knowing the boys' habit of writing their own dialogue as the cameras roll, I feel that this is quite a change at that.

"The only trouble," Lou says with a straight face, "is that so far no drama school has accepted Abbott's application to learn how to act. I even offered to subsidize Pasadena Playhouse and pay for a coach, but they slammed the door in my face."

"Lou's only got one thing in common with Ernie Borgnine, and it isn't acting," Abbott comes back with a friendly insult. "They both like spaghetti."

Producer Bob Goldstein comes along just in time to save the situation from becoming a good-natured verbal free-for-all. "Given the proper situation in a script," he says, "Lou can mix pathos, comedy and drama with great skill. I believe our new presentation of Abbott and Costello is going to have tremendous appeal."

But the same old Bud and Lou are in evidence between scenes, even when director Charlie Barton tells them they have a tear-jerking scene coming up. "I'm in a real crying mood, Charlie," says Lou. "Abbott beat me at gin rummy this morning."

And when I comment on the number of kids on the set, Bud says, "They'll not only steal your heart, but steal our scenes. That's our problem."

"Yeah," chirps Lou. "They're so good you'd think they were sent here by Martin and Lewis to sabotage us."

When I leave, this kind of dialogue is still going on, and I'm waiting until the preview to decide if there's been a change in Abbott and Costello.

Devery Freeman visited the set on several occasions. "One of the reasons I stayed with the picture was it was a fun thing and I had two kids who were the right age at that time and were given parts as extras in the mob scenes. Lou was so sweet and dear about the whole thing and seemed to love the kids so genuinely. His arms were always around them and he would hug them and kiss them like he was their father. This was *him*. He exhibited himself at that time as an emotional person with a lot of sensitivity."

BUD AND LOU'S SCENES

Lou looks healthier and even chubbier than he did in *Meet the Mummy*. But Bud seems to have aged during the hiatus.

Dance With Me, Henry avoids lapsing into Abbott and Costello routines per se, but does permit the boys some amount of cross-talk. Yet the team seems to have lost its edge on occasion. As Bud explained in an interview, "Well, the script was so interesting and to us was so funny, that we just stuck to lines, which we've never done before." Perhaps it is this inexperience working with cues that is responsible for throwing the team's rhythm off.

One curious sequence permits Lou some pantomime with gags. After the police have finished interrogating him, he pulls out a hot water bottle filled with coffee and pours himself a cup. He adds cream from his fountain pen, and produces a sandwich from his wallet. After he's done eating, he hops onto the desk and prepares to nap, donning sunglasses to overcome the room's interrogation light.

Bud's funniest moment comes when he shows up at Mushie's apartment ludicrously disguised in a long beard and dark glasses. Bud, in fact, gets a few laughs in the film. At the end party sequence, he nearly drops a tray of food. Bootsy exclaims, "Watch out. You nearly dropped it." "Aw, I never dropped anything in my life," boasts Bud. "Oh no?" Bootsy says. "What about the ten g's you dropped to Big Frank that got Popsy in trouble?" Devery Freeman remarked, "The thing that I thought was so nice about Lou is that he said, 'Abbott is the comedian in this one,' but he said it without any jealousy, like he was glad to have this change."

DELETIONS AND ADDITIONS

Bud asks Lou for money to pay off Big Frank, and Lou explains that he doesn't have enough to help him. The original script indicated that the boys' were to go into their classic "Loan Me $50" routine.

In a deleted sequence, following his release from jail, Lou dreams of Shelly singing opera while he conducts an orchestra. After she completes one aria to a thunderous ovation, Lou taps his baton to signal the start of a second. However, the orchestra, to Lou's consternation, segues into the song, "Dance With Me, Henry." Lou dashes over to each musician to try and stop them, but they continue playing. Then Lou looks off-screen and is shocked to see Ernie dancing with Shelly. He tries to separate them, but Ernie begins dancing with Lou. Finally, Lou is roused from his dream by Dutch, who takes him to Big Frank's hideout.

The chase sequence at Kiddyland originally did *not* include the kids. In one scene, Lou tries to fill a balloon with helium so he can float the incriminating record out of the amusement park. But Bud distracts him, and *Lou* fills with helium and starts to float away! (Some of the poster art for the film depicts an inflated Lou floating in the air.) The script's original ending took place at Lou's house. Bud and Lou smugly think they're going to receive a $10,000 reward for Big Frank's recorded confession. But when they put the record on, it turns out to be "Dance With Me, Henry." The boys are stunned as Ernie comes bopping through the door. Bud wails, "Ten thousand dollars down the drain!" Lou sighs, "So it shouldn't be a total loss," and starts to dance with Ernie for the fade-out.

REVIEWS

Variety: "Carrying more story line than in most past A-C entries, film generally is quick-tempoed and spotted with enough laughs to satisfy comic's followers, particulary moppets, in the program market. . . . Charles Barton, who directed many of comics' earlier films, is back again on the job, his know-how responsible for the pair's smooth routines and fast wind-up. . . ."

New York Herald-Tribune: "This time the team is more sedate. Mr. Costello doesn't take a

Leo Durocher presents Bud and Lou with the Hall of Fame plaque commemorating "Who's On First?"

pushing around from Mr. Abbott, who has mellowed to the extent of feeling sorry for the rotund comedian. In fact, Mr. Costello is developing along the lines of a Chaplinesque character, pathetic and the victim of a conniving world."

Hollywood Reporter: "Bud Abbott and Lou Costello are moderately amusing in 'Dance With Me, Henry', but they are restricted by a script that is more frantic than funny and situations that seldom give them an opportunity to get going in any of the routines in which they have been so successful in the past. The title is not much help, since it is out of date now and has nothing particularly to do with the picture. 'Dance With Me, Henry' will do to fill a double bill, mostly on the strength of the Abbott-Costello names."

The New York Times: "An impression derived from the long past that any change in the stereotyped format of a Bud Abbott and Lou Costello film could only be for the better was knocked into a cocked hat by the arrival of 'Dance With Me, Henry'. . . . [I]t is perfectly clear that any attempt to lend dramatic dimension to the simple and egregious fantasy expected of an Abbott and Costello venture can be fraught with the makings of a loud backfire. . . . In reaching for a few sticky values possibly slanted for the family market, Mr. Abbott and Mr. Costello have inadvertently clipped the wings of their usual lark, however it might have been valued."

POSTSCRIPT

While *Dance* was in production, the team's "Who's On First?" routine was inducted into the National Baseball Hall of Fame in Cooperstown. (A tape of the routine from *The Naughty Nineties* runs continuously today.) "This is better than getting an Oscar," Lou said. "Every year there's another group of Oscar winners. But to have a place alongside Babe Ruth's bat, Ty Cobb's glove, and other displays of immortal baseball names, is a greater glory. We're deeply grateful."

Ironically, as Abbott and Costello's most famous routine was being celebrated, Bud and Lou were busy trying to disavow the rest of their classic sketches. They shelved, as contracts expired, all fifty-two episodes of their TV series to pave the way for a potential new situation comedy series. In December 1956, Bud and Lou were also reportedly scheduled to host a Saturday morning quiz show for kids, *A Penny For Your Thoughts,* on ABC. Lou spoke optimistically in an interview on NBC's newsmagazine *Monitor:* "We sort of have a very bright future as far as Bud and I are concerned after making this last picture. I think Bud and I are going to stay around for quite a while as long as Devery Freeman or some other writers can write the same kind of stories."

LOU AFTER THE SPLIT

On November 21, 1956, Lou was the subject on Ralph Edwards' *This Is Your Life.* It was strangely prophetic to recount his career at this point. Two weeks later, he and Bud opened at the Sahara in a Las Vegas revue that was destined to be Abbott and Costello's final engagement. Produced and written by Sid Kuller, *Miltown Revisited,* with the exception of "Who's On First?," was comprised of brand-new, topical sketches. Kuller recalled how the show led to the end of the partnership. "On opening night the first show was absolutely sensational! Bud and Lou got standing ovations, the kids were brilliant, and everything was just right on. We had a packed house. After the first show Bud went out into the casino and started to gamble. You know what happens when you sit there at a table. They start pushing the drinks on you. Came time for the midnight show—the show that all the NBC brass was attending—and Bud was absolutely out of it. They got out on the stage and it was the disaster of all times. Bud didn't even know what "Who's On First?" was. I remember that Lou called Eddie Sherman and said, 'I'm through. I'll never forgive him for what he did out there tonight! I've had it! He'll never do this to me again.' "

However, Stan Irwin, who was then vice president and director of entertainment at the Sahara, recalls, "During the engagement, Lou was very sharp and alert onstage. Bud, however, was not as energetic. The straight man sets up the timing for the comic, and it threw Lou off that Bud wasn't delivering the right timing. I'm sure that added to the tension between them. Nonetheless, I cannot recall any time when Lou had to lead a drunk Bud Abbott off the stage." At the end of the two weeks, Lou simply said to Bud, "Maybe we just better go our own ways from now on." Bud replied, "If that's the way you want it, Lou, go ahead. Do what you have to do. I'll wait for you."

Many factors converged to cause the team's break-up. Some insiders point to the gradual degradation of their personal relationship. But Lou had always wanted to try his hand at serious roles. He realized that Abbott and Costello had had their time in the spotlight—an unusually long time, to be sure—but it was rapidly coming to a close. A new generation of stand-up comics told their jokes about sex, politics, and the Cold War, making the team's old sketches anachronisms. At sixty-one and fifty, and in dubious health, Bud and Lou were plainly too old for the rigors of physical comedy. Almost exactly twenty-one years after it began, after unprecedented successes on Broadway, on radio, in movies, and on television, the partnership was dissolved. Their thirty-six feature films (more than any other comedy team) had earned $85,000,000 up to that time. It was time to move on and try new things.

On February 10, 1957, Lou began making occasional guest appearances on the *Steve Allen Show,* which was broadcast Sunday nights at eight pm on NBC. It wasn't until his third appearance, on June 23, that a correspondent from the Associated Press cornered him and he confirmed that he and Bud had dissolved their partnership. "It's funny, but I was seen as a

Lou in "The Blaze of Glory" episode of *GE Theater* (broadcast Sept. 21, 1958).

single by millions of people on the *Steve Allen Show* and lots of other national TV shows and you're the first to ask me why. I guess, after twenty years, no one would believe that Abbott and Costello have split up." Lou remarked that he did not want another partner. "Oh, I might try and work with Dean Martin," he quipped.

Eddie Sherman presumed to speak for Bud and confirmed the amicable split. "Every time I call Bud up about jobs he turns them down, saying he's not ready to come back for a while," Sherman said. "Bud is fixed well, and he's in good shape with the income tax people. He just wants to take it easy after many years in show business. He may change his mind after a while."

Bud, however, set the record straight himself. "I can't retire. I never intended to retire. The break-up was Lou's idea. I didn't know anything about it until Lou calls me in the office and says, 'Bud, I guess we'd best go it alone.' I said, 'OK, if you want it that way.' Lou took the *Steve Allen Show* and never asked me to go on it. I'm always being accused of refusing work. I can't afford to refuse. I owe the government too much money. They've attached all my property. The comedian always wants to go alone, not the straight man who feeds him. Ever since Jerry Lewis went alone, Lou has wanted to. I wish him all the luck in the world and I wish he'd stop being advised by outsiders. I'm broken-hearted Eddie Sherman acted this way, but I know that Lou and I will still be good friends."

The reporter contacted Lou for further comment. "Sherman has done nothing to hurt Bud. Bud has misinterpreted everything. Bud says he wants to work. This isn't true, or if it is, he should have told me when I first talked to him and told him I wanted to go alone. In the last few years we haven't done any good things. In sixteen years of Abbott and Costello pictures we did all that we possibly could. How many times can you get slapped in the face and make an audience laugh? It worked for a good many years, but now that's over. I thought Bud understood this when I first spoke to him. He didn't raise any objections. I figured Bud likes to take it easy and relax and so do I, but I have a big family to support. I don't think Bud has to worry for money.

"We're very good friends. I love him to death. His heart is as big as all Los Angeles. We had a big fight in 1945, but this isn't the same. It's not the same as Martin and Lewis. Bud can't sing and neither can I. I want to do some constructive comedy with fresh writers and Lord knows I need them. I've done the old routines for years. They're dead. I think everyone will benefit from this, including Bud even though he may not see it now."

Costello revealed plans to star in a biography of Fiorello La Guardia; perform in Las Vegas; and host a new quiz show (a la Groucho Marx, perhaps?). He denied rumors that he would portray a priest in *Heaven Only Knows,* to be filmed on location in a small Italian village. By the end of 1957, Lou had made seven appearances on the Steve Allen program while still searching for a new niche in television or films. "I feel like a baby starting to walk," he told United Press. "I want so much to make the right move in my career that I'm afraid to say yes to what's offered. My intuition tells me to choose carefully, take my time. Look at Ed Wynn. Look how long he waited for the right thing! [The television version of *Requiem for a Heavyweight* in 1956.] Somewhere in this world, there must be a guy who has *the* format for me. I've been looking, looking hard, but I haven't had any luck. I've been accused of being too cautious, but I don't think that's the case. It's just that I can't afford a flop, not at this point in my career. What I'm looking for is something with pathos instead of slapstick. I don't want to be the brash, pie-in-the-face clown anymore. Unfortunately, I've been associated with slapstick and that's the sort of thing I'm offered."

Probably Lou's last publicity still, taken for *The 30-Foot Bride of Candy Rock* (1959).

The following year saw Lou play light comedy in an episode of *GE Theater* (broadcast September 21, 1958) and straight drama in an episode of *Wagon Train* (October 22, 1958) for the show's producer, Howard Christie. "That's right—straight drama," Lou emphasized. "This is a Lou Costello nobody has ever seen before. I play it with a heavy beard and all—and not a laugh in the whole show," he told an Associated Press reporter in August. His sincere performance garnered good reviews and other producers began to take notice. (Reportedly Lou was considered for the role of Debbie Reynolds' father in *The Mating Game* [1959]. Actor Paul Douglas won the part, and turned in a memorable performance shortly before his death.)

"I've never felt so good in my life," Lou enthused. "When I used to come home from the studio when we were doing the comedies, I was mentally and physically exhausted. Nobody knew it, but I was almost sick. All those pratfalls! They take a lot out of you. I'd go to the studio feeling tired the next morning. But when I did those two dramatic shows, I felt terrific. I could hardly wait to go to work each day. Think what I've been missing all these years!"

At the same time, however, Lou just couldn't let go of the routines he and Bud made famous. He performed "Crazy House," "The Lemon Bit," "The Drill Scene," "The Dice Game" and other routines on the Steve Allen program. Then, in August of 1958, Lou reprised more classic gags at the Dunes in Las Vegas in *Minsky's Follies of 1958,* with Sid Fields filling in as his straight man. Lou Costello's career had come full circle. Ironically his last success was in a burlesque show bearing the Minsky name, where his career was launched twenty-five years earlier.

THE 30-FOOT BRIDE OF CANDY ROCK

After the engagement, Lou accepted an offer for a feature film. The screenplay, originally titled "The Secret Bride of Candy Rock Mountain," was intended as a spoof of such films as *The Amazing Colossal Man* (1957), *War of the Colossal Beast* (1958) and *The Attack of the 50-foot Woman* (1958). Here is where the film may have been doomed from the start. These science fiction films are ludicrously funny themselves; parodying something that's already hilarious is foolish. Lou portrays Artie Pinsetter, junk collector for the desert town of Candy Rock and amateur inventor, who creates a talking "time-space" machine named "Max." Artie's fiancée, Emmy Lou Raven, runs into the mysterious Dinosaur Springs and emerges a thirty-foot giantess. Eventually, Max figures out how to return her to normal size. Producer Lew Rachmil recalled, "The project was brought to Columbia by Jack Rabin and Irving Block, who were special effects people. When the studio bought the idea, it assigned me to produce the picture because these men didn't have enough experience making pictures."

Director Sidney Miller recalled, "I was enthralled by the script because it read like a very, very funny science fiction comedy. Lou expressed how much fun it was going to be." But Miller's enthusiasm over the script was dampened by the film's budget. "The producers had a very tight budget which would not allow us to build a giant arm, leg or foot, like *King Kong*. They wouldn't spend the money. We were all disappointed. So I had to resort to shooting Lou against a process screen, where they projected her blown-up image. To me, it looked fake. But what could we do? The shoot must go on, and on it did."

Production Start:
December 3, 1958

Production End:
December 22 (?), 1958

Copyright Date:
August 1, 1959

Released: August 6, 1959

Running Time:
75 minutes

Directed By: Sidney Miller

Produced By:
Lewis J. Rachmil

Executive Producer:
Edward Sherman

Screenplay By: Rowland
Barber and Arthur Ross

Original Story By:
Lawrence L. Goldman

Story Idea By:
Jack Rabin,
Irving Block

Director of Photography:
Frank G. Carson ASC

Art Direction:
William Flannery

Lou was at his most inventive with a prop. Imagine the fun he might have had with a giant hand or foot. But the film's budget prohibited such luxuries. Lou was further handicapped by having to play his scenes to thin air. Emmy Lou's image and Max's voice would both be added later in post-production. Thus, calling it Costello's solo film is something of an understatement.

Lew Rachmil explained, "As I recall, Lou was a little overwhelmed at the time by one, not having Bud Abbott as his foil, and two, not having a visible being for his foil. He had no rhythm and no timing because he had nobody to play off of. I can remember many times he said, 'How do I do this?' Because there would be nothing—a blank screen—and Lou would ask, 'Where is she supposed to be? How high up?' All of these things threw him. He was kind and considerate, and he would say, 'I'm sorry, I'm sorry. Would you let me do it again?' He knew when it wasn't quite right and he was always apologetic. Then Dorothy Provine was equally embarrassed about how she was going to look thirty feet tall. And the two of them would get together and say, 'Gee, how did we get involved in this?!' [laughs] She felt equally strange because she played scenes when Lou wasn't there."

Miller recalled, "There was nothing Lou wouldn't do if he could do it. He tired a bit, but he'd sit down and rest. He had several chases to do, and Lew Rachmil permitted us to have a double; Lou's brother Pat took that job. He had his brother's movements and gestures down pat."

But the picture took a great toll on Lou. Chris Costello recalls. "I know he was ill when he made that film. I remember him coming home one night looking gray and just exhausted. But I think he had to prove something to himself."

Nine weeks after completing 30-Foot Bride, Lou collapsed of a heart attack on February 28, 1959. He was hospitalized and seemed to be improving when a second attack on March 4 claimed him. Two days later he would have been fifty-three. His devoted wife, Anne, followed him on December 6, 1959, at the age of forty-seven. They were married for twenty-five years and left three daughters, Paddy, Carole, and Chris, and three grandsons.

Ironically, when Eddie Sherman telephoned Bud with the news, Bud was watching a TV rerun of the Abbott and Costello Show that featured "Who's On First?" "Tell me, why was I watching that picture at that particular time?" Bud sobbed. "I never watch it. After all, I've seen it a thousand times. And yet, there were Lou and I. . . . What can I say? I've lost my best friend."

Lew Rachmil confided, "The film didn't make it for two reasons. Number one, when the effects were all finally done, they weren't all that slick. The second was, Lou had just died when the picture came out. The immediacy of that had a serious effect. Plus, the picture didn't come off as funny as it should have. I can blame some of it on a poor script. But our feeling was that the effects and Lou's dynamics would help it. But it just never jelled in my opinion." Lou's widow, Anne, leaving the preview, remarked, "This would have killed Lou." Ironically, 30-Foot Bride was released a few months before the Three Stooges feature, Have Rocket, Will Travel; a film that rejuvenated that team's career and proved that slapstick comedy had not died. In the wake of that picture, it is interesting to speculate what might have happened to Lou, and to Abbott and Costello, had Lou lived longer.

BUD AFTER THE SPLIT

For Bud, more grief lay ahead in 1959. The Internal Revenue Service, after a seven-year audit, disallowed a half-million dollars in deductions, then slapped him with an equal amount in penalties, fines, and interest. Although it took the sale of his showplace in Sherman Oaks and a sizeable chunk of his estate, Lou managed to settle his tax problems before his death.

A little over a year later, Bud had cleared his account with the IRS by selling his Encino estate, a ranch in Ojai, and the residual rights to all but seven of his films to Universal. The Abbotts moved into a comfortable home in Woodland Hills, and Bud refused to work during the period, explaining, "Why should I work when they take all the money and leave me with nothing to pay tax on the salary I earned?"

Later in 1960, however, Bud planned a comeback with comedian Candy Candido. "So far we've been rehearsing the routines Lou and I used to do," Bud told the Associated Press. "Later on, we'll do some different things. I don't think we'll break in the act in nightclubs. We're thinking in terms of doing a television pilot. I think the public is ready for some good, rowdy comedy. The only ones who are doing it nowadays are the Three Stooges, who have made a phenomenal comeback. Why can't I do the same?"

Early in 1961 the new team of Abbott and Candido opened at the Holiday House in Pittsburgh to enthusiastic reviews. *Variety* wrote, "Youngsters filled the air with their laughter at what was new to them, and adults were roaring at the familiar material so perfectly delivered." Bud later recalled, "That was the biggest challenge of all—to see, after twenty-four years of working with Lou, if I could make another man funny. I found out I could. I put Candy through a lot of our old routines—yes, even 'Who's On First?' You know something? It was just as funny as before. Candy did some of his own routines, too; he wasn't just imitating Lou. He never said 'I'm a baaad boy.' He used his own trademark, 'I'm feeling mighty low.' Believe me, it was a real thrill to read those headlines, 'New Comedy Team Is Born.' " Although the tour (and, subsequently, the partnership) ended when Bud became ill on a flight to Chicago, Bud had proven something to himself the same way Lou had.

Bud's next venture would be a minor dramatic role on an episode of *GE Theater* (broadcast April 16, 1961). It marked the first time he had returned to Universal Studios since *Abbott and Costello Meet the Mummy*. "I'm not nervous," Bud told the Associated Press. "It does seem a little strange not working with the little guy. But what the heck—acting is acting, whether you're doing 'Who's On First?' or a dramatic scene. I think I can handle it." As he looked around the studio lot, he reflected, "Remember those poker games me and Lou used to have between scenes? We had two or three thousand dollars riding on every pot. We were crazy." Bud also discussed the split: "Lou just told me he thought he could do better on his own. He was the victim of bad advice. Lou's own mother told me the split killed Lou. Later he was laying an egg in Vegas and he told Eddie Sherman to send for me. But Lou wanted to pay me only $500, and Eddie wouldn't do it. I wish I had known. I would have done it for nothing."

THE WORLD OF
ABBOTT AND COSTELLO

ABOVE LEFT: The new team of Abbott and Candido in 1961. ABOVE: Bud in a recording session for the Abbott and Costello cartoons, 1967.

Abbott and Costello's names would appear on theater marquees one more time. In 1965, Universal assembled *The World of Abbott and Costello,* a compilation of routines, gags and scenes from eighteen of the team's twenty-eight features made at the studio. Universal no doubt took its cue from the popular compilation films of Robert Youngson. Beginning with *The Golden Age of Comedy* in 1957, Youngson released a string of films celebrating the silent comedies of Chaplin, Keaton, Langdon, Lloyd, and Laurel and Hardy. These included *When Comedy Was King* (1960), *Days of Thrills and Laughter* (1961), and *30 Years of Fun* (1963). In 1964, when Youngson produced *MGM's Big Parade of Comedy,* which included Abbott and Costello's classic washing machine sequence from *Rio Rita,* Universal was reminded that it, too, had its own wealth of material to draw upon.

The producers mixed scenes from some of Bud and Lou's best and worst films. Included were sequences from *Abbott and Costello Meet Frankenstein; Wistful Widow of Wagon Gap; The Naughty Nineties; Buck Privates; In the Navy; In Society; Who Done It?; Ride 'Em Cowboy; Hit the Ice; Buck Privates Come Home;* as well as *Abbott and Costello Go to Mars; Abbott and Costello Meet the Mummy; Lost in Alaska; Abbott and Costello in the Foreign Legion; Little Giant; Mexican Hayride; Comin' Round the Mountain;* and *Abbott and Costello Meet the Keystone Kops.*

Some ten films remained untouched, while certain stand-out routines were ignored in the films that were included. If *The World of Abbott and Costello* did well at the box office, a sequel could easily be assembled from the remaining footage.

When *World* was released, Bud Abbott was recuperating from a mild stroke he'd suffered just before the start of the new year. Bud remained in retirement until 1967, when Hanna-Barbera began production on 156 Abbott and Costello cartoons. Bud supplied his own voice, and Stan Irwin impersonated Lou. The cartoons bear little resemblance to the team's on-screen characters, but it's gratifying to hear Bud's raspy voice again.

Bud lived to see a nationwide revival of the team's work when Universal released its entire Abbott and Costello catalogue into television syndication in 1971. By then, the team's television series had already achieved classic status and hasn't been off the air since it entered syndication in the late 1950s. Bud frequently received fans from all over the United States in his home, and he enjoyed watching his old movies with them. He never failed to praise Lou as the greatest natural born comic that ever lived, and it was obvious to visitors that Bud still missed and loved Lou very much.

Bud Abbott succumbed to cancer on April 24, 1974. He was seventy-eight. Groucho Marx eulogized Bud as "the greatest straight man ever." Bud and Betty had been married for fifty-five years. Betty passed away in 1981 at the age of eighty. They are survived by two children, Bud Jr. and Vickie, and four grandchildren.

Perhaps the best testament to Bud and Lou's work is in its staying power. Their films and television shows continue to run in markets across the country on cable networks and local stations, garnering yet another generation of fans. In addition, many of the team's movies have been released on videocassette to excellent response.

Bud and Lou depicted classic characters and relationships that audiences can still identify with. Bud could at times represent a parent or a teacher. Mostly he was like an older brother, instigating pranks to get the little brother in trouble or to throw all the risk on him. The younger brother was too naive to know better, and too trusting to question anything. Lou was the little kid who knew better than his parents, his teacher, or even his older brother. His way of doing or seeing things was just as valid as the adult way. Other comedians used the character of the little boy, most notably Red Skelton and Harpo Marx. But Skelton's character was the malicious "mean wittle kid," while Harpo's pixie could often be lecherous. Costello's character was never mean or lecherous, just sweet.

As long as little kids are afraid of monsters and the dark; as long as they are confused—and amused—by puns; as long as their curiosity leads them into trouble; and as long as baseball is the national pastime . . . Bud and Lou will always be fresh and funny, and always have a place in their hearts.

Released: April 8, 1965

Running Time:
75 minutes

Produced By:
Max J. Rosenberg
and Milton Subotsky

Associate Producer:
Norman E. Gluck

Narrated By:
Jack E. Leonard

Narration Written By:
Gene Wood

Musical Supervision:
Joseph Gershenson

Editorial Direction:
Sidney Meyer

Assistant: Nina Feinberg

Title Design: Gil Merit

WHO'S ON FIRST?

(from *The Naughty Nineties*)

ABBOTT: Strange as it may seem, they give ball players nowadays very peculiar names.

COSTELLO: Funny names?

ABBOTT: Nicknames. Pet names. Now, on the St. Louis team we have Who's on first, What's on second, I Don't Know is on third—

COSTELLO: That's what I want to find out. I want you to tell me the names of the fellows on the St. Louis team.

ABBOTT: I'm telling you: Who's on first, What's on second, I Don't Know is on third—

COSTELLO: You know the fellows' names?

ABBOTT: Yes.

COSTELLO: Well, then, who's playin' first?

ABBOTT: Yes.

COSTELLO: I mean the fellow's name on first base.

ABBOTT: Who.

COSTELLO: The fellow playin' first base for St. Louis.

ABBOTT: Who.

COSTELLO: The guy on first base.

ABBOTT: Who is on first.

COSTELLO: Well, what are you askin' *me* for?

ABBOTT: I'm not asking you—I'm telling you. Who is on first.

COSTELLO: I'm asking *you*—who's on first?

ABBOTT: That's the man's name!

COSTELLO: That's who's name?

ABBOTT: Yes.

COSTELLO: Well, go ahead and tell me!

ABBOTT: Who.

COSTELLO: The guy on first.

ABBOTT: Who.

COSTELLO: The first baseman!

ABBOTT: Who is on first!

COSTELLO: Have you got a first baseman on first?

ABBOTT: Certainly!

COSTELLO: Then who's playing first?

ABBOTT: Absolutely!

COSTELLO: When you pay off the first baseman every month, who gets the money?

ABBOTT: Every dollar of it! And why not, the man's entitled to it.

COSTELLO: Who is?

ABBOTT: Yes.

COSTELLO: So who gets it?

ABBOTT: Why shouldn't he? Sometimes his wife comes down and collects it.

COSTELLO: Who's wife?

ABBOTT: Yes. After all, the man earns it.

COSTELLO: Who does?

ABBOTT: Absolutely.

COSTELLO: All I'm trying to find out is what's the guy's name on first base?

ABBOTT: Oh, no, no, What is on second base.

COSTELLO: I'm not asking you who's on second.

ABBOTT: Who's on first.

COSTELLO: That's what I'm trying to find out!

ABBOTT: Well, don't change the players around.

COSTELLO: I'm not changing nobody!

ABBOTT: Now, take it easy.

COSTELLO: What's the guy's name on first base?

ABBOTT: What's the guy's name on second base.

COSTELLO: I'm not askin' ya who's on second.

ABBOTT: Who's on first.

COSTELLO: I don't know.

ABBOTT: He's on third. We're not talking about him.

COSTELLO: How did I get on third base?

ABBOTT: You mentioned his name.

COSTELLO: If I mentioned the third baseman's name, who did I say is playing third?

ABBOTT: No, Who's playing first.

COSTELLO: Stay offa first will ya?!

ABBOTT: Well, what do you want me to do?

COSTELLO: Now what's the guy's name on third base?

ABBOTT: What's on second.

COSTELLO: I'm not asking ya who's on second.

ABBOTT: Who's on first.

COSTELLO: I don't know.

ABBOTT: *He's* on third.

COSTELLO: There I go back on third again.

ABBOTT: Well, I can't change their names.

COSTELLO: Will you please stay on third base?

ABBOTT: Please. Now what is it you want to know?

COSTELLO: What is the fellow's name on third base?

ABBOTT: What is the fellow's name on second base.

COSTELLO: I'm not askin' ya who's on second!

ABBOTT: Who's on first.

COSTELLO: I don't know.

ABBOTT and COSTELLO: Third base!

COSTELLO: You got an outfield?

ABBOTT: Oh, sure.

COSTELLO: St. Louis has a good outfield?

ABBOTT: Oh, absolutely.

COSTELLO: The left fielder's name?

ABBOTT: Why.

COSTELLO: I don't know, I just thought I'd ask you.

ABBOTT: Well, I just thought I'd tell you.

COSTELLO: Then tell me who's playing left field?

ABBOTT: Who's playing first!

COSTELLO: Stay out of the infield!

ABBOTT: Don't mention any names out here!

COSTELLO: I want to know what's the fellow's name in left field?

ABBOTT: What is on second.

COSTELLO: I'm not asking you who's on second!

ABBOTT: Who is on first.

COSTELLO: I don't know!

ABBOTT and COSTELLO: *Third base!*

ABBOTT: Now take it easy, take it easy, man.

COSTELLO: And the left fielder's name?

ABBOTT: Why.

COSTELLO: Because!

ABBOTT: Oh, he's center field.

COSTELLO: Wait a minute. You got a pitcher on the team?

ABBOTT: Wouldn't this be a fine team without a pitcher.

COSTELLO: I dunno. Tell me the pitcher's name.

ABBOTT: Tomorrow.

COSTELLO: You don't want to tell me today?

ABBOTT: I'm telling you, man.

COSTELLO: Then go ahead.

ABBOTT: Tomorrow.

COSTELLO: What time?

ABBOTT: What time what?

COSTELLO: What time tomorrow are you gonna tell me who's pitching?!

ABBOTT: Now listen. Who is not pitching! Who is on—

COSTELLO: *I'll break your arm if you say who's on first!*

ABBOTT: Then why come up here and ask?

COSTELLO: I want to know what's the pitcher's name?

ABBOTT: What's on second!

COSTELLO: I don't know!

ABBOTT and COSTELLO: *Third base!*

COSTELLO: You gotta catcher?

ABBOTT: Yes.

COSTELLO: The catcher's name?

ABBOTT: Today.

COSTELLO: Today. And Tomorrow's pitching.

ABBOTT: Now you've got it.

COSTELLO: That's all. St. Louis got a couple of days on their team, that's all.

ABBOTT: Well, I can't help that. All right. What do you want me to do?

COSTELLO: Gotta catcher?

ABBOTT: Yes.

COSTELLO: I'm a good catcher too you know.

ABBOTT: I know that.

COSTELLO: I would like to play for the St. Louis team.

ABBOTT: Well I might arrange that.

COSTELLO: I would like to catch. Now I'm being a good catcher, Tomorrow's pitching on the team, and I'm catching.

ABBOTT: Yes.

COSTELLO: Tomorrow throws the ball and the guy up bunts the ball—

ABBOTT: Yes.

COSTELLO: Now when he bunts the ball—me being a good catcher—I want to throw the guy out at first base, so I pick up the ball and throw it to who?

ABBOTT: Now, that's the first thing you've said right.

COSTELLO: I DON'T EVEN KNOW WHAT I'M TALKING ABOUT!

ABBOTT: Well, that's all you have to do.

COSTELLO: Is to throw it to first base?

ABBOTT: Yes.

COSTELLO: Now who's got it?

ABBOTT: Naturally!

COSTELLO: Who has it?

ABBOTT: Naturally.

COSTELLO: Naturally.

ABBOTT: Naturally!

COSTELLO: O.K.

ABBOTT: Now you've got it.

COSTELLO: I pick up the ball and throw it to Naturally.

ABBOTT: No you don't, you throw the ball to first base.

COSTELLO: Then who gets it?

ABBOTT: Naturally!

COSTELLO: O.K.

ABBOTT: All right.

COSTELLO: I throw the ball to Naturally.

ABBOTT: You don't! You throw it to Who!

COSTELLO: Naturally.

ABBOTT: Well, that's it. Say it that way.

COSTELLO: That's what I said.

ABBOTT: You did not.

COSTELLO: I said I throw the ball to Naturally.

ABBOTT: You *don't*. You throw it to *Who*.

COSTELLO: Naturally.

ABBOTT: Yes!

COSTELLO: So I throw the ball to first base and Naturally gets it.

ABBOTT: No! You throw the ball to first base—

COSTELLO: Then *who* gets it?!

ABBOTT: Naturally.

COSTELLO: *That's what I'm saying!*

ABBOTT: You're not saying that.

COSTELLO: I throw the ball to Naturally!

ABBOTT: You throw it to Who!

COSTELLO: Naturally!

ABBOTT: Naturally. Well, say it that way.

COSTELLO: *That's what I'm saying!*

ABBOTT: Now don't get excited. Now don't get excited.

COSTELLO: I throw the ball to first base—

ABBOTT: Then Who gets it!

COSTELLO: *He better get it!*

ABBOTT: Alright, now don't get excited. Take it easy.

COSTELLO: Now I throw the ball to first base, whoever it is drops the ball, so the guy runs to second. Who picks up the ball and throws it to What. What throws it to I Don't Know. I Don't Know throws it back to Tomorrow—a triple play.

ABBOTT: Yeah. It could be.

COSTELLO: Another guy gets up and hits a long fly ball to Because. Why? I don't know. He's on third. And I don't care!

ABBOTT: What was that?

COSTELLO: I said, I DON'T CARE!

ABBOTT: Oh, that's our shortstop!

INDEX

ABBOTT & COSTELLO
ON VIDEOCASSETTE

Abbott and Costello Meet Dr. Jekyll
and Mr. Hyde

Abbott and Costello Meet
Frankenstein

Buck Privates

Hit the Ice

Hold That Ghost

The Naughty Nineties

The Time of Their Lives

Who Done It?

Watch for new releases
coming soon on videocassette.

AVAILABLE
WHEREVER
VIDEOCASSETTES
ARE SOLD.

MCA
UNIVERSAL
HOME VIDEO